general editors John M. MacKenzie and Andrew S. Thompson

When the 'Studies in Imperialism' series was founded more than twenty-five years ago, emphasis was laid upon the conviction that 'imperialism as a cultural phenomenon had as significant an effect on the dominant as on the subordinate societies'. With more than ninety books published, this remains the prime concern of the series. Cross-disciplinary work has indeed appeared covering the full spectrum of cultural phenomena, as well as examining aspects of gender and sex, frontiers and law, science and the environment, language and literature, migration and patriotic societies, and much else. Moreover, the series has always wished to present comparative work on European and American imperialism, and particularly welcomes the submission of books in these areas. The fascination with imperialism, in all its aspects, shows no sign of abating, and this series will continue to lead the way in encouraging the widest possible range of studies in the field. 'Studies in Imperialism' is fully organic in its development, always seeking to be at the cutting edge, responding to the latest interests of scholars and the needs of this ever-expanding area of scholarship.

Livingstone's 'Lives'

Manchester University Press

SELECTED TITLES AVAILABLE IN THE SERIES

Heroic Imperialists in Africa: The promotion of British and French colonial heroes, 1870–1939
Berny Sèbe

European Empires and the People: Popular responses to imperialism in France, Britain, the Netherlands, Belgium, Germany and Italy
Edited by John M. MacKenzie

Museums and Empire: Natural history, human cultures and colonial identities
John M. MacKenzie

Writing Imperial Histories
Edited by Andrew S. Thompson

Representing Africa: Landscape, exploration and empire in Southern Africa, 1780–1870
John McAleer

Livingstone's 'Lives'
A METABIOGRAPHY OF A VICTORIAN ICON

Justin D. Livingstone

MANCHESTER
UNIVERSITY PRESS

Copyright © Justin D. Livingstone 2014

The right of Justin D. Livingstone to be identified as the author of this work has been asserted by him in accordance with the Copyright, Designs and Patents Act 1988.

Published by Manchester University Press
Altrincham Street, Manchester M1 7JA, UK
www.manchesteruniversitypress.co.uk

British Library Cataloguing-in-Publication Data is available

Library of Congress Cataloging-in-Publication Data is available

ISBN 978 1 5261 0679 7 *paperback*

First published by Manchester University Press in hardback 2014

This edition first published 2017

The publisher has no responsibility for the persistence or accuracy of URLs for any external or third-party internet websites referred to in this book, and does not guarantee that any content on such websites is, or will remain, accurate or appropriate.

Printed by Lightning Source

For my parents

CONTENTS

List of illustrations viii
General editor's introduction x
Acknowledgements xiii
List of abbreviations and a note on spelling xv

1	Bio-diversity: metabiographical method	*page* 1
2	Styling the self: making *Missionary Travels*	19
3	Death: lamenting Livingstone	69
4	Empire: imperial afterlives	114
5	Nation: Scotland's son	178
6	Fiction: laughing at Livingstone?	222
7	Revisionism: sins, psyche, sex	272

Index 292

ILLUSTRATIONS

1. Manuscript of *Missionary Travels and Researches in South Africa* (1856–57). MS 42428-9, John Murray Archive. Courtesy of the National Library of Scotland, Edinburgh. — page 37
2. 'The Missionary's Escape from the Lion'. *Missionary Travels and Researches in South Africa* (London: John Murray, 1857). Courtesy of the National Library of Scotland, Edinburgh. — 45
3. 'Dr. Livingstone Reading the Bible to his Men'. Supplement to the *Graphic* (25 April 1874). Courtesy of the National Library of Scotland, Edinburgh. — 81
4. 'Stanley Meeting Livingstone'. In J.E. Chambliss, *The Life and Labors of David Livingstone* (Philadelphia: Hubbard Bros., 1875). Courtesy of the National Library of Scotland, Edinburgh. — 93
5. 'The Scene at the Pier, Southampton'. Supplement to the *Graphic* (25 April 1874). Courtesy of the National Library of Scotland, Edinburgh. — 98
6. Ernest Prater, front cover of Basil Mathews, *Livingstone the Pathfinder* (London: Oxford University Press, 1912). Courtesy of the National Library of Scotland, Edinburgh. — 122
7. Ernest Prater, 'Livingstone Preaching to the Makololo'. In Basil Mathews, *Livingstone the Pathfinder* (London: Oxford University Press, 1912). Courtesy of the National Library of Scotland, Edinburgh. — 123
8. Ernest Prater, 'A Large Spear Grazed Livingstone's Back'. In Basil Mathews, *Livingstone the Pathfinder* (London: Oxford University Press, 1912). Courtesy of the National Library of Scotland, Edinburgh. — 143
9. Front cover of R.B. Dawson, *Livingstone the Hero of Africa* (London: Seeley, Service, 1918). Courtesy of the National Library of Scotland, Edinburgh. — 147
10. 'Susi's Party Meets Cameron's at Unyanyembe'. Photograph from *The Last Journey* by Alan Paton. Courtesy of The Alan Paton Centre & Struggles Archive, University of KwaZulu-Natal. — 248

ILLUSTRATIONS

11 'Livingstone Dies at Ilala'. Photograph from *The Last Journey* by Alan Paton. Courtesy of The Alan Paton Centre & Struggles Archive, University of KwaZulu-Natal.   249
12 C. d'O. Pilkington Jackson, *Mercy: Freeing a Slave Gang*. Courtesy of the David Livingstone Centre, Blantyre.   251
13 'Slaver and Slaves'. Photograph from *The Last Journey* by Alan Paton. Courtesy of The Alan Paton Centre & Struggles Archive, University of KwaZulu-Natal.   252

GENERAL EDITOR'S INTRODUCTION

Walking along a Bergen street in 2012, I was startled to see the 'Dr. Livingstone Travellers' Café'. On investigation, it certainly referred to *that* Dr. Livingstone. Even in Norway, the name of Livingstone seemed to conjure up the notion of travel, not to mention solid food on a restricted budget. Such is the universality of the Livingstone 'brand'. It leads me to think that, although Justin Livingstone's essay in 'metabiography' is inevitably and properly restricted to Anglophone and mainly British (with one or two excursions into the Caribbean, South Africa and elsewhere) representations of the Livingstone life and reputation, it is almost certainly the case that another book could be constructed out of his profile in territories of the former British Empire, throughout Europe, and in other international settings. As in Bergen, Livingstone and journeys have become synonymous, well illustrated by advertisements from travel companies such as Voyages Jules Verne.

But it is a special pleasure for me to write the general editor's introduction to *this* book. When I came to consider Livingstone in the context of imperial propaganda over twenty years ago, it soon became apparent that the 'afterlife' was for me more interesting than the life itself (although the two cannot of course be entirely disconnected). For this afterlife was indeed extraordinary. I could think of few other historical figures who had been the subject of so many biographies, who had maintained a posthumous reputation over such a lengthy period, and whose name had been bent to so many causes, political and religious, social and scientific. As Justin Livingstone points out, it is indeed remarkable that the almost inevitable 'debunking' process only really began one hundred years after Livingstone's death. Lytton Strachey had dealt with more recently prominent personalities in 1918. The attack upon the reputation of T.E. Lawrence, Lawrence of Arabia, had occurred a mere twenty years after his death with the publication of Richard Aldington's *Lawrence of Arabia: A Biographical Enquiry* in 1955. Yet, in 2013, the bicentennial of the birth of Livingstone, his prominence seems to have been re-established in a whole range of fields. His medical and scientific legacy has been seriously reviewed by some distinguished practitioners in these fields. And the respect in which he is held in many parts of Africa has been re-emphasised even as others have sought to attack or at the very least reinterpret his reputation and significance.

Biography is of course a highly attractive form. It is, as has often been pointed out, the nearest non-fictional form of writing to fiction itself.

GENERAL EDITOR'S INTRODUCTION

It is a story, re-created as an imaginative narrative, with a clearly linear form from birth (beginnings) through the life (achievements, failings, controversies, reputations) to the death (the climactic ending). It sweeps up, and often illuminates the lives of, an entire cast of characters drawn from both the obscure and the famous. Through the connections between the central figure and these other 'cast members', the subject's character and activities are developed and explored. It is also clearly related to the travel narrative since a life involves a journey from birth to death, with personality development, relationships with others (often including marriage and procreation), with the intellectual, spiritual, creative and emotional landscapes encountered en route. Invariably, there is also a strong element of visuality. A life is imaginatively envisioned through both text and images, through events, encounters and topographical contexts. Livingstone's life includes all of these aspects in heightened form, as well as constituting a genuine and highly dramatic travel narrative which, as in the Bergen café, has made his name synonymous with such journeying. But in addition to all of that, Livingstone's life carried on beyond the death at Ilala in Zambia. He became, in many senses, an ancestor figure, a patron saint, a touchstone, a court of appeal, also an object of abuse, to so many causes. His life is so closely connected to central issues of recent history, to 'exploration' (a term which has itself been subjected to much complex reconsiderations), to Christian missionary endeavour, to colonialism and imperialism, to race relations, to Western scientific and medical developments, to European cultural appropriation and proselytism throughout the world, to decolonisation, neo-colonialism and all sorts of intellectual processes, as well as the global political and social arrangements through which all of these are expressed.

Justin Livingstone's book considers many of these uses and abuses of Livingstone through the technique of 'metabiography'. Indeed, this book is so significant that it considerably develops this methodology as a key approach to the cultural, social and political embedding of biographical production. It contains much that is entirely new even in the apparently over-developed Livingstone biographical industry. We have here an analysis of Livingstone's book *Missionary Travels and Researches in South Africa* which breaks new ground in considering the hand-written manuscript of the book, its relationship to the published version and the correspondence with the publisher through which it was formed for public consumption. There is an extensive analysis of the way in which the extraordinary death rites can be connected with Victorian concepts and 'production' of the drama and instrumentality of mourning. Moreover, the moulding of Livingstone's reputation is considered in terms of the imposition and development

GENERAL EDITOR'S INTRODUCTION

of late nineteenth-century imperialism as well as the emergence of a Scottish cultural and historical renaissance in the period. And, intriguingly, there is a highly original consideration of the ways in which Livingstone has indeed been considered in various forms of fiction and both didactic and satirical entertainment. Yet the Livingstone afterlife is so protean that much remains to be done. As well as the additional book I proposed in my opening paragraph, we can still explore the ways in which the name of Livingstone has been repeatedly invoked, often in wholly contrary causes, in so many controversies associated with empire and its demise in the twentieth century, with cultural and political issues in the United Kingdom in the same period, and in the identities formed in the Scottish diaspora throughout the world. But in all of these there can be no doubt at all that this book constitutes a key text which all future writers on Livingstone will have to take note of. It is indeed high time that we should junk that fateful reviewer's 'famous last word', 'definitive', but there are still books which define the current state of play. This is one of them.

John M. MacKenzie

ACKNOWLEDGEMENTS

I owe a debt of thanks to many people who made this book possible. Firstly I am grateful to Aaron Kelly for his support, encouragement and insight throughout much of my research. Many conversations with him helped to clarify my thinking and point me in new directions. Ian Campbell, too, was always ready to discuss ideas and for many years he has provided me with counsel and academic guidance. I am greatly indebted to Clare Pettitt for her perceptive feedback on an earlier draft. Her engagement provided both the specialist knowledge and critical perspective that this project needed. Other scholars have offered comments and conversation, and have encouraged this project in a number of ways. Prominent among these are Bill Bell, Roy Bridges, Lawrence Dritsas, Felix Driver, Louise Henderson, Joanna Lewis, John MacKenzie, Brian Murray, Brian Stanley, Jack Thompson, Jonathan Wild and Adrian Wisnicki. Max Jones, the reader for Manchester University Press, provided particularly strong insights and helped to make this book much better than it would have been otherwise. I am very grateful for his advice.

Some parts of this monograph have been published elsewhere in earlier forms. Sections from Chapter 2 appeared as 'The Meaning and Making of *Missionary Travels*: The Sedentary and Itinerant Discourses of a Victorian Bestseller' in *Studies in Travel Writing* (15: 3 (2011), 267–92). My thanks to the editor, Tim Youngs, and to the publisher, Taylor & Francis Ltd, for permission to reuse this material. Likewise, sections of Chapter 3 were published as 'A "Body" of Evidence: The Posthumous Presentation of David Livingstone' in *Victorian Literature and Culture* (40: 1 (2012), 1–24). Again I'm grateful to the editors, John Maynard and Adrienne Munich, and Cambridge University Press for granting me their permission.

Many curators and librarians lent crucial support by helping me to gain access to the material that I have worked on. I particularly appreciate conversations with David McClay, from the National Library of Scotland, who was exceedingly generous with this time and gave invaluable advice on the holdings in the John Murray Archive. I thank the National Library of Scotland for the kind permission to quote its material and to reproduce many of the illustrations included in this book. Thanks as well to the David Livingstone Centre, Blantyre, and particularly Anne Martin, for allowing me to reproduce another of the images. I am also indebted to Jewel Koopman and

ACKNOWLEDGEMENTS

Estelle Liebenberg-Barkhuizen of the Alan Paton Centre & Struggle Archives in the University of KwaZulu-Natal, for sending me material relating to the unpublished play *The Last Journey*. I thank the Alan Paton Centre & Struggle Archives, and its head librarian Nazim Gani, for permitting me to quote the play and to use the photographs that are included here. I must also acknowledge the Carnegie Trust for the Universities of Scotland for their financial support. I am very grateful for their scholarship which enabled me to undertake this project. My current fellowship at the University of Glasgow also enabled me to bring this book to completion. Thanks to my colleagues, Megan Coyer, Rhian Williams, Andrew Radford, Nigel Leask and especially Christine Ferguson, the School of Critical Studies has provided a supportive and engaging intellectual environment.

Many friends over the years have listened to me talk at length about my work. They are far too numerous to list in full here. Special thanks, however, must go to Lizzie Dearden for the depths of her patience and for taking me away from my work to have some much needed breaks. My biggest debt is to my family. Emma and Paul, also great friends, have always opened their home to me. They've been ready with words of encouragement and – just as important – a lot of fun. My mum continually offered a listening ear when I needed it most. She read this book with a sharp eye, which speaks volumes about her generosity. My dad has been an academic inspiration. Time and again he has given critical advice, and in his own work he has shown me what real scholarship looks like.

ABBREVIATIONS AND A NOTE ON SPELLING

Abbreviations

LMS   London Missionary Society
RGS   Royal Geographical Society
UMCA Universities' Mission to Central Africa

Note on spelling

Today, the river that Livingstone hoped would open the African continent to commerce and Christianity is spelt 'Zambezi'. Throughout this book, however, I have followed Livingstone's spelling, 'Zambesi', for the sake of consistency.

CHAPTER ONE

Bio-diversity: metabiographical method

> Someone else, in my limited experience, never gets things quite right. The exact socio-economic tone, the muddle and eddy of peculiar circumstances are almost inevitably missed.
> John Updike, 'On Literary Biography'

John Updike reportedly once remarked that biographies are nothing but 'novels with indexes'.[1] This delightfully scathing quip epitomises a certain sense that biography is a spurious enterprise, a genre to be defined in terms of its limits, and best approached with a healthy dose of suspicion. Even where it has not been brushed aside with quite such dismissive disregard, it is notable that biography has not been the subject of serious critical examination until fairly recently. The result is that, for those now writing on the subject, it has become almost axiomatic to pass comment on its lack of theorisation. David Ellis, for instance, refers to on the surprising 'dearth of analytic enquiry' that the genre has inspired.[2] In one of the most recent discussions, by Michael Benton, the familiar complaint is sounded once again as he notes that 'it has become something of a truism to declare that biography has failed to establish any theoretical foundations'.[3] On the whole, argues the practitioner and professor of biographical studies Richard Holmes, the academy 'has not been very keen to recognize biography'. For the most part, it has been left to itself, 'outside the established institutes of learning, and beyond the groves of academe'.[4] These complaints, however, while once valid, have now largely passed into obsolescence. In the last decade or so, research into biography has begun to thrive and a burgeoning, theoretically inclined literature has been produced.[5] As the discipline has established itself, increasing attention has been directed to the changing nature of biography, across both time and space. It is no homogenous genre, but one that has adapted in order to meet different cultural needs and to serve a variety of interests. As Peter

France and William St Clair put it in *Mapping Lives*, 'biography is not the same, and does not perform the same tasks, at different times and in different places'. Consequently, the form of criticism they pursue is one that scrutinises 'the functions which it can serve and has served in different societies, its *uses*'.[6]

The mode of enquiry that this book adopts is broadly similar in intent. Its subject is the use, function, and evolution of the biographical tradition that has drawn sustenance from the Victorian period's foremost missionary and explorer, David Livingstone. As John M. MacKenzie has noted, since his death Livingstone 'has become the subject of a major biographical industry'.[7] We might add that he has sustained something of an academic industry as well, and one that appears to be far from exhausted. In examining the discursive strata that have sedimented around Livingstone, no single or essential image of the hero emerges. Instead, it becomes clear that he has been represented in diverse ways and put to work in a variety of socio-political contexts. The heterogeneity of Livingstone's posthumous identity has of course received a certain amount of attention. MacKenzie has remarked on the way in which he appears to have 'lent himself to any number of iconic images'.[8] Indeed, as I will argue, Livingstone has been moulded variously by writers emerging from differing socio-cultural locations and with contrasting political purposes. His historical reputation has, in short, shown a remarkable malleability. The aim of this project then is to investigate Livingstone's legacy, or as it is perhaps better to say, his legacies. MacKenzie has ably sketched the rough shape of Livingstone's afterlife, but the task remains to open up more fully the plurality of identities that he has acquired since his demise. This book, then, is not another biography. Its terrain is not the chronicle of Livingstone's life from factory 'piecer' to international superstar, nor an account of his missionary activity and explorations in southern and central Africa. It is, rather, a book about biography, an examination of the ways in which one subject has been used, abused, represented and remembered.

In recent decades, Livingstone scholarship has become increasingly interdisciplinary and has turned in many productive intellectual directions. Livingstone has, for instance, played an integral role in studies of nineteenth-century expeditionary science and the culture of exploration,[9] as well as in scholarship concerned with the Victorian press and the rise of celebrity.[10] Livingstone has long been considered part of the 'prelude to imperialism',[11] but he is now also discussed in the context of 'imperial literature' and the genesis of the 'dark continent' mythos.[12] Social anthropologists, moreover, particularly Isaac Schapera, have paid close attention to Livingstone's ethnographic observations about local African life in various regions.[13] Even in the Comaroffs' critical study of cultural collision – a book in which missionaries are cast as agents of the 'colonization of consciousness' – notable credit is given to his commentaries on the cultural and linguistic particularities of the Tswana ethnic group.[14] Indeed Livingstone offers one of the very few eyewitness accounts for certain areas of mid-Victorian Africa, and so his writings – from field diaries and journals to bestselling publications – have proven vital to Africanists attempting historical reconstruction.[15] This same written output has likewise proven significant for work on the Victorian publishing industry and the production of travel literature and geographical knowledge.[16] Mission historians have also analysed Livingstone's theories – which were not always conventional – as well as the extent of his impact on later missionary enterprises.[17] Within mission research more generally, studies on topics as varied as racial and gender politics,[18] the family unit,[19] missionary linguistics,[20] natural science,[21] and expeditionary photography[22] have all included reference to Livingstone. Medical historians have likewise anatomised his role as a practitioner, trained in the Scottish system, who produced an extensive body of epidemical commentary. Indeed, Livingstone's perceptions regarding febrile disease and prophylactic treatment are considered important contributions in the development of tropical medicine.[23]

The scholarship constituting Livingstone studies is clearly considerable and comprises diverse academic projects. Nevertheless, within the field, this book is the first extended account of Livingstone's lengthy posthumous reputation and multiple afterlives.[24] While it offers the fullest study of his remembrance to date, it does so within parameters that are resolutely textual. The countless statues, exhibitions and commemorative events that he has inspired could certainly sustain their own monograph-length treatment. Here, however, such forms of memorialisation have largely been laid to one side in order to offer detailed engagement with the ways that Livingstone has been written. Indeed, in documenting Livingstone's 'lives', the methodology I have employed is what might be called metabiographical analysis. This framework, essentially a biography of biographies, was developed by the historian of science Nicolaas Rupke. Surveying the reputation of Alexander von Humboldt, Rupke reflects on what he calls 'a striking plasticity of the historical record'.[25] Humboldt acquired a suite of posthumous identities, and his numerous biographers, across generations of German culture, 'offered a diversity of reasons for honouring him': they addressed largely the same biographical material, but 'molded it differently, developing distinct narrative lines, supported at times by specific hermeneutic and research strategies'.[26] In examining the diverse versions of Humboldt, Rupke stresses that his aim is not to discover some 'essential' identity, or to finally retrieve the 'real' Humboldt from historical misappropriation. Rather, he argues, the task of metabiography is 'primarily to explore the fact and the extent of the ideological embeddedness of biographical portraits, not to settle the issue of authenticity'.[27] The purpose is not to offer the last word on the debate, but instead to interrogate representational difference and its underlying preoccupations. In itself, the existence of variant portrayals of the same life could seem a rather trivial observation. However, metabiography is not just interested in subjective constructions of any historical subject. Its deeper concern is their ideological and institutional 'embeddedness' within the 'remembrance culture of any one period of political history':[28] in other words, what is important is the way in which one life can be recreated according to contemporaneous needs. While of course each reinterpretation of an historical figure will be subjective to a degree, Rupke argues that the constructions are more often than not 'collective' in nature.[29] Political culture is frequently of greater significance than merely individual predilections. While I will argue that, with Livingstone at least, it is often possible to discern competing versions of his identity at one chronological moment, he has been perpetually constructed in dialogue with the contemporary political environment of his biographers.

In offering a metabiography of Livingstone, this project can be situated within a growing body of research that is concerned with the ideology of representation over and against the pursuit of the subject's authentic identity.[30] Recently, several studies have applied similar methodologies to the afterlives of historical figures. While Rupke has offered the most sophisticated formulation of the metabiographical framework, the same term is used by Lucasta Miller in her examination of the 'Brontë myth'. In exploring the 'years of cultural accretion' that have generated the mythology, Miller does not aim to 'sweep away all previous "false" versions of the story and resurrect the "true" Brontës in their place'.[31] Instead of engaging in iconoclastic demystification, in order to reveal the 'real' Brontës, she offers 'a book about biography, a metabiography', which exposes 'just how malleable the raw material' of life-writing can be.[32] Patricia Fara takes largely the same approach to 'Newton's posthumous reputations'. Without explicitly declaring a metabiographical outlook, she states that her work 'is emphatically *not* a conventional biography', for 'one of its central arguments is that no "true" representation of Newton exists';[33] the succeeding reinterpretations of his life were perennially 'laden with ideological import'.[34] Metabiographical elements are evident too in Steven Aschheim's work on the 'transformational nature of the Nietzsche legacy' in Germany. He rejects an essentialist approach that evaluates the vascillating interpretations of the philosopher with a 'prior interpretive construction of the "real" Nietzsche'.[35] From a cultural historical perspective, the task is not to assess the validity of different interpretations but to 'map their agendae, contexts and consequences'.[36] Metabiography is not as interested in the question of the subject's true selfhood, as in the malleable and historically situated nature of posthumous identity. Accordingly, this project is less concerned with making its own claims about the 'real' David Livingstone than with charting the claims that have been made by so many others.[37]

The influence of several distinct intellectual currents can be readily detected in metabiographical analysis. Two of these are signalled by Rupke, who considers both reception theory and developments in postmodern approaches to historiography to be precursors to his project. In this sense metabiography weds theories of reading and writing; it is a theory of both hermeneutics and narrative, interpretation and inscription.

The indebtedness of metabiography to the flourishing industry of reception theory lies in its insights into the contrasting production of meaning in differing readerships. Important to the genesis of this movement by way of intellectual influence, and thus a critical foundation to metabiography, were the philosophical hermeneutics of Hans Georg Gadamer. As Robert Holub points out, Gadamer, more than any other thinker has been 'concerned with the situated nature of our interpretations' and 'the historical nature of understanding'.[38] For Gadamer, when we read, our inescapable human setting, our locatedness, is necessarily implicated in the production of any meaning that will be 'discovered'.[39] Since our historical boundedness is inexorable, the present situation and past experience of 'knowers' become 'constitutively involved in any process of understanding'.[40] Rehabilitating the idea of prejudice, Gadamer argues that our preconceptions and presuppositions should not be considered obstacles to understanding: rather, they are actually enabling. As Holub writes, prejudices are in reality 'a fundamental part of any hermeneutic situation'.[41] The notion of the horizon, which Gadamer so famously developed, is a potent metaphor that is intended to encompass 'our situatedness in the world' and everything that we bring to bear on interpretation: the horizon is that 'over which we cannot see'.[42]

In Gadamer's wake, one of his students and one of reception studies' early theorists, Hans Robert Jauss, began to take account of 'the reader's constructive activity' in approaching a text, and the importance of the 'paradigms, beliefs and values' that they brought to bear upon it.[43] Following his teacher, Jauss's 'methodological centerpiece' was his notion of the 'horizon of expectations', which Robert Holub broadly defines as the 'structure of expectations, a "system of references" or a mind-set that a hypothetical individual might bring to any text'.[44] In a similar vein, another reader-oriented critic, Stanley Fish, argues that meaning should not be understood simply as an inherent quality residing in a text, but rather '*as an event*, something that is happening between the words and in the reader's mind'.[45] In the wake of these theorists, subsequent reception studies have turned increasingly to real readers, in an effort to determine the impact of historical and geographical location in the construction of discrete textual meanings. As James Machor and Philip Goldstein observe, working from 'Jauss's assumption that as positive constructive influences the prejudices of the reader establish his or her subjective horizon and divide it from the historical other', modern reception study 'examines the changing horizons of a text's many readers':[46] its overarching concern is the 'the sociohistorical contexts of interpretive practice'.[47] They are aware, as Fish has argued, that readerly habits depend on one's historical situation, on the social group and 'interpretive communities' to which one belongs.[48] As with texts, the meaning of a life can never be fixed. It inevitably lies open to interpretation and revision. In a sense, metabiography can be considered the consequence of extending hermeneutic logic to the ways in which people and legacies are multifariously interpreted. It is thus an important argument of this book that the historicality and horizons of David Livingstone's biographers inevitably impinged upon the way in which he was interpreted and deemed to have significance.

But while metabiography is 'a hermeneutic of biography', it makes claims that go beyond reception theory.[49] Indeed, the point is that in life-writing the biographical subject is not just interpreted, but constructed: the biographee not only is reread, but is recreated. Metabiography is not solely a theory about reading but also one about writing. In this respect it is indebted, in a restricted sense at least, to the insights of the postmodern challenge to conventional historical enquiry.[50] Metabiography necessarily engages with 'the way we frame historical questions, our attempts to capture past meaning, and the relationship of these to ideology, politics and power'.[51] Although Rupke does not make any explicit link, there is an obvious resonance, even in the name, with Hayden White's project of 'metahistory'. As White argues, it is important to take seriously 'the essentially provisional and contingent nature of historical representations and of their susceptibility to infinite revision'. Historical writing, he contends, has not been sufficiently appraised as a form of narrative. For White, it is vital to examine the historical text as a literary artefact, a discourse whose explanatory power lies in its ability to make 'stories out of *mere* chronicles'.[52] As White puts it, 'The events are *made* into a story by

[6]

the suppression or subordination of certain of them and the highlighting of others, by characterization, motif repetition, variation of tone and point of view, alternative descriptive strategies, and the like.'[53] In other words, the facts of the historian have to be selected and then 'emplotted' into the narrative form that readers receive.[54] In this sense historians are involved in making history rather than simply retrieving it. The importance of this perspective for metabiography is White's observation that the same historical events can be emplotted in disparate ways. The raw biographical material of Livingstone's life, it will become clear, has been integrated into a variety of plots and inscribed with an array of meanings across different contexts. Our socio-cultural locatedness is thus relevant not only to the way in which we interpret, but to the narratives we choose to write and the way in which we choose to write them. To this degree, the project of metabiography is engaged with the relationship between the writing of history and questions of politics and ideology.

To argue this is not necessarily to cast the historical method aside as irredeemably fictive, or to lapse into a debilitating relativism. Metabiographical analysis is itself an historical endeavour, a mode of enquiry that presumes the capacity to detect the agendas at work in the biographical representations it explores. Rather than wallowing in the limits of our capacity to effect historical insights, the challenge is to approach the task of recovering the past in a chastened manner. While historians and biographers may not be in the business of tracking down objective truth, it is nonetheless the case that there are varying degrees of warrant for the claims they make. Some versions of history will clearly have greater credibility than others. It is worth pointing out that, to some extent, the partiality of historical research has long been acknowledged in practice. It is now over fifty years since E.H. Carr enjoined scholars to 'study the historian before you begin to study the facts'.[55] Few historians naively believe they are in the business of capturing unambiguous truth; they are under no illusion that their findings are anything more than provisional. The encounter with postmodernism then, has most conspicuous benefit when it heightens such reflexivity in the practice of both history and biography. As one of its foremost critics, Richard J. Evans, observes, postmodernism at its best can encourage 'historians to look more closely at documents, to take their surface patina more seriously, and to think about texts and narratives in new ways', while interrogating 'their own methods and procedures as never before'.[56] In this way, it has the potential to have a self-referential therapeutic effect on research. Despite the postmodern influences on my metabiography of Livingstone, I do not deny that some biographical portrayals are more plausible than others. Yet, the respective quality and authenticity of the representations is a question that this study, and all metabiography, must set to one side in order to prosecute its fundamental argument: all biographies, regardless of sophistication, intersect with the socio-political cultures from which they emerge.

Further to the impact of reception theory and postmodernism, recent developments in biographical studies have added credence to the metabiographical project. While they may not have influenced Rupke's formulation directly, they are striking in their intellectual compatibility. As Richard Holmes has pointed out, one of the most notable features of life-writing as a genre is the way in which biographies continually pass into redundancy, to be supplanted by others offering a fresh take on the life in question. The process by which biographies re-envision their subjects in the light of the present registers how 'social and moral attitudes' and 'standards of judgement' evolve between generations.[57] Biography's inherent dynamic of perpetual reinterpretation functions as a barometer of broader societal changes. Its 'shifts and differences – factual, formal, stylistic, ideological, aesthetic' are some of the genre's most stimulating features and, for Holmes, they warrant the founding of 'virtually a new discipline' for which he offers the epithet 'comparative biography'. Such a project would entail an examination of 'the handling of one subject by a number of different biographers, and over several different historical periods'.[58] Metabiography is at the very least intimately related to this enterprise, yet one could even consider it to be a fully articulated response to the disciplinary appeal for comparative biography.

That a life can be rewritten from ever-new angles indicates that a perennial feature of biography is debate. This duly raises questions about the nature of the genre itself: just what kind of writing is it, where dispute is the life-blood? One feature that recent criticism has commented on is its inability to truly capture its subject, the sense that the biographee always remains elusive. Lucasta Miller suggests that 'Patchwork, rather than photographic likeness, is all the biographer can truly hope to achieve.'[59] Even the fullest representation of a life will never be more than partial. In the same vein, criticism has also drawn attention to biography's irremediable subjectivity. As Hermione Lee writes, it can never offer 'an entirely objective treatment' of a life since 'we write from a certain position, constructed by our history, nationality, race, gender ...'.[60] This is of course true, broadly speaking, of all life's interpretive endeavours, for we are inherently located beings. A stronger version of this argument, however, goes so far as to contend that every biography is really a kind of autobiography, revealing as much about the author as about the subject.[61] While this is overstating the case, and implies a pessimistic view of our capacity to comprehend the other, the autobiographical function of biography is a suggestive notion. Indeed, many of those who wrote 'lives' of Livingstone did recreate him in their own image. He was continually constructed so as to instantiate the politics and cherished values of those producing him.

Related to the charge of subjectivity is the contention that biography incorporates 'fictive' elements. This stems from the way in which, through narrative, it imposes form on the facts of its subject's existence. As Miranda Seymour points out, 'Life in the raw is often shapeless; the biographers must create their persuasive narrative by inserting a connecting thread.'[62] Biographies are thus subject to aesthetic considerations and the compulsion to create a compelling and satisfying story. It has even been suggested that the creative impulse is more complex in biography than in fiction. Michael Benton argues, developing an observation of David Cecil's, that 'the novelist's creativity shows itself mainly in invention, in the power to create characters, to put them in scenes'. '[T]he biographer's creativity', on the other hand, 'shows itself in interpretation, in a capacity to discover in the scenes and anecdotes and the mass of other raw material the dominant thematic life story to be fashioned into a work of art.'[63] The deeply interpretive nature of life-writing, its artistic mores and its formal proximity to fiction are thus integral features of the genre.

Yet it seems self-evident that biography is not purely fictional. While David Ellis notes that both biographers and novelists 'use many of the same literary devices and methods', he argues that outward semblance should not be taken to mean that the two forms are identical.[64] A key difference of course is 'the imaginary pact' that biographers make to respect the information to which they have access.[65] Any story that they tell must coalesce with the evidence they have assembled. In other words, biographers and novelists deal with a different order of events; the former are bound to aspire towards a faithful depiction of what really happened and what their subject was really like, even if this remains difficult to grasp. While biographies are interpretive, and so are necessarily underdetermined by the facts of a life, the possibility of true representation must at least serve as a regulative principle for good biographical practice. All this rubs up, however, against that ever-present imperative to translate a life into a compelling tale. It is this tension that has led recent critics to theorise biography as a genre that occupies the space between fiction and history. As Holmes suggests, 'all good biographers struggle with a particular tension between the scholarly drive to assemble facts as dispassionately as possible and the novelistic urge to find shape and meaning'.[66] Michael Benton similarly argues that biography 'lies between history and fiction', and that its 'main generic feature' is a 'concern to document facts driven by a strong narrative impulse'.[67] Biography shares terrain with fiction in aesthetics, but parts company in its function and subject matter. This leads critics like Lucasta Miller to call it 'an amphibious art form'.[68] Or as Benton puts it, biography is 'hybrid'.[69] The difficulty with these descriptions, however, is that they could be taken to imply that biography is in some way a corrupted or inferior genre. Indeed, as Ben Pimlott observes, biography has sometimes been seen as 'neither chalk nor cheese: limited in imaginative range, and of its nature insufficiently grounded in the historical method'.[70] Emphasising biography's hybridity could thus enforce the unfortunate notion that it is not quite one thing or the other. As Pimlott reminds us, however, biography 'can claim to be as ancient as any other written form'. It is not the little cousin of two great genres: rather, 'Biography is itself.'[71] However, as long as it is understood to be an entity in its own right, the recognition of biography's amphibian and hybrid character can be productive. These concepts helpfully draw attention to the dualistic and interstitial nature of an enduringly popular literary form.

Given the complex makeup of life-writing, Benton suggests that we should describe and study it as 'biomythography'.[72] In supplying this moniker, he seeks to counterbalance the received notion that biography offers unmediated access to its subject by drawing attention to the process of myth-making that is so prevalent in its literature. While taking biography's concern with the documentary record seriously, Benton aims to subvert 'any concept of life-writing based on a simplistic account of supposed "facts"'.[73] His model is intended to serve as a reminder that a life can never quite be textually captured and that consequently, no biography can ever be considered truly 'definitive'. Biomythography has clear resonances with the metabiographical project, for it is interested in the mutability of biographical representation and the tendency of each generation to rewrite its celebrated lives anew according to contemporary concerns and conventions.

In addition to its roots in reception theory and the postmodern encounter with history, metabiography thus clearly rises to meet certain disciplinary demands in biographical studies. It fulfils the petition for biomythography by attending to the interpretive and fictive dimensions of life-writing: in fact, the contingent and constructed nature of biography is the *sine qua non* of this project. Furthermore, metabiography also responds to Holmes's suggestion that comparative analysis is one of the most productive means of studying the genre. It is not merely a theoretical paradigm, but a direct call to detailed empirical study across a range of contexts. In examining the shifting legacy of a single figure, David Livingstone, questions of history will therefore be paramount. In addition, comparative analysis necessitates a discussion of location, for geographical situatedness bears upon biographical narration. Metabiography will thus be attentive to what Stephen Daniels and Catherine Nash describe as the relationship 'between script and space in the making of life histories'.[74]

Before going on to examine Livingstone's afterlife, the next chapter sets out to consider his own self-representation by critically analysing his bestselling travelogue, *Missionary Travels and Researches in South Africa* (1857). Despite being one of the most celebrated travel texts of the nineteenth century, and a cornerstone of his posthumous reputation, the book has received surprisingly little critical attention. Treating the text as a mechanism of self-projection, the chapter discusses the narrative strategies by which Livingstone managed his image and cultivated his authority as an explorer. In writing *Missionary Travels*, he drew on a number of genres in order to create a hybrid text and thereby present a multifaceted persona to the public. The body of letters between Livingstone and his publisher, John Murray, which deal with the process of the book's publication, are central to the argument of this chapter. Through this correspondence, *Missionary Travels* is revealed to be a censored text, subject to a process of rigorous 'impression management'. Livingstone's editing practices, and indeed the pressures of the marketplace, become yet clearer when the published version of the book is compared with the original handwritten manuscript. While this manuscript has been routinely overlooked in Livingstone scholarship, it contains a number of significant variations to the print version. Most importantly, Livingstone had originally included a protracted diatribe against the role of the British in the Cape Frontier Wars. Engaging in counterfactual speculation, we might surmise that his posthumous reputation might have been rather different had he not excised this powerful extract. Livingstone's text had an active imperialist afterlife, deeply influencing the way in which Victorian Britain perceived the African continent. Some of the material that he removed for publication, however, might not have been quite so appealing to imperialist sensibilities. Yet, even as it stands in its published version, *Missionary Travels* should be considered a highly complex text and one that cannot be unproblematically categorised as imperialist. Indeed, it is likely that Livingstone has been able to sustain such diverse posthumous interpretations because of the protean nature of his text, which has offered readers a range of exploitable quotations to draw upon. This is, of course, true only to a limited extent, for the interpretive practices and prejudices of his biographers were of the utmost consequence.

In the third chapter, I proceed to explore Livingstone's Victorian commemoration by focusing on the ways in which he was constructed in 1874, the year in which his body was returned to British soil after his death in the African continent. When Livingstone passed away in Chitambo, Ilala, after a long battle with debilitating illness, his attendants removed and buried his innards and dried and preserved his body, before transporting it to the coastal town of Bagamoyo in a journey of over a thousand miles. From there, his remains were shipped to Britain, where he was granted a national funeral in the tomb of heroes, Westminster Abbey. The news and circumstances of Livingstone's death quickly took on sensational proportions and were reported, discussed and debated in the contemporary press. He was venerated in numerous obituaries and eulogies, as well as in a profusion of elegiac poetry. Focusing solely on the year of Livingstone's interment presents a unique opportunity to explore this wealth of previously unexamined literature, which was of course integral to the constitution of his legacy. This process of memorialisation opens a window on the Victorian cult of the hero and the period's culture of death and mourning. More important than this, however, is the fact that Livingstone was not always commemorated in the same manner. By examining the differing ways that he was produced in diverse social spaces, Livingstone's name and legacy are revealed to be the subject of dispute; he was, to some degree at least, a space for debate. While Livingstone was certainly the hero of Victorian culture, he is perhaps better thought of as a hero who had multiple meanings for a plurality of Victorian cultures.

The fourth chapter takes up Livingstone's post-mortem imperialist reputation, which can be considered the hegemonic dimension of his afterlife. Most of the texts that use Livingstone in this way can be described as 'exemplary lives' – or even 'hagiography' – in that they idealise their subject, presenting him entirely without blemish. While saintly writing of this stripe was predominantly a Victorian penchant, such biographical practices broke the confines of the nineteenth century. The first argument of this chapter is that the many hagiographic representations of Livingstone were imperialist in their effects. They often emplotted him into a romance narrative in which he played the role of the questing hero. Applied to an African context, this construed a racial dynamic in which the white explorer was elevated into a conquering champion, while indigenous peoples were reduced to obstacles that barred his path and confronted him with disorder. After exploring the logic of hagiography, the focus of the chapter turns to the way in which Livingstone was routinely shaped by his biographers in order to meet the demands of the changing face of empire. Expanding on John M. MacKenzie's account of Livingstone's legacy, I argue that, as the poster-boy of imperialism, he was remoulded and re-presented with each major shift in colonial policy in a pattern that persisted into the empire's twilight years. Yet it is an important argument of this chapter that he was not presented homogenously at any one chronological moment. Certainly, shifts in colonial attitude were decisive, but Livingstone was used by his biographers to enter into dialogue with their contemporary environment. Indeed, while he was continually found to speak to present-day politics, Livingstone was actually constructed according to a range of imperialisms. This chapter also explores a less-developed dimension of Livingstone's legacy that resisted the hegemonic colonialist representation. Certain authors countervailed the norm by using him to offer a limited critique of imperialism. For several of his biographers dating from the mid-twentieth century, Livingstone foreshadowed sensitive intercultural engagement and even cultural relativism.

In recent years, a considerable amount of Livingstone scholarship has been devoted to his Scottish identity and his position within the nation's social and intellectual history. In keeping with this critical trajectory, my fifth chapter takes up Livingstone's Scottish legacy. The aim, however, is not to discuss the formative influence of his cultural background or the Scottish bent of his ideas and vision. Rather, the purpose is to ask both how his Scottishness has been represented, and more specifically, how he has been represented by Scots. The chapter begins by considering those biographies that were not particularly interested in his Alban roots at all. Indeed, for some, Livingstone embodied an 'English' national character, while, for others, he exemplified supposedly 'Anglo-Saxon' qualities. In these Anglocentric representations, Livingstone's Scottishness was not quite effaced but was certainly relegated to the sideline. Yet, for his northern biographers, the explorer's national identity has been of vital importance and has functioned in a variety of contexts. Under the Celtic revival, from the late nineteenth century, researchers took it upon themselves to delve into Livingstone's Gaelic lineage. In an effort to confront Anglo-Saxonism, and to increase the prestige of the Gàidhealtachd, Livingstone was soon connected with a range of Highland heritages. In contrast to the polarised Anglo-Saxon and Celtic representations, other authors were attracted to Livingstone because he could represent a fusion of races. While his ancestry was Highland and Jacobite on his father's side, it was Lowland and Covenanting on his mother's. Given the longstanding antipathy between the Highland and Lowland regions, it was fitting that Scotland's foremost champion could serve as a unifying figure for the entire nation. At the same time, I argue, many authors sought to use Livingstone for an even broader purpose, in order to assert a Scottish national consciousness within the confines of the Union and empire. In the late nineteenth century, and leading up to the First World War, those who were keen to assert Scotland's prestige within the imperial project insisted on the vital influence of Livingstone's nation of origin in shaping his character and talents. One of the effects of the preoccupation with Livingstone's Scottishness, however, was the production of many biographies redolent of Kailyard literature. Presenting his life in terms of Scotland's best-known genre was ambivalent in its effects: on the one hand, it conveyed a limited and parochial vision of the nation, but on the other, it served to direct attention to Livingstone's identity as a Scot. The chapter concludes by revisiting the period of the Scottish National Memorial to David Livingstone, which opened in 1929.[75] Since it enshrined him as a distinctly national hero, this is generally thought of as the era in which the connection between Livingstone and Scottish identity was at its strongest. While this is true to a large extent, I offer some revision of this perspective. By chronicling the longer history of Livingstone's Scottish legacy, I argue that the memorial should be understood as both an intensification and modification of a longstanding national reputation.

Following this coverage of Livingstone's extensive biographical legacy, the sixth chapter examines the ways in which he has been represented in fiction and drama. The creative literature that David Livingstone inspired has not been subjected to sustained interrogation; in fact, it has been almost universally ignored. This is surprising, for even while they are outweighed in volume by the numerous biographical portraits, fictional portrayals constitute a significant dimension of his reputation in their own right. The most interesting of this work emerges in the aftermath of the political and intellectual shifts that were inaugurated by decolonisation. Under the auspices of postcolonialism, Livingstone was radically rewritten: he served as a cherished icon of empire, and thus as a focal point against which to direct critique, vandalism and the project of 'writing back'. In symbolic capacity, he was employed to debunk the Western myth of 'discovery', to 'laugh back' at the imperial centre and to offer comment on both the linguistic legacy of imperialism and the complex relationship between Christianity and colonialism. But while the politico-intellectual project of postcolonialism spawned some of the most creative re-evaluations, an alternative image of Livingstone emerged from the oppressive context of South African apartheid. For certain authors with liberal and radical agendas, he symbolised in varying degrees the breakdown of division and the possibility of positive racial interaction.

Although Livingstone has been scrutinised extensively by historians, historical geographers and historical anthropologists, it is perhaps a perspective derived from a background in literary analysis that permits an original contribution to the field. It is close engagement with textuality, literary genre and authorship that enables this book to offer a critical exploration of David Livingstone's multifaceted legacy, covering ground from his own self-staging to his Victorian commemoration, and from imperial and Scottish representations to fictional re-creations. Interpreting the term 'biography' broadly – so as to encompass forms of life-writing such as elegy, obituary, drama and the novel – this metabiography traces the rich range of contexts in which Livingstone has found meaning and maps the evolution of these reputations over a considerable historical period. Of course even in the span of a lifetime, the meaning of a self is never stable. As Richard Jenkins argues, selfhood should not be conceived of as 'a fixed entity' that persists in stasis throughout life's duration, but instead should be 'understood *as* process, as "being" or "becoming"'.[76] Indeed, as Charles Taylor and Alasdair MacIntyre have suggested, the self can be grasped as a story, an unfolding and developing narrative.[77] And this narrative, as my study shows, does not conclude with an individual's death. The subject's identity is not left to rest in peace, but persists in an afterlife of continued revision which generates fresh meanings in ever new contexts.

Notes

1. In his essay 'The Proper Study', which appeared in *Mapping Lives*, Richard Holmes attributed this quotation to an article by Updike in the *New York Review of Books* (4 February 1999). The phrase, however, does not actually occur anywhere within Updike's piece, which is entitled 'One Cheer for Literary Biography'. Others who have cited this comment, like Hermione Lee in *Biography: A Very Short Introduction*, quote it indirectly from *Mapping Lives*.
2. David Ellis, *Literary Lives: Biography and the Search for Understanding* (Edinburgh: Edinburgh University Press, 2000), p. 3.
3. Michael Benton, *Literary Biography: An Introduction* (Chichester: Wiley-Blackwell, 2009), p. 3.
4. Richard Holmes, 'The Proper Study?', in Peter France and William St Clair (eds), *Mapping Lives: The Uses of Biography* (Oxford: Oxford University Press, 2002), p. 7.
5. Indeed, Holmes's own appointment to a chair of 'Biographical Studies' in East Anglia signals the change in intellectual climate.
6. Peter France and William St Clair, 'Introduction', in Peter France and William St Clair (eds), *Mapping Lives: The Uses of Biography* (Oxford: Oxford University Press, 2002), p. 4.
7. John M. MacKenzie, 'David Livingstone and the Worldly After-Life: Imperialism and Nationalism in Africa', in John M. MacKenzie (ed.), *David Livingstone and the Victorian Encounter with Africa* (London: National Portrait Gallery, 1996), p. 203.
8. John M. MacKenzie, 'The Iconography of the Exemplary Life: The Case of David Livingstone', in Geoffrey Cubitt and Allen Warren (eds), *Heroic Reputations and Exemplary Lives* (Manchester: Manchester University Press, 2000), p. 102.
9. Lawrence Dritsas, *Zambesi: David Livingstone and Expeditionary Science in Africa* (London: I.B. Tauris, 2010); Felix Driver, *Geography Militant: Cultures of Exploration and Empire* (Oxford: Blackwell, 2001); James R. Ryan, *Picturing Empire: Photography and the Visualization of the British Empire* (London: Reaktion Books, 1997).

10 Clare Pettitt, *Dr. Livingstone, I Presume? Missionaries, Journalists, Explorers, and Empire* (Cambridge, Mass.: Harvard University Press, 2007); Beau Riffenburgh, *The Myth of the Explorer: The Press, Sensationalism, and Geographical Discovery* (Oxford: Oxford University Press, 1994).
11 H.A.C. Cairns, *Prelude to Imperialism: British Reactions to Central Africa Society, 1840–1890* (London: Routledge & Kegan Paul, 1965); Tim Jeal, *Livingstone* (New Haven: Yale University Press, 2001).
12 Daniel Bivona, *British Imperial Literature, 1870–1940: Writing and the Administration of Empire* (Cambridge: Cambridge University Press, 1998); Patrick Brantlinger, *Rule of Darkness: British Literature and Imperialism, 1830–1914* (New York: Cornell University Press, 1988).
13 Isaac Schapera (ed.), *David Livingstone: Family Letters, 1841–1856* (London: Chatto & Windus, 1959); *Livingstone's Private Journals, 1851–1853* (London: Chatto & Windus, 1960); *Livingstone's Missionary Correspondence, 1841–1856* (London: Chatto & Windus, 1961); *David Livingstone South African Papers, 1849–1853* (Cape Town: Van Riebeeck Society, 1974, 1975).
14 Jean Comaroff and John L. Comaroff, *Of Revelation and Revolution*, vol. 1 (Chicago: University of Chicago Press, 1991), p. xi.
15 Roy. C. Bridges, 'Nineteenth-Century East African Travel Record with an Appendix on "Armchair Geographers" and Cartography', *Paideuma*, 33 (1987), 179–96; Adrian S. Wisnicki, 'Victorian Field Notes from the Luala River, Congo', in Justin D. Livingstone (ed.), 'Livingstone Studies: Bicentenary Essays', special issue, *Scottish Geographical Journal*, 129: 3–4 (2013), 210–39.
16 Leila Koivunen, 'Visualising Africa – Complexities of Illustrating David Livingstone's *Missionary Travels*', paper presented at 'Ennen & Nyt', the Nordic Conference on the History of Ideas, Helsinki, 2001; Leila Koivunen, *Visualizing Africa in Nineteenth-Century British Travel Accounts* (New York: Routledge, 2009); Louise Henderson, '"Everyone will die laughing": John Murray and the Publication of David Livingstone's *Missionary Travels*', Livingstone Online, Wellcome Trust Centre for the History of Medicine at UCL (n.d.), www.livingstoneonline.ucl.ac.uk/companion.php?id=HIST2 (accessed 7 June 2010).
17 Jeffrey Cox, *The British Missionary Enterprise since 1700* (New York: Routledge, 2008); John McCracken, *Politics and Christianity in Malawi 1875–1940: The Impact of the Livingstonia Mission in the Northern Province* (Cambridge: Cambridge University Press, 1977); John McCracken, *A History of Malawi: 1859–1966* (Woodbridge: James Currey, 2012).
18 Esme Cleall, *Missionary Discourses of Difference: Negotiating Otherness in the British Empire, 1840–1900* (Basingstoke: Palgrave Macmillan, 2012).
19 Emily Manktelow, *Missionary Families: Race, Gender and Generation on the Spiritual Frontier* (Manchester: Manchester University Press, 2013).
20 Rachael Gilmour, 'Missionaries, Colonialism and Language in Nineteenth-Century South Africa', *History Compass*, 5: 6 (2007), 1761–77.
21 Patrick Harries, 'Natural Science and *Naturvölker*: Missionary Entomology and Botany', in Patrick Harries and David Maxwell (eds), *The Spiritual in the Secular: Missionaries and Knowledge about Africa* (Grand Rapids: Eerdmans, 2012), pp. 30–71.
22 T. Jack Thompson, *Light on Darkness? Missionary Photography of Africa in the Nineteenth and Early Twentieth Centuries* (Grand Rapids: Eerdmans, 2012).
23 Michael Gelfand, *Livingstone the Doctor: His Life and Travels: A Study in Medical History* (Oxford: Blackwell, 1957); Christopher Lawrence, 'David Livingstone's Medical Education', 'Fever in the Tropics' and 'Medicine and Science in Livingstone's Letters', Livingstone Online (n.d.), www.livingstoneonline.ucl.ac.uk/companion.php?category=historical (accessed 31 July 2013); Debbie Harrison, 'A Pioneer Working on the Frontiers of Western and Tropical Medicine', in Sarah Worden (ed.), *David Livingstone: Man, Myth and Legacy* (Edinburgh: National Museums Scotland, 2012), pp. 69–81.
24 Dorothy O. Helly has previously published an excellent study of Livingstone's 'legacy', but her focus is primarily on Horace Waller's role in shaping the myth

by editing Livingstone's *Last Journals*. Helly is concerned with Livingstone and Waller's influence on the Victorian missionary movement and imperialism, whereas my own study is occupied with the different identities that Livingstone has acquired over a longer period. See Dorothy O. Helly, *Livingstone's Legacy: Horace Waller and Victorian Mythmaking* (Athens, O.: Ohio University Press, 1987).

25 Nicolaas A. Rupke, *Alexander von Humboldt: A Metabiography* (Chicago: University of Chicago Press, 2008), p. 203.
26 Ibid., p. 16.
27 Ibid., p. 215.
28 Ibid., p. 18.
29 Ibid., p. 208.
30 The very idea of a singular or essential self is not an uncontested notion. As Charles Taylor argues, the nature of selfhood is 'complex and many-tiered' and takes shape in relation to the orientations and identifications provided by our 'horizon' experience. See Charles Taylor, *Sources of the Self: The Making of the Modern Identity* (Cambridge, Mass.: Harvard University Press, 1989), p. 29.
31 Lucasta Miller, *The Brontë Myth* (London: Jonathan Cape, 2001), p. x.
32 Ibid., pp. x, 109.
33 Patricia Fara, *Newton: The Making of Genius* (London: Picador, 2003), p. xvi.
34 Ibid., p. 196. Similarly, Rebekah Higgitt situates her study of Newton within a growing field of 'reputational studies'. See Rebekah Higgitt, *Recreating Newton: Newtonian Biography and the Making of Nineteenth-Century History of Science* (London: Pickering & Chatto, 2007), p. 1.
35 Steven E. Aschheim, *The Nietzsche Legacy in Germany, 1890-1990* (Berkeley: University of California Press, 1994), p. 4.
36 Ibid., p. 5.
37 For an introduction to 'Livingstone Studies', see Justin D. Livingstone, 'Writing and Remembrance: New Directions in Livingstone Studies', in Livingstone (ed.), 'Livingstone Studies: Bicentenary Essays', 137–49.
38 Robert C. Holub, *Reception Theory: A Critical Introduction* (London: Methuen, 1984), p. 36.
39 David Linge, 'Introduction', in Hans-Georg Gadamer, *Philosophical Hermeneutics*, trans. David Linge (Berkeley: University of California Press, 1976), p. xv.
40 Ibid., p. xiv.
41 Holub, *Reception Theory*, p. 41.
42 Ibid., p. 42; Hans-Georg Gadamer, *Truth and Method*, trans. Joel Weinsheimer and Donald E. Marshall (London: Bloomsbury, 2013).
43 James L. Machor and Philip Goldstein, 'Introduction', in James L. Machor and Philip Goldstein (eds), *Reception Study: From Literary Theory to Cultural Studies* (London: Routledge, 2001), p. xi.
44 Holub, *Reception Theory*, p. 59.
45 Stanley E. Fish, *Is there a Text in this Class? The Authority of Interpretive Communities* (Cambridge, Mass.: Harvard University Press, 1980), p. 28.
46 Machor and Goldstein, 'Introduction', p. xi.
47 Ibid., p. xii.
48 Fish, *Is there a Text in this Class?*, p. 14.
49 Rupke, *Alexander von Humboldt*, p. 214.
50 'Postmodernism' is term of contention defying simple definition. As Simon Malpas argues, finding 'a simple, uncontroversial meaning for the term "postmodern" is all but impossible'. Consequently, it is perhaps best characterised as a 'space for debate'. My use of the term, however, can be broadly taken to refer to that work within historical theory whose 'focus frequently falls on the act of writing history, and the social and political questions evoked by different narrative strategies'. See Simon Malpas, *The Postmodern* (London: Routledge, 2005), pp. 4, 97.
51 Rupke, *Alexander von Humboldt*, p. 216.
52 Hayden White, *Tropics of Discourse: Essays in Cultural Criticism* (Baltimore: Johns Hopkins University Press, 1978), p. 82.

53 Ibid., p. 84.
54 Ibid., p. 85.
55 Edward H. Carr, *What is History?* (London: Macmillan, 1961), p. 23.
56 Richard J. Evans, *In Defence of History* (London: Granta, 1997), p. 248.
57 Holmes, 'The Proper Study?', p. 15.
58 Ibid., pp. 15, 16.
59 Lucasta Miller, 'Stuff with Raw Edges', in Mark Bostridge (ed.), *Lives for Sale: Biographers' Tales* (London and New York: Continuum, 2004), p. 145.
60 Hermione Lee, *Biography: A Very Short Introduction* (Oxford: Oxford University Press, 2009), p. 12.
61 Ibid., p. 12.
62 Miranda Seymour, 'Shaping the Truth', in France and Clair (eds), *Mapping Lives*, p. 264.
63 Benton, *Literary Biography*, p. xx.
64 Ellis, *Literary Lives*, p. 14.
65 Ibid., p. 15.
66 Holmes, 'The Proper Study?', pp. 16–17.
67 Benton, *Literary Biography*, pp. 3, 18. Benton acknowledges that neither history nor fiction should really be thought of as entirely autonomous concepts: 'History is conveyed through narrative ... conversely, fictional narrative is dependent upon history.' See Benton, *Literary Biography*, p. 42. Despite this relationship, it is useful to conceive of biography as a narrative form caught between two discourses that deal with a different order of events.
68 Miller, *The Brontë Myth*, p. 169.
69 Benton, *Literary Biography*, p. xv.
70 Ben Pimlott, 'Brushstrokes', in Bostridge (ed.), *Lives for Sale*, pp. 165–6.
71 Ibid., p. 165.
72 Benton, *Literary Biography*, p. 48.
73 Ibid., p. 63.
74 This issue of the *Journal of Historical Geography* dealt with the relationship between geography and biography. In drawing attention to questions of spatiality, Daniels and Nash suggest that life-histories can also be understood as 'life geographies'. Stephen Daniels and Catherine Nash, 'Lifepaths: Geography and Biography', *Journal of Historical Geography*, 30 (2004), 450.
75 The Scottish National Memorial to David Livingstone is now known as the David Livingstone Centre.
76 Richard Jenkins, *Social Identity* (London: Routledge, 1996), p. 4.
77 Taylor, *Sources of the self*, p. 47; Alasdair MacIntyre, *After Virtue: A Study in Moral Theory*, 3rd ed. (London and New York: Bloomsbury, 2013), pp. 245–6.

CHAPTER TWO

Styling the self: making *Missionary Travels*

> I think I may declare to you that you will not find me cantankerous or unreasonable or difficult to deal with in any other matter but I must positively resist any attempts to tamper with or emasculate this book.
> David Livingstone, letter to John Murray, 31 May 1857

In November 1857, David Livingstone's *Missionary Travels and Researches in South Africa*, published by the renowned John Murray, was released to an eager British public. The text, consisting of almost 700 pages, was immediately met with rapturous response not least for its breadth and scope of content. As the *Leeds Mercury* put it, the book seemed to add 'as many facts and thoughts new to the European world as have ever before been compressed within that compass'.[1] Indeed, for the *Glasgow Herald*, *Missionary Travels* was the 'book of the season', if not what the *Caledonian Mercury* called 'the work of the age'.[2] As contemporary scholars point out, the text played a substantial role in both cultivating Livingstone's public image and consolidating his popularity. Despite its early acclaim, and the current critical realisation of its importance, however, there has been a dearth of in-depth studies of the book itself. While the Livingstone biographical industry has thrived from the nineteenth century, and while he has been the subject of any number of academic volumes, the majority of this discourse has paid little attention to *Missionary Travels* as a literary and rhetorical product. The major studies, of course, have mined the narrative for evidence of Livingstone's ideas and activities and for information on mid-Victorian Africa.[3] Yet inspecting and interpreting the text in detail is, as Adrian Wisnicki puts it, something that 'few recent critics have done'.[4]

Wisnicki has himself gone some considerable way in correcting this absence. Where he is largely interested in the imagined geography of *Missionary Travels*, however, and its role in the modern 'invention' of south central Africa, this chapter explores the book primarily as a vehicle of self-projection and impression management before the British public. Through close analysis of the text's narrative, in terms of literary genre and stylistic device, I explore the various ways in which Livingstone negotiated his public identity and authority as an explorer. Furthermore, by examining the body of correspondence between Livingstone and John Murray, which discusses the publication of *Missionary Travels*, I highlight the process of editing and censorship by which the bestseller came into being. Important to this argument too is the original handwritten manuscript of Livingstone's text. If *Missionary Travels* has received little critical attention, the unpublished manuscript has suffered from scholarly neglect altogether. Yet the significant discrepancies between the published and unpublished versions of the book throw light on the persona that Livingstone chose to exhibit to his readership.

Of particular interest is a lengthy passage on the Cape Frontier Wars, critical of both settler and British imperial actions, that Livingstone removed prior to publication. While *Missionary Travels* functioned as imperialist in the extent to which it inspired British interest and intervention in the African continent, this excised section indicates that the book as it was originally conceived might have been less attractive to future generations of empire-builders. Indeed, the fact that Livingstone was capable of writing such a passage should encourage us to pay closer attention to the published text as well. This chapter thus closes with a rereading of *Missionary Travels* which reveals it to be a complex and heterogeneous document. Through colonial discourse analysis, I demonstrate the ways in which the book operated as imperialist while also arguing that this interpretation fails to do justice to its ambivalent nature. *Missionary Travels* is certainly implicated in the field of imperialist discourses, but there are many elements at work in the text that render such classification problematic.

While the remainder of this metabiography will concentrate on Livingstone's diverse afterlives, beginning with an analysis of *Missionary Travels* serves to indicate the complexity of the primary documents on which biographers have relied. Even though my focus later will predominantly be the socio-political locatedness of Livingstone's many interpreters, I would suggest that he has been able to sustain such diverse meanings because of the multivalent nature of his writing. At least as far as Livingstone's imperialist legacy is concerned, the heterogeneous complexity of his text facilitated those who would later exercise him in a range of different ways. As his primary platform before the British public, and as a major resource for his many biographers, *Missionary Travels* played an important role in the constitution of Livingstone's posthumous reputation. It must be acknowledged that his other writings were also vital in this process, particularly, as Dorothy O. Helly has shown, his posthumous and heavily edited *Last Journals*.[5] Nevertheless, *Missionary Travels* fully warrants the principal focus it is given here as Livingstone's *magnum opus* and major intellectual statement.

Livingstone's self-construction

Generic heterogeneity

In examining the construction of identity in *Missionary Travels*, this chapter follows Casey Blanton's suggestion that the 'self' is often travel writing's primary theme: 'the traveler/narrator's well-being and eventual safe homecoming become the primary tensions of the tale, the traveler's encounter with the other its chief attraction'.[6] In other words, the travelogue has an autobiographical function and so to some extent can be considered a form of life-writing. In thinking about *Missionary Travels* in this way, it becomes clear that the text signals towards, and serves to constitute, Livingstone's public persona. In fact, even by electing to write his narrative of exploration Livingstone made a statement about his identity. As Laura Marcus has observed in *Auto/biographical Discourses*, in the nineteenth century the view was prevalent that 'only certain "lives" [were] worthy of record'; the 'legitimacy' of writing about the self was intimately bound up with 'status and public importance'.[7] In composing his weighty tome, Livingstone declared that his was a significant life, worthy of the written word. John Sturrock argues that those who write about their self-experience are generally determined to mark 'him or herself off from other people, as an individual who has come to distinction'. They seek to parade how they have broken 'with the stage army of the anonymous, or that undifferentiated human mass whose members may be assumed to have no story to tell'.[8] A reviewer in the *Athenaeum* certainly felt that this was something Livingstone had achieved; he was nothing less than the 'author of a Livingstoniad'.[9]

In order to interrogate this 'Livingstoniad', and the self-image that its author presented, the first section of this chapter subjects *Missionary Travels* to genre analysis. As Tzvetan Todorov puts it, genres 'function as "horizons of expectation" for readers and as "models of writing" for authors'.[10] In other words, genres are fundamental to textual understanding; they are not mere form, but are in themselves content. In recent theory, it is suggested that texts often engage with a multiplicity of genres, rather than belonging comfortably in a single category. As John Frow argues, we should think of texts as individual literary 'acts' which 'use' or 'perform' genre in various ways.[11] Instead of belonging to a single class, each text is shaped, Dell Hymes suggests, by its 'relationships' to a number of forms.[12] They participate in 'a field or economy of genres, and their complexity derives from the complexity of that relation'.[13] In approaching *Missionary Travels* then, I will remain sensitive to the heterogeneous generic elements that it incorporates into structural unity.

Travel-writing scholars have frequently pointed to the hybridity of their field of study. Tim Youngs and Glenn Hooper note that 'one of the most persistent observations regarding travel writing ... is its absorption of differing styles and genres'.[14] These various styles, furthermore, are recognised to be value-laden. For one thing, a choice of genre could impinge upon a text's readership; to some degree, the selection of form was also a determination of audience. As Louise Henderson writes, travel 'publications tailored their contents for their intended readers, each contributing information about the latest expeditionary ventures in highly specific ways'.[15] Genre, however, not only signified something about the text's audience, but also about its author. Indeed, as Jan Borm argues, the 'form of travel writing one will practice depends on what kind of writer one is or wants to be'.[16] A choice of literary form, then, can be taken as a symptom of the identity the traveller-author wished to convey to his readers. Through genre criticism, we can probe the ways in which the various narrative paradigms co-residing in Livingstone's text emit messages about his identity.

In *Missionary Travels* it is possible to trace a number of generic influences. These literary modes, I would suggest, signify the nature of the expansive identity that Livingstone sought to carve for himself. As Timothy Holmes has observed, when it came to penning *Missionary Travels* he had a number of antecedent models. The 'missionary perspective' was provided by Dr John Philip's *Researches in South Africa* and by his father-in-law's *Missionary Labours and Scenes*.[17] In writing and publishing an account of his experience on return from the field, Livingstone was following a pattern well established by previous agents of the London Missionary Society (LMS).[18] A different precedent was offered by Richard Burton's 'swashbuckling adventure stories', which were 'interwoven with "Believe it or Not" information'. Darwin's *Voyage of the Beagle*, the report of a cartographer and naturalist, offered yet another diegetic option.[19] Livingstone refused to embrace a single template and instead drew upon them all; in consequence he would be part missionary, part adventurer and part field-scientist. Something of this is even indicated by his book's title, *Missionary Travels*, which distinctly refuses the traditional concept of a missionary as a stationary and settled individual who would invest in the people of one tongue and tribe over a considerable period.[20]

STYLING THE SELF: MAKING *MISSIONARY TRAVELS*

A few examples suffice to indicate the influence of these various traditions of travel literature on Livingstone's book. Its relationship to the missionary genre is tangible in his references to his evangelical activity. While at the outset he explains that he does not 'intend to specify with any prominence the evangelistic labours to which the love of Christ has impelled me', numerous, although often brief, references to attempted proselytising pepper the text.[21] For instance, Livingstone mentions his efforts in 'reading a small portion of the Bible and giving an explanatory address' and his attempts to expound the 'nature of true worship'.[22] In addition, he gives an account of the conversion and baptism of the Bechuana chief, Sechele, who soon learnt to conduct prayer 'in his own simple and beautiful style'. 'During the space of two years and a half', writes Livingstone, Sechele 'continued to profess to his people his full conviction of the truth of Christianity.'[23] Despite this, however, *Missionary Travels* contains few archetypal conversion narratives which proclaim the transformative nature of the gospel by parading the 'before' and 'after' stories of indigenous Christians. Indeed, Livingstone was actually quite critical of the expectation that missionaries would quickly produce 'model Christians'. The idea should not be entertained, he thought, by those 'who know their own hearts enough' to concede that they might not be models of faith themselves.[24] Perhaps Livingstone was shy on conversion narratives because, as it is well known, he was not the most successful evangelist. The continual movement essential to the role of 'missionary pioneer' was likely not conducive to imparting the Christian message. Nonetheless, Livingstone sought to display a soupçon of change in those he encountered in various locations: 'Some begin to pray to Jesus in secret as soon as they hear of the white man's God ... and no doubt are heard by Him who, like a father, pitieth his children.'[25] In one passage, he reports too how he had witnessed 'Baba, a mighty hunter' who had shed not a tear when mangled by a rhinoceros, 'sink down to the ground weeping', overcome by 'the gracious words of Christ'.[26]

Yet a sense of frustration and resignation often underpins Livingstone's account of evangelistic labours. He explains how he would preach of 'the Son of God having come down', but bemoans the fact that if this 'fails to interest them, nothing else will succeed'.[27] Even when reporting that some warmed to his message of 'peace on earth', he reminds his readers that 'they of course did not understand the full import of the message'.[28] After delivering one religious address, he hopes, or rather pleads, that 'surely some will remember the ideas conveyed, and pray to our merciful Father, who would never have thought of Him but for this visit'.[29] To this extent, Livingstone construes the African continent as a domain of spiritual need, requiring an escalation of missionary activity.[30] In integrating dimensions of the missionary genre, demonstrating his evangelistic stoicism and his fulfilment of expected protocol, Livingstone created a text amenable to the field of evangelical readers.

Daniel Bivona suggests that 'Missionary Travels is remarkable in the way it seems to refuse dramatic possibilities.' For the most part, Livingstone abstains from 'conventionally heroic self-characterization' and resists casting himself 'as the hero of the kind of epic adventure narrative into which Stanley so readily inserts himself'.[31] While this is the prevailing impression of Missionary Travels, the adventure narrative did, nonetheless, provide the text with another source of logic. Indeed, the most celebrated episode in the entirety of the book was undoubtedly Livingstone's encounter with the lion, in which he won his infamous shattered elbow. But this scene, to which I will return later in the chapter, was only one among many. He also relays his close call with a poisonous snake whose 'cold scaly skin twine[d] round a part of my leg' and the assault on his boat by an angry hippopotamus.[32] The reader follows him as one of his men is tossed by a raging buffalo and another seized by an alligator.[33] Even while Livingstone was critical of the senseless destruction of African wildlife, the bloody hunting escapades that punctuate the narrative offer moments of exhilaration.[34] Risky encounters with unpredictable chiefs are also staple fodder, and Livingstone never fails to outdo them in nerve and grit. On one occasion, he describes the uncertainty of his reception by a powerful chief named Shinte. In a tribal demonstration, his soldiers came 'armed to the teeth, running and shouting towards us ... for the purpose, I thought, of trying whether they could not make us take to our heels'.[35] Later, he describes how at a village of the Batoka a man 'came forward howling at the top of his voice in the most hideous manner; his eyes were shot out, his lips covered with foam'. While somewhat alarmed, Livingstone determined that he 'would not show fear' and instead endured the intimidation until his 'courage had been sufficiently tested' and the man was removed.[36] While Livingstone arguably did not exploit the heroic potential of these episodes to the utmost, their presence ensured that many readers would interpret his text, Bivona points out, as an 'epic narrative'. Indeed, the 'heroic reticence' of Livingstone's narratorial voice actually served to heighten his heroic reputation.[37]

The generic interplay between adventure narrative and missionary tract which is integral to Missionary Travels was also important to Livingstone's public success. Tim Barringer has rightly suggested that it was his ability to effectively combine these two identities that made him so unusual: Livingstone's 'amalgam of active heroism and religious conviction singled him out as the ultimate muscular Christian and was irresistible to the Victorian reading public'.[38] Yet there were other important generic influences on *Missionary Travels*. Most conspicuously, the text incorporated the scientific aspect. Projecting itself as a naturalist's treatise, it was filled with cartographic measurements, flora and fauna, and ethnological detail. As Isaac Schapera has noted, Livingstone stood out from contemporary missionaries and explorers in 'the diversity of his interests. He wrote voluminously and accurately on geography, botany, zoology, disease, linguistics, and what would nowadays be called anthropology, and for his own period he is by far the most comprehensive source of information on South-Central Africa.'[39] Certainly, in its abundance of information about southern African population groups – for instance, the Tswana – *Missionary Travels* contributed to the development of missionary ethnography.[40] Furthermore, with its Buxtonian ideas of commerce and Christianity, the text participated in a lengthy tradition of abolitionist writing. The premise underwriting the book was the termination of east and central African slavery by opening a pathway for legitimate trade to the centre of the continent. At the end of *Missionary Travels* Livingstone advertised his next venture, an expedition along the Zambesi, by which he hoped that 'an effectual blow will be struck at the slave-trade'.[41] In addition, we might add that in providing schemes for the development of African resources, *Missionary Travels* should also be considered what Oliver Ransford calls a 'feasibility project'.[42] Or, to follow Adrian Wisnicki, the text was an 'administrative document' that represented the African continent as an 'inviting field' for British intervention.[43] In addition to his identities as missionary, adventurer and naturalist, Livingstone thus construed himself as both an abolitionist and as a surveyor and prospector of African potentiality.

The result of integrating several literary modes, and negotiating multiple identities, was a text in which discursive shifts and odd juxtapositions were commonplace. Something of this was recognised by Livingstone's first major biographer, William Garden Blaikie, professor of apologetics and pastoral theology at New College, Edinburgh. While he certainly praised *Missionary Travels* for demonstrating the 'wonderful power' of Livingstone's mind, which could pass 'with the utmost rapidity, not only from subject to subject, but from one mood or key to another', he felt obliged to account for its fragmented nature.[44] '[T]he book is more a collection of pieces than an organised whole: a fault inevitable, perhaps, in some measure, from its nature, but aggravated, as we believe, by the haste and pressure under which it had to be written.'[45] One example of such disjointedness occurs in a passage in which Livingstone fulfils his role as missionary by baptising a dying child, 'commend[ing] its soul to the care and compassion' of Christ. Livingstone then notices how the mourning women present 'used a small musical instrument, which produced a kind of screeching sound, as an accompaniment of the death wail'. His anthropological interest leads to the immediate description of the instrument's construction out of 'caoutchouc'.[46] The narrative thus modulates abruptly from the tragic to the mundane, from the personal to the ethnographical. Despite the awkwardness resulting from what Fredric Jameson would call *'generic discontinuities'*, the important point is that *Missionary Travels* is essentially a 'symbolic act' which draws into unity and harmonises 'heterogeneous narrative paradigms' in order to propagate a powerful popular image which would appeal to diverse constituencies.[47]

We can discern that Livingstone aimed to cultivate the widest possible interest base for his book from the body of letters that he wrote to his publisher, John Murray, in the spring and summer of 1857. On 29 April, Livingstone wrote explaining how Mr Binney, who was providing literary assistance, had 'advised a few sentences on the change in the feelings in my history without which many religious people would set the book down as a merely intellectual affair and that I was not a religious missionary at all'.[48] In incorporating a section on his spiritual affairs and in relaying his evangelistic activities, he sought to undermine the arguments 'which some might use against it'. Similarly, on 24 August, he declared that he would incorporate his astronomical observations as an appendix in order to 'add interest to the book among the scientific'.[49] Murray was not so sure, however, that they would increase the text's attraction, arguing, as Livingstone put it in a letter to Henry Toynbee, that the 'majority of readers care little for these details'; they 'would not be valued except by a very few'.[50] For Murray, this addition would require considerable expense but would not yield a significant profit margin. As Louise Henderson has pointed out, a compromise was found: the full observations were published by the Royal Geographical Society (RGS), while a table of latitudes and longitudes was included in *Missionary Travels*.[51] Livingstone's desire to include this dimension of his work indicates that he had envisaged his book as even more hybrid than it turned out to be. The negotiations between author and publisher, however, prevented his conception from becoming reality. In his letter to Murray on 24 August, Livingstone suggested that his observations might make a 'better appendix' than 'the grammar'.[52] Presumably, Livingstone was referring here to his work on the 'Sichuana' language, which, like his observations, never made it into *Missionary Travels*. But Livingstone's one-time intention to incorporate his linguistic work reveals the scope of his imagined text, the hybrid ideal to which *Missionary Travels* fell short.

While the text did not encompass quite all that Livingstone had intended, it was, nonetheless, the book's diverse nature that appealed most to its contemporary reviewers. The *Leeds Mercury* proclaimed that Livingstone 'has made a book in which the child will revel, whilst the philosopher is fascinated by it. Adventures the most romantic attended him at every stage of his journeys.' His story was 'full of information of high interest to the geographer, the geologist, the ethnologist, the naturalist, the physician, the astronomer, the merchant, and the Christian philanthropist'.[53] Certainly, as Timothy Holmes has argued, *Missionary Travels* simply 'contained something for everyone ... The missionary spirit is roused ... The abolitionist is inspired ... Medical men are intrigued ... Empire-builders, millowners and engineers are excited ... The geographer, the naturalist, the geologist are fascinated.'[54] As Felix Driver expresses it, much of the 'power of the Livingstone myth' lay 'precisely in the fact that it appealed simultaneously to all these different interests' and networks.[55] In ensuring that *Missionary Travels* clearly resonated with a number of recognisable literary genres, Livingstone constructed his own expansive public identity while also broadening the horizons of his text's appeal.

Style and self: authority and credibility

While generic hybridity was crucial to the image that Livingstone projected in *Missionary Travels*, literary style was also of great significance. It was by his mode of expression that Livingstone sought to establish both his authority and his credibility as an explorer. Indeed it is important to note that travellers' tales have always been beset by the issue of trustworthiness.[56] The distance between the field and the centre meant that the legitimacy of travellers' claims were always at stake. Steven Shapin, the sociologist of science, summarises it neatly in *A Social History of Truth*:

> The problem with crediting travelers' tales was twofold. If the tales were regarded as worth telling, they frequently, and naturally, conflicted with what was already known about the world, hence they possessed inherent credibility-handicaps. Second, they were commonly told by people about whom one knew little or nothing, by people to whom one might legitimately impute an interest ... in fabricating testimony or embroidering the truth.[57]

Since, as Charles Withers observes, travellers' claims to truth were so integrally linked to trust, 'the social status of practitioners' and their moral credentials came to bear fundamental importance.[58] Like any traveller, then, Livingstone had to display his moral authority and credibility in order to be granted legitimacy.

Yet apprehension about reliability was not merely confined to explorers and field agents. In the nineteenth century considerable anxiety also surrounded the ethics of self-writing. It centred, Laura Marcus argues, on the mercenary incentives of notoriety and financial gain that might motivate authorship. In addition, the 'apparently self-eulogising nature and function of "self-biography"' left it open to 'charges of vanity and egotism'. Although this disquiet primarily concerned introspective literature there was some sense that heroic tales, 'recounted by their actor', could lead to an 'unwelcome parade of self'.[59] As both traveller and self-writer, then, Livingstone was under a dual compulsion to avoid egocentrism and cultivate trust.

Livingstone's correspondence to Murray makes it clear that style occupied his attention. A trivial indication of this was his request, on 26 May, for copies of both 'Roget's thesaurus of synonyms – and Maunders treasury of words'. But in the same letter he also asked, 'Will Kane's style be of any help to me?', referring to *Arctic Explorations* by Elisha Kent Kane, published in the previous year.[60] Since Kane was, as Larzer Ziff writes, 'By training a physician and by vocation an explorer', Livingstone perhaps wondered whether he might learn from the narrative of another travelling doctor.[61] He was likely attracted too by the book's popularity and by its success in inspiring others to turn towards the author's field of exploration.[62] While *Arctic Explorations* and *Missionary Travels* are quite different books, Livingstone shares Kane's 'restless eye' and habits of observation, and like the Arctic author he gathers a mix of 'narrative incidents, pictorial descriptions, and scientific explanations into a work of imposing size'.[63] While Livingstone only mentions Kane in passing, his interest in the other traveller's prose demonstrates his concern with fitting his style to his subject.

This becomes clearer in a series of letters in which Livingstone protests against 'the utterly unwarrantable liberties' inflicted on his text by an editor in Murray's employ.[64] On one level, his complaint seems to be the loss of his distinctive voice. He reminded his publisher of the pleasure that Whitwell Elwin, another reader of Murray's and the editor of the *Quarterly Review*, had 'experienced in reading what I had written in my own style', and that Professor Owen, Sir Roderick Murchison and Mr Binney all felt his style to be more 'popular and saleable' than the corrupted version of this inferior editor. Livingstone complained that the reader – who can be identified as John Milton, one of Murray's advisers – marked many sections of the text with the words 'meaning obscure'.[65] If he accepted these corrections, Livingstone argued, the text would soon resemble a mere children's 'penny primer'. Fearing that the expansions and explanations that Milton demanded would over-simplify the book, he felt justified in rejecting the changes

STYLING THE SELF: MAKING *MISSIONARY TRAVELS*

'in toto'; 'every iota of his labour must go'.⁶⁶ While Livingstone wanted his book to be popular, he was clearly wary of it becoming too popularised. Yet he did not only feel that the editor made his work appear juvenile; there was another level to his vehement expostulations. In a letter of 30 May, he described the alterations as 'namby pambyism' and indeed even went so far as to send Murray two versions of an extract from *Missionary Travels* on 3 June, one entitled 'the text' and the other 'the emasculation'.⁶⁷ Livingstone makes a repeated and strenuous objection: 'you will not find me cantankerous or unreasonable or difficult to deal with in any other matter but I must positively resist any attempts to tamper with or emasculate the book'.⁶⁸ The man must be given 'leave to quit',⁶⁹ and in his place Livingstone would 'get a man who has some sympathy with African travel'.⁷⁰ Livingstone thus set out to avoid effeminacy and to pursue what he felt to be a manly style, for only such diction would be in 'sympathy' with the text's content. For Livingstone, a book of African travel demanded a masculine prose in order to appear 'forcible', 'popular' and authentic.⁷¹

In establishing trust and warrant, Livingstone had several other stylistic tactics. In the first place, he engaged in what we might call 'virtual witnessing'. Steven Shapin has previously employed this term when discussing the 'literary technology' that experimental scientists like Robert Boyle employed in cultivating their credibility.⁷² Boyle, as a pioneer of the experimental method, advocated the important role of witnesses in consolidating the reliability of the facts generated in observational science. But as important as embodied witness, argues Shapin, was the 'virtual witnessing' constructed in his reports. This, in effect, was a literary device which involved 'the production in the reader's mind of such an image of an experimental scene as obviates the necessity for either its direct witness or its replication'.⁷³ In other words, the way a report was written would create a sense of verisimilitude for readers, as though they had actually been present.

For travellers, who likewise needed to demonstrate their texts' trustworthiness, virtual witnessing or a semblance of presence also proved an effective device. Livingstone achieved this in *Missionary Travels* through the vividness of his descriptions and by providing extensive circumstantial detail. In a verbose passage, portraying a 'picturesque' valley, Livingstone writes:

> The open glade, surrounded by forest trees of various hues, had a little stream meandering in the centre. A herd of reddish-coloured antelopes (pallahs) stood on one side ... while gnus, tsessebes, and zebras gazed in astonishment at the intruders ... A large white rhinoceros came along the bottom of the valley with his slow sauntering gait without noticing us ... It being Sunday, all was peace.⁷⁴

In scenes like these, Livingstone sought to convey a sense of immediacy to his readers. Indeed, when he came to write his later text, *Narrative of an Expedition to the Zambesi*, Livingstone explained at the outset that this was his intention. He hoped that incorporating extracts from his brother Charles's journal would add the 'freshness which usually attaches to first impressions ... many remarks made by the natives, which he put down at the moment of translation, will convey to others the same ideas as they did to ourselves.'[75] On the whole, virtual witnessing is actually more detectable in Livingstone's later book. In communicating a wealth of first-hand detail, he frequently moves into the present tense in order to convey a sense of real presence to the reader:[76] 'The dark woods resound with the lively and exultant sound of the kinghunter (*Halcyon striolata*), as he sits perched on high among the trees. As the steamer moves on through the winding channel, a pretty little heron or bright kingfisher darts out in alarm from the edge of the bank.'[77] Authenticity is secured as Livingstone's audience experiences Africa vicariously. As the author's co-witness to the continent's many sights, the reader becomes a virtual companion on a textual journey.

Yet while Livingstone showed descriptive flair in creating a sense of immediacy, he also fostered credibility by adopting, for the most part, a simple and unembellished style. This served to cultivate trust since the equation between plainness and honesty, rhetoric and duplicity has been longstanding in scientific discourse.[78] Consequently, while *Missionary Travels* might appear plodding in places to the modern reader, its prosaic features were considered to be virtues by contemporary reviewers. For instance, the *Era* compared the text favourably with those products of the 'deceptive art of book-making' which seduce readers into trivia through their 'artistic effects' and smooth flowing sentences.[79] Similarly the *Glasgow Herald* lauded Livingstone's style as 'clear and vigorous, and free from all meretricious decoration'.[80] In the reviews, his unadorned phrasing was generally taken to signify veracity. On 4 December 1857, the *Caledonian Mercury* mourned that there are 'comparatively few travellers whose narratives can be accepted without some reservation. Most men have an innate disposition to exaggerate, and ... it need not excite surprise that there should occasionally be found descriptions in which imagination occupies as large a place as fact.'[81] However, the reviewer held that no charge of exaggeration could be laid on David Livingstone: 'Whether he writes about himself or about others – what he did or what he saw – his statements may be accepted without suspicion.' And this trust was granted because of style: 'The natural, modest, unassuming manner in which he narrates the most thrilling adventures disarms the sceptic; indeed, the internal evidence furnished in this way by his volume is sufficient to quiet any doubt as to the thorough honesty of every statement which he makes.' Veracity was something to be determined not by external authority, but by the internal. Because there was 'no effort at word painting – no attempt to excite the reader by a superabundance of adjectives and adverbs to strengthen and intensify scenes', Livingstone's narrative was deemed reliable.[82] Without feeling obliged to provide any evidence, *John Bull* stated on 19 December that Livingstone '*evidently* writes within the truth, and carefully avoids any colouring that is in any way inconsistent with facts' (emphasis added).[83] As Charles Withers puts it, in travel writing it is clearly 'not just what is said' but 'the nature of communication itself' that 'matters in securing trust and credibility'.[84]

It is notable too that Livingstone's claim to have come rather loathly to authorship was also deemed to attest authenticity. The *Athenaeum* praised his 'evident reluctance to quit the ingle-nook, and mount an author's seat and discourse glibly from a literary platform'.[85] His expression of hesitancy helped him to avoid suspicion, for it created distance from those writers who engaged in self-eulogy. Indeed, Livingstone's declaration that he 'would rather cross the African continent again than undertake to write another book' was felt to augur an appropriate antipathy to fame.[86] The *Athenaeum*'s reviewer noted approvingly that 'Dr Livingstone apparently prefers the grip of an actual lion to the uncomfortable position occupied by popular and metaphorical potentates.'[87] This supposed aversion to the spotlight purified his motivations and so certified *Missionary Travels*; for Livingstone's reviewers, humility was a signifier of credibility.

In spite of all this, style and literary technique would never have been enough to fully legitimise Livingstone: something more was needed. Indeed it is important to realise that personal networks played a crucial role, for they enabled judgements about character and reliability to be adequately formed. In other words, as Withers argues, relationships were vital in establishing the 'bases of believability'.[88] Certainly, one of the most important ways in which Livingstone became established as a public figure was through his association with Sir Roderick Murchison, President of the Royal Geographical Society and hearty advocate of African exploration. Livingstone paraded this alliance by dedicating *Missionary Travels* to his willing patron: the book was 'affectionately offered as a Token of Gratitude for the kind interest he has always taken in the Author's pursuits'.[89] Forming part of what Gérard Genette calls the 'paratext',[90] the dedication to one of Britain's foremost geographical illuminati served to indicate Livingstone's affiliation with the scientific establishment. As Felix Driver argues, the relationship between the two men was one of mutuality, characterised by the 'public exchange of gifts'.[91] Livingstone had received the RGS's gold medal, and in his dedication he returned the favour. At one stage, however, Livingstone had contemplated including the astronomer Thomas Maclear in the inscription as well, and he wrote to Murray to enquire whether there was any precedent for such a 'double dedication'.[92] Although, in the end, Livingstone settled on his primary patron alone, he gestured throughout his book to the relationships he had cultivated with an array of eminent men. Livingstone's personal networks were vital in granting him validation and he signalled to these in *Missionary Travels*.

In a variety of ways, then, Livingstone sought to establish credibility. Through the stylistic technology of virtual witnessing and unvarnished prose, by performing humility and by signalling connections to the scientific virtuosi, *Missionary Travels* was given warrant. As we have seen, it was critically acclaimed as a travelogue that effused truthfulness. The irony, of course, is that *Missionary Travels* soon became the object of disenchantment. From a number of quarters, Livingstone was later accused of having underplayed the difficulties of travel and of having exaggerated the potential of the continent. This was epitomised in the reaction of James Stewart, when he came to Africa in 1862 to survey the possibilities of a Free Church of Scotland mission. In a dramatic gesture of disenchantment, he cast his copy of *Missionary Travels* into the Zambesi, proclaiming it to be a book of lies. While Stewart and others regained their faith in Livingstone in the years following his death, it is nonetheless true that the text, as Timothy Holmes argues, was almost utopian in its optimism.[93] When this is taken into consideration, Livingstone's success in stylistically generating trust is all the more striking.

Textual censorship: Livingstone's impression management
Through literary genre and stylistic technology, Livingstone worked to forge his self-image in *Missionary Travels*. Indeed, in my examination of the travelogue as a medium of life-writing it should have become clear that the textual persona does not exist in a simplistic mimetic relationship with the authorial self. Rather, to some extent at least, the subject is constructed within the narrative.[94] Yet we do not need to press the fictive nature of self-writing to agree with Harold Rosen that 'all autobiography operates within very specific constraints – the reluctance to give offence to living persons, the deliberate omission of sensitive material, the effort to conform to an image'.[95] It thus remains to interrogate some of the pressures on Livingstone and the ways in which he correspondingly shaped himself. As the sociologist Erving Goffman famously argued, individuals engage in strategies of

'impression management' in the social encounters of everyday life, as they attempt to control the signals they send forth about themselves.[96] In this way, self-identity is embedded in social practice and performative in nature. But the notion of 'impression management' also proves fertile for thinking about the self as it is performed within narrative. As Fredric Jameson has commented, just as 'indications and signals' litter everyday speech acts in order to ensure their appropriate reception, 'the art of writing' is similarly absorbed with the ultimately '(impossible) attempt to devise a foolproof mechanism for the automatic exclusion of undesirable responses to a given literary utterance'.[97] While Livingstone's diverse afterlives indicate just how difficult it is to control interpretation, I would suggest that he was deeply aware of his audience and so acted as a self-censor in *Missionary Travels*. This can be detected in his representation of his religious conviction, national identity, and social class and, mostly explicitly, his views on imperialism. By comparing Livingstone's published text with his original manuscript, we will see the extent of the editing practices by which he constructed his public image.

Discussing the mediation of his religious identity, Timothy Holmes notes that 'one has to read *Missionary Travels* very carefully indeed to learn that Livingstone was a minister at all'. This silence, he surmises, was part of an attempt 'to disarm the snobbery of the overwhelmingly Anglican establishment'.[98] By obscuring his identity as an ordained Independent clergyman, to some degree, Livingstone increased the likelihood of rallying the support of the established Church. While he was candid about joining the LMS, he failed to be explicit about the organisation's role in his medical education and the theological training he received at Ongar.[99] Clearly, Livingstone did not wish to be known as too dogmatically Independent. In consequence, he asserted his inclusive ecclesiastical outlook: 'I never, as a missionary, felt myself to be, either Presbyterian, Episcopalian, or Independent, or called upon in any way to love one denomination less than another.'[100] Holmes also argues that Livingstone, even while describing his profound religious commitment, felt it necessary to demonstrate that he had an unprejudiced and open mind.[101] In his autobiographical introduction, he described his love of science flourishing in accompaniment to his faith. He delighted in reading Dr Thomas Dick's work, in which 'it was gratifying to find [his] own ideas, that religion and science are not hostile, but friendly to each other, fully proved'.[102] While I would not deny that Livingstone really was little concerned with denominational divisions or that he really was convinced of the harmonious nature of science and religion, the moderate, ecumenical and enlightened Christianity that he presented in *Missionary Travels* was undoubtedly amenable to the establishment whose patronage he required.

A more significant dimension of Livingstone's impression management, however, was his treatment of national identity. As George Shepperson pointed out, there appears to have been 'a certain ambivalence in Livingstone's attitude towards his native land'.[103] Although much recent scholarship has focused on his Scottishness, one might suggest that there is actually little to identify him in this way in *Missionary Travels*. After the opening autobiographical chapter in which Livingstone outlines his Scots upbringing, he repeatedly refers to himself as one of the 'English'. Thus, while not erasing Scottish identity, Livingstone at least downplays it. Perhaps, in the grips of Anglophilia, he hoped to demonstrate his cultural ascendancy and his newfound standing with the ruling classes. We might interpret his attitude as a symptom of what Judith Listowel rather disparagingly described as his 'almost childish enjoyment of aristocratic circles in London'.[104] Or, if we were to follow the critical trajectory of Craig Beveridge and Ronald Turnbull, we might suggest that Scottishness has been 'eclipsed' in *Missionary Travels* and that this should be understood as an instance of 'inferiorisation', a theory developed by Frantz Fanon which they apply to Scottish culture. Summarising Fanon, they write that 'the native comes to internalise the message that local customs are inferior to the culture of the coloniser'.[105] Through 'a relationship of national dependence' the colonised comes 'to doubt the worth and significance of inherited ways of life and embrace the styles and values of the coloniser'.[106] Since Livingstone seldom refers to himself as a Scot, and so frequently identifies himself with the dominant metropolitan culture, he could possibly be interpreted as a product of inferiorising forces. Certainly, it is important to remember that the binary representations of Scotland and England – dark and enlightened, backward and advanced – were remarkably persistent. In 1861 H.T. Buckle felt able to write, in his *History of Civilisation in England*, that 'In no civilised country is toleration so little understood as in Scotland.'[107]

The story, however, is more complicated, and I would suggest that Livingstone uses the label 'English' with greater self-awareness than the inferiorisation argument allows. To some degree at least, his self-portrayal is likely to have been a market-oriented decision. As John Corbett argues, Livingstone wrote with the assumption that his audience would be primarily English and would hold 'anglocentric beliefs and values'.[108] In an effort to negotiate this readership he thus cast himself appropriately. Furthermore, it should be remembered that Livingstone was following the nineteenth-century pattern in employing the term 'English' to mean 'British'. And while he clearly did not reject the Anglo-oriented vocabulary of the day, Livingstone made it clear that his conception of Englishness was by no means narrow and exclusive, but one which incorporated all the national groups in the British Isles. He explains that the 'Bachuana', when addressed with 'any degree of scorn', would strongly declare that '"we are not inferior to any of our nation," in exactly the same sense as Irishmen or Scotchmen, in the same circumstances, would reply, "We are Britons," or "We are Englishmen."'[109] In this quotation, Livingstone affirmed a shared sense of identity across the United Kingdom and, significantly, the equality of the 'margins' with the centre. While he continued to use the label 'English', he ensured that it would be understood to encompass the United Kingdom's diversity.

It is also important to note that Livingstone's Scottish identity is not entirely effaced from *Missionary Travels* even if it receives less articulation than we might expect. Something of an underlying Scottish frame of reference can be detected. For instance Livingstone tends to liken African rivers and landscape to the Clyde and its surrounding features. Scottish scenery remained, as Clare Pettitt puts it, 'imaginatively present' to him throughout his travels.[110] The banks of the Zouga are thus described as 'very beautiful, resembling closely many parts of the River Clyde above Glasgow' while the range of hills at Lupata gorge is 'not so high in appearance as the Campsie Hills when seen from the Vale of Clyde'.[111] Even when describing Victoria Falls, Livingstone observes that the streams that formed the columns of vapour 'ascending from this strange abyss' 'seemed each to exceed in size the falls of the Clyde at Stonebyres'.[112] Similarly, as John Corbett notes, Livingstone tended to draw on the Scottish bard, Robert Burns, as his 'literary touchstone'.[113] Although this is less true of *Missionary Travels* than of his letters, Livingstone does describe his family home as resembling a scene from the 'Cottar's Saturday Night'.[114] Although one has to read carefully for these fleeting moments in the book, they are important to our understanding since, as Robert Crawford urges, in interpreting books by Scots we must 'remain alert to nuances of cultural politics ... which set them apart from Anglocentric assumptions'.[115]

Furthermore, the autobiographical sketch which opens *Missionary Travels* – in which Livingstone both recalls his great-grandfather's death at Culloden and reflects on his formative years in Blantyre – should inflect our interpretation of the remainder of the text. As Corbett points out, Livingstone vacillates in the opening section between a description of the working people of Scotland as an 'object, and a first-person assertion of his solidarity with the Scottish poor'.[116] When he uses the first-person plural pronoun, telling his readers that '*we* are content to respect our laws till we can change them' (emphasis added), Livingstone grammatically identifies himself with the Scottish poor.[117] This introduction, if it provides a hermeneutic frame on *Missionary Travels*, casts different light on Livingstone's later self-positioning as 'English'. He can instead be understood to imply that a Scotsman can act legitimately as a representative of Englishness. On one occasion he describes how, on discovering that a fellow countryman had failed to remunerate his indigenous assistants, he 'upheld the English name by paying his debts'.[118] Having articulated and established his Scottish identity early in the text, Livingstone the Scot now casts himself as a defender of English values. In fact, he is a much better representative of the national ideal than the one who swindled his African carriers. Livingstone also suggests that he was able to retain the trust of his own assistants, who feared being sold into slavery, by reminding them that he had always behaved in accordance with his role 'as an English teacher'.[119] Once again, in manifesting the 'English character', he indicates that it is something that a Scot can successfully embody.[120] On the whole, Livingstone's treatment of his national identity is more complex than it might first appear. While he may have identified himself as a Scot less than we might anticipate, he did not so much mask his identity as manage it.

Livingstone's autobiographical introduction is significant too for other reasons. By comparing the published book with his original manuscript, we can gather that the opening section was particularly, and very literally, subject to impression management and self-censorship. In fact Livingstone actually excised a significant portion of text pertaining to his social class. As it stands, the narrative concentrates on Livingstone's working-class origins and his strenuous endeavours to raise himself by self-help. While subdued in tone, the chapter fashions Livingstone as an exceptional individual who has impressively defied the odds and beaten the hand that he was dealt in life. As I previously mentioned, Livingstone identifies himself with the 'Scottish poor' and elects to speak as a representative of the working classes. As Corbett argues, his 'mission here is to explain his nation and his class to his fellow Britons'.[121] In a pacifying statement, Livingstone contends that Scottish workers have no intention of overthrowing authority: 'we ... hate those stupid revolutions which might sweep away time-honoured institutions, dear alike to rich and poor'.[122] Since an important dimension of Britishness from 1789 was its opposition to France as the centre of European revolutionary Republicanism, Livingstone's anti-revolutionary sentiments were no doubt pleasing to the establishment and to a broadly conservative British national identity. Timothy Holmes suggests that in so writing, Livingstone was 'respectful, deferential' and demonstrated 'that he would present no possible danger to the governing class'. While disclosing his working-class roots on the

1. Manuscript of *Missionary Travels and Researches in South Africa* (1856–57).

one hand, he 'sought to reassure the establishment that he accepted the prevailing social order unreservedly' on the other.[123]

While this appears to be true of the published *Missionary Travels*, the original manuscript reveals impression management of greater complexity (see Fig. 1). Indeed, in the portion that Livingstone excised, he considered the state of the Scottish poor and discussed an analogy, put forth by 'our American cousins', which characterised 'factory life' as a form of 'white slavery'.[124] Much of this edited material appears fairly conservative and unthreatening to the establishment. Rejecting the equivalence between factory workers and slaves, Livingstone praises the 'English' for never tolerating 'the shabbiness of expecting services from an inferior class without payment'.[125] He describes the nation as having the most 'true liberty with the greatest amount of happiness for the greatest possible number'.[126] However the reasons for Livingstone's act of censorship soon become clear. In the deleted passage he states that workers are the 'victims of great social evils arising from overpopulation' and are paid wages that are 'often far too low'.[127] Declaring his 'warmest sympathies' with the poor in no uncertain terms, Livingstone proclaims that he would 'denounce any oppression' of them 'no matter by whom practised'.[128] Furthermore, Livingstone rejected the parallel between factory work and slavery in large part because it was unjust 'to speak of those as slaves whose blood boils at the thought of oppression'.[129] The implication is that the character of the working poor would by no means tolerate enslavement. A most telling sentence is omitted from the published *Missionary Travels*: 'If slavery were attempted to be imposed on such people no human power could restrain their vengeance'.[130] It appears then that while Livingstone ultimately assured his readers that the labouring classes were 'no revolutionary levellers', his first draft was actually tantamount to a warning, if not a threat, to those who engaged in exploitative practices.[131] The text that Holmes perceives as 'safe' and reassuring was clearly the product of a political decision to edit the threatening class material. By rescinding his forthright declarations, Livingstone ultimately retreated from controversy and at the same time created a book that would be marketable to a socially significant audience.

Livingstone's autobiographical introduction was not the only heavily edited passage in *Missionary Travels*, and a comparison with the manuscript reveals another, even more substantial act of literary censorship. In fact, in his original draft Livingstone had included an extended diatribe on the Cape Frontier Wars, the protracted series of border disputes between European settlers and the Xhosa that spanned a century in length.[132] In his manuscript, Livingstone had railed against the actions of both colonial settlers and imperial authority.

STYLING THE SELF: MAKING *MISSIONARY TRAVELS*

In a massive act of editing, however, before publication he removed more than twenty pages in which he had criticised the abuse of martial power, the infringement of African rights, and corruption at the Cape.

It should be acknowledged that Livingstone's support for the Xhosa in their war against the British colonisers has been explored before, by Christopher Petrusic. He points out that Livingstone championed African interests and articulated this in an article on the War of Mlanjeni in 1852, which was rejected for publication.[133] In letters to his family, he decried the English as having 'lost character and honour' in the conflicts, and he even sent a copy of a speech, by the rebel Ngqika chief Sandile, to his brother in the United States in the hope of disseminating Xhosa grievances to a larger audience.[134] But while it has been observed that Livingstone possessed such views, and that he failed to articulate them more publicly in *Missionary Travels*, it has not hitherto been realised that he had at one stage intended to use his travelogue to broadcast his opposition. It is worth exploring this excised section in some detail, not least because it has never before been addressed, but also because it indicates what a radically different book *Missionary Travels* could have been.

The repressed block of text begins by condemning unsavoury military practices. Livingstone bemoans the abandonment of Lord Glenelg's principles – what he calls a 'philanthropic policy' – which had presupposed that Africans 'had some sort of natural title to their lands', and suggests that the extremely violent actions of subsequent authorities were misguided and impracticable.[135] He writes, 'if we follow the fighting policy we can only hope for a permanent peace when we have depopulated all the country between Graham's Town and Timbuctu'. But to judge by the current military performance the accomplishment of such a grisly task, he jests, would require 'a postponement of the millennium'.[136]

Livingstone goes on to explore at length the substantial confusion surrounding the causes of the wars. While some blamed 'the restless thievish propensities of our savage neighbours' rather than 'any injustice or aggression either on the part of the government or of the inhabitants of the Frontier', Livingstone was not so sure. For him, an equally viable explanation was that 'the native population becomes worse and not better from its contact with civilization and a professedly Christian people … the grasping encroachment of the white man from year to year on the native lands is rather an unlikely mode of teaching the Kaffirs that honesty is one of the virtues'.[137] In the manuscript, Livingstone gives pride of place to the Xhosa understanding of the ongoing conflicts. He offers up a passage from an impassioned speech by the Paramount Chief of the Rharhabe Xhosa, Sandile: 'Is it God who gave this book bids him think of blood? Some white men come and say "the Kaffirs steal," but the white men are the robbers. God made a boundary by the sea and white men cross it to rob us of our country ... We are tired of the Englishman on account of his bad conduct.'[138] Livingstone concedes that Sandile's speech perhaps contains too 'much of the recriminatory character', but for him it is a no less trustworthy version of events than that of the 'Shopocracy', his own neologism for those who profited financially by war and by the purportedly 'philanthropic business of aiding the troops.'[139] Livingstone argues that 'there is a small party which has grown great by Kaffir wars'. These warmongers profited by confusion: 'they are especially divided in their opinions as to the causes of the outbreaks but always stoutly hold to the doctrine that England must pay the expenses'.[140] In such a context, suggests Livingstone, it would be well to consult the African understanding of the conflict. This is his frequent appeal: 'In all our wars we have had but one side of the question. We never hear the Kaffir version.'[141] 'Let us hear both sides and not go blundering on.'[142] '[T]he mother country' too was guilty, since it had gratified the 'Shopocracy's' 'whim for Kaffir wars as the most leech-like position of humanity could desire.'[143]

Livingstone also offers some commentary in the manuscript on the Kat River Rebellion of 1851, in which the Khoikhoi revolted despite their former support for the British in the wars of 1834–35 and 1846–47. He expresses his sympathy with the rebels, arguing that they had no option but to join the British enemy on the outbreak of conflict, situated as they were, unarmed and surrounded. But he suggests too that they had legitimate grievances, having been 'most unjustly deprived of their arms and some of their lands'.[144] Indeed Livingstone condemns the land-lust of those who would possess the Kat river: 'That which renders the unblushing greediness of this small portion of our empire peculiarly odious is the altogether un-English wish displayed for aggrandizement at the expense of the degraded races in their security and of the blood of the English soldier.'[145] He reflects too on the conduct of the Cape's judicial system in the aftermath of the revolt, in which the field cornet Andries Botha was convicted of high treason. Having been only briefly involved in the rebellion, this soldier served as a rather convenient scapegoat. For Livingstone the whole hearing was a problematic affair, reliant on dubious witnesses whose testimonies were compromised.[146]

The original manuscript of *Missionary Travels* thus included a protracted digression on colonial injustice and the rights of existing communities. But of course Livingstone decided on censorship: in his correspondence with Murray, he wrote only that he had 'curtailed the Caffre war subject and sweetened it'.[147] Unfortunately, since this rather amusing understatement is the only mention of this editorial decision, it is difficult to ascertain for certain who prompted the excision of this radical material. Certainly, as David Finkelstein has shown, the process of production and publication could play a vital role in shaping narratives of exploration. As he illustrates in the case of John Speke, traveller's texts could be significantly revised, even in ways that contravened authorial intention.[148] It is possible, then, that John Murray prompted the censorship: he would undoubtedly have been prepared to suggest such a substantial alteration if he thought it would affect commercial success. Yet, as Livingstone's insistence on stylistic matters would indicate, he was ever ready to resist undue interference with his writing. Since the removal of over twenty pages was dealt with so briefly in the correspondence, and occurred without traceable protest, it seems likely that the resolution was Livingstone's. But whether on his own whim, or at the prompting of the respectable John Murray publishing house, the anti-British sentiment in *Missionary Travels* was certainly tempered in order to make it more palatable to the public who he hoped would buy his book and invest in the African continent. It is perhaps significant that it was in April, the month in which this portion was removed, that Lord Clarendon was persuaded by Murchison to employ Livingstone as consul in central Africa. While Livingstone may, or may not, have known of this decision, he was clearly becoming more wary of courting controversy as he was increasingly integrated into the establishment.

In a variety of ways, then, Livingstone played the role of self-censor in *Missionary Travels*. Motivated by concern for his public image, he carefully managed his religious and national identity. Yet Livingstone's impression management is at its clearest in those radical passages, relating to social class and particularly to imperial exploitation, that the pressures of the literary marketplace encouraged him to excise.

Sedentary and itinerant discourses

The sedentary text

The censored extract criticising the Cape Frontier Wars casts interesting light on the nature of *Missionary Travels*. In its published form, the text had imperialist effects since it radically altered the contemporary imagination of Africa. As Adrian Wisnicki argues, the book successfully 'reinvent[ed] south central Africa in a manner which invite[d] British intervention and colonization': Livingstone sought to '*map* the cultural and physical geography of southern African in a way that responded to the sacred and secular desires of the British public'.[149] In advocating 'legitimate commerce' and in urging traders, explorers and missionaries to work together towards the grand end of elevating humankind, there is no doubt that – in certain respects – Livingstone's vision was an imperial one. The force of his anti-slavery rhetoric certainly helped to inaugurate the potent connection between humanitarianism and imperial intervention that would prove so important towards the end of the nineteenth century.[150] Yet while the published version of *Missionary Travels* surely did entice empire-builders, the original manuscript – which unveils Livingstone's radical act of editing – suggests that things might well have been rather different. In fact, it seems unlikely that the book would have appealed to imperialist fantasies to such an extent had he not removed his substantial critique of the Cape Frontier Wars. We might engage in counterfactual speculation and suggest that if Livingstone had permitted his lengthy section to stand, *Missionary Travels* would have had a less pervasive imperialist influence.

Furthermore, the fact that *Missionary Travels* was written by an individual who was capable of expressing such sustained criticism should also encourage us to revisit the published text. Even though future imperialists were inspired by its image of Africa, I would argue that on closer inspection it proves to be a more ambivalent document than has previously been acknowledged. Few critics have examined the text in detail, but those who have tend for the most part to position it categorically as imperialist. Yet the ambiguity of *Missionary Travels*, its competing impulses and contrary drives, problematise such unequivocal categorisation. By bearing in mind the critical and cautionary elements that Livingstone had originally incorporated into the book, we can read the travelogue in a manner attuned to its discursive complexity. In the remainder of this chapter, then, I intend to develop the discussion of the book as an imperialist text, particularly by exploring its mechanics of 'othering' and its representations of Africa. At the same time, however, I also seek to demonstrate that there are elements of the text that significantly complicate this interpretation. My question is thus not only the extent to which *Missionary Travels* extends imperialist discourse, but the extent to which the narrative resists it.

In bringing the notion of colonial discourse to bear on *Missionary Travels*, my approach is indebted to Edward Said's *Orientalism* (1978), in many ways the founding text of postcolonial studies. For Said, imperialism and colonialism were not just phenomena reliant on economic and political structures but were dependent on, as Peter Hulme summarises, 'an ensemble of linguistically-based practices unified in their common deployment in the management of colonial relationships'.[151] These features were so ubiquitous, appearing in such diverse texts, that they could not be reduced to the predilections of individual authors. Instead, borrowing the vocabulary of Michel Foucault, Said insisted that these regularities indicated a pervasive belief system that was 'structured by discursive frameworks' and 'given credibility and force by the power relations found in imperialism'.[152] Said was interested not just in a specific body of texts, but in the 'practices and rules' and 'methodological organisation of thinking' that underlay them.[153] Of course Said's implementation of discourse analysis has subsequently come under significant criticism. As Sara Mills points out, critics have rejected the notion of a singular and homogenous imperial 'discourse', and have instead argued that there were 'various *discourses* circulating within the colonial period' (emphasis added).[154] But while Said's notion has been complexified, his turn to discourse emphasised, as Peter Hulme writes, that 'during the colonial period large parts of the non-European world were *produced* for Europe through a discourse that imbricated sets of questions and assumptions, methods of procedure and analysis, and kinds of writing and imagery'.[155]

In this understanding, Livingstone's book participates in imperialist discourse to the extent that it is constructed along the lines of a 'discovery narrative'. Indeed, for Leon de Kock, one of the few scholars to adopt a literary approach to *Missionary Travels*, Livingstone's narrative epitomises 'the greatest height of consensual Western self-delusion' in its 'appropriating fantasy of "discovering" Africa'. The text operates, he argues, on an 'absurd' rationale, 'as though natural phenomena came into full and proper existence only once the imperial western eye fell upon them'.[156] Drawing on Mary Louise Pratt's notion of anti-conquest, de Kock characterises Livingstone's 'act of witness' as in reality 'an act of appropriation by Western knowledge'.[157] Such an understanding of *Missionary Travels* is indicative of the contemporary concern with what Derek Gregory has called the relationship between 'claims to knowledge and the metaphorics of vision', and the workings of power in 'visual appropriations of the world'.[158] And certainly the 'benign' and yet possessive logic of the 'seeing-man' is present in *Missionary Travels*, perhaps most conspicuously in Livingstone's famous description of the Victoria Falls, that natural wonder which had 'never been seen before by European eyes'. Livingstone begins with an aesthetic discourse, describing a vista so spectacular that 'no one can imagine the beauty of the view ... scenes so lovely must have been gazed upon by angels in their flight'.[159] But he rapidly settles on the narrative commentary of the natural historian to communicate the sight to his readers. The falls were:

> bounded on three sides by ridges 300 or 400 feet in height ... I peered into a large rent which had been made from bank to bank of the broad Zambesi, and saw that a stream of a thousand yards leaped down a hundred feet, and then became suddenly compressed into a space of

fifteen or twenty yards. The entire falls are simply a crack made in a hard basaltic rock ...[160]

Through statistical reportage, Livingstone encompasses the mind-boggling sight before him into his descriptive paradigm. For Adrian Wisnicki, this passage is a 'phallic-like visual penetration', an attempt to bring the falls 'under the western gaze'.[161] Furthermore, in rechristening the locally known 'Mosioatunya' with an 'English name',[162] Livingstone's narrative enacts the appropriative logic of discovery which Pratt characterises as 'a gesture of converting local knowledges (discourses) into European and continental knowledges'.[163] Elsewhere Livingstone makes it clear that something is 'discovered' only when it received European certification; 'native' information needed to be borne out by Western authority. Discussing information on the Zambesi, received from 'Balonda and native traders', Livingstone is sure to write, 'All, being derived from native testimony, is offered to the reader with diffidence, as needing verification by actual explorers.'[164] *Missionary Travels* is thus an imperialist text at least to the degree that the 'myth of discovery' is an imperialist discourse.

Leon de Kock argues that, as the account of a 'gentlemanly scientist', meticulously observing his way around Africa, Livingstone's narrative 'emphasizes a mastery over nature'.[165] But it is not just scientific narrative that achieves this end. Those episodes of adventure, to which I referred earlier, produced the same effect. Indeed, Livingstone's confrontation with nature's force is exemplified best in the passage recounting the ferocious lion attack. Despite being left physically maimed, Livingstone emerges victorious as the round of ammunition he has opened into the beast belatedly takes effect.[166] His triumph is of course figuratively rich. As Glenn Hooper and Tim Youngs write, 'It is a truism that animals signify the border between nature and the wild on the one hand, and civilization and human on the other. Thus the presence of the beast can represent a threat to order, but its narrative expression contains it.'[167] Livingstone's passage displays human vulnerability before a hostile environment on the one hand, but his victory domesticates it effectively on the other. The defeat of the lion ultimately carries the symbolic weight of civilisation's conquest of untamed nature (see Fig. 2).[168]

The lion passage is also conspicuous for another reason. Although an episode of adventure, it merges with Livingstone's scientific discursive mode. The whole scene departs from readerly expectations when he begins to discuss his mauling as though it were a specimen for analytic observation: 'The shock produced a stupor similar to that which seems to be felt by a mouse after the first shake of the cat. It caused a sort of

STYLING THE SELF: MAKING *MISSIONARY TRAVELS*

2. 'The Missionary's Escape from the Lion'. *Missionary Travels and Researches in South Africa* (London: John Murray, 1857), p. 13

dreaminess, in which there was no sense of pain or feeling of terror.'[169] In recounting this incident Livingstone communicates his mastery, not only by displaying the power of the gun, but by treating his experience as an experiment.

Missionary Travels can thus be found to resonate with various imperialist discourses. Furthermore, the text relies on what, following Syed Manzurul Islam, we might characterise as 'sedentary' practices of racial representation. Islam explains how on reading travelogues it dawned on him that 'all these intrepid travellers, despite moving so much and so far in space, did not seem to have travelled at all'.[170] This sedentary motion 'involves a movement across geographical and textual space, but it settles for a representational practice that scarcely registers an encounter with the other'. Sedentary travellers journeyed with their domestic habits of mind secure, 'driven by the need to secure a vantage point from which to carry out a representation of difference'.[171]

Certainly, Livingstone is sedentary to the extent that he offers up scenes figuring the encountered groups as alien and unfamiliar. And for the cultivation and maintenance of domestication, Livingstone has a number of textual strategies. Perhaps his most unusual method is to deploy the label 'insane' when confronted with seemingly incomprehensible behaviour. On coming face to face with Tlapane, a '"senoga" – one who holds intercourse with the gods', and who can enter a 'mesmeric state', Livingstone dismisses him as having 'a touch of insanity'.[172] On another occasion, when witnessing a dance of 'men standing nearly naked ... each roaring at the loudest pitch of his voice', Livingstone again muses, 'If the scene were witnessed in a lunatic asylum it would be nothing out of the way, and quite appropriate even, as a means of letting off the excessive excitement of the brain.'[173] In the same way, the disappearance of a trusted guide, Monahin, is reduced to 'a sudden fit of insanity', the product of excessive mental strain.[174] When Livingstone finds particular forms of behaviour alienating, the labels 'insane' and 'mad' vindicate his inability to engage. They cement the boundary between him and 'them'.

There are other textual mechanisms to which Livingstone resorts more routinely in representing the 'other'. One of the most basic is to contrast African and European capabilities, so as to leave the reader in little doubt as to their relative powers. For instance, Livingstone relays how, at Kolobeng, he 'took notes of the different numbers of elephants killed in the course of the season by the various parties which went past our dwelling'. To make the kill, 'success depended mainly on the courage which leads the huntsman to go close to the animal ... the average for the natives was under one per man, for the Griquas one per man, for the Boers two, and for the English officers twenty each.' He concludes, 'It would thus appear that our more barbarous neighbours do not possess half the physical courage of the civilized sportsman.'[175] Such unfavourable juxtapositions are common currency in *Missionary Travels* and have the simple effect of reiterating the physical and cultural ascendancy of Europeans.

In establishing self-supremacy and cultivating difference from local populations, Livingstone intermittently grants his readers barbaric spectacles. One of the more graphic is his verbal depiction of the slaughter of an elephant and her calf:

> After the first discharge she appeared with her sides red with blood, and, beginning to flee for her own life, seemed to think no more of her young ... the calf had taken refuge in the water and was killed ... It was by this process of spearing and loss of blood that she was killed; for at last, making a short charge, she staggered round and sank down and died in a kneeling posture ... I turned from the spectacle of the destruction of noble animals, which might be made so useful in Africa, with a feeling of sickness.[176]

Livingstone presents himself watching at a symbolic removal from the orgy of blood. Other episodes of barbarism and superstition likewise serve the same end. On meeting the Batoka, for instance, Livingstone expresses his horror at their 'mode of salutation':

> They throw themselves on their backs on the ground, and, rolling from side to side, slap the outside of the thighs ... The men being totally unclothed, this performance imparted to my mind a painful sense of their extreme degradation ... The sight of great naked men wallowing on the ground ... made me feel thankful that my lot had been cast in such different circumstances.[177]

Such indecent exposure offended Livingstone's European sensibilities and offered the opportunity for brief reflection on both his own and his readers' superiority.

Livingstone does not, of course, only put savagery on display: he also demonstrates his triumph over it. Whereas confrontations with beasts and a hostile environment conveyed Livingstone's mastery over nature, collisions with barbaric men enabled him to construct ascendancy over the encountered. He relates how:

> Njambi collected all his people, and surrounded our encampment ... some even pointed their guns at me and nodded to each other, as much to say, 'This is the way we shall do with him.' I sat on my camp-stool, with my double-barreled gun ... One young man made a charge at my head from behind, but I quickly brought round the muzzle of my gun to his mouth.[178]

Similarly, when a chief in the 'Chiboque territory' mounted an attack, 'the sight of the six barrels gaping into his stomach, with [Livingstone's] ghastly visage looking daggers at his face, seemed to produce an instant revolution in his martial feelings'. With implacable courage Livingstone mounted his ox, saying to his men: 'Tell him to observe that I am not afraid of him.'[179] These instances show something of the repetitive nature of the scene, in which Livingstone coolly surmounts hostility.[180] Such passages function, as Martin Green reminds us, to portray the protagonist as 'a hero, eminent in virtues such as courage, fortitude, cunning, strength, leadership, and persistence'.[181] 'Native' obstacles serve as a foil against which the central character can achieve self-definition.

In *Missionary Travels* it is not only the hostile locals, but also the amicable and welcoming, who facilitate Livingstone's self-construction. Indeed he is preoccupied with demonstrating his influence upon those willing to learn. Recounting the story of a theft among Sekeletu's people, Livingstone notes how 'the simple mode of punishment, by forcing a criminal to work out a fine, did not strike the Makololo mind until now'. This new system was of course 'immediately introduced', in place of the 'customary mode of punishing a crime' by casting 'the criminal into the river'.[182] In this way, Livingstone construes himself in the capacity of a teacher, imparting the benefits of civilised culture to eager recipients. He furthers this self-image too by appropriating local speech. The Kololo women, we are told, gave him 'copious supplies of shrill praises', shouting out cries of '"great lords" and "great lions"'. While Livingstone proclaims his modesty, by explaining that he asked them to adopt 'more humble expressions', the recital of their excessive adulation enables him to project his pre-eminence.[183] Indeed such speech appropriation is a recurring strategy throughout *Missionary Travels*. His trusty 'sextant and artificial horizon', writes Livingstone, led the inhabitants around Tete to exclaim that 'the Son of God had come,' who could 'take the sun down from the heavens and place it under his arm!'[184] Similarly, tales of British manufacturing elicited the exclamation, 'Truly ye are gods!'[185] In this way, *Missionary Travels* ensures that Livingstone's supremacy and the ascendancy of Western technology and culture appear to be confirmed by African voices.

It seems clear that *Missionary Travels*, as a document of discovery and adventure narrative, participates in certain ways in imperialist discourse. The text is woven too with practices of 'sedentary' representation that serve to cultivate a sense of distance from the African 'other'. A number of textual strategies, from savage scenes to speech appropriation, ensure that *Missionary Travels*, at points at least, bolsters a European self-image of superiority and domesticates the cultures encountered.

The hybrid text

But while it is apparent that *Missionary Travels* can be situated as imperialist to some degree, this argument requires complication. The notion of a univocal discourse of the dominant has been problematised by Homi Bhabha's pioneering work on ambivalence and hybridity. For Bhabha, it is continually the case that '"denied" knowledges enter upon the dominant discourse and estrange the basis of its authority'.[186] In other words, 'the effect of colonial power is seen to be the *production* of hybridization rather than the noisy command of colonialist authority or the silent repression of native traditions'.[187] The point is that the subversive presence of the 'other' impinges on the coloniser's discourse; rather than being in easy possession of control, the coloniser was hesitant and unstable.[188]

Livingstone's text exposes such vulnerability by displaying what Helmers and Mazzeo call 'the dialogic nature of vision'. In other words, *Missionary Travels* demonstrates that in cultural encounter the 'observer is also observed'.[189] For instance, Livingstone describes the way in which he appeared strange and startling and how his hair

STYLING THE SELF: MAKING *MISSIONARY TRAVELS*

particularly was 'considered a curiosity': it seemed to be 'the mane of a lion, and not hair at all'.[190] A shift in the subject–object dichotomy occurs in the text, in which Livingstone becomes a spectacle on the receiving end of scrutiny.

Becoming an object, rather than subject, signifies a loss of authority and control. As Chloe Chard notes, certain explorers, such as Mungo Park, embraced the experience and 'eagerly reproduce[d] the plot of crossing over to the side of the spectacle'.[191] She observes, however, that such writers employed rhetorical strategies to compensate for the challenge to their authority. Often, they strived to return the scrutiny, to remain a spectator even while a spectacle.[192] Certainly Livingstone tries to conserve his position through gentle humour. When the locals joke that his hair is like a lion's mane, he inwardly laughs that theirs is like 'the wool of sheep'.[193] At the same time, it was useful for Livingstone to display his spectacle status since it certified his unique claim to be the first European many Africans had seen. Relating a conversation with Sansawe, a Bashinje chief, Livingstone tells how 'the difference between their wool and our hair caused him to burst into a laugh'.[194] It provoked this reaction, of course, because straight hair had never before been beheld. Nonetheless, even if Livingstone deployed his experience as a spectacle tactically, and worked to control it, the reciprocity of vision forces the reader to experience the strange sensation of being different.

Livingstone's text further reveals its ambivalence in those moments in which local ridicule, with its power to estrange, surfaces disruptively within the text. On one occasion we read of his attempt to explain hunting for 'sport' to a group of Kwena questioners. They interrogated him about the hunting practices of his British companions: 'Have these hunters, who come so far and work so hard no meat at home?' they asked. When Livingstone replied that these British men were wealthy enough to 'slaughter oxen every day', his interlocutors were left in astonishment. To his regret, the explanation that one might hunt '"for the sake of play besides" (the idea of sport not being in the language)' produced 'a laugh, as much as to say ... "Your friends are fools"'. Livingstone was left concerned by 'the low estimation in which some of my hunting friends were held' and of course 'anxious that a higher estimate of my countrymen should be formed'.[195] Once again, the trace of the 'other' is disturbing; with a subversive laugh the familiar becomes strange as a world is encountered in which hunting for 'sport' is a nonexistent and nonsensical concept.

Humour also surfaces several times when Livingstone explains his attempts to impart the Christian message. Describing his efforts to communicate the idea of prayer to the Bakalahari, he notes that 'when we kneel down and address an unseen Being, the position and the act often appear to them so ridiculous that they can not refrain from bursting into uncontrollable laughter'.[196] Again, recounting a religious service with the Kololo, Livingstone complains of the way solemnity so easily descended into mirth. When the women knelt to pray, they 'bent over their little ones', who immediately 'set up a simultaneous yell'; this 'so tickled the whole assembly there was often a subdued titter, to be turned into a hearty laugh as soon as they heard Amen'.[197] The repetitive presence of such humour is of especial interest in light of the body of postcolonial theory on the nature of laughter in colonial situations. Much of this, following Bakhtin, has focused on its potential agency and subversive power. Laughter from the margins should not be understood as a token of frivolity, but instead as something that can undertake the serious work of unsettling the centre.[198] It is interesting that Livingstone, on the first occasion at least, strives to contain the disruptive mirth by rapidly passing on to describe a more positive reception of the Christian message: 'I was once present when a missionary attempted to sing among a wild heathen tribe of Bechuanas, who had no music in their composition ... tears actually ran down their cheeks.'[199] Despite this attempt at resolution, the narrative leaves the reader with the disturbing possibility of ironic response.

The itinerant text

While the hybridising power of 'the other' certainly does permeate Livingstone's text, I would argue that something more subversive is going on in *Missionary Travels*. The text actually exhibits considerable evidence of an attempt to challenge its readers by passing on the experience of encounter. Something of this may already be detectable in the textual space that Livingstone grants to encountered humour and the inversion of the gaze. A notion of narrative rupture takes us only so far; we need to move beyond Bhabha's conception of the hybrid text if we are to do justice to the radical strand in Livingstone's book.

As Dennis Porter has argued in his critique of Edward Said, the idea of colonial discourse perhaps allows insufficient conceptual space for disjunction, tension and heterogeneity within texts. In order to demonstrate the limitations of an overly monolithic conception of discourse, Porter reread both Marco Polo's *Travels* and T.E. Lawrence's *Seven Pillars of Wisdom*, calling attention to their 'counter-hegemonic' dimensions and 'contradictory energies'.[200] In even 'canonical' imperialist works, he revealed, dissenting discourses can surface. To read *Missionary Travels* solely for its imperial dimensions, then, would fail to do justice to the discursive complexity of the text.

Indeed, over the last two decades many studies in travel writing have pointed to the potentially destabilising nature of travelogues. From

STYLING THE SELF: MAKING *MISSIONARY TRAVELS*

these ventures, a number of models have emerged that resist interpreting such texts simply as vehicles for imperialist ideology. Brian Musgrove, for one, has suggested that 'the formal basis of the travel genre is in the structure of rites of passage', and more particularly the 'border-crossing', a period of profound 'unsettlement' which promotes reflexivity in the traveller.[201] Under this framework, the travelling subject 'is by no means the self-assured colonist' but instead reveals 'points of unravelling, conflict and uncertainty'.[202] Derek Gregory and James Duncan provide another analytical model, suggesting that travel writing operates as a space of 'translation' involved in 're-presenting other cultures and other natures'. While this translative act is always 'shot through with relations of power and of desire', it nonetheless leads travellers to 'constantly rub against the hubris that their own language-game contains the concepts necessary to represent another language-game'.[203] These paradigms are only two of those that have sought, as Steven Clark puts it, 'to resist the reduction of cross-cultural encounter to simple relations of domination and subordination'.[204]

The remainder of this chapter will follow in this critical trajectory, destabilising the imperialist reading of *Missionary Travels* by highlighting those textual dimensions that disrupt the discourses which we have so far discerned at work. I conceptualise this as Livingstone's 'itinerant' discourse, by which I aim to encapsulate those textual practices that run against the grain of his sedentary representation. By using a metaphor of movement, I hope to bring into focus both the reflexivity granted by the experience of travel and cultural encounter, and the ways in which Livingstone attempts to transmit this to his audience.[205] Reading for Livingstone's itinerant discourse makes space for the points at which he questions the authority of home and disrupts domestic expectations. In all this, Livingstone resonates with what Islam calls 'nomadic' travel, a mode of passage that breaks with the 'route of power', the 'travelling incarceration' of 'the same', in which the sedentary traveller moves.[206] The term, however, is not fully appropriate for Livingstone, since he cannot be said to satisfy Islam's criterion for 'ethical' travel as a 'performative enactment of becoming other'.[207] Yet the more limited concept of itinerant discourse allows that Livingstone at least approximates to nomadic encounter when he comes 'face to face with the other, without the paranoia of othering'.[208] By examining the itinerant dimensions of Livingstone's book, I will show that *Missionary Travels* is a heterogeneous text with intermingling discourses that resists too facile categorisation as imperialist.

Livingstone reveals a degree of his itinerancy in passages that exhibit some ability to reflect on the relativity of cultural standards. Even when discussing polygamy, a practice he never condoned, Livingstone attempts to convey its normalcy within its own cultural context. For instance, Livingstone discusses the way in which marriage bonds enabled Sechele to consolidate his leadership when he rose to the chieftainship of the Kwena, thanks to the military intervention of the famed Kololo leader Sebituane: 'Sechele married the daughters of three of his under-chiefs, who had, on account of their blood relationship, stood by him in his adversity. This is one of the modes adopted for cementing the allegiance of a tribe.' Indeed, a leader always 'attaches the under-chiefs to himself and his government by marrying'.[209] For Livingstone, then, there were viable political reasons for polygamous practice. There were social dimensions too, since he spotted a connection between polygamy and hospitality. The duty of welcoming strangers was taken with such seriousness among the Kololo 'that one of the most cogent arguments for polygamy is that a respectable man with only one wife could not entertain strangers as he ought'. This argument had force in its context, Livingstone points out, particularly in regions dependent on female labour, where 'women are the chief cultivators of the soil'.[210]

It seems clear that Livingstone approaches customs with an effort to comprehend, even when discussing practices with which he disagrees on point of principle. As Andrew Ross puts it, he seeks to demonstrate that the seemingly alien dimensions of African life developed as a 'rational reaction to their environment or as a result of their particular history'.[211] This is most powerfully communicated in one of Livingstone's most publicised scenes, the dialogue with the 'rain doctor'. The reported discussion took place during Livingstone's early period as a missionary to the Kwena at Kolobeng. The passage is conspicuous not least for the considerable textual space granted to an African voice. The rain doctor, we are told, responded to Livingstone's accusation that he was a deceptive fraudster by confronting him with this challenge: '*We* do not despise those things which you possess, though we are ignorant of them. We don't understand your book, yet we don't despise it. *You* ought not to despise our little knowledge, though you are ignorant of it.'[212] And when Livingstone persisted in his doubting enquiry, the rain doctor continued:

> I use my medicines, and you employ yours; we are both doctors, and doctors are not deceivers. You give a patient medicine. Sometimes God is pleased to heal him by means of your medicine; sometimes not – he dies. When he is cured, you take the credit of what God does. I do the same. Sometimes God grants us rain, sometimes not. When he does, we take the credit of the charm. When a patient dies, you don't give up trust in your medicine, neither do I when rain fails. If you wish me to leave off my medicines, why continue your own?[213]

Livingstone admits that he failed to deliver a response and so leaves the reader with the resonating challenge of this claim to epistemic equivalence. He writes, 'The above is only a specimen of their way of reasoning, in which ... they are perceived to be remarkably acute ... I never succeeded in convincing a single individual of their fallacy, though I tried to do so in every way I could think of.'[214] While dismissing the rainmaker's arguments as clearly false, Livingstone concedes his own inability to answer them sufficiently.

In this section, Livingstone willingly hosts the rainmaker's voice and attempts to explain the epistemological power of his argument. He points out the feeling of frustration that would arise from being subject to the climate and unable to alter adverse weather conditions. In a context of powerlessness, 'The natives, finding it irksome to sit and wait helplessly until God gives them rain from heaven, entertain the more comfortable idea that they can help themselves by a variety of preparations.'[215] While Livingstone's tone is somewhat condescending, he argues that the attempt to make rain was driven by the very human desire to alter one's circumstances and to reject passivity. In fact, he goes so far as to contend that 'were we as much harassed by droughts, the logic would be irresistible in England in 1857'.[216] In other words, the belief in the rain doctor's powers, while undoubtedly mistaken, was reasonable in its own cultural parameters.

In even as critical a study as the Comaroffs' *Of Revelation and Revolution*, the exceptional nature of this scene is remarked upon. While many missionaries recorded their attempts to engage rainmakers, Livingstone was alone in describing 'his debate with a Kwena practitioner in such a way as to suggest that there was little to choose between their positions'.[217] His 'parallel use of the title "doctor"' also implied, perhaps ironically, that they were on 'equal ontological ground'. Indeed, such a unique passage, they suggest, might be read as an anticipation of Edward Evans-Pritchard's 'spirited defence of the rationality of African "magical" thought'.[218] It is worth noting that the original manuscript of *Missionary Travels* includes several additional and important sentences on the subject of rainmaking. Here, Livingstone actually presses the logic of the argument further by suggesting that many in his home nation rely on the same rationale manifested in rainmaking. His argument is that that the British following for homeopathic treatments stemmed from the same sense of helplessness in adversity, and the same desire to alleviate one's situation, that lay behind the Kwena confidence in 'medicine'. Both practices, African and British, emerge from what he calls '"the every man his own doctor" feeling'.[219] Livingstone makes it clear that there is no more reasonable evidence for homeopathic medicine than for rainmaking; both reach unwarrantable conclusions and rely on fallacious *post hoc ergo propter hoc* logic: 'Have we aught else in support of the powers of the homeopathic globule' than mere 'inference', he enquires.[220] By demonstrating rainmaking's equivalence with certain kinds of domestic reasoning, Livingstone attempted to prevent a scornful dismissal of a seemingly alien practice.

In connecting a local African custom with something in British life, this excised portion reveals a strategy that Livingstone would employ when presenting facets of culture that were irrevocably foreign to his audience. Ross briefly notes that by this literary manoeuvre, contrasting something in African life with 'something in the experience of the white reading public', Livingstone aimed to strike his readers with 'their common experience, their shared humanity'.[221] At one point in *Missionary Travels*, Livingstone elaborates on the fashion of Kololo women, describing their ornamental brass anklets, which were 'so heavy that the ankles are often blistered by the weight'. Yet, in the face of this custom, Livingstone likens the ability to bear this pain so 'magnanimously' to the equally foolish endurance of 'tight lacing and tight shoes among ourselves'.[222] Rather than focusing on the strangeness of the practice, he compels his readers to realise that the trends of home are equally arbitrary. The juxtaposition of Kololo and British women works to undermine difference. Livingstone employs the tactic again when discussing the same 'profusion of iron rings', which led Sheakondo's wife 'to make a tinkling as she walked in her mincing African style'. Rather than holding her up for pure mockery, Livingstone reminds the reader that 'the same thing is thought pretty by our own dragoons in walking jauntily'.[223]

In this way, Livingstone resisted the greater extremes of racial stereotyping. Although he showed some interest in racial classification, an aversion to caricatures is a conspicuous feature of *Missionary Travels*: 'With every disposition to pay due deference to the opinions of those who have made ethnology their special study', writes Livingstone, 'I have felt myself unable to believe that the exaggerated features usually put forth as those of the typical negro characterize the majority of any nation of south Central Africa.'[224] Livingstone distances himself from physical typecasting, but also from intellectual and character profiling. He resists the 'stupid prejudice against colour'[225] and what he describes in the later *Narrative of an Expedition to the Zambesi*, co-authored with Charles Livingstone, as 'the heaps of nonsense which have been written about the negro intellect'.[226] These images, he suggests, are projections of the white man's own deficiencies. It was only those Europeans 'who were much addicted to lying on their backs smoking' who 'complained of the laziness of the negroes'.[227] His experience in Africa had taught him the superficiality of the stereotype and the shared complexity of humanity: 'After long observation, I came to the conclusion that they are just such a strange mixture of good and evil as men are everywhere else ... By a selection of cases of either kind, it would not be difficult to make these people appear excessively good or uncommonly bad.'[228]

One particularly interesting literary strategy that Livingstone employs against the stereotype is the inversion of racial perception. In *Missionary Travels* Livingstone renders white skin strange; whiteness becomes 'other'.[229] His readers have the unsettling experience of reading that 'The sight of a white man always infuses a tremor into their dark bosoms': 'When a little child, unconscious of danger, meets you in the street, he sets up a scream at the apparition'.[230] For a short time, his audience is compelled to see itself as bizarre and even disgusting. Livingstone frequently returns to this point in the *Narrative*, in which he writes, 'There must be something in the appearance of white men, frightfully repulsive to the unsophisticated natives'; 'Blue eyes appear savage and a red beard hideous.'[231] Indeed, he even goes as far as to say that 'One feels ashamed of the white skin; it seems unnatural, like blanched celery or white mice.'[232] By estranging whiteness in an African context, Livingstone's texts force their white-skinned readers onto the receiving end of typecasting. They are exposed to the defamiliarising experience of cultural encounter. Indeed, Livingstone describes his own alienation in becoming something of a 'hobgoblin' figure, a bogyman used to terrify naughty children into obedience.[233] Using the experience of typecasting he encourages his readers to confront the constructed nature of their own stereotypes.

Missionary Travels is clearly a text that confronts its audience with the reflexivity of cultural contact; it strives towards empathy, resists racial stereotypes, and grants space to voices from existing communities. The travelogue attempts an act of translation, an effort to re-present and make the 'other' not so other at all. But should these itinerant dimensions be thought of as progressive? For Andrew Ross, Livingstone was part of a radical evangelical tradition that was pre-Victorian in attitude. Although Livingstone lived until 1873, Ross points out that he had been cut off from Britain for much of his life; his was the worldview of those such as Wilberforce, Buxton and Philip, who believed in the unity of humanity and the potential of every race for redemption. Ross argues that, working from this tradition, *Missionary Travels* was written as 'an attempt to undermine the ignorance and the positive prejudice in Britain' and to combat the racism that ran counter to these evangelical notions.[234] While Ross touches on an important point, he perhaps avoids the sedentary dimensions of Livingstone's discourse in an effort to distance him from a later generation of imperialists.

Adrian Wisnicki suggests a more complex interpretation. For him, *Missionary Travels* occupies an 'interstitial space' between the older evangelical discourse of 'conversionism', to which Ross gestures, and an emerging 'trusteeism'.[235] This new paternalistic discourse emphasised that the firmly 'superior' Anglo-Saxon race must show caring responsibility towards the 'inferior' races, whom by duty it was bound to 'develop'. Emerging out of the ideology of the new imperialists, trusteeism came into being as the more humane, although still firmly hierarchical, cousin of 'scientific racism' which insisted on absolute black inferiority. For Wisnicki, *Missionary Travels* resonates with both discourses: it is a 'transitional text' between conversionism and the newer trusteeism.[236] Under this argument, Livingstone's sedentary dimensions, in which he domesticated Africans and cultivated European superiority, might be understood as part of the trustee discourse. And what I have characterised as itinerancy, in which Livingstone recognised African complexity and individuality, would be part of the diminishing conversionism. Livingstone's seemingly radical dimensions would thus be part of an older tradition and indeed not really radical at all.

Wisnicki's interpretation is one of the most sensitive readings of *Missionary Travels*, particularly since it shows close attention to the competing discourses and shifting positions within the text. Yet portraying the book as 'transitional', leading towards trusteeism, perhaps underplays its subversive dimensions. Certainly I agree that much of Livingstone's thought is rooted in the conversionist tradition, but it remains highly important that he mobilised these views against newer forms of racialism that he encountered in figures like Richard Burton. Andrew Ross has noted that Livingstone and Burton actually came into conflict over their respective opinions on Africans in 1865 when both men gave evidence before the House of Commons committee examining British policy in west Africa. While Burton deemed mission work to be wasted on Africans, whom he considered inherently inferior beings, Livingstone testified to the opposite and declared their inherent worth.[237] Even if many of Livingstone's ideas were conversionist in origin, the way in which he implemented them can be considered progressive.

It is also significant that some of Livingstone's more radical sentiments can be shown to have origins that lie outside the confines of earlier evangelical thought. John Corbett has argued that to understand Livingstone's comparatively 'admirable' attitude to Africans we need to turn to 'the particularities of [his] Scottish origins and his understanding of his heritage'.[238] Livingstone had such 'sympathy with his African acquaintances' in contrast to his contemporary missionaries, argues Corbett, because he believed they occupied a similar position to his own Highland ancestors, who had been Roman Catholic, Jacobite and Hebridean Gaels before being 'improved' by Protestantism and civilisation.[239] His understanding of this cultural inheritance enabled self-identification with Africans, who he believed had the same scope for development. While the earlier evangelical tradition significantly influenced Livingstone, Corbett's article reminds us that there were local factors too involved in shaping his attitude. This gives us reason to resist reducing the progressive dimensions of *Missionary Travels* solely to remnants of the diminishing conversionist discourse.

All this is further consolidated by the fact that Livingstone's attitude to Africans was perceived to be quite unusual even by his contemporaries. Clare Pettitt notes that Livingstone's obituary in *The Times* declared that 'his success depended, from first to last, in an eminent degree upon the great power which he possessed of entering into the feelings, wishes, and desires of the African tribes and engaging their hearty sympathy'.[240] Such remembrances, of which there are many, suggest to Pettitt that there was a 'reciprocity in Livingstone's relationships with Africans which was unheard of at the time'.[241] This may be slightly overstating the case, but – as will become clear in my next chapter – the sense that Livingstone interacted in an exceptional way was certainly echoed in other contemporary obituaries and eulogies. Given Livingstone's opposition to the advocates of scientific racism, the importance of his specific cultural heritage and the contemporaneous perception that he had an unusual affinity with Africans, it seems correct to make space in *Missionary Travels* for a discourse that goes beyond conversionism. By casting such salient moments as itinerant, my framework leaves room for those occasions in which Livingstone employs this older discourse to radical effect and even exceeds its parameters altogether.

Missionary Travels, on close inspection, has been revealed to be a deeply complex text. It participates in and extends imperial discourse, yet in certain ways resists it. On the whole, then, Livingstone's book defies any simple categorisation as imperialist. This mode of enquiry was stimulated by Livingstone's original manuscript, which contained radical material that he excised for the published text. The fact that, at an earlier stage of textual production, Livingstone had seen fit to include such a substantial challenge to colonial power and practice confirms the importance of scrutinising his text for ambivalence, hesitancy and itinerant discourse. While the few critics who have examined the text in detail have tended to position it unequivocally within imperial discourse, revisiting *Missionary Travels* has proven it to be more ambiguous than such an interpretation allows.

This chapter has brought the tools of literary analysis to bear on one of the bestselling travelogues of the Victorian period. It has examined the text as a mechanism of self-construction, a means by which Livingstone projected himself to the British public. Beginning with genre analysis, I have argued that *Missionary Travels* resonates with a number of literary modes. By drawing on diverse genres of travel, Livingstone created a heterogeneous book that was at once missionary text, adventure narrative, naturalist's report, administrative document and abolitionist manifesto. And in performing these genres, of course, Livingstone not only appealed to a wide range of audiences but constructed for himself an almost polymathic identity. I have also examined Livingstone's narrative style; as his correspondence with John Murray indicates, he sought a style to suit his subject and resented undue interference with his writing. Furthermore, it was through the 'literary technology' of virtual witnessing and unadorned prose that Livingstone was able to negotiate the issues of authority and credibility that have perennially plagued travellers. His success on this front is abundantly clear in the glowing reviews that his book received.

In treating *Missionary Travels* as a form of life-writing, the concept of impression management has proved productive. I have sought to explore the pressures of the literary marketplace and the ways in which Livingstone responded in the performance of his identity. In this section, the previously unexamined handwritten manuscript of *Missionary Travels* has been crucial in establishing that Livingstone acted as a self-censor, removing a body of radical material from the text prior to publication. The result of this editorial process was the production of a book that was more appealing to the sensibilities of empire-builders than it might otherwise have been. While the text had an undeniable impact on the empire, it was originally conceived as a more ambivalent document than it finally became. Yet the material in the manuscript compels a re-reading of the published *Missionary Travels* itself. As I have argued, even in its final form the book defies easy categorisation: *Missionary Travels* is certainly imperialist to an extent, but it is not as self-evidently so as has sometimes been assumed.

By discursively analysing *Missionary Travels* we have been able to perceive the sheer heterogeneity of the document. At the outset of a metabiography, this serves to demonstrate the complexity of at least some of the raw material that future biographers would rely on in writing their lives of Livingstone. While the horizons and locatedness of his biographers have been the most decisive factors in reshaping Livingstone, it remains the case that not just any individual could sustain so many different representations. This is particularly relevant to his legacy as an icon of empire, which will be discussed in a later chapter. Approaching his oeuvre with a hermeneutic of selectivity, Livingstone's biographers were able to put him to work for a variety of imperialist and, more rarely, counter-imperialist purposes. At least to some degree, it was the protean nature of *Missionary Travels* that facilitated this range of posthumous interpretations and that made him a figure so ripe for reconstruction.

Notes

1 'Dr. Livingstone's Book', *Leeds Mercury* (7 November 1857), 4.
2 'Dr. Livingstone's Missionary Travels and Researches in South Africa', *Glasgow Herald* (11 November 1857), 2; 'Literature', *Caledonian Mercury* (21 December 1857), 3.
3 Andrew Ross, *David Livingstone: Mission and Empire* (London: Hambledon and London, 2002); Tim Jeal, *Livingstone* (New Haven: Yale University Press, 2001); Oliver Ransford, *David Livingstone: The Dark Interior* (London: John Murray, 1978).
4 Adrian S. Wisnicki, 'Interstitial Cartographer: David Livingstone and the Invention of South Central Africa', *Victorian Literature and Culture*, 37 (2009), 256.
5 Horace Waller (ed.), *The Last Journals of David Livingstone, in Central Africa, from 1865 to his Death* (London: John Murray, 1874); Dorothy O. Helly, *Livingstone's Legacy: Horace Waller and Victorian Mythmaking* (Athens, O.: Ohio University Press, 1987).
6 Casey Blanton, *Travel Writing: The Self and the World* (New York: Routledge, 2002), p. 2.
7 Laura Marcus, *Auto/biographical Discourses: Theory, Criticism, Practice* (Manchester: Manchester University Press, 1994), pp. 30, 32.
8 John Sturrock, *The Language of Autobiography: Studies in the First Person Singular* (Cambridge: Cambridge University Press, 1993), p. 289.
9 'Reviews', *Athenaeum* (7 November 1857), 1381.
10 Tzvetan Todorov, *Genres in Discourse*, trans. Catherine Porter (Cambridge: Cambridge University Press, 1990), p. 18.
11 John Frow, *Genre* (London and New York: Routledge, 2006), pp. 23–4.
12 Dell Hymes, 'Ways of Speaking', in Richard Bauman and Joel Sherzer (eds), *Explorations in the Ethnography of Speaking* (Cambridge: Cambridge University Press, 1974), p. 443.
13 Frow, *Genre*, p. 2.
14 Glenn Hooper and Tim Youngs, 'Introduction', in Glenn Hooper and Tim Youngs (eds), *Perspectives on Travel Writing* (Aldershot: Ashgate, 2004), p. 2.
15 Louise Henderson, '"Everyone will die laughing": John Murray and the Publication of David Livingstone's *Missionary Travels*', Livingstone Online, Wellcome Trust Centre for the History of Medicine at UCL (n.d.), www.livingstoneonline.ucl.ac.uk/companion.php?id=HIST2 (accessed 7 June 2010).
16 Jan Borm, 'Defining Travel: On the Travel Book, Travel Writing and Terminology', in Hooper and Youngs (eds), *Perspectives on Travel Writing*, p. 25.
17 Timothy Holmes, *Journey to Livingstone: Exploration of an Imperial Myth* (Edinburgh: Canongate, 1993), p. 117.
18 See Chris Wingfield, 'Remembering David Livingstone 1973–1935: From Celebrity to Saintliness', in Sarah Worden (ed.), *David Livingstone: Man, Myth and Legacy* (Edinburgh: National Museums Scotland, 2012), pp. 117–18.
19 Holmes, *Journey to Livingstone*, p. 117.
20 It is important to note that the different identities that Livingstone pulled together are by no means mutually exclusive. Dorinda Outram notes for instance how the 'field natural historian' was long associated with 'ideals of heroic, manly endeavour'. See Dorinda Outram, 'New Spaces in Natural History', in Nicholas Jardine, James A. Secord and E.C. Spary (eds), *Cultures of Natural History* (Cambridge: Cambridge University Press, 1996), p. 259. Similarly, missionaries often acted as

field agents of natural history. Yet despite such interaction, I would suggest that Livingstone was unusual in the degree to which he sought to cultivate an expansive identity.

21 David Livingstone, *Missionary Travels and Researches in South Africa* (London: John Murray, 1857), p. 4.
22 Ibid., pp. 188, 219.
23 Ibid., p. 17.
24 Ibid., p. 116.
25 Ibid., p. 236.
26 Ibid., p. 552.
27 Ibid., p. 317.
28 Ibid., p. 553.
29 Ibid., p. 496.
30 This idea is derived from Daniel Bivona, who suggests that H.M. Stanley's *How I Found Livingstone* sought to construct the continent as a place of economic 'need' that promised opportunity for Europe. See Daniel Bivona, *British Imperial Literature, 1870–1940: Writing and the Administration of Empire* (Cambridge: Cambridge University Press, 1998), p. 43.
31 Ibid., pp. 45, 47.
32 Livingstone, *Missionary Travels*, pp. 143, 497–8.
33 Ibid., pp. 588, 254–5.
34 Livingstone criticised those hunters who 'fired away indiscriminately'. If 'great numbers of animals are wounded and allowed to perish miserably, or are killed on the spot ... for the sole purpose of making a "bag",' he mused, 'then I take it to be evident that such sportsmen are pretty far gone in the hunting form of insanity'. See ibid., pp. 161–2.
35 Ibid., p. 291.
36 Ibid., p. 549.
37 Bivona, *British Imperial Literature*, p. 48.
38 Tim Barringer, 'Fabricating Africa: Livingstone and the Visual Image 1850-74', in John M. MacKenzie (ed.), *David Livingstone and the Victorian Encounter with Africa* (London: National Portrait Gallery, 1996), p. 179.
39 Isaac Schapera (ed.), *David Livingstone: Family Letters, 1841–1856* (London: Chatto & Windus, 1959), pp. xvi–xvii.
40 Livingstone's importance as an ethnographer is indicated by the significant interest that social anthropologists, such as Isaac Schapera, have taken in his work. For discussions of missionary ethnography, see George Stocking, *Victorian Anthropology* (New York: The Free Press, 1987); Patrick Harries and David Maxwell (eds), *The Spiritual and the Secular: Missionaries and Knowledge about Africa* (Grand Rapids: Eerdmans, 2012); Patrick Brantlinger, *Taming the Cannibals: Race and the Victorians* (New York: Cornell University Press, 2011).
41 Livingstone, *Missionary Travels*, p. 680. Livingstone's subsequent book, *Narrative of an Expedition to the Zambesi*, owed yet more to the abolitionist genre, and it offered lengthy descriptions of the horrors of slavery. Describing his experience on the Shire river, Livingstone wrote: 'No words can convey an adequate idea of the scene of widespread desolation ... the slave-trade must be deemed the chief agent in the ruin' and 'Dead bodies floated past us daily ...'. See David Livingstone and Charles Livingstone, *Narrative of an Expedition to the Zambesi and its Tributaries* (London: John Murray, 1865), pp. 455–6, 449–50.
42 Ransford, *David Livingstone*, p. 135.
43 Wisnicki, 'Interstitial Cartographer', p. 257.
44 William Garden Blaikie, *The Personal Life of David Livingstone* (London: John Murray, 1880), p. 62.
45 Ibid., p. 209.
46 Livingstone, *Missionary Travels*, pp. 433, 434.
47 Fredric Jameson, *The Political Unconscious: Narrative as a Socially Symbolic Act* (New York: Cornell University Press, 1981), p. 144.

48 David Livingstone, letter to John Murray, 29 April 1857, MS 42425, John Murray Archive, National Library of Scotland, Edinburgh.
49 David Livingstone, letter to John Murray, 24 August 1857, MS 42425, John Murray Archive.
50 David Livingstone, letter to Henry Toynbee, 22–7 August 1857 MS 7329/70, Wellcome Library, London.
51 Henderson, '"Everyone will die laughing"'.
52 Livingstone, letter to John Murray, 24 August 1857.
53 'Dr. Livingstone's Book', *Leeds Mercury* (7 November 1857), 4. In spite of this, the attempt to meet the demands of different readerships and to embrace plural identities did leave some with a sense of dissatisfaction. On 11 November 1857, the *Scotsman* compared his text rather unfavourably with the work of 'Bruce, the Abyssinian traveller'. 'Any one who chooses to compare [Bruce's] story of the poor pilot in the storm … with the feebly-related anecdotes of Livingstone, will at once recognise the immeasurable superiority, as a writer, of the earliest traveller … he is so entirely deficient in imagination.' This reviewer was clearly hoping for a book packed with adventure and found the 'minute and trifling details' too monotonous for his taste. See: 'Literature', *Scotsman* (11 November 1857), 3. The Catholic periodical the *Dublin Review*, while taking a surprisingly warm attitude to a Protestant missionary, did observe however that Livingstone's expedition seemed to be 'three quarters scientific and one quarter missionary'. See 'Recent African Explorations', *Dublin Review*, 44: 87 (1858), 131.
54 Holmes, *Journey to Livingstone*, p. 124.
55 Felix Driver, *Geography Militant: Cultures of Exploration and Empire* (Oxford: Blackwell, 2001), p. 73.
56 The issue of credibility has become a major field of study within the sociology of science, as interest has turned towards the criteria by which a claim takes on the status of knowledge. Steven Shapin points out the reason for this preoccupation in the discipline: 'science, like finance, is a credit economy: there are activities in which, if you subtract credibility, there is no product left'. See Steven Shapin, 'Cordelia's Love: Credibility and the Social Studies of Science', *Perspectives on Science*, 3 (1995), 258. Within this discussion of warrant, the ambiguous status of travellers' tales has come under focus since they have been integral in the development of Western science at least since the seventeenth century.
57 Steven Shapin, *A Social History of Truth: Civility and Science in Seventeenth-Century England* (Chicago: University of Chicago Press, 1994), pp. 246–7.
58 Charles W.J. Withers, 'Travel and Trust in the Eighteenth Century', in John Renwick (ed.), *L'invitation au voyage: Studies in Honour of Peter France* (Oxford: Voltaire Foundation, 2000), p. 48.
59 Marcus, *Auto/biographical Discourses*, pp. 13, 39.
60 David Livingstone, letter to John Murray, 26 May 1857, MS 42425, John Murray Archive.
61 Larzer Ziff, 'Arctic Exploration and the Romance of Failure', *Raritan: A Quarterly Review*, 23: 2 (2003), 58.
62 There were critical differences between Livingstone's book and Kane's. While *Arctic Explorations* was what Ziff calls a 'romance of failure', *Missionary Travels* recounted Livingstone's highly successful trans-continental sojourn.
63 Ziff, 'Arctic Exploration', p. 75.
64 David Livingstone, letter to John Murray, 31 May 1857, MS 42425, John Murray Archive.
65 John Milton's father, Henry Milton, had also served as a reader for the Murrays. The connection between the firm and the Milton family had been established by John Murray II in the early 1840s. For discussion, see Angus Fraser, 'A Publishing House and its Readers, 1841–1880: The Murrays and the Miltons', *Papers of the Biblographical Society of America*, 90: 1 (1996), 4–47.
66 Livingstone, letter to John Murray, 31 May 1857.
67 David Livingstone, letter to John Murray, 30 May 1857, MS 42425, John Murray

Archive; David Livingstone, letter to John Murray, 3 June 1857, MS 42425, John Murray Archive.
68   Livingstone, letter to John Murray, 31 May 1857. It is perhaps significant that Livingstone wrote in this letter that he had 'come to this decision reading Kane's book today'.
69   Livingstone, letter to John Murray, 30 May 1857.
70   Livingstone, letter to John Murray, 31 May 1857.
71   Livingstone, letter to John Murray, 30 May 1857. This episode of course also demonstrates that *Missionary Travels* was subject to debate. A growing body of scholarship on travel and exploration, influenced by book-historical methods, has revealed the role that editors and publishers played in shaping travel texts into the final products offered to readers. This work problematises a simple notion of authorship, by revealing that travelogues were often heavily mediated and subject to a process of negotiation. See David Finkelstein, 'Unraveling Speke: The Unknown Revision of an African Exploration Classic', *History in Africa*, 30 (2003), 117–32; Charles W.J. Withers and Innes M Keighren, 'Travels into Print: Authoring, Editing and Narratives of Travel and Exploration c.1815-1857', *Transactions of the Institute of British Geographers*, 36: 4 (2011), 560–73. For further discussion of the negotiations involved in publishing *Missionary Travels*, see Henderson, '"Everyone will die laughing"'; Justin Livingstone, '*Missionary Travels*, Missionary Travails: David Livingstone and the Victorian Publishing Industry', in Sarah Worden (ed.), *David Livingstone: Man, Myth and Legacy* (Edinburgh: National Museums Scotland, 2012), pp. 33–51. For analysis of the issues involved in illustrating the book, see Leila Koivunen, 'Visualising Africa – Complexities of Illustrating David Livingstone's *Missionary Travels*', paper presented at 'Ennen & Nyt', the Nordic Conference on the History of Ideas, Helsinki, 2001; Leila Koivunen, *Visualizing Africa in Nineteenth-Century British Travel Accounts* (New York: Routledge, 2009), pp. 132, 166–7.
72   Steven Shapin, 'Pump and Circumstance: Robert Boyle's Literary Technology', *Social Studies of Science*, 14: 3 (1984), 484.
73   Ibid., pp. 490, 491.
74   Livingstone, *Missionary Travels*, pp. 172–3.
75   Livingstone and Livingstone, *Narrative*, p. 13.
76   While the *Narrative* often aims for effects of immediacy, the book is predominantly written in the third person. Ostensibly the text demanded this mode of diegesis, for it was co-authored with Livingstone's brother Charles. Yet, given that the book was written during a dip in Livingstone's popularity in the aftermath of the Zambesi expedition, and that it sought to defend him against criticism over the deaths of the missionaries of both the Universities' Mission to Central Africa (UMCA) and the LMS, the third-person narration surely provided a distancing effect and helped to lend the appearance of objective reportage.
77   Livingstone and Livingstone, *Narrative*, p. 20.
78   John Christie and Sally Shuttleworth argue that the idea arose in the seventeenth century that, 'As a writing practice, science would now forego the whole realm of rhetorical persuasion and of figuration'. They note that the frontier between scientific and literary discourse is not a 'feature of a natural landscape' but 'a cultural artefact'. See John Christie and Sally Shuttleworth, *Nature Transfigured: Science and Literature, 1700–1900* (Manchester: Manchester University Press, 1989), p. 2.
79   'Missionary Travels and Researches in South Africa', *Era* (28 March 1858), 10.
80   'Dr. Livingstone's Missionary Travels and Researches in South Africa', *Glasgow Herald* (11 November 1857), 2.
81   'Literature', *Caledonian Mercury* (4 December 1857), 2.
82   Ibid.
83   'Literature', *John Bull* (19 December 1857), 810.
84   Withers, 'Travel and Trust', p. 52.
85   'Reviews', *Athenaeum* (7 November 1857), 1381.

86 Livingstone, *Missionary Travels*, p. 8.
87 'Reviews', p. 1381.
88 Withers, 'Travel and Trust', p. 48.
89 Livingstone, *Missionary Travels*, p. iv.
90 Gérard Genette, *Paratexts: Thresholds of Interpretation*, trans. Jane E. Lewin (Cambridge: Cambridge University Press, 1997), p. 1.
91 Driver, *Geography Militant*, p. 78.
92 David Livingstone, letter to John Murray, 4 August 1857, MS 42425, John Murray Archive.
93 Holmes, *Journey to Livingstone*, p. 351.
94 Life-writing's reliance on narrative should not be considered disabling, for recent scholarship has pointed to the importance of narrative as 'a constitutive part of human identity – that we are, as it were, formed by narrative structures'. We impose order on our lives by the stories we tell about it. See Marcus, *Auto/biographical Discourses*, p. 243. Hermione Lee suggests that current philosophical arguments can ease 'Biographical anxieties about how a narrative construction can represent a "real" life'. She argues that 'If, in the philosopher Alasdair MacIntyre's formulation, "human actions" are "enacted narratives", and if we "understand our lives in terms of the narratives that we live out", then "the form of narrative is appropriate for understanding the actions of others"', and of course, the self. There is no need to fear that 'to give a narrative account of a human life is necessarily to falsify it'. See Hermione Lee, *Biography: A Very Short Introduction* (Oxford: Oxford University Press, 2009), p. 104.
95 Harold Rosen, *Speaking from Memory: The Study of Autobiographical Discourse* (Stoke-on-Trent: Trentham, 1998), p. 44.
96 Erving Goffman, *The Presentation of Self in Everyday Life* (Edinburgh: University of Edinburgh Social Sciences Research Centre, 1956), p. 132.
97 Jameson, *The Political Unconscious*, pp. 106–7.
98 Holmes, *Journey to Livingstone*, p. 121.
99 Ibid.
100 Livingstone, *Missionary Travels*, p. 118.
101 Holmes, *Journey to Livingstone*, p. 120.
102 Livingstone, *Missionary Travels*, p. 4.
103 George Shepperson, 'David Livingstone the Scot', *The Scottish Historical Review*, 39 (1960), 113.
104 Judith Listowel, *The Other Livingstone* (New York: Charles Scribner's Sons, 1974), p. 208.
105 Craig Beveridge and Ronald Turnbull, *The Eclipse of Scottish Culture: Inferiorism and the Intellectuals* (Edinburgh: Polygon, 1989), p. 1.
106 Ibid., p. 5. The idea that Scotland experienced what Michael Hector called 'internal colonialism' is contentious, not least because of the significant role that the country played in British imperialism. See Michael Hector, *Internal Colonialism: The Celtic Fringe in British National Politics, 1536–1966* (Berkeley: University of California Press, 1975), p. xiii. Certainly, Scotland's situation cannot be equated in any simple way to that of former colonies in Africa or Asia.
107 Quoted in Beveridge and Turnbull, *The Eclipse of Scottish Culture*, p. 8.
108 John Corbett, 'The Missionary's Positions: David Livingstone as a British Scot in Africa', *Scotlands*, 5: 1 (1998), 82.
109 Livingstone, *Missionary Travels*, pp. 200–1.
110 Clare Pettitt, *Dr. Livingstone, I Presume? Missionaries, Journalists, Explorers, and Empire* (Cambridge, Mass.: Harvard University Press, 2007), p. 20.
111 Livingstone, *Missionary Travels*, pp. 69, 655.
112 Ibid., p. 522.
113 Corbett, 'The Missionary's Positions', p. 86.
114 Livingstone, *Missionary Travels*, p. 3.
115 Robert Crawford, *Devolving English Literature* (Edinburgh: Edinburgh University Press, 2000), p. 6.

116 Corbett, 'The Missionary's Positions', p. 82.
117 Livingstone, *Missionary Travels*, p. 7.
118 Ibid., p. 152.
119 Ibid., p. 374.
120 Since Livingstone so often called himself English, it is interesting to note that there is a significant point in his second book, *Narrative of an Expedition*, in which he departs from this pattern. After the failure of the UMCA and its retreat from the Shire highlands, Livingstone suggests that 'had the Scotch perseverance and energy been introduced, it is highly probable that they would have reacted, most beneficially, on the zeal of our English brethren, and desertion would never have been heard of'. See Livingstone and Livingstone, *Narrative*, p. 310. For the most part, Livingstone uses the label 'English' to invoke a common sense of British identity, but when reacting against what he perceived as English and Anglican weakness, he invokes his more specific cultural identity as a Scot.
121 Corbett, 'The Missionary's Positions', p. 82.
122 Livingstone, *Missionary Travels*, p. 7.
123 Holmes, *Journey to Livingstone*, p. 120.
124 David Livingstone, manuscript of *Missionary Travels and Researches in South Africa*, vol. 1, 1856–57, MS 42428-9, p. 14, John Murray Archive. This was a common analogy. As Janice Carlisle observes, 'Factory life was often called "white slavery," as if its horrors could be conveyed only by comparing it unfavorably to the forced labor of black slaves'. See Janice Carlisle, 'Introduction', in James R. Simmons (ed.), *Factory Lives: Four Nineteenth-Century Working-Class Autobiographies* (Peterborough, Ont.: Broadview, 2007), pp. 18–19.
125 Livingstone, manuscript vol. 1, p. 15.
126 Ibid., p. 16.
127 Ibid., p. 15.
128 Ibid., p. 14.
129 Ibid., p. 15.
130 Ibid., p. 16.
131 Livingstone, *Missionary Travels*, p. 7.
132 The Cape Frontier Wars consisted of nine conflicts, the first of which began in 1779, and the last of which ended in 1878 in South Africa's Eastern Cape. See J.O. Sagay and D.A. Wilson, *Africa: A Modern History (1800–1975)* (London: Evan Bros., 1978), pp. 140–5.
133 Christopher Petrusic, 'Violence as Masculinity: David Livingstone's Radical Racial Politics in the Cape Colony and the Transvaal, 1845–1852', *The International History Review*, 26: 1 (2004), 24.
134 Ibid., pp. 32, 29. Some of this opposition does appear in *Missionary Travels*. For instance, Livingstone argued that the British had too often 'engaged in most expensive wars with them without once inquiring whether any of the fault lay with our frontier colonists': if the 'border colonists' were less sure that the government would 'bear them out in their arrogance, we should probably hear less of Caffre insolence. It is insolence which begets insolence.' See Livingstone, *Missionary Travels*, pp. 370, 372. This opposition, however, is considerably less sustained than in his private correspondence.
135 Livingstone, manuscript vol. 1, pp. 195, 196.
136 Ibid., p. 199.
137 Ibid., p. 200.
138 Ibid., p. 201. Livingstone's spelling of 'Sandile' in the manuscript is 'Sandillah'.
139 Ibid., pp. 210, 202.
140 Ibid., p. 203.
141 Ibid., p. 219.
142 Ibid., p. 205.
143 Ibid., p. 206.
144 Ibid., p. 215.

145 Ibid., p. 216.
146 Ibid., pp. 212–13.
147 David Livingstone, letter to John Murray, 6 April 1857, MS 42425, John Murray Archive.
148 Finkelstein, 'Unraveling Speke', p. 118.
149 Wisnicki, 'Interstitial Cartographer', pp. 267, 256.
150 See Felix Driver, '*Missionary Travels*: Livingstone, Africa and the Book', in Justin D. Livingstone (ed.), 'Livingstone Studies: Bicentenary Essays', *Scottish Geographical Journal*, 129: 3–4 (2013), 175.
151 Peter Hulme, *Colonial Encounters: Europe and the Native Caribbean 1492–1797* (London: Methuen, 1986), p. 2.
152 Sara Mills, *Discourse* (London: Routledge, 1997), p. 106. Said drew on Foucault's 'understanding of how the will to exercise dominant control in society and history, has also discovered a way to clothe, disguise, rarefy, and wrap itself systematically in the language of truth, discipline, rationality, utilitarian value, and knowledge'. See Edward Said, *The World, the Text, and the Critic* (London: Faber, 1984), p. 216. For further analyses of Said's role in emphasising the discursive dimensions of Orientalism and colonialism, see Benita Parry, 'The Institutionalization of Postcolonial Studies', in Neil Lazarus (ed.), *The Cambridge Companion to Postcolonial Literary Studies* (Cambridge: Cambridge University Press, 2004), pp. 66–80; and Robert J.C. Young, *Postcolonialism: An Historical Introduction* (Oxford: Blackwell, 2001).
153 Mills, *Discourse*, p. 107.
154 Ibid., p. 117.
155 Hulme, *Colonial Encounters*, pp. 106–7.
156 Leon de Kock, *Civilising Barbarians: Missionary Narrative and African Textual Response in Nineteenth-Century South Africa* (Johannesburg: Witwatersrand University Press, 1996), pp. 163, 167.
157 Ibid., p. 168. In *Imperial Eyes*, Pratt employs the term 'anti-conquest' 'to refer to the strategies of representation whereby European bourgeois subjects seek to secure their innocence in the same moment as they assert European hegemony ... The main protagonist of the anti-conquest is a figure I sometimes call the "seeing-man," an admittedly unfriendly label for the white male subject of European landscape discourse – he whose imperial eyes passively look out and possess.' She develops the term in order to explore the 'mutual engagement between natural history and European economic and political expansionism'. The 'system of nature as a descriptive paradigm' helped create an 'innocent vision of European global authority'. See Mary Louise Pratt, *Imperial Eyes: Travel Writing and Transculturation* (New York: Routledge, 2008), pp. 9, 37–8.
158 Derek Gregory, 'Human Geography and Space', in R.J. Johnston, Derek Gregory, Geraldine Pratt and Michael Watts (eds), *The Dictionary of Human Geography*, 4th ed. (Oxford: Blackwell, 2000), p. 770.
159 Livingstone, *Missionary Travels*, p. 519.
160 Ibid., p. 520.
161 Wisnicki, 'Interstitial Cartographer', pp. 266–7.
162 Livingstone, *Missionary Travels*, p. 518.
163 Pratt, *Imperial Eyes*, p. 197.
164 Livingstone, *Missionary Travels*, p. 458.
165 de Kock, *Civilising Barbarians*, pp. 165, 167.
166 Livingstone, *Missionary Travels*, p. 12.
167 Hooper and Youngs, 'Introduction', p. 7.
168 John M. MacKenzie argues that, since Livingstone was 'saved by one of his African followers', the scene demonstrates not only 'the necessity for co-operation between European and African, but the absolute necessity of such co-operation if Africa is to be redeemed'. See John M. MacKenzie, 'The Iconography of the Exemplary Life: The Case of David Livingstone', in Geoffrey Cubitt and Allen Warren (eds), *Heroic Reputations and Exemplary Lives* (Manchester: Manchester University Press,

169   2000), p. 95. However, it is surely significant that the lion is not actually killed by African hands but by Livingstone's bullets. When his companion, Mebalwe, attempts to shoot the lion his gun misfires, and when another attempts to spear it he is himself mauled. The scene may suggest cooperation to some degree but it is only the technology of the gun, as wielded by Livingstone, which secures victory.
169 Livingstone, *Missionary Travels*, p. 12.
170 Syed Manzurul Islam, *The Ethics of Travel: From Marco Polo to Kafka* (Manchester: Manchester University Press, 1996), p. vii.
171 Ibid., p. viii.
172 Livingstone, *Missionary Travels*, p. 87.
173 Ibid., p. 225.
174 Ibid., p. 619.
175 Ibid., p. 166.
176 Ibid., p. 562.
177 Ibid., p. 551.
178 Ibid., p. 340.
179 Ibid., pp. 445, 446.
180 While Livingstone does display hostile encounters, he frequently stresses the benefits of a peaceful disposition and good character over and against force. Even in the encounter with Njambi, he explains that he had aspired to 'the principles of peace and conciliation'. Elsewhere, he writes that 'Much of my influence depended upon the good name given me by the Bakwains, and that I secured only through a long course of tolerably good conduct. No one ever gains much influence in their country without purity and uprightness.' See Livingstone, *Missionary Travels*, pp. pp. 342–3, 513.
181 Martin Burgess Green, *Dreams of Adventure, Deeds of Empire* (New York: Basic Books, 1979), p. 23.
182 Livingstone, *Missionary Travels*, p. 235.
183 Ibid., p. 246.
184 Ibid., p. 633.
185 Ibid., p. 271.
186 Homi K. Bhabha, *The Location of Culture* (Abingdon and New York: Routledge, 2004), p. 162.
187 Ibid., p. 160.
188 Robert Young summarises Bhabha's project well. Bhabha demonstrates that 'the discourse of colonial authority loses its univocal grip on meaning and finds itself open to the trace of the languages of the other'; the colonial voice undermines itself by 'inscribing and disclosing the trace of the other'. See Robert J.C. Young, *Colonial Desire: Hybridity in Theory, Culture and Race* (London: Routledge, 1995), p. 23.
189 Marguerite H. Helmers and Tilar J. Mazzeo, 'Unraveling the Traveling Self', in Marguerite H. Helmers and Tilar J. Mazzeo (eds), *The Traveling and Writing Self* (Newcastle: Cambridge Scholars, 2007), p. 2.
190 Livingstone, *Missionary Travels*, p. 274.
191 Chloe Chard, 'Women who Transmute into Tourist Attractions: Spectator and Spectacle on the Grand Tour', in Amanda Gilroy (ed.), *Romantic Geographies: Discourses of Travel* (Manchester: Manchester University Press, 2000), p. 117.
192 Ibid., p. 118.
193 Livingstone, *Missionary Travels*, p. 274.
194 Ibid., p. 362.
195 Ibid., p. 59.
196 Ibid., p. 157.
197 Ibid., p. 187.
198 For discussions of humour and the postcolonial see Susanne Reichl and Mark Stein (eds), *Cheeky Fictions: Laughter and the Postcolonial* (Amsterdam: Rodopi, 2005); and Graeme Dunphy and Rainer Emig (eds), *Hybrid Humour: Comedy in Transcultural Perspectives* (Amsterdam: Rodopi, 2010).
199 Livingstone, *Missionary Travels*, p. 157.

STYLING THE SELF: MAKING *MISSIONARY TRAVELS*

200 Dennis Porter, 'Orientalism and its Problems', in Patrick Williams and Laura Chrisman (eds), *Colonial Discourse and Post-Colonial Theory: A Reader* (Hemel Hempstead: Harvest Wheatsheaf, 1993), pp. 154–5.
201 Brian Musgrove, 'Travel and Unsettlement: Freud on Vacation', in S.H. Clark (ed.), *Travel Writing and Empire: Postcolonial Theory in Transit* (London and New York: Zed Books, 1999), pp. 31, 39.
202 Ibid., pp. 39, 44.
203 James S. Duncan and Derek Gregory, 'Introduction', in James S. Duncan and Derek Gregory (eds), *Writes of Passage: Reading Travel Writing* (London: Routledge, 1999), pp. 4–5.
204 Steven H. Clark, 'Introduction', in Clark (ed.), *Travel Writing and Empire*, p. 3.
205 This resembles to some degree one of the newer paradigms for studying travel writing: that of 'mobility'. The term, however, expresses something of the doublesidedness of travel and travelogues. As Paul Smethurst argues, European mobility played a crucial role in forming empire, for by it 'knowledge was garnered and returned, often haphazardly, to imperial centres'. Imperialist travel writing can thus be considered 'mobility in the service of empire'. Yet on the other hand, mobility simultaneously possesses the potential to be 'a destabilising force': 'if mobility is enabling for the imperialist traveller, it is also potentially threatening and disorderly'. See Paul Smethurst, 'Introduction', in Julia Kuehn and Paul Smethurst, *Travel Writing, Form, and Empire: The Poetics and Politics of Mobility* (New York: Routledge, 2009), pp. 1, 2, 7. While Smethurst thinks that the challenging and heterotopian potential of mobility is largely domesticated in the travelogue, some of its effects remain detectable. Such moments are what I aim to emphasise by using the term 'itinerant'.
206 Islam, *The Ethics of Travel*, p. 143.
207 Ibid., p. vii. There are other reasons too for resisting the term 'nomad'. John Noyes considers theory's use of the nomad as a model of critical thought to be a problematic appropriation, since the existence of real nomadic peoples is one of material dispossession. See John Noyes, 'Nomadism, Nomadology, Postcolonialism: By Way of Introduction', *Interventions*, 6: 2 (2004), 159–68.
208 Islam, *The Ethics of Travel*, p. vii.
209 Livingstone, *Missionary Travels*, p. 15.
210 Ibid., p. 196. Livingstone's approach was similar too when discussing the rites of the 'boguera', a ceremony of initiation that had horrified earlier missionaries. He argued it was a 'civil rather than a religious rite' and aimed to render it explicable within its context. It was 'intended to harden the young soldiers' and served as 'an ingenious plan for attaching the members of the tribe to the chief's family'. See Livingstone, *Missionary Travels*, pp. 147–8.
211 Andrew Ross, 'Livingstone and Race', in *David Livingstone and Africa: Proceedings of a Seminar Held on the Occasion of the Centenary of the Death of David Livingstone at the Centre of African Studies, University of Edinburgh, 4th and 5th May 1973* (Edinburgh: University of Edinburgh, Centre of African Studies, 1973), p. 76.
212 Livingstone, *Missionary Travels*, p. 24.
213 Ibid., p. 25.
214 Ibid.
215 Ibid., p. 22.
216 Ibid., p. 23.
217 Comaroff and Comaroff, *Of Revelation*, p. 210.
218 Ibid., p. 211; see Edward Evans-Pritchard, *Witchcraft, Oracles and Magic among the Azande* (Oxford: Clarendon Press, 1937).
219 Livingstone, manuscript vol. 1, p. 44.
220 Ibid., p. 45.
221 Ross, 'Livingstone and Race', p. 76.
222 Livingstone, *Missionary Travels*, p. 187.
223 Ibid., p. 273.

224 Ibid., p. 379.
225 Ibid., pp. 30, 371.
226 Livingstone and Livingstone, *Narrative*, p. 67. As Lawrence Dritsas points out in his recent book, *Zambesi*, the *Narrative* drew on the journals of both Livingstone brothers. David added 'his own observations, polemics and basic information, and he also omitted parts of Charles's writing'. The question of authorship is thus complex and is heightened by the number of people involved in its production. Livingstone had editorial assistance from his daughter Agnes, from the Webb family and to a lesser degree from John Kirk and Horace Waller. Nonetheless, argues Dritsas, 'David's ideology rings through the text loud and clear'. See Lawrence Dritsas, *Zambesi: David Livingstone and Expeditionary Science in Africa* (London: I.B. Tauris, 2010), p. 25. See also Gary W. Clendennen, 'Who Wrote Livingstone's Narrative?', *The Bibliotheck: A Scottish Journal of Bibliography and Allied Topics*, 16 (1989), 30–9.
227 Livingstone and Livingstone, *Narrative*, p. 36.
228 Livingstone, *Missionary Travels*, pp. 510–11.
229 In reflecting on the strangeness of white skin, Livingstone was using a strategy with roots in the abolitionist tradition. For example, the former slave turned abolitionist Olaudah Equiano described his perception of his strange white-skinned captors. He assumed he would 'be eaten by those white men with horrible looks, red faces, and loose hair'. See Olaudah Equiano, *The Interesting Narrative of the Life of Olaudah Equiano* (London: Black Classics, 1998), p. 28.
230 Livingstone, *Missionary Travels*, p. 465.
231 Livingstone and Livingstone, *Narrative*, pp. 181, 127.
232 Ibid., p. 379.
233 Livingstone, *Missionary Travels*, p. 465.
234 Ross, 'Livingstone and Race', p. 75.
235 Wisnicki, 'Interstitial Cartographer', p. 261.
236 Ibid.
237 Ross, *David Livingstone*, p. 196.
238 Corbett, 'The Missionary's Positions', p. 83.
239 Ibid.
240 Quoted in Pettitt, *Dr. Livingstone, I Presume?*, p. 144.
241 Ibid. Certainly, at a number of points Livingstone reveals his reliance on local goodwill. In the towns of the Kololo, 'kindness was manifested by all ... my heart glows with gratitude'. Indeed, he was 'dependent on their bounty, and that of other Africans, for the means of going from Linyanti to Loanda, and again from Linyanti to the east coast' and was 'deeply grateful' for it. See Livingstone, *Missionary Travels*, pp. 250, 516.

CHAPTER THREE

Death: lamenting Livingstone

David Livingstone: Risky profession we're in. You know of course that I was mauled by a lion. (opens his shirt) He only chewed my shoulder.

Richard Burton: (opens his own shirt and points) Bullet hole. Single bore.

David Livingstone: (unbuttons his breeches) Scorpion bite.

Richard Burton: (pulls up his trouser leg) Cellulitis.

Mountains of the Moon

Authority ultimately derived, if not from premature death itself, then at least from the corporeal evidence of heroic travel – the noble empowering stigmata of scarred and disfigured bodies.
Michael Heffernan, '"A Dream as Frail as Those of Ancient Time"'

It is Tuesday 27 January, 1874, and a telegram from Her Majesty's Acting Consul-General at Zanzibar reaches the Foreign Office, confirming the breaking news of the death of Dr David Livingstone.[1] In the weeks that follow, an incredulous British public struggles to disbelieve and discredit the account. Months later and after an agonising delay, the Peninsular and Oriental Company's steamship *Malwa* arrives, bearing a broken and wizened body to port in Southampton. Waiting is a public throng, in mourning for its hero. Later he is laid to rest in a teeming Westminster Abbey, the resting place of the nation's chosen idols.

The chronicle of Livingstone's death and burial has fascinated biographers and scholars alike. Undoubtedly, he passed away in truly exceptional circumstances. In 1873, when he could at last go no further, Livingstone had been on his famous 'last journey' for seven years and had travelled through vast portions of east and central Africa, spanning the areas that today include Mozambique, Malawi, Tanzania, Zambia and the Democratic Republic of Congo. In 1871, having been 'found' by Henry Morton Stanley in Ujiji, he had famously declined to return to Britain, persisting instead in his effort to trace the central African water system; he refused to relinquish his mission to use exploration to advance Christianity, commerce and civilisation, and thereby usher in the end of the slave trade. After a long struggle with fever and anal bleeding, his health continued to spiral downwards until, at the end of April, he died in a makeshift hut in the village of Chitambo (now Chipundu, Zambia). At this point, Livingstone's retinue elected to remove and bury his innards, embalm his body and transport it to the east African coast for delivery to his home nation. Whether motivated by a sense of duty to a great man – or for reasons more prosaic, like securing their wages – this group of men and women undertook an arduous, hazardous and profoundly admirable journey of over a thousand miles to return his papers, instruments and remains. On meeting the Livingstone search expedition under the leadership of Lieutenant Verney Lovett Cameron at Unyanyembe in October, they were urged to bury their cargo. Refusing, they pressed on towards the coast and reached Bagamoyo in February 1874. Immediately paid and summarily dismissed, Livingstone's body was then sent by mail ship, via Zanzibar and Aden, reaching British soil on 15 April. Received with considerable ceremony in Southampton, he was conveyed to the rooms of the Royal Geographical Society in Savile Row, London. There he lay in state, was visited by distinguished citizens, and was examined by the eminent surgeon Sir William Fergusson. Dean A.P. Stanley had offered burial space in Westminster Abbey, and after lobbying from the RGS and pressure from the public, the government funded an impressive funeral. Attended by the great and the good, and honoured by the Queen's empty carriage and public-crowded streets, the interment of the missionary and explorer who had died thousands of miles away was an affair of considerable ceremony.[2]

It is those days and months around the time of Livingstone's public obsequies and civic memorial that are the subject of this chapter. Subsequently, this book will go on to consider the plasticity of Livingstone's multifaceted posthumous identity over a longer chronological period, but the aim first is to rigorously examine the way in which he was constructed in just one year, 1874, immediately after his body returned to British soil. Such a brief historical juncture – the days immediately following demise – represents a critical moment in the judging of a life, and so sharply focuses the manufacturing of its meaning on the borderland between a living past and a dead present. This temporal fulcrum point also presents an opportunity to scrutinise a body of unexplored literature, a wealth of obituaries, eulogies and commemorative poetry, which delivered some of the foundation stones of Livingstone's posthumous reputation.[3] Approaching these representations metabiographically entails attention to difference, to their located and historically contingent nature. In what follows I investigate the differing ways in which Livingstone was produced as a hero in diverse social spaces, or what I call 'sites of construction', and I thereby reveal his name and legacy to be – to some extent at least – spaces of contestation.

This is a rather different approach from that taken in previous discussions of Livingstone's heroic cult. Much of this criticism has engaged in the important work of seeking explanations for the way in which he so fascinated the Victorian imagination. Andrew Ross, for instance, suggested that the low public morale succeeding the Crimean War led the British nation 'to a thirst for stories about heroes and heroines'.[4] Livingstone, it would seem, burst on the scene at a time ripe for fame. Another biographer, Tim Jeal, has argued that 'There is no one reason that accounts for Livingstone's sudden emergence as a national hero'; instead he points to the irreducible complexity of his popularity, to a litany of factors ranging from his spectacular exploratory feats to his exceptional ability to combine 'patriotism and Christianity' and to the patronage of the 'various interested parties' that sought to make him famous.[5] Adrian Wisnicki, who recently summarised the various postulations that have aimed to account for Livingstone's surprising celebrity, notes how a number of critics have seen 'the actual narrative of *Missionary Travels* as key to the success of both text and missionary'.[6] He develops this line himself to some extent, by suggesting that Livingstone's acclaim resulted in part from the successful narrative creation in *Missionary Travels* of an 'ideal space – an interstitial, idyllic domain that cater[ed] to deeper British imperial fantasies'.[7] This chapter, however, moves away from the quest to explain Livingstone's popularity and instead scrutinises the very nature of his heroic identity. Instead of seeking to account for his fame, it illuminates the competing representations to which he was subject and perpetually asks which hero is being celebrated. While Livingstone was broadly extolled and was certainly the champion of Victorian culture, it becomes clear this should not be thought about in a purely monolithic sense; he was rather a suite of heroes of multiple identities produced out of a plurality of Victorian cultures.

Dealing with death: Livingstone and elegy

Before considering the conflicting constructions of Livingstone that will occupy the bulk of this chapter, it is important to register that certain features pervaded his textual production more generally. While

I aim to broadly illustrate early episodes in a contested legacy, it would be mistaken to suggest that there is no unity underlying Livingstone's posthumous representation. This commonality can be discerned in reported tributes and public speeches as the remains of the nation's favourite explorer-missionary were laid to rest. It is evident too in the numerous, though surprisingly neglected, elegiac poems that burgeoned in the press in the months around the time of Livingstone's burial. By focusing on those genres of literature that exist to deal with dying, the first part of this chapter offers reflections on the Victorian cultures of death and mourning and the characteristics that made his life worthy of commemoration. In consequence these deathly poetics, and the discourse surrounding his interment more generally, enable us to form the very broad image of Livingstone, the backdrop of shared agreement against which my story of constructed multiplicity is forged.

A certain amount of critical attention has been devoted before to the representation of Livingstone's final days and hours. Dorothy O. Helly, for one, explores the influence that the anti-slavery campaigner Horace Waller exerted in shaping the Livingstone myth. Responsible for editing Livingstone's *Last Journals*, Waller aimed to ensure that his hero would appear as a saintly figure whose name might become 'symbolic of a British commitment to African development in the name of antislavery', a champion who might tug the heartstrings and purse-strings of the British public.[8] A crucial part of this process of idealisation involved the depiction of Livingstone's passing: he hoped to construct a final ideal journey that would culminate in an ideal death. From a few conversations with the carriers, James Chuma and Abdullah Susi, Waller created a powerful drama of sacrifice out of Livingstone's death at the heart of the continent. Since he died on his knees, Waller presented it as death in prayer and freely speculated that the content of his petition was a plea for the completion of his life's work. Was it too much to think that 'David Livingstone, with a dying effort, yet again besought Him for whom He [sic] laboured to break down the oppression and woe of the land?'[9] The result was to model an iconic image that would become 'symbolic of the man's life'.[10] It would prove to be an episode that would powerfully convey his essence and live on in public memory.

Yet before Waller's edition of the journals was published, Livingstone's death was attracting the attention of a number of poets who sought to memorialise the nation's hero in verse.[11] That the circumstances of Livingstone's demise fascinated poets and public should perhaps be unsurprising, for the Victorian period was an era whose interest in death and mourning bordered on the obsessive. This was the case partly, as James S. Curl has argued, because they 'were aware of death as something not remote, but an ever-present part of life'.[12] In an era of urbanisation, with the unhygienic conditions and low life expectancy that attended it, death could not be easily ignored. The period's culture of lamentation was epitomised, as Erik Gray suggests, by the ruling monarch Queen Victoria – the 'widow at Windsor' – who spent over forty years of her reign in mourning.[13] It was a time in which cemeteries were built, mourning attire was developed, and funeral services became ever more ornate. In other words, thanatology was deeply woven into the fabric of Victorian culture.

For a period distinguished by its preoccupation with death, it is fitting that some of its most celebrated poems were elegies: indeed, to Erik Gray, the Victorian era can appropriately be called 'an Elegiac age'.[14] The poetry that memorialised Livingstone was primarily of this ilk, and titles such as 'In Memoriam', 'Dr. Livingstone: An Epitaph' and 'Burial of Livingstone in Westminster Abbey: A Dirge' soon flooded the pages of the press.[15] '"The great, lone land" has yielded up the dead', mourned a poet known only as W.F.H. in 'David Livingstone', printed in *John Bull*.[16] In another verse of the same name, and by the same author, it was bemoaned that Livingstone was '*Dead!* – ere his work was ended'.[17] In the same way, an anonymous poet in *Punch* lamented that finally all doubts that he was deceased must yield 'To the chill certainty of death'.[18] For the most part, in the elegiac form, the loss of the individual is deemed to be 'a critical, even catastrophic event'.[19] Certainly this is the case with the Livingstone elegies. Yet in these poems, the loss expressed is less personal or individual than it is collective; they articulate a communal grief on the nation's behalf. As W.F.H. put it, 'A race doth mourn, an empire makes his grave.'[20] Similarly, a poet in *Fun* addressed a posthumous Livingstone with the words: 'A nation's tears shall consecrate / your grave.'[21] In conveying this shared sorrow the poems tend to instruct both country and reader to proper commemoration. A poet who signed himself P.M.F. cried out, 'Throw wide the Minster's gate – a Hero comes', 'Lay him in glory, while the organ's peal / Its solemn requiem rolls above his tomb.'[22] W.H. Dowding's 'In Memoriam' followed suit by calling the nation to 'Mourn, Britain, mourn! a hero hath departed',[23] while James Hurnard's 'Dirge' urged the public to 'Bow low each head.'[24] These appeals demonstrate the extent to which Livingstone was deemed worthy of a hero's burial and national mourning. They testify that there was a desire to see him rightly remembered, an imperative to memorialise him in a manner that befitted his life.

Further to displaying his merit for remembrance, the elegies also paid considerable attention to the way in which Livingstone died. Joanna Lewis has argued that his death 'deeply upset the Victorians', who were aware that he had perished 'depressed, dejected' and 'with an acute sense of failure'.[25] The story proved potent, she suggests, in part because his was a fundamentally bad death. This is true to some extent, for the circumstances were undeniably imbued with qualities of the tragic. Yet if the death proved disturbing in the first instance for the Victorians, I would argue that it equally came to be seen to be a fitting end. Indeed, in the elegies there is a general sense that his death came as repose, at the close of a life worthily spent. 'Sleep well!' wrote the poet in *Fun*, 'You have accomplished all / Ambition hoped, or science dreamed', 'Sleep well! / You nobly did your part.'[26] In his poem 'David Livingstone: An Epitaph', W. Sumpter stated, in a Pauline allusion, that for Livingstone 'the victor's wreath is waiting / For the race so nobly run!'[27] It was felt to be important that Livingstone passed away while still in the pursuit of his work. For P.M.F., the nation should have 'Pride that he should have fallen on the way, / While struggling to complete the task nigh done.' It was 'better thus – that he should sink alone, / Where all alone he laboured to fulfil' than that 'He should have ris'n unscathed from the strife, / To reap his worldly meed of honours rich and rife.'[28] Death while engaged in toil was deemed to be an end eminently appropriate to Livingstone's lifetime of labour. As Hermione Lee observes, biographies, and we may extend the point to other forms of life-writing, often seek to ensure that death encapsulates the subject's existence and meaning. She points to the tendency 'to make the moment of their subject's death sum up and conclude the whole story of their life'.[29] By emphasising that Livingstone died in the continued pursuit of his goal, his elegists provided a fitting climax to what they saw as his period of sacrificial service.

In fact, while Livingstone's death was undeniably 'bad' in certain respects – he was disappointed, ill and isolated – I would suggest that the poems sought to demonstrate that there were ways in which he died 'well'. Death is one of the few certainties in life, but the way in which it is conceived and experienced is to some degree culturally bound. As Michel Vovelle puts it, death 'is a constant which is quite relative': 'people's relationships with death have changed, as have the ways in which it strikes them'.[30] For the Victorians, the primary model of dying was the evangelical 'good death'. Under the influence of the 'religion of the heart', argues Pat Jalland, the idea came to flourish that a good death 'required piety and fortitude in the face of suffering'.[31] '[S]piritual readiness was crucial', and the manner in which an individual ended life 'could provide the final proof of salvation'.[32] Of course, since Livingstone's death in Africa was profoundly undomestic, and since he was at a great distance from friends and family, his demise was not a conventional evangelical good death. Yet in focusing on how he bore his sufferings until transported to the celestial realms, his elegists were clear that in important respects he died well. Readers were to take consolation that Livingstone was now, as Sumpter put it, 'pressing / To realms beyond the sun – / To realms of light eternal.'[33] '[S]ay not he is dead, ye mourners', wrote W.H. Dowding, but 'rather / Say he is now at home with the Good Father.'[34] The heavenly reward that awaited Livingstone was nothing short of certain. And, in spite of the adversity he faced, there was no doubt about his state of spiritual preparation. A poet who signed himself W.F.C. put it thus: 'Could terror of the Pale King make *thee* start / From couch of pain at touch of the cold scythe? / Nay!' Livingstone was fully ready to approach 'the Great White Throne'.[35] In a poem entitled 'David Livingstone: The Seeker of the Founts of the Nile', J. Hoskyns-Abrahall mentioned in a footnote that Livingstone's 'last words were – "I am going home".'[36] While he was incorrect in this assertion, it reflects the Victorian preoccupation with the final words of the dying. Such expressions were deemed to indicate an individual's spiritual readiness and potentially to impart heavenly wisdom.[37] By placing weight on last words and final hours, the Victorians invested death-bed scenes with didactic value. Indeed, in emphasising Livingstone's preparedness and the consolation of the afterlife, his elegists almost used him to demonstrate *ars moriendi* or the art of dying. If the agony and isolation of his end were distressing, the way in which he faced it was nothing short of exemplary. Of course, in his sacrificial demise and certain reward in the hereafter, Livingstone far surpassed the conventional demands of the typical good death: in this way he was less a figure for emulation than for awe.

Adventurer and master

The poetic tributes grant insight into the Victorian cultures of death and indicate the extent to which Livingstone's passing was considered a public loss. Yet these poems, alongside other eulogies and obituaries, also demonstrate the shared agreement over why his life was one of worth. Firstly, in the commemorative literature a vital dimension of Livingstone's significance was his reputation as an adventurous explorer, opening up new terrain and perpetually facing challenges and overcoming adversity. In my previous chapter I argued that he partially represented himself in this way by ensuring that *Missionary Travels* resonated with the genre of the adventure narrative. The literature that memorialised him, however, lost all sense of his heroic reticence and the strain of ambivalence detectable in his travelogue. Without restraint, Livingstone was interpreted as a heroic adventurer *par excellence*. It is noticeable that this dimension of his identity was forged in juxtaposition and contradistinction to both the people and the place of Africa. The African body and topography served as textual tropes against which his identity could be fashioned. This analysis is informed by Edward Said's powerful disclosure of the 'non-innocence' and power relations at work in any act of representation and particularly in 'imaginative geographies', those constructions of other 'peoples and landscapes, cultures and "natures"'. In these imaginative geographies, places and races are endowed with 'figurative values' which are critically implicated in occidental identity-formation.[38] As we shall see, Livingstone's reputation as an adventurer depended upon the correlative imagination of the African 'other'.

For Livingstone to take shape as an adventurer he needed to be portrayed as one who battled against a hostile climate, lethal life-forms and indigenous opposition. Indeed, the image of the adventurer is integrally linked to the array of impediments that he (and it is almost always a he) successfully surmounts. Franco Moretti clarifies the nature of such challenges: 'lions, heat, vegetation, elephants, flies, rain, illness and natives. All mixed up, and at bottom all interchangeable in their function as obstacles.'[39] Many of the death poems certainly created a portrait of environmental resistance in which Livingstone and landscape were cast as opponents locked in perpetual conflict.

In these, the climate is described in adjectival overload: in one poem the hero faced 'forests' that were 'dense o'erarched', and a sun 'wild red' and full of 'fire',[40] while in another he is celebrated for trekking 'through *wilds*, vast, drear & dread'.[41] In a 120-page epic poem on Livingstone, Roden Noel offers his readers a scene of 'lurid evenings, crimson, warm, like blood'.[42] Yet, just as Moretti observed in reference to the colonial romance, a conspicuous feature of these poetics is the way in which the environmental, faunal and indigenous challenges merge indiscriminately in their function as hindrances. The poets luxuriate in haphazard hybridising:

> He warred where in the jungle and the swamp,
> Repulsive life of man and beast is seen ...
> Where desolation undisputed reigns,
> And man, debased to lowest creature, crawls.[43]

Standing in opposition to this fusion of impediments, the heroic figure materialises full of tenacious persistence, courage and vigorous strength.

As the above quotation suggests, those elegies and obituaries that presented encountered peoples as obstacles relied upon the conventional dehumanising tropes of savagery. In 'Muelala-Bisa Country', by a poet initialled 'J.H.S.', the intrepid Livingstone becomes one who 'in the Manyuema land' had '... seen the handsome dark-brown race / Who eat their captured enemies / With all the *savant* in their face.'[44] Although Livingstone himself claimed to have encountered very little of the cannibalism supposedly rife throughout the continent, it is introduced here by way of trope to symbolise, as Martin Green puts it, the 'archetype of everything monstrous and appalling'.[45] Roden Noel's *Livingstone in Africa* follows suit, imagining a cave 'Strewn with fresh bones of men, that hideous ghouls / In human form, foul anthropophagi, / Have gnawn for food.'[46] Indeed, Noel devotes considerable textual space to sketching the human horrors he speculated were burrowed deep in the continent. Livingstone faced:

> Dark unimaginable human lives;
> Wearing what uncouth forms, allied to some
> Misshapen horrors of the forest wild
> Weird startling mockery of immortal man.[47]

In contrast to such human chaos and depravity, Livingstone is able to stand as an exemplar of civilisation, order and culture. As Syed Manzurul Islam observes of the representative practices of colonialism, those who are 'other' are reduced to 'negatives, the site of non-values; their sole purpose is to be [his] shadow that [he] may shine in splendour'.[48]

Livingstone was cast therefore as a figure of mastery and authority. Despite the fact that *Missionary Travels* contains ambivalent and even progressive racial sentiments, Livingstone's encounter with Africans was performed in the press so as to establish an unmistakable socio-racial hierarchy. Under this logic, Livingstone was represented as a commander of unquestioning and juvenile native servants. The *Daily News*, reporting on the arrival of Livingstone's body at Southampton, described one of his African companions, Jacob Wainwright, as 'the boy – for although he is one-and-twenty years of age, he seems but a boy', and commended him for 'respectfully and gracefully doff[ing] his cap'.[49] Wainwright's childlikeness establishes black inferiority while his respectful demeanour implies deference to his betters. Again, versified commemorations articulated this dynamic of power effectively. A stanza in Hoskyns-Abrahall's poem produced the hierarchy by appropriating native speech: '"Good morning, master dear!" (such the command / The master's self has spoke) the servant cries.'[50] Through their own mouths, the Africans accept their auxiliary role and inferior status; through linguistic manoeuvre the master–servant dichotomy is naturalised. In Lord Houghton's poem 'Ilala – May, 1873', the naturalisation of Livingstone's leadership and the infantilisation of the indigenous are achieved by paternalistic metaphor: as Livingstone lay dying, his 'swarthy followers stood aloof / Unled – unfathered'.[51]

Just as his obstacles were deemed to be both human and climatic in nature, so Livingstone's mastery was seen to extend not only to men but to the environment. Indeed, for Roden Noel, the land the hero infiltrated was a 'Vast immeasurable Void', a mythological place outside the 'imperial march of History'.[52] By contrast, Livingstone 'reclined' in imposing command while his penetrating 'falcon eyes explore[d] the moonèd East': he would enter 'undiscover'd worlds' and 'lay [his] hand upon the Mystery!'[53] The language of 'mystery' confers mastery on the one who has peered behind the African veil. In Noel's poem, Livingstone's piercing stare signifies his easy dominance over the inscrutable and 'undiscover'd' terrain. His all-encompassing vision metaphorically suggests both power and possession. In this way, Livingstone is portrayed as what Mary Louise Pratt has theorised as the 'seeing man', 'he whose imperial eyes passively look out and possess'.[54] Noel creates a 'monarch-of-all-I-survey scene', in which Livingstone's penetrating gaze, set upon the unknown, is deemed to perceive 'all there is'.[55]

Livingstone's cartographic accomplishments also serve as a metaphor for his totalising grasp of the continent. As Richard Phillips points out, the idea of *terra incognita* has often been the starting point of adventure. It has invited writers and readers to 'dream of the world(s) they might find, the adventures they might have, the kinds of men and women they might become'.[56] But Livingstone was known as one who had filled in unknown spaces in the blank African canvas. 'The map of the interior of Southern Africa we owe almost entirely to him', the *Northern Echo* told its readers.[57] Or as the elegy 'On Livingstone' more poetically put it: 'Look on the map: Where once was blank and void, / Now rivers, lakes and fertile planes appear.'[58] Livingstone is endowed here with creative power, as though generating the very value in the landscape. His cartographic ability was thus a semiotic declaration of authority and environmental mastery.[59] Yet for *Punch*'s poet, mapping implied dominance over the environment because of the intense struggle that was required in its production. Livingstone died so 'That our maps may stand / Their blanks filled in with names and figures.' But the blank spaces to be filled and labelled had to be forcefully 'wrung', at the cost of life and limb, from nature's reluctant, resistant and 'close-clenched hand'.[60]

Livingstone's environmental mastery, as a 'seeing-man' and a cartographer, was closely related to the tools that he employed as an exacting field scientist. Indeed, a substantial focus of the literature surrounding Livingstone's interment was the scientific apparatus that was conspicuously exhibited at the chambers of the Royal Geographical Society preceding the public ceremonial. The record of the *Daily News* drew attention to the array of tables on which were displayed 'the spoils of many a bloodless victory in the field of science'. On show were Livingstone's 'marvellous specimens of careful penmanship' and his instruments of natural science, 'a sextant, chronometer, thermometer ...'.[61] They were set up to demonstrate the superiority of the Western technology that granted Livingstone his authority. These instruments, wrote the *Daily News*, always 'created a great sensation amongst the natives, causing them to exclaim that a white man was coming who brought down the sun and moon, and carried them under his arm. Here were the instruments bearing full marks of active service'.[62] In the discourse surrounding his interment then, Livingstone came to represent science as an endeavour of triumph and conquest.

Man of faith and freedom: the nation's ideal

While Livingstone was valorised as an adventurer, leader of men and master of his environment, he was also pervasively represented as a Christian and spiritual hero. Something of this should already be clear from the depictions of his demise; Livingstone, as I argued, died a Christian death. But he was not just any normal individual who died well. He was, as the *Western Mail* put it, 'a martyr to the cause he had so ardently espoused'.[63] During the 1870s, challenges to religious certainties were gathering pace. The previous decade had seen the publication of unsettling works of biblical criticism like *Essays and Reviews* (1860) and Bishop Colenso's *The Pentateuch and Book of Joshua Critically Examined* (1862). With evolution in the air following Darwin's *The Origin of Species* (1859) and *The Descent of Man* (1871), and well-publicised exchanges like the Wilberforce–Huxley debate of 1860, humanity's place in the cosmos was no longer quite so secure. In the midst of this uncertainty, a hero of Christian conviction and character would no doubt have had considerable appeal. Such a hero might renew faith and offer reprieve in an increasingly materialist universe. A crucial part of Livingstone's appeal certainly lay in his status as a spiritual paragon; he was consistently represented as a paradigmatic 'muscular Christian' who combined manly vigour with Christian virtue.[64] Indeed, a suite of spiritual tropes accumulated around him in accompaniment to the general fascination with his physicality. An obituary in the *Daily News* on 29 January praised his 'dauntless spirit and unconquerable faith',[65] while the *Glasgow Herald* maintained that 'in his large toleration and unfailing charity for all mankind, the most superficial observer could not but recognise the devoted follower of his Divine Master'.[66]

Yet Livingstone's spiritual staging exceeded traditional religious phraseology. In the *Leeds Mercury*, he was granted the energy of the

Hebraic lawgivers as the paper mourned 'another Patriarch' who 'has been carried up by tender hands out of the Nile'.[67] This connection was heightened too by members of the clergy. Dean Stanley, preaching at Livingstone's Westminster interment, chose as one of the lessons 'the Scripture narrative relating to the death of Aaron on Mount Hor in the midst of the desert of Zin', a text 'singularly applicable to the circumstances under which the great traveler passed away amidst the wilderness of Central Africa'.[68] Similarly, the Rev. H.W. Hamilton took a text from Deuteronomy 32 for his own homily at a memorial service in Livingstone's hometown: 'he found him in a desert land, and in the waste howling wilderness'.[69] Livingstone struggled like the nation Israel, but was led, protected and chosen by God. The death of such a religious figure provided an opportunity for spiritual lessons, and his life immediately came to provide didactic source material. From the centre of Anglicanism to local Presbyterianism, Livingstone was routinely preached on from the pulpit. This reminds us, as John Wolffe has argued, that an important part of Livingstone's heroic cult lay in 'the non-sectarian character of his profound Christian commitment'. Since he was 'baptized a Presbyterian, lived a Congregationalist, and was buried by Anglicans', Livingstone was sufficiently ecumenical to be adopted by the established church and varieties of nonconformism.[70]

To secure a place in sermons across such denominational boundaries, Livingstone clearly had a spiritual stature that was almost unrivalled. The biblical rhetoric that surrounded him in the press and poetry really was unrelenting and hyperbolic. The *Glasgow Herald* saw fit to connect him to John the Baptist: 'no man in these days realized more completely the great work of the forerunner ... no man of our time has done more the work of the Baptist ...'.[71] In other articles, he was even invested with messianic proportions. The account of Livingstone's last days in *The Times*, which depicts his approach to his final resting place on the back of a 'donkey', consciously resonates with Christ's triumphant entry into Jerusalem. We are told that Livingstone 'suffered greatly, groaning night and day. On the third day he said "I am very cold".'[72] The moans and 'third day' reference implicitly suggest the agony of the crucifixion. Henry Morton Stanley, in an extensive piece in the *Graphic*, was more explicit in his messianic allusions (see Fig. 3). In this article, Livingstone became 'a man of humble aspect and poor garb; a despised and rejected man by his countrymen at Magabesberg'.[73] The passage rings of the 'Suffering Servant' (Isaiah 53.1–12), and the description of Christ as a 'prophet without honour' in his hometown (Mark 6.4). He was truly, as John MacKenzie argues, a 'protestant saint' who 'almost uniquely, attracted the language of canonisation'.[74]

3. 'Dr. Livingstone Reading the Bible to his Men'. Supplement to the *Graphic* (25 April 1874), 393

Indeed, H.M. Stanley also called Livingstone the 'Apostle of Africa', an epithet that his contemporaries and later biographers would adopt.[75] Apostleship of course suggests a spiritual watershed, a new paradigm for worship and religious practice: to be an apostle is to be the elected bearer of God's message. Presumably, Livingstone was deemed to warrant this title for his claim to be the first missionary to reach and teach in various parts of central Africa. The poem 'On Livingstone', printed in *Lloyd's Weekly Newspaper*, followed the pattern in describing him as 'One of the apostles of the present age'. Yet the verse goes on to adapt the spiritual rhetoric: significantly, it is explained that 'Work was his gospel and his simple creed.'[76] The phrase 'Gospel of Work', as Martin Danahay points out, more or less 'sums up the mixture of self-discipline and piety that constituted a broad middle-class consensus in the period'.[77] As it was most famously formulated by Carlyle, work was deemed to be a moral and divine imperative and one that was inherently ennobling. The dominant 'Gospel of Work', argues Rob Breton, was intended 'to counter economic, rationalistic thinking'. It ran in opposition to self-interest and utility and instead emphasised 'effort in itself', 'work for its own sake'.[78] In the context of the Victorian moral valorisation of labour, Livingstone could thus be celebrated for his pattern of industry and eschewal of personal reward. In the *Aberdeen Journal* he was commended for his 'downright, dogged perseverance to accomplish and perfect whatever he took upon himself to perform'.[79] His ethos was repeatedly depicted in metaphorical terms. As an obituary in the *Examiner* by William Hughes put it, Livingstone persisted in his travels 'with his harness on his back'.[80] Or as it was expressed in *Punch*'s poem 'David Livingstone', he never 'looked back, nor hand from plough refrained'.[81] The biblical nature of the metaphors indicates the proximity between the gospel of work and Victorian Christianity. As Danahay reminds us, 'Work ... was the most frequently used term in the Victorian lexicon after God.'[82]

Further to being a spiritual paragon and a disciplined, ideal worker, Livingstone was also construed in obituary and verse as a great emancipator bringing liberation to the captive people of central Africa. 'After centuries of darkness and oppression', wrote *The Times*, Africa would 'at length be emancipated' in the wake of Livingstone's efforts.[83] Many poets took it upon themselves to illustrate the conditions of enslavement that he opposed. Roden Noel, for one, imagined a scene from a slave-hunt:

> A sudden deafening crash of musketry!
> Hundreds of blithe love-dreaming youths and maidens,
> Bathed in their own life-blood, and one another's
> Fall, with one last death-quivering embrace.[84]

DEATH: LAMENTING LIVINGSTONE

He described the 'stolen journeying slave', 'shackled, starved, and goaded', stumbling 'Under the sunblaze' until 'she faints and falls!'[85] Working against such chaos, Livingstone's primary incentive is seen to be devotion to the abolitionist cause. Likewise, W.H. Dowding declared in his sonnet 'In Memoriam' that Livingstone's 'whole career was a sublime endeavour / To make the Negro's cruel bondage lighter / And cheer his soul with better hopes and brighter.'[86] Yet it is conspicuous that in these lines the force keeping Africans in 'cruel bondage' remains unnamed. Indeed, superstition and savagery are as likely as the slave trade to be the subjugating agency. This is clearer in W.F.H.'s poem 'David Livingstone', in which the explorer enters 'lands where vice and darkness man enslave'.[87] In other words, while the motif of slavery in the poems often refers to real and material bondage, it also functions to signify 'backwardness'. Livingstone is thus seen not only to oppose physical servitude, but mental and spiritual bondage as well: the boundaries between these, however, remain hazy.[88]

In bringing clemency in all its forms Livingstone was typically staged as a force stimulating vital transformation in those he encountered. In the words of the poem 'David Livingstone: Westminster Abbey', signed only by 'A.', he 'Struck off the gyves which manacled the slave, / Bade him be free – a brother and a man!'[89] In this instance, Livingstone transfigured the African from object to subject, as though endowing the newly unchained with the full status of humanity. His presence was a civilising one, and those he had apparently reconditioned became an important stamp of authority that validated his mission. The same poem praised his native carriers for their faithfulness in transporting his corpse to the coast, announcing that they might:

> Look England's statesmen in the face and say
> That Afric's children, like thyself, can be,
> With gentle treatment, culture, pious care,
> And guarantees of liberty and right,
> As loyal, earnest, resolute of will,
> And brave, and pure, as aught of humankind.[90]

The tremendous efforts of the body-bearers were used to confer glory on Livingstone as the one who had moulded them into such impressive models of indigenous capacity. For instance, in *The Times's* account of the funeral service, Jacob Wainwright, the token African present, became identified explicitly as a signifier of Livingstone's success. He was 'a manumitted and Christianized young African, whose presence *symbolized* the beneficent work of the master whom he tended so faithfully to the last' (emphasis added).[91]

The extent to which Livingstone was idealised in the Victorian press should be clear by this point. As a spiritual paragon, he was deemed to have transcended the conventional demands of piety. As a tireless worker and one who vigorously opposed slavery, Livingstone was an example of dedicated devotion, one who had achieved a higher existence and lived a life of action on behalf of the public good. In such exaltation, there was an extent to which he appeared as a representative of an idealised national character. Certainly, the valorisation of Livingstone's civilising and emancipating presence correlated well with Britain's self-image as an abolitionist country. As Patrick Brantlinger has pointed out, while the nation had originally been a world-leader in slavery, the success of the abolition movement meant that 'the British began to see themselves less as perpetrators of the slave trade and more as potential saviors of the African'.[92] Livingstone, who had cast himself in the abolitionist mode in *Missionary Travels*, served to consolidate this aspect of British self-perception. Indeed, in Noel's epic poem the campaign against slavery is clearly portrayed as the national mission. When confronted by enslavement, Livingstone gives forth that he 'will flash the light of Europe's eyes / Full on the tyrant' slavery; he calls 'England, inviolate Ark of Freedom' to 'launch / Thy thunder as of old' and 'Fulfil thy mission!'[93] Later in the poem, Livingstone makes the same appeal: 'with a gauntlet of stern iron crush out, / England! the foul snake coil'd voluminous / About this desolate land, feeding on blood!' He warns his countrymen not to 'dare neglect the mission of the strong, / To bind the oppressor, and to help the poor!'[94] The 'England' that Livingstone represents here is one firmly committed to the ongoing cause of emancipation.

Furthermore, the fact that Livingstone could provide the subject of an epic poem suggests in itself that he was being used to envision the nation. As Herbert F. Tucker argues, 'it is the very idea of epic to tell a sponsoring culture its own story, from a vantage whose privilege transpires through the successful articulation of a collective identity that links origins to destinies by way of heroic values in imagined action'.[95] The epic imagines historical and cultural unity and so has often been the chosen genre of those seeking to legislate the idea of the nation.[96] While Livingstone's opposition to slavery enabled Noel to adequately represent his vision of Britain as an abolitionist nation, there was an additional reason behind his choice of subject. His epic, Noel's preface tells his readers, was intended to be a heroic narrative on the person of 'the modern Explorer'. This, he argued, was 'a subject peculiarly modern, peculiarly English'.[97] Livingstone was thus, for Noel, a representative of a nation whose character compelled it to explore. This sentiment was echoed and clarified by others elsewhere.

DEATH: LAMENTING LIVINGSTONE

At a luncheon in the Corporation Galleries in Glasgow, organised to entertain Sir Bartle Frere, William Stirling Maxwell was reported to have announced that 'a passion for travel and exploration was almost instinctive in the boyhood of an island race': for him, the 'spirit of adventure' was the 'spirit of the race'. While 'Portugal . . . had almost ceased to navigate', and 'the native country of Columbas ha[d] ceased to be animated with the spirit of the great 15th century', and 'a modern Italian ha[d] an unhappy dislike to taking off his gloves', in Britain 'the spirit of Livingstone [was] still rife amongst his countrymen'.[98] 'On Livingstone', a poem in *Lloyd's*, similarly sought to valorise this dimension of the national disposition. The sons of Britain 'Have long disdained their bounds', noted the author. '[O]nward still they pressed / To victory or to death: this spirit 'tis Inspires and animates our national life.'[99] Not only did Livingstone represent the nation's anti-slavery commission, but he typified Britain's self-image as an 'island race' with a mandate to explore. For many of those who commemorated Livingstone, then, he was an idealised embodiment of qualities that were central to their conception of the national character.

Since Livingstone was framed as a national ideal, obituarists and poets were able to employ him to critique the values of the present. For a writer in *Lloyd's* he represented a repository of principles seemingly abandoned by a materialistic society. Livingstone scorned the contemporary 'money standard', 'seeking neither the jewels nor the gold-dust that might lie in strange hands, but only knowledge for his fellows'.[100] Criticism of the acquisitive ethos was common too in the Livingstone poetic corpus. In his sonnet 'In Memoriam', Dowding cast him as one free from the 'greedy grovelling after sordid gold / Or from the thirst for empty adulation!'[101] In the same way, 'On Livingstone' disparaged those whose question is 'What the profit?' 'What the cost?', and who 'deeds of daring weigh with paltry pelf'. Such a line of reasoning, the poet declared, would spell the death of the national character: 'For then, farewell our fame, our national life.'[102] *Punch*'s poet likewise mounted a challenge to those who would 'use / Mammon's equivalents of loss and fain' to evaluate the worth of Livingstone's endeavour. Must society be 'so base / In its appraisement, that "What use?" must be / The measure of our judgments', the poet enquired.[103] In all these cases Livingstone was seen to defy monetarist and utilitarian ethics of appraisal; he was a yardstick against which to measure the nation's values. Such use of Livingstone of course fitted well with the contemporary ideology of the press in the so-called 'golden age' of the 1860s and 1870s. As Alan J. Lee notes, 'liberty, progress, knowledge and even salvation were virtues commonly attributed to the newspaper'.[104] The press was envisaged to operate as part of 'improvement', and to be a valuable resource for information, education and guidance.[105] In this context, Livingstone was put to work in order to elevate and instruct. Indeed, for many poets, Livingstone appeared to transcend present standards of judgement and so provided a means to stand judgement on the present.[106]

Competing constructions

The collective mourning that Livingstone's death inspired manifests the extent to which his heroic image achieved national proportions. But while he was invested with the qualities of a national ideal, it would be insufficient to rest content with revealing the common features of his construction. The celebration of a hero is one thing but the meaning attached to such heroism is another. For all the shared agreement over a life of worth, Livingstone was no monolithic hero. Lurking beneath the surface of exterior harmony is a story of difference and dispute, in which Livingstone was put to use in strikingly different ways. And so, rather than focusing on homogeneity, it is the complex nature of competing representations emerging from different socio-cultural locations that I will now explore. The methodology of metabiography insists on the located and ideologically embedded nature of all forms of life-writing, whether this be formal biography, obituary or eulogy. Consequently, the remainder of this chapter will emphasise the ways in which Livingstone was fashioned in different 'sites of construction'.[107] To use Gadamer's term, the aim here is to reveal the impact that the 'horizons' of Livingstone's interpreters had in shaping the meaning they gave to his heroism.[108] Those with different frameworks, with their distinct values and identifications, found different significances in Livingstone's life and so they constructed him accordingly.

I will begin my exploration of the sites of construction in which Livingstone was differently produced by contrasting the emphases of scientific and religious arenas, two spaces which distinctly made the hero in their own image. Among scientific sites, the medical journal the *Lancet* perhaps most clearly demonstrates the creation of Livingstone out of a specific horizon. The medical profession continually emphasised his role as physician. One letter to the editor, from the eminent surgeon William M. Fergusson, stressed, 'Livingstone, besides his holy occupation, belonged to our profession. In my own mind I have a strong impression that a considerable portion of his great works resulted from that part of the education which he imbibed in our professional schools.'[109] Given the medical mould in which this construction was cast, it is unsurprising that Livingstone's significance became so bound up with his physician's training. Indeed, Livingstone even became an iconic emblem of the medical character; in embarking upon 'the devious and dangerous career of missionary explorer,' one contributor wrote, he exemplified 'the unmercenary character of the student of nature'.[110] Here professional calling and moral virtue were seamlessly interwoven. Yet another article, pondering the reasons for the small number of doctors entering the navy, concluded that 'It cannot be that they are deterred by ignoble motives of personal safety and comfort, or are less imbued with a spirit of adventure than the rest of their countrymen: a long distinguished role of men, from Park and Livingstone' onwards would indicate otherwise.[111] So Livingstone was enshrined as a distinctly medical hero. He gave ammunition to a fantasy, becoming an embodied representative of an idealised self-image. And the medical world was by no means unaware of the esteem that Livingstone was able to bestow upon them. The *Lancet* traced the discussion surrounding the erection of a 'Memorial Missionary Training Institution' and the creation of a 'Livingstone scholarship'; together these 'would at once express our regard for his memory, and show that we are not insensible to the great honour which Livingstone has conferred upon us'.[112]

Certain religious spaces similarly claimed Livingstone as their own distinctive kind of hero. An article in the *British Quarterly Review*, a magazine directed to Congregationalists and Baptists, claimed to show 'how the work that made this man so justly famous grew out of the noble nature of his soul'; 'Never perhaps in all the history of human enterprise was a career of physical discovery so ... constantly crowned by religious devotion.'[113] Just as the *Lancet* staked its claim to medical training as the wellsprings of his success, this religious journal declared his piety to be foundational. While Livingstone was generally recognised as a hero of the faith, as we have already seen, the *British Quarterly Review* strongly staked a claim to him by arguing that his spiritual status was really the primary way to understand his importance: 'His career, if read aright, should teach the world that religion is not a speciality of dogmas and ceremonials, but a great satisfying influence, catholic enough to embrace all forms of fruitful labours.'[114] In this understanding, the most legitimate interpretation of Livingstone's career was one that drew upon his energy to bolster Christianity and more particularly the independent brand of low worship practice.

A key difference between the scientific and religious zones was one of emphasis; the former tended toward a results-based discourse, while the latter preoccupied itself with character and devotion. In *Nature*, for example, the concern was always Livingstone's 'grand results' and the ways in which 'various departments of science [have] been enriched by his observations'.[115] The scientific value of his journals, and their expression of disciplined empiricism, were constantly extolled; 'nearly every sentence is a statement of an observed fact', and 'there is so little of what is superfluous'.[116] For the *British Quarterly Review*, however, a results discourse was not so appealing. Of course a religious paper would have no desire to focus on the fruits of scientific and cartographic fieldwork, but neither did it choose to concentrate upon the results of Livingstone's evangelistic efforts. Since he had few converts to show – those typical signifiers of missionary success – it was better to lay the emphasis on Livingstone as one of those 'whose characters have been a more precious legacy than any of their practical achievements'.[117] His greatness lay in his embodiment of Christian virtue, in his moral influence, rather than in the more seemingly tangible outcomes of his work. In both these spheres, then, the scientific and the spiritual, what Gadamer calls the 'prejudices' of the interpreters, mediated the way in which Livingstone was understood.[118] For Gadamer, an act of understanding must bridge the gap between the alien object and the familiar world that is already understood.[119] And so Livingstone became encompassed by and assimilated into the familiar horizons of his interpreters. Both sites clearly presented Livingstone as a hero in terms that they valued, as a champion in their own image. They created him out of contrasting economies of virtue for particular readerly communities who inhabited the same network of esteem.

By creating Livingstone in such self-mimetic fashion, both sites revealed their preoccupation with status and their desire to cultivate greater prestige by fostering their connection with the explorer. As William J. Goode argued, the need for respect and approval is an almost fundamental human condition.[120] Individuals as well as 'Organizations from clubs to nations constantly try to change their own internal prestige payments ... so as to reward and support one type of activity rather than another.'[121] In the competing constructions of Livingstone, he actually entered into this process of status negotiation by functioning as a sort of symbolic capital. Those writing about him sought to claim him as one of their own and to draw upon his substantial reserves of honour in order to bolster their societal position. Both spaces, scientific and spiritual, presented him in such a way as to profit through association with a name that was an exceedingly powerful cultural commodity. Livingstone was not constructed in order merely to reflect competing horizons, but was drawn on in order to consolidate them.

It would be mistaken of course to cast the debate over Livingstone in the tired and clichéd dichotomy of science versus religion. The obituary printed in the *Proceedings of the Royal Geographical Society*, and composed as part of Sir Bartle Frere's presidential address to the RGS, complicates such a binary model. Of course, given its audience, Livingstone's importance as a geographer and scientist received most textual space. Bartle Frere, a former Governor of Bombay, quoted Lord Ellesmere on the quality of Livingstone's writings: 'I believe I may say that there is more sound geography in the sheet of a foolscap which contains them than in many volumes of much more pretension.' Livingstone's career was nothing less than a metamorphosis 'from that of the quiet but active missionary ... to that of the bold and vigorous explorer'. Frere self-consciously alluded to Livingstone's debt to the RGS and reminded his readers of how it championed him: 'Such honours as it was in our power to bestow were quickly his.'[122] By so presenting Livingstone, Bartle Frere mobilised his reputation to raise the profile of the society and geographical endeavour. Yet this obituary is evidence of both the way in which the projections of the explorer can overlap and interlink, and the complex nature of the horizons which mediated his interpretation. For Frere also happily acknowledged that 'the wide and extended view he had of the duties of his sacred calling, gave to his character an elevation and power far beyond what the highest mental or physical gifts could have commanded'.[123] In articulating the spiritual underpinning of his vocation, Frere's obituary demonstrates that scientific and religious constructions of Livingstone were not mutually exclusive. Each site of construction was not hermetically sealed from its neighbours, but was an intellectual space where a particular image of Livingstone took shape with greater or lesser intensity.

The complicated nature of the spaces of production can be seen in internal conflict within their own borders. As I pointed out earlier, it has long been realised that an important dimension of Livingstone's celebrity lay in his ability to appeal across denominational boundaries to different factions of Victorian Christianity. At the same time, it is important to note that his representation across these borders was not always entirely homogenous. It was certainly a common trend in the newspapers to represent Livingstone as an ecumenical hero with a 'thoroughly unsectarian Christianity,' but at the same time he became embroiled in factional struggle.[124] The nonconformist *Northern Echo*, for one, used Livingstone as ammunition against the established Church in April 1874, quoting at length a letter he had written to the *New York Herald* in which he castigated the Anglican practice of 'sheep stealing' by placing bishops in areas where other missions had done the groundwork.[125]

Such sentiments, unsurprisingly, had not exactly received a favourable hearing among some sections of the Church of England. Indeed, when Livingstone's letter was publicised it provoked a firm rebuttal from the Rev. J.L. Barnett at a meeting of the Society for the Propagation of the Gospel (14 April 1874). In his counterattack he took it upon himself to destabilise Livingstone's status as a spiritual hero. While he was 'great as a discoverer; great as an adviser of the statesmen of the age', Livingstone was no theologian or 'representative of the Church of God' and so was without religious authority; he was certainly 'not great as a judge of the policy and action of the Catholic Church'.[126] Barnett, however, could not escape censure from Livingstone enthusiasts. The *Northern Echo* firmly took an opposing stance. An article that appeared on 16 April railed against the clergyman's comments, even denouncing the established church as guilty not only of 'flagrant violation of both the letter and the spirit of the religion they profess, but of that more deadly sin, too often committed now-a-days, of identifying Christianity with the most hateful intolerance, and parading as the spirit of the Church of CHRIST the very spirit of those who crucified the Saviour'. The *Northern Echo* stormed at the *Church Herald* too for its earlier 'unfavourable comments upon Dr. Livingstone's interment' and described it with loathing as 'that organ of Antichrist'. Indeed, Barnett was merely 'an indiscreet member of a great and growing party in the Establishment, whose ideal seems to be to disgust all rational Englishmen with religion, and to drive the masses of the country into atheism'.[127] In all this, the *Northern Echo* was able to use Livingstone's weight as a weapon against the Anglican Communion. The perhaps foolish criticism of a national hero provided a welcome opportunity for a nonconformist paper to lambast the theological opposition. Clearly, Livingstone had become a pawn in a larger politico-ecclesiastical struggle between the established and dissenting church communities. He had become a resource for culture wars, a territory on which theological battles could be fought out.

National negotiation

The scientific and religious are two of the more important venues among the many where the meaning of the Livingstone phenomenon was actively constructed. In their conspicuous difference, moreover, they are indicative of the more general principle that differing horizons critically impinged upon the way in which Livingstone was created. But there were also sites of a broader nature, operating at a different scale, which overarched these intra-cultural struggles. Indeed, contemporary geopolitical horizons came to play a key role in shaping the nature of Livingstone's heroic persona. The differing representations to which he was subject in both Scottish and American spaces attest to something of how Livingstone was marshalled in the cause of broader national agendas.

DEATH: LAMENTING LIVINGSTONE

Newspaper obituaries from north of the border reveal that Livingstone was valued and enshrined as a specifically Scottish icon; his Blantyre roots, his Glaswegian education and his Scots 'character' all came to be valorised. But how should these claims to Livingstone be read? The strong declaration of his Scottish identity could perhaps be taken as an expression of nationalism. One letter to the *Glasgow Herald* forcefully asserted Livingstone's Scottishness by contesting his burial in Westminster Abbey. 'One can hardly help feel that Livingstone himself would have shrunk from this trumpet-blaze of fame at his interment, and would have liked a less famous resting-place.' The author tried to reclaim Livingstone by urging that he should be laid to rest on Scottish soil: 'there is no town that has more pre-eminent claims than Glasgow to be the resting-place of the illustrious Livingstone'. 'All his early associations were with the West of Scotland and its capital. What place, then, more suited for his final repose than our ancient Cathedral?'[128] Underpinning this epistle could be an irritated nationalist force that aimed to reclaim Livingstone from the appropriation of a grasping south. Another writer, adopting a more humorous tone, noticed that the London *Times* 'had a leader about the departed being a great "Englishman?"' and joked that 'the coffin plate will a little disturb the Cockneys', who 'to their great disgust must call him a Scotsman'.[129] Again, a note of resentment that Livingstone's Scottish identity was so often overlooked can be most clearly detected. Both letters bristled at the tendency to stage Livingstone as the embodiment of 'English' character.

While a strand of nationalist sentiment is arguably detectable here, what are just as conspicuous are the efforts made by Scottish partisans to use Livingstone to negotiate British identity itself. Paul Ward warns against the historiographical tendency to interpret every 'assertion of non-English identity' purely 'as an implication of nationalism'.[130] Instead, echoing Homi Bhabha, he insists that 'Britishness has always been unstable' and is constantly 'in a process of formation';[131] a nation is recursively 'caught, uncertainly, in the act of "composing" its powerful image'.[132] Scottish identity has been perennially capable of co-habiting with a British one since, as Linda Colley has famously written, 'identities are not like hats. Human beings can and do put on several at a time.'[133] Despite deep tensions in Britishness, 'since 1870 the majority of Britons, that is people living in the United Kingdom, have adopted cultural and political identities associated with the existence of this multi-national polity'.[134] In the late nineteenth century, 'the complicity of many of the Scottish in imperialism was utilised as a method of enhancing a distinctive Scottish identity, but at the same time Scottish men made the Empire truly British'.[135] And so the repeated, if often gentle, assertions of Livingstone's Scottishness served to remind the United Kingdom of Scotland's integral role in Britain's identity and in its international adventures. In other words, Livingstone had become part of a prestige struggle on a national scale. British rivalry was performed on the platform of his name. So whether all this is read as one episode in a wider struggle to negotiate Britishness, or as symptomatic of a simmering nationalist sentiment, a Scottish cultural landscape is clearly conspicuous as a critical horizon against which Livingstone was projected.[136]

Within Scotland itself, moreover, Livingstone was subjected to regional claims. One letter to the *Glasgow Herald* mourned that 'Glasgow was lacking somewhat in her characteristic energy' when it allowed the honour of a memorial to Livingstone, 'rightly hers', to pass to Edinburgh.[137] It was felt that a statue in Glasgow was appropriate, the *Glasgow Herald* later reported from a meeting in the city's Council Chambers to establish a fund for the monument, since 'Livingstone might be considered as one of our fellow-citizens, born in the neighbourhood'. Just as the *Lancet* recognised medicine's gain in prestige by connection with Livingstone, so it was acknowledged that through a memorial Glasgow 'would honour herself'.[138] Thus Scotland's industrial city lamented the missed chance to be the first to draw upon Livingstone's symbolic reserves. Rival regions vied over the cultural capital associated with Livingstone's name. The hero was not, then, constructed out of merely national horizons: here, Livingstone became local.

Britishness and Scottishness were not the only geographical identities at stake in the posthumous representation of Livingstone. Clare Pettitt convincingly argues that Livingstone's connection with Henry Morton Stanley, the journalist from the *New York Herald,* had significance for transatlantic relations. Their famously comic encounter in Africa in 1871 had been 'a fitting symbol of a thaw in Anglo-American relations after all the bitter feeling over the American Civil War' (see Fig. 4).[139] Britain's tacit support for the Confederate cause, in building ships for the Southern states, despite their official neutrality and opposition to slavery, had left considerable tension between the two nations. The United States had demanded reparations, known as 'Alabama claims', and in 1872 'Stanley's handshake was timely, reported as it was alongside the successful settlement of the claims that same summer'.[140] Now Stanley was certainly interested in self-promotion and exploited his connection with Livingstone to such an extent that he was satirised in the *Examiner*, which, in writing 'of the distinguished reception given to Mr. Stanley in Westminster Abbey', noted 'the opportunity taken at the same time of interring there

4. 'Stanley Meeting Livingstone'. In J.E. Chambliss, *The Life and Labors of David Livingstone* (Philadelphia: Hubbard Bros., 1875), p. 695

an individual of the name of Livingstone'.[141] But there were deeper agendas at work in Stanley's construal of Livingstone. He sought to convey a hero who could appeal to both Americans and the British and so, in order to cultivate transatlantic brotherhood, he drew upon the concept of the 'Anglo-Saxon'. This was 'a means of consolidating and legitimating a new identity for America – as a global force for good'.[142]

After his death, Livingstone continued to serve the cultivation of transatlantic partnership. Stanley closed his lengthy article on Livingstone published in the *Graphic* by promoting the shared role of the United States and Britain as 'the shepherds of the world', who must protect 'the feeble and oppressed races of Africa'.[143] The *New York Herald*, the paper behind the scheme to 'find Livingstone,' also drew attention again and again to the Stanley connection. James Gordon Bennett, its editor, considered it his duty to keep the British press well supplied with letters from Livingstone to Stanley that expressed the Scot's great indebtedness to the younger American. In one letter that Bennett sent to *The Times*, Livingstone told Stanley, 'I felt, and still feel, that I had not expressed half the gratitude that wells up in my heart for all the kind services you have rendered to me.'[144]

However, the American depiction of the Livingstone–Stanley encounter was more than an exercise in the forging of transatlantic comradeship. According to Pettitt, Bennett presented Stanley's success in 'finding' Livingstone as an American victory over the 'Royal Geographical Society of London, backed by the ready purses of the whole English nation'.[145] Stanley's 'scoop' became 'the emotive story of the ordinary American man overcoming the massed power of the old-world elite' and displayed 'the force and purposefulness' of the United States.[146] It seems that Bennett meant not to imply fellowship between Britain and America but rather to suggest the latter's superiority as the new leading world power. If Britain and the United States were members of the same family, there was to be no doubt who was the big brother. When Livingstone died, this parade of predominance persisted. In fact Bennett actually capitalised on the hype surrounding Livingstone's demise by appropriating his energy to an American hero. Stanley too sometimes seemed less concerned with transatlantic solidarity than with cultivating American triumphalism. Preparing for travel in November 1874, for instance, Stanley publicised his 'enlistment of all the "faithfuls" who have at various times accompanied Livingstone, Speke, Burton, Grant, and himself'.[147] Did this manoeuvre suggest affinity between the United States and Britain, between himself and the other explorers, or did it suggest that both he and his country far surpassed the old? In life and in death, Livingstone found himself embroiled in the negotiation of the United States both as a British ally and as a younger, more vigorous, nation. In these representations, Livingstone's relationship with Stanley went way beyond the personal; he was the foil to an American hero.

In both these spaces, Scottish and American, we see what David Linge calls 'the constitutive role of the interpreter's own facticity in all understanding'.[148] The historical positioning and political situation of the interpreters were inescapable facts that inevitably bore on the significance read in Livingstone. Indeed, understanding and interpreting always involve an act of 'translation' into the terms of one's present horizon. Livingstone's representation was thus mediated through contemporary political realities. The undercurrents of the national concerns of both Scotland and the United States were clearly reflected in their respective constructions.

Spaces of dissent: questioning Livingstone's heroism

In nearly every portrayal of Livingstone considered so far, he has been treated as a hero. The differing images have all arisen against a backdrop of a shared sense that his life was one of worth and that association with him was something to be desired. This, however, was not always the fate of explorers. According to Felix Driver, more often than achieving heroic status they 'were represented as controversial figures who challenged rather than defended orthodoxy'.[149] Even with Livingstone, certain reservation is detectable in the midst of copious celebration. There were, I would argue, occasions on which his heroism was questioned and individuals for whom he could never be an unambiguous celebrity.

During his lifetime, of course, there were some quarters in which Livingstone was by no means deemed to be a hero. Portuguese officialdom was deeply suspicious of his exploratory work in east and central Africa and perceived his presence to be a sign of British aspirations in the interior. This attitude was most forcibly articulated by José Maria de Lacerda, whose *Viagens do Doutor Livingstone*, also translated into English, sought to contest the pre-eminence of Livingstone's discoveries while also casting aspersions on his motivations. Lacerda argued that 'under the pretext of propagating the Word of God (this being the least in which he employed himself)', Livingstone had sought to ensure 'the loss to Portugal of the advantages of the rich commerce of the interior, and in the end, when a favourable occasion arose, that of the very territory itself'.[150] Even in his home country too, Livingstone was not entirely free from censure.[151] This was most strongly felt after the tragic deaths of members of both the Helmore–Price and UMCA missions during the Zambesi expedition.[152] As Oliver Ransford observes, after his second period in Africa there was an extent to which 'Livingstone had fallen from his pedestal'. Disillusion set in, especially when the Zambesi river, 'God's Highway', failed to offer an accessible route to the centre of the continent. The expedition was fraught with disagreement and consequently he 'had made a host of enemies among the relatives and friends of Bedingfeld, Baines, Thornton, Kirk and Stewart'.[153] One member of the UMCA, Henry Rowley, did considerable harm to Livingstone's reputation by publishing a critical letter in Cape Town, reprinted in *The Times* in November 1862, in which he accused him of a course of aggression in releasing slaves. 'He hunted for slaving parties in every direction', wrote Rowley, 'and when he heard of the Ajawa making slaves in order to sell to the slavers, he went designedly in search of them, and intended to take their captives from them by force'.[154] Following this letter, as Ransford observes, Livingstone was publicly admonished by a group of clerics for his supposed abuse of physical offence.[155]

It would be mistaken to suggest that Livingstone's reputation was in tatters at this point, for he continued to receive a considerable amount of favourable coverage in the press. It would not be long, moreover, before his heroic stature was fully restored, beginning when his whereabouts in Africa became uncertain and culminating when he was relieved by Stanley.[156] Judith Listowel suggests that when Stanley set about renewing Livingstone's celebrity, the troubled past was allowed to lie undisturbed; 'no questions were asked, no memories revived'.[157] Yet I would argue that it is important to realise that the critical perspective on Livingstone was never fully extinguished and even persisted in the midst of the hero-worship offered up on his demise. In fact, after his death Rowley again cast doubts on Livingstone's character in an article for the *Cornhill Magazine*. While, for the most part, he showed that his position had changed and he applauded Livingstone's service to humanity, his powerful faith and non-sectarian character, there were points at which he did not spare his censure. Livingstone, he declared, was 'scarcely fitted to be the leader' of the Zambesi expedition at all. 'His arbitrary, not to say unjust, dismissal of some; his distrust of others, who were worthy of confidence; and the sense of failure, and consequent vexation of spirit, which beset not only him but all others associated with him, had practically broken up the Expedition before it was abruptly recalled.'[158]

The point is that Livingstone's heroic status was not undisputable, and that for some he was a risky and questionable character. Notwithstanding the continual lionising and memorialising that came his way, such niggling doubts call attention to the conflictual nature of myth-making.[159] The transfiguration from man into icon could never occur seamlessly without resistance. The dubious leadership that Rowley so condemned, alongside his refusal to be open and frank with his companions, his utter obsession with conquering the Cabora Bassa rapids and his unpredictable and brooding character certainly complicated his celebration as a hero in certain domains. Even while he was becoming canonised as a saint, there remained a strand of thought casting Livingstone as a potentially dangerous figure.

Of course, there were certain deep anxieties that surrounded explorers more generally. Many worried that they would 'go native' and abandon their European civilised standards. The suspicion of degeneration even touched Livingstone, whose strange accent and deeply tanned skin created something of a stir on his visits to the imperial centre. Bartle Frere, lecturing in Glasgow City Hall before the news of Livingstone's death had broken in Britain, felt the need to address those who wondered at 'the degree ... he has naturalized himself in Africa and become like one of the Africans'. While of course Frere declared him 'to be still, and to have always been ... a missionary of the Cross', the necessity of meeting such concerns at all indicates the reservations that surrounded explorers who spent such lengthy periods away from the homeland.[160] Some also found themselves anxious about Livingstone's attitude to the indigenous population. While his humanitarianism routinely received praise, some considered his sympathy with Africans to be excessive. On 21 April, for instance, the *Scotsman* warned against 'illusions and prejudices of love, as well as those of hatred', implying that Livingstone was so deceived when it came to the 'negro': it was the hideous slave trade which 'prompted him to clutch more passionately to his heart the down-trodden victim, and to overlook his faults'.[161] Several months later, on 30 July, the same paper described his viewpoint as typical of the 'negrophilists', at the opposite pole from Richard Burton and Samuel Baker, who 'always assigned to the negro a rather low place in nature'.[162] In these cases, Livingstone's progressive racial politics were seen as an embarrassment needing to be explained away. For those who were particularly strong advocates of racial hierarchy, of the 'anthropological' persuasion, he could not be simply praised without qualification.[163] While such qualms are of a different sort from the reports of his unpredictable character, together they express some disquiet that Livingstone was a radical free spirit who might transgress accepted societal bounds. Indeed, personal antipathy and political persuasion could situate an author on the continuum of dissent, where celebrating Livingstone was not unproblematic and where his heroic stature was not simply a given.

The 'body' of evidence

So far we have seen that Livingstone, from the very moment of his demise, was subject to conflicting constructions and competing claims to his name. His persona was malleable and mouldable, able to take on various meanings for different people and groups. Something of this struggle was reflected in his spectacular funeral in Westminster Abbey. Pettitt, engaging in a semiotic exercise, suggests that the whole spectacle 'drew attention as much to the mourners as to the mourned' and revealed at least two ways of reading Livingstone's life. She argues that the presence of the aristocracy and his entombment in Westminster Abbey signified that he was embraced by the ruling classes, while the presence of Sir Fowell Buxton, the anti-slavery campaigner, the radical MP John Bright and other 'notable radicals and critics of the empire' emitted a distinctively different message.[164] As Felix Driver writes, 'each of the pall-bearers on that day in April 1874 were staking a claim upon his name as well as his body'.[165] Thus Livingstone was symbolically connected with radical British politics even while simultaneously being canonised as the establishment's hero. 'Even as the funeral staged the triumphalist power of empire and of "England", the forces of resistance and criticism were present.'[166] Different visions of Livingstone competed while he was consigned to the grave, as groups with diverging politics simultaneously laid claim to him (see Fig. 5).

5. 'The Scene at the Pier, Southampton'. Supplement to the *Graphic* (25 April 1874), 404

What is particularly interesting here is the way in which a single event took on different meanings for different people. But this analysis can be pushed even further. Livingstone's mangled corpse, no less than his funeral, was itself a site of multiple and conflicting significations. His carcass actually became a symbolic space on which a wider debate over the capacity and authority of black Africans could be played out. Underlying the entire discourse of the remains, their return and identification, was a trial of native reliability and black capability. Indeed, it was partly because of its significance as a testing ground for African credentials and trustworthiness that the trans-continental journey of his body, from the heart of Africa to Westminster Abbey, attracted such extensive textual space and became a national obsession.

When the first rumours of Livingstone's passing began to reach British ears at the end of January 1874, there were mixed reactions. Some believed and began to mourn, while others were more dubious, remembering comparable tales propagated by Livingstone's 'Johanna men' which had proved false not so long ago.[167] Since these new reports similarly originated with Africans, for many in Britain they emphatically could not be trusted. Indeed, some of Livingstone's most famed companions cast doubt on African truthfulness, revealing a deep-set distrust of indigenous authority. Dr John Kirk, for one, immediately aired his suspicion; for him the story was pure fiction. After all he was one who knew at first hand 'how rumours grow in Africa'.[168] The future editor of Livingstone's *Last Journals*, Horace Waller, had similar reservations. He pointed to 'the habit the natives have of using an exaggerated expression which leads one to suppose a man is dead when he is only seriously disabled'.[169] As it became increasingly likely that Livingstone really was dead, some doubts continued to be voiced. David Leslie, for instance, writing to the *Glasgow Herald* as late as 23 February, sought to discredit native witness and to pitch the authoritative weight of his own experiences in Africa against it. It was on his superior knowledge of tribal life that he 'ground [his] doubts as to the truth of the reports'. No matter how seemingly honest, native reports should always be greeted with a healthy dose of suspicion. 'The Johanna men were also "faithful servants",' he pointed out, 'and they lied.'[170] So why trust these new and equally dubious rumours? Continually, reasons were dug up to doubt the native report. Surely, some complained, preserving a body in salt would be impossible in the African climate. And surely, others argued, the Africans' terror of corpses and their lack of respect for the dead were even greater grounds for doubt. Albert J. Mott expressed the underlying logic: it would be premature to pronounce the hero dead when so few facts had yet been certified by the 'evidence of Europeans'.[171]

Indeed, the only decisive body of evidence that would eradicate doubt was Livingstone's body itself. Only by an examination of the corpse could the question finally be settled; it would take Western scrutiny to authorise a tale of African origin. When Livingstone's remains arrived in the United Kingdom, the prestigious surgeon Sir William Fergusson was called upon to identify the body and so put all anxieties to rest. In his post-mortem Fergusson described himself as 'one of those who entertained hopes that the last reports of Livingstone's death might, like others, prove false'. But when he examined the largely unrecognisable remains, the discovery of Livingstone's infamous 'false' arm joint 'set [his] mind at rest'. Livingstone's men could now be counted trustworthy, having been vindicated by an 'oblique fracture', 'Exactly in the region of the attachment of the deltoid to the humerus'.[172] As Dorinda Outram has perceptively written, 'the oldest locus of authority is the human body'.[173] In Livingstone's case it became a means of verifying the stories of those who, by their ethnicity, were cast aside as lacking in credibility.

When Livingstone's native companions were finally vindicated and their constancy confirmed, their fortunes changed; they became heroic figures publicly praised. But even then the dialogue surrounding

Livingstone's body did not entirely cease; the discourse instead shifted from a discussion of African reliability to African capability. In other words, while the truthfulness of Livingstone's men was no longer at stake, some suggested that the body's successful trans-continental journey was in actuality owed to European assistance at the critical moment. A series of letters, printed in the pages of *The Times*, passionately disputed the matter of the glory due for its spectacular return. Did the credit belong to his self-sacrificing African followers, or to the Europeans of Lieutenant Lovett Cameron's party who accompanied the men in the final stages of their journey?[174] The debate was spurred by a letter from Clements Markham, Secretary of the Royal Geographical Society: 'The time has, I think, come when I may ask you to bring the Cameron – Livingstone Expedition more prominently than has hitherto been done before the notice of your readers.' Given the society's considerable institutional investment in African exploration and in both travellers, Markham presented Cameron as Livingstone's heir apparent; his attempt to reclaim the hero's papers at Ujiji was nothing less than an act of 'obedience to the dying request of Dr. Livingstone'. But most critically, Markham contended that 'it was owing to aid given by Lieutenant Lovett Cameron's party that Dr. Livingstone's body was sent down in safety to the coast'.[175] While the trustworthiness of those who bore the body was no longer the issue, Markham's letter certainly sought to shift the glory and confer it upon Cameron.

Markham's missive immediately provoked a response from Livingstone's son Thomas, whose brusque letter to *The Times* of 9 July fuelled a dispute which would eventually be terminated by the editor a month later as a most 'ungrateful controversy'.[176] In his first epistle, Thomas rebutted Markham's 'grievous error in supposing that but for meeting Mr. Cameron's party, the brave fellows who had carried my father's body ... would not have reached the coast'. His retort was that Susi and Chuma 'should have reached Zanzibar much earlier had they not been obliged to escort Dr. Dillon and Lieutenant Murphy', other members of the expedition. Thomas Livingstone defended his father's African retinue from those who would belittle them: 'One cannot allow anything to pass that might in the slightest degree detract from the splendid feat accomplished by my father's attendants.'[177] The body's return proved the capacity and competence of Africans, and he was intent on advocating their cause.

At this stage a relative of Cameron's, the Rev. C. Lovett Cameron, took up the cudgels.[178] In reply to Thomas he asserted that 'Lieutenant Cameron sent out succour to the explorer's servants before their reaching Unyanyembe, and furnished them with supplies for the journey to Zanzibar.' It was, apparently, due to 'Lieutenant Murphy's management' that the bearers 'secured the unmolested conveyance of the remains through the Ugogo country'. The likelihood that they would have completed the march without this aid was 'improbable' at best, especially in light of 'the misconduct of the great majority of them at Unyanyembe'.[179]

But the matter was not allowed to lie. Thomas responded again to what he considered the preposterous claims made by Cameron's companion, Murphy, to have provided critical aid and protection for the indigenous carriers. His letter, on 10 August, struck at what he called 'a masked battery' against his father's men. He lashed out at Murphy, calling him an 'infant in exploration' compared with Chuma and Susi, who were 'old enough in experience to be his great grandfather'. These men were certainly 'able to shift for themselves after eight years' tramping' with Livingstone, and so he doubted their need for any assistance at all. For rhetorical support Thomas Livingstone quoted his father's journal, which condemned those who dismissed Africans lightly: 'Nothing but the most pitiable puerility would lead any manly heart to make their inferiority a theme for self-exaltation. However, that is often done, as if with the vague idea that we can, by magnifying their deficiencies, demonstrate our immaculate perfections.'[180] In all this Thomas positioned himself as an advocate of Africans, championing their cause against those who would appropriate the credit due to them. He took the side of the indigenous, resisting those who would try to reveal a fundamental foundation of European assistance.

Native capability was not all that was at stake in this debate in *The Times*. Cameron's and Murphy's advocates were undoubtedly on a campaign to promote these explorers as heroes in the Livingstonian mould, for a symbolic connection with his name could significantly enhance the reputations of less illustrious travellers. Perhaps, then, another logic at work in Thomas Livingstone's vigorous defence of the indigenous, and his confrontation with Cameron and Murphy, was to do with resisting these new heroic claims. He was anxious, indeed admirably so, to defend his father and to prevent the eclipse of his memory so soon after his demise. In protecting Chuma and Susi's achievement Thomas simultaneously defended his father's reputation, for it was commonplace to attribute their astonishing perseverance to Livingstone's civilising influence. David Leslie's letter to the *Glasgow Herald* is a case in point:

> if [Livingstone] has died as we are told, the greatest proof to my mind of the ascendancy he gained in Africa, of the power which his very name was possessed of, would be the fact of his men having carried his remains to Zanzibar, and having been allowed to do so by the inhabitants of the villages through which they passed.[181]

In other words, Livingstone's men had become signifiers of his success, emblems of his supreme authority. In defending them, Thomas protected the father he had so recently lost; their success was proof of the civilising mission so precious to Livingstone.

Issues of indigenous credentials certainly wove their way through the discourse surrounding Livingstone's mortal remains, as did the matter of his own credibility. But there was another way, yet more fundamental, in which authority was bound to his body. As I argued in my previous chapter, matters of warrant and dependability have always surrounded travellers who would return home bearing incredible tales from remote and exotic lands – stories that often seemed just too fantastic to be true. Unlike other scientific discoveries, travellers' reports from overseas could not be replicated and tested in any simple way; they simply had to be trusted. Since it was difficult to ensure that the explorer was an honest and reliable reporter, emphasis was laid on the importance of proven good character; authentication came to rely on the traveller's moral calibre. Michael Heffernan sheds light on the resolution of credibility quandaries when he reveals how warrant often came to reside in the bodily wounds and scars won in exploration; they came to serve as signs of reliability, signifiers of moral authority. Heffernan argues that 'Authority ultimately derived, if not from premature death itself, then at least from the corporeal evidence of heroic travel – the noble empowering stigmata of scarred and disfigured bodies.'[182] Livingstone's mangled remains, I would argue, sealed his status and proved his heroism. The extraordinarily graphic examination report by Sir William Fergusson, reprinted in the popular press and hungrily consumed by the public, was an anatomical eulogy fit for a martyr:

> The lower limbs were so severed from the trunk ... The soft tissues seem to have been removed to a great extent from the bones ... There had been made a large opening in front of the abdomen, and through that the native operators had ingeniously contrived to remove the contents of the chest ... Every-where was that shrivelling ... The features of the face could not be recognised ... A moustache could not be recognised, but whiskers were in abundance.[183]

Most attention was given to his ancient badge of authority, the arm shattered in a lion attack, of which *Lloyd's Weekly Newspaper* wrote, 'No dust of hero in the Abbey bears a more honourable scar than this!'[184] His disfigured arm and crushed remains bore testimony to his credentials.[185] He had been prepared to go to the extremes in pursuit of his cause and his body had borne the consequences.

Clare Pettitt, analysing the sensation surrounding the return of the 'withered remains', argues that they 'were reassuringly unbodily' by the time they arrived in Southampton. The delay had allowed his corpse to be 'purified of all suspicion of material corruption', and so, wizened like a saint's body, 'Livingstone had been both literally and imaginatively transformed from mortal remains to immortal relic', to what Lord Houghton called a 'sacred crust'.[186] There is merit to this argument, for poets like Roden Noel employed similar metaphors: to him, the 'rude grey bark' that bore Livingstone's body was 'a holiest ark'.[187] Moreover, as Chris Wingfield has recently observed, some of Livingstone's friends and family treated his embalmed remains like that of a saint's by obtaining mementoes – or 'bodily relics' – such as matted locks of hair.[188] Yet it equally seems to me that there was such fascination with his body because it was a mangled corpse. The story of the gruesome embalming procedure, with the bloody removal of guts, was a major source of public captivation. And as Debbie Harrison comments, in its macabre detail Fergusson's autopsy was actually rather 'gothic' in character.[189] It was physicality and corporality that enthralled the people every bit as much as a sacred relic. Livingstone's brokenness spoke of adventure and sacrifice, and firmly sealed his status as the ultimate explorer-hero in the eyes of the public.

Livingstone's body was the site of multiple meanings, a site of clashing horizons. It was an arena in which debates about native warrant and indigenous potential could be dramatised. But the story of the body's return also provided the opportunity to negotiate and debate the prestige of other explorers, who would profit by association. On another level the whole body discourse was crucially bound up with the issue of Livingstone's own authority. The successful return of his remains signified his civilising influence in moulding such exceptional men, while his battered carcass spoke volumes about sacrifice.

This chapter began by exploring the general characteristics of Livingstone's commemoration in the nineteenth-century print media. As the subject of numerous elegies and eulogies, the body of literature that appeared on his demise grants insight into the Victorian conception of death and a culture of mourning that now seems excessive to the contemporary reader. This written remembrance gave prominence to the way in which Livingstone perished, focusing on his spiritual preparation and the consolation of the afterlife. While his death was undoubtedly bad in certain respects – and undeniably tragic – Livingstone fulfilled the Victorian ideal of sacrifice. In fact in this regard, and in the way that he faced his end, he was actually offered as an exemplar of a 'good' Christian death. Of course, in dying as a martyr while in the harness of labour, Livingstone exceeded the contemporary evangelical conception of dying 'well'.

The scope of Livingstone's memorialisation reveals the extent to which his decease was considered a tragedy to be lamented on a national level. Yet the deathly poetics, and other obituaries, also reveal the shared features that lay behind his public celebrity. Livingstone, I argued, was enshrined as an explorer extraordinaire who battled a series of obstacles in human, animal and environmental form. To this end, he was constructed in opposition to the imagined, and brutalised, people and place of Africa. Livingstone was construed as a master, a figure of authority exerting easy control over the encountered indigenous. And more than this, he metaphorically became master of his environment, one who opened the dark and mysterious spaces of the continent to European knowledge. Another of Livingstone's most pervasive images was that of the Christian hero, and consequently he was surrounded by a ubiquitous spiritual discourse. He exceeded the discourse of Christian manliness and was invested with prophetic, apostolic and even pseudo-messianic proportions. The extent to which Livingstone was idealised in this manner indicates that he was envisaged to be a national ideal. This, I suggested, is particularly detectable in the reputation that he sustained as an emancipator due to his campaign against the slave trade. Since Livingstone was deemed to be participating in a national mission, he served to consolidate Britain's self-image as an abolitionist nation. Furthermore, his portrayal as an exemplar of the roving disposition supposedly inherent in the 'island race' makes it clear that he was imagined as a representative of the national character.

Despite the commonality of construction that is detectable in the aftermath of Livingstone's death, however, this chapter has sought to escape the notion that Livingstone was enshrined in any homogenous way. While the heterogeneity of Livingstone's longer heroic history has hitherto attracted some degree of critical attention, to date no one has explored in detail the plural nature of his identity at the height of his fame and the competing discourses surrounding his demise. From the very moment of his interment, Livingstone was subject to rival claims, and so divergent meanings have been perpetually attached to him.[190] While this should not mask the important unifying elements of Livingstone's remembrance, it is vital to note that underneath the umbrella of his name was an array of heroic identities, constructed out of a plurality of Victorian cultures. Debated and created in disparate intellectual and socio-political sites, he was diversely produced by communities possessing contrasting horizons of significance. And being created in the image of his creators, Livingstone became deployed as symbolic capital in order to enhance status and prestige. As a cultural commodity his name became involved in diverse disputes that ranged from the theological to the national and even the international. Quiet voices of dissent for whom Livingstone was a potentially transgressive figure persisted and complicated his consecration.

Livingstone's corpse had powerful symbolic value: it too became a space for debate. An altercation over extra-European authority and reliability found its focal point in the remains. Indeed, the contemporary clash in notions about Africans was played out in the diverging stories about the body and its return to Britain. But all this also had implications for Livingstone's own credibility. The trans-continental journey seemed to signify his tremendous elevating influence, while the actual battered carcass put the final authorisation upon his discoveries and heroic status. A final couplet from one of the many poetic venerations seems an appropriate way to conclude: 'His name on history's brightest page, / Shall shine for evermore unchanged.'[191] These words now hold ironic weight; Livingstone's name simply never carried just one meaning that could remain in eternal stasis.

Notes

1 This was reported in *The Times*: 'Death of Dr. Livingstone', *The Times* (28 January 1874), 8.
2 For discussions of Livingstone's reception and funeral, see John Wolffe, *Great Deaths: Grieving, Religion, and Nationhood in Victorian and Edwardian Britain* (Oxford: Oxford University Press, 2000); Joanna Lewis, 'Southampton and the Making of an Imperial Myth: David Livingstone's Remains', in Miles Taylor (ed.), *Southampton: Gateway to the British Empire* (London; New York: I.B. Tauris, 2007), pp. 31–48. Wolffe notes that the government was originally reluctant to organise a public funeral for Livingstone. It was not standard practice to stage such events for missionaries or, for that matter, explorers. There also was the possibility that the body returning in the *Malwa* would prove not to be authentic, and they feared being caught out by a hoax. In the end, it was 'press-inspired public interest and pressure' and 'the convergent interests of the RGS and of Dean Stanley' that resulted in his stately funeral. See Wolffe, *Great Deaths*, pp. 139–40. More recently, Joanna Lewis has argued that the reception of Livingstone's remains in Southampton prompted London to escalate its own preparations. For Southampton, the arrival of Livingstone's body provided an opportunity for the port town 'to display civic prowess to an international audience'. See Lewis, 'Southampton', pp. 35, 42.
3 Uncovering the numerous sources discussed here has been made possible by recent digitisation projects that provide extensive access to a range of nineteenth-century newspapers and periodicals.
4 Andrew Ross, *David Livingstone: Mission and Empire* (London: Hambledon and London, 2002), p. 109.
5 Tim Jeal, *Livingstone* (New Haven: Yale University Press, 2001), pp. 163–4.
6 Adrian S. Wisnicki, 'Interstitial Cartographer: David Livingstone and the Invention of South Central Africa', *Victorian Literature and Culture*, 37 (2009), 256.
7 Ibid., p. 267. In my previous chapter, I also gave credence to the vitality of *Missionary Travels* by arguing that it was a crucial vehicle of self-construction and a heterogeneous text that facilitated the diversity of his posthumous representations.
8 Dorothy O. Helly, *Livingstone's Legacy: Horace Waller and Victorian Mythmaking* (Athens, O.: Ohio University Press, 1987), p. 247.

9 Quoted in ibid., p. 109.
10 Ibid., p. 108.
11 There is a parallel to here with the memorialisation of Captain Scott. As Max Jones observes, while Scott's journals were instrumental in shaping his posthumous reputation, the process of commemoration began – through the press and various societies – before they were ever published. See Max Jones, *The Last Great Quest: Captain Scott's Antarctic Sacrifice* (Oxford: Oxford University Press, 2003), p. 157. For information on the publication of Scott's last journals, see Max Jones (ed.), *Journals: Captain Scott's Last Expedition* (Oxford: Oxford University Press, 2006).
12 James Stevens Curl, *The Victorian Celebration of Death* (Stroud: Sutton, 2004), p. 202.
13 Erik Gray, 'Victoria Dressed in Black: Poetry in an Elegiac Age', in Karen Weisman (ed.), *The Oxford Handbook of the Elegy* (Oxford: Oxford University Press, 2010), p. 275.
14 Ibid., p. 272.
15 W.H. Dowding's poem on Livingstone, 'In Memoriam', clearly alluded to the most famous poem of the Victorian period, *In Memoriam A.H.H.*, by Alfred, Lord Tennyson, the Poet Laureate. See W.H. Dowding, 'In Memoriam', *Bristol Mercury* (25 April 1874), 6; W. Sumpter, 'David Livingstone: An Epitaph', *Lancet*, 103: 2642 (1874), 572; James Hurnard, 'Burial of Livingstone in Westminster Abbey: A Dirge', *Manchester Times* (18 April 1874), 124.
16 W.F.H., 'David Livingstone', *John Bull* (25 April 1874), 280.
17 W.F.H., 'David Livingstone', *John Bull* (7 February 1874), 100.
18 'David Livingstone', *Punch* (7 February 1874), 52.
19 Gray, 'Victoria Dressed in Black', p. 279.
20 W.F.H., 'David Livingstone', p. 280.
21 'David Livingstone', *Fun* (7 February 1874), 56.
22 P.M.F., 'Livingstone', *Birmingham Daily Post* (20 April 1874), 6.
23 Dowding, 'In Memoriam', 6.
24 Hurnard, 'Burial of Livingstone in Westminster Abbey', 124.
25 Lewis, 'Southampton', p. 33.
26 'David Livingstone', *Fun* (7 February 1874), 56.
27 Sumpter, 'David Livingstone', 572.
28 P.M.F., 'Livingstone', *Birmingham Daily Post* (20 April 1874), 6.
29 Hermione Lee, *Body Parts: Essays in Life-Writing* (London: Chatto & Windus, 2005), p. 209.
30 Michel Vovelle, *Ideologies and Mentalities*, trans. Eamon O' Flaherty (Cambridge: Polity, 1990), p. 65.
31 Patricia Jalland, *Death in the Victorian Family* (Oxford: Oxford University Press, 1999), pp. 2–3.
32 Ibid., pp. 28, 21.
33 Sumpter, 'David Livingstone', 572. By concentrating on his heavenly reward after death, the Livingstone elegies were fulfilling the function of the genre. As Erik Gray argues, most elegies 'move in a more or less continuous arc through stages of grief, generally towards a form of consolation'. See Gray, 'Victoria Dressed in Black', p. 273. Oftentimes this solace was spiritual in nature. Linda K. Hughes reminds us that in Victorian poetry 'response to grief most often took the form of religious consolation'. See Linda K. Hughes, *The Cambridge Introduction to Victorian Poetry* (Cambridge: Cambridge University Press, 2010), p. 180.
34 Dowding, 'In Memoriam', p. 6.
35 W.F.C., 'Livingstone', *Glasgow Herald* (30 December 1874), 5.
36 J. Hoskyns-Abrahall, 'David Livingstone: The Seeker of the Founts of Nile, after a Brief Stay in a Temporary Hut, has at Dawn of Day Departed', *Jackson's Oxford Journal* (9 May 1874), 5. When Horace Waller published the *Last Journals*, he claimed that in Livingstone's final conversation he asked 'How many days is it to the Luapula?' On hearing it was still at some distance, Livingstone 'half sighed, half

said, "Oh dear, dear!"' In Waller's account, his very last words, spoken 'in a low feeble voice', were to Susi telling him he could depart from the hut: 'All right; you can go out now.' See Horace Waller (ed.), *The Last Journals of David Livingstone, in Central Africa, from 1865 to his Death*, vol. 2 (London: John Murray, 1874), p. 307. In the elegiac poetry published prior to the *Last Journals*, however, it was generally taken that Livingstone's last words were 'build me a hut to die in'. These words, or variations on them, which clearly served to indicate a state of readiness, were recited in at least four poems: Sumpter, 'David Livingstone', 572; J.H.S., 'Muelala-Bisa Country', *Glasgow Herald* (3 April 1874), 4; 'On Reading Livingstone's Last Words in the Account of his Death', *The Monthly Packet of Evening Papers for Members of the English Church* (1 July 1874), 22; and Roden Noel, *Livingstone in Africa* (London: Sampson Low, Marston, Low and Searle, 1874).

37 Jalland, *Death in the Victorian Family*, p. 33.
38 Derek Gregory, 'Imaginative Geographies', in R.J. Johnston, Derek Gregory, Geraldine Pratt and Michael Watts (eds), *The Dictionary of Human Geography*, 4th ed. (Oxford: Blackwell, 2000), p. 372.
39 Franco Moretti, *Atlas of the European Novel, 1800–1900* (London; New York: Verso, 1999), p. 60.
40 P.M.F., 'Livingstone', p. 6.
41 Hoskyns-Abrahall, 'David Livingstone', p. 5.
42 Noel, *Livingstone in Africa*, p. 13.
43 P.M.F., 'Livingstone', p. 6.
44 J.H.S., 'Muelala-Bisa Country', p. 4.
45 Martin Burgess Green, *Dreams of Adventure, Deeds of Empire* (New York: Basic Books, 1979), p. 81.
46 Noel, *Livingstone in Africa*, p. 22. Dorothy Hammond and Alta Jablow note that 'in the imperial period writers were far more addicted to tales of cannibalism than ... Africans ever were to cannibalism'. See Dorothy Hammond and Alta Jablow, *The Africa that Never Was: Four Centuries of British Writing about Africa* (New York: Twayne, 1970), p. 94.
47 Noel, *Livingstone in Africa*, p. 20.
48 Syed Manzurul Islam, *The Ethics of Travel: From Marco Polo to Kafka* (Manchester: Manchester University Press, 1996), p. 44.
49 'Arrival of Dr. Livingstone's Remains', *Daily News* (16 April 1874), 5.
50 Hoskyns-Abrahall, 'David Livingstone', 5.
51 Richard Monckton Milnes (Lord Houghton), 'Ilala – May, 1873', *The Times* (20 April 1874), 12.
52 Noel, *Livingstone in Africa*, p. 12.
53 Ibid., pp. 1, 2.
54 Mary Louise Pratt, *Imperial Eyes: Travel Writing and Transculturation* (New York: Routledge, 2008), p. 9.
55 Ibid., pp. 200–1.
56 Richard Phillips, *Mapping Men and Empire: A Geography of Adventure* (London; New York: Routledge, 1997), p. 3.
57 'The Dead Hero', *Northern Echo* (25 February 1874), 3.
58 'On Livingstone', *Lloyd's Weekly Newspaper* (8 February 1874), 5.
59 Recent theories on cartography have been interested in what Svetlana Alpers has called the 'aura of knowledge' that emanates from maps, their seeming power to display the world as it 'really is'. See Svetlana Alpers, *The Art of Describing: Dutch Art in the Seventeenth Century* (Chicago: University of Chicago Press, 1983), p. 133. Maps, argues Richard Phillips, 'circumscribe geography' by 'their propensity to ignore, suppress and negate alternative geographical imaginations'. See Phillips, *Mapping Men*, pp. 14–15.
60 'David Livingstone', *Punch* (7 February 1874), 52.
61 'Funeral of Dr. Livingstone', *Daily News* (20 April 1874), 3.
62 Ibid.
63 'The Last Hours of Livingstone', *Western Mail* (31 March 1874), 6.

64 Norman Vance has criticised the term 'muscular Christian' for misleadingly 'draw[ing] attention more to muscularity than to Christianity'. Certainly, in Livingstone's case, spirituality was of equal importance to physical prowess. Vance suggests the replacement term 'Christian manliness' to denote more accurately a discourse which 'represented a strategy for commending Christian virtue by linking it with more interesting notions of moral and physical prowess'. See Norman Vance, *The Sinews of the Spirit: The Ideal of Christian Manliness in Victorian Literature and Religious Thought* (Cambridge: Cambridge University Press, 1985), pp. 2, 1.
65 *Daily News* (29 January 1874), 4–5.
66 'Livingstone – his Last Journey', *Glasgow Herald* (30 March 1874), 5.
67 'The Family of Dr. Livingstone', *Leeds Mercury* (31 April 1874), 2.
68 'Funeral of Dr. Livingstone', *Daily News* (20 April 1874), 3.
69 'Funeral Service at Hamilton', *Scotsman* (20 April 1874), 5. The Rev. Hamilton also led a short service in the premises of the RGS at Savile Row, London, on the morning of the Westminster funeral service (18 April). He returned to Scotland that night in order to preach in Hamilton the following day (19 April).
70 Wolffe, *Great Deaths*, p. 138.
71 'Livingstone – his Last Journey', p. 5.
72 '... Dr. Livingstone', *The Times* (30 March 1874), 7.
73 Henry Morton Stanley, 'The Life and Labours of David Livingstone', supplement to *Graphic* (25 April 1874), 402.
74 John M. MacKenzie, 'Heroic Myths of Empire', in John M. MacKenzie (ed.), *Popular Imperialism and the Military* (Manchester: Manchester University Press, 1992), p. 124.
75 Stanley, 'The Life and Labours', p. 394.
76 'On Livingstone', 5.
77 Martin A. Danahay, *Gender at Work in Victorian Culture, Literature, Art and Masculinity* (Aldershot: Ashgate, 2005), p. 23.
78 Rob Breton, *Gospels and Grit: Work and Labour in Carlyle, Conrad and Orwell* (Toronto: University of Toronto Press, 2005), pp. 4, 6. Following Rob Breton, we should note that the 'idea of a single, unified Gospel of Work shared by all Victorian is grossly inadequate'. Rather, we need to think in terms of multiplicity: the various 'Gospels of Work have to be disentangled'. See Breton, *Gospels and Grit*, p. 6. My description here is thus intended only as a broad sketch of the most culturally pervasive version.
79 'Dr. Livingstone', *Aberdeen Journal* (4 February 1874), 3.
80 William Hughes, 'Livingstone', *Examiner* (31 January 1874), 107.
81 'David Livingstone', *Punch* (7 February 1874), 52.
82 Danahay, *Gender at Work*, p. 24. It was Livingstone's status as a spiritual hero and exemplary worker that attracted the attention of the Christian children's press of the period. As is to be expected, such literature put him to work for didactic purposes. In the *Child's Companion*, readers were told that Livingstone learned early in life 'to know that he was a sinner and Jesus Christ is a Saviour ... his great concern was to give his whole life to His service'. See 'Young Livingstone and his Latin-Grammar', *Child's Companion* (1 May 1874), 66. Such Christian moralising sits squarely alongside an emphasis on enterprise and effort. As Joseph Bristow argues, the ethos of boys' periodicals was 'fashioned by the liberal principles of Samuel Smiles'; they championed 'independent citizenship' and the 'virtues of thrift and hard work'. See Joseph Bristow, *Empire Boys: Adventures in a Man's World* (London: Harper Collins Academic, 1991), p. 33. In the same article from the *Child's Companion*, the lesson drawn from 'the spinner-boy who became a missionary' is that 'where God has given us a work to do, we must, assisted by His grace, try to do it. Nothing truly worth having is to be got without hard work.' See 'Young Livingstone', p. 66.
83 'Dr Livingstone's Body', *The Times* (14 April 1874), 9.
84 Noel, *Livingstone in Africa*, p. 94.

85 Ibid., p. 95.
86 Dowding, 'In Memoriam', *Bristol Mercury* (25 April 1874), 6.
87 W.F.H., 'David Livingstone', p. 280.
88 The fact that these two conceptions of slavery merge consolidates Patrick Brantlinger's argument that in the imperial period, sensational and brutalising descriptions of the indigenous meant that slavery came to look 'more and more like a direct extension of African savagery'. See Patrick Brantlinger, *Rule of Darkness: British Literature and Imperialism, 1830–1914* (New York: Cornell University Press, 1988), p. 179.
89 A., 'David Livingstone: Westminster Abbey', *Western Mail* (18 April 1874), 6.
90 Ibid.
91 'Funeral of Dr. Livingstone', *The Times* (20 April 1874), 12.
92 Brantlinger, *Rule of Darkness*, p. 177.
93 Noel, *Livingstone in Africa*, p. 17.
94 Ibid., p. 102.
95 Herbert F. Tucker, *Epic: Britain's Heroic Muse, 1790–1910* (Oxford: Oxford University Press, 2008), p. 13.
96 Tucker points out that after the French Revolution, both radicals and reactionaries articulated their positions in nationalist terms. At this time, numerous verse narratives of diverse ideological positions appeared in the press to express their vision of Britain and its destiny. According to Tucker, the Victorians received this 'generic bequest' 'with ambivalence'. With doubts about national unity and the national mission, Victorian poets encountered epic 'as a compound trial'. See Herbert Tucker, 'Epic', in Richard Cronin, Anthony Harrison and Alison Chapman (eds), *A Companion to Victorian Poetry* (Oxford: Blackwell, 2002), pp. 27, 28. Poets who attempted national epics were thus in danger of accusations of excess. Noel's poem certainly fell into this trap, and was described by the *Daily News* as 'overwrought, swollen, and bombastic'. See 'Current Literature', *Daily News* (10 September 1874), 2.
97 Noel, *Livingstone in Africa*, p. xi.
98 'Luncheon in the Corporation Galleries', *Scotsman* (9 January 1874), 5.
99 'On Livingstone', *Lloyd's Weekly Newspaper* (8 February 1874), 5.
100 'The Death of Dr. Livingstone', *Lloyd's Weekly Newspaper* (1 February 1874), 6.
101 Dowding, 'In Memoriam', p. 6.
102 'On Livingstone', p. 5.
103 'David Livingstone', *Punch* (7 February 1874), 52. It has been observed that Victorian elegies often mourned not only the passing of a person, but the passing of an age. As John D. Rosenberg argues, the Victorians were in '"an age of transition", caught between a vanishing past and an uncertain future'. This led them to seek 'points of purchase, as it were, in an imagined past that appeared more stable than the present'. Elegiac poetry tended to hark back to an apparently 'cohesive past' and fret over a 'menacing future'. Those poems, then, which present Livingstone as a repository of values that had seemingly faded, reveal their concern over the paucity of contemporary society. See John D. Rosenberg, *Elegy for an Age: The Presence of the Past in Victorian Literature* (London: Anthem Press, 2005), pp. 1, 2, 3.
104 Alan J. Lee, *The Origins of the Popular Press in England, 1855–1914* (London: Croom Helm, 1976), p. 21.
105 Ibid., p. 27.
106 In spite of this it is important to remember, as Alan J. Lee reminds us, that 'Rhetoric and ideology aside, the Victorian newspaper was … for those who ran it first and foremost a business.' See Lee, *The Origins*, p. 49. This truth would become much more conspicuous in the 1880s with the advent of the more explicitly commercial 'new journalism'. This style of reportage aimed for human interest and sensation in order to accrue profit, and so the relationship between reader and paper began to move 'from the ideal one of a tutorial and intellectual nature, to one of market character'. See ibid., p. 121. Of course, neither market motivation nor sensation was 'new'; however, the new journalism did exemplify a shift in the

balance. Livingstone perhaps served an interstitial function in a period when the nature of journalism was evolving. Thus, while he was congenial to the demands of the older liberal ideology which aimed to elevate readers, he also helped to meet the growing focus on selling papers and making profit. In the years before new journalism became established, Livingstone thus provided a satisfactory compromise between human interest and didactic potential.

107 This approach is indebted to the insight that location is an important category in both the production and the consumption of knowledge. A considerable body of research in human geography over the past two decades has been directed to what has become known as the spaces of knowledge. See Felix Driver, *Geography Militant: Cultures of Exploration and Empire* (Oxford: Blackwell, 2001), p. 12; David N. Livingstone, 'The Spaces of Knowledge: Contributions Towards a Historical Geography of Science', *Society and Space*, 13: 1 (1995), 5–34; David N. Livingstone, *Putting Science in its Place: Geographies of Scientific Knowledge* (Chicago and London: University of Chicago Press, 2003), pp. 5–12.
108 Hans-Georg Gadamer, *Truth and Method*, trans. Joel Weinsheimer and Donald G. Marshall (London: Bloomsbury, 2013).
109 W.M. Fergusson, 'Examination and Verification of the Body of Dr. Livingstone', letter, *Lancet*, 103: 2642 (1874), 566.
110 'Medical Annotations', *Lancet*, 104: 2671 (1874), 674.
111 'The Naval Medical Service', *Lancet*, 104: 2671 (1874), 665.
112 J.M.B., 'Memorial to the Late Dr. Livingstone', letter, *Lancet*, 103: 2643 (1874), 607.
113 'David Livingstone', *British Quarterly Review*, 59: 118 (1874), pp. 507, 494.
114 Ibid., p. 514.
115 'Livingstone's "Last Journals"', *Nature*, 11: 269 (1874), 143.
116 'Livingstone's "Last Journals" II', *Nature*, 11: 271 (1875), 183.
117 'David Livingstone', *British Quarterly Review*, 59: 118 (1874), p. 487.
118 David Linge, 'Introduction', in Hans-Georg Gadamer, *Philosophical Hermeneutics* (Berkeley: University of California Press, 1976), xv.
119 Ibid., p. xii.
120 William J. Goode, *The Celebration of Heroes: Prestige as a Social Control System* (Berkeley: University of California Press, 1978), p. 7.
121 Ibid., p. 54.
122 Bartle Frere, 'Address to the Royal Geographical Society', *Proceedings of the Royal Geographical Society*, 18: 5 (1874), 506.
123 Ibid., p. 502.
124 *Daily News* (29 January 1874), 4.
125 'Sacerdotal Insolence', *Northern Echo* (16 April 1874), 2.
126 'Society for the Propagation of the Gospel', *Leeds Mercury* (15 April 1874), 5. At the same meeting, the Rev. J.H. McCheane disagreed with Barnett's comments, stating that 'He regarded Dr. Livingstone as one who, if he was not a priest of the Church, yet was at any rate a prophet of the living God and of our Saviour Jesus Christ.'
127 'Sacerdotal Insolence', 2.
128 'Where should Livingstone be Interred?', letter, *Glasgow Herald* (11 March 1874), 7.
129 'A Glasgow Man on his Travels', letter, *Glasgow Herald* (2 May 1874), 7.
130 Paul Ward, *Britishness since 1870* (London; New York: Routledge, 2004), p. 143.
131 Ibid., p. 3.
132 Homi K. Bhabha, *Nation and Narration* (London: Routledge, 1990), p. 3.
133 Linda Colley, *Britons: Forging the Nation, 1707–1837* (New Haven and London: Yale University Press, 1992), p. 6.
134 Ward, *Britishness*, p. 2.
135 Ibid., p. 150.
136 The range of Scottish representations of Livingstone is explored in full in Chapter 5.
137 'A Statue to Livingstone in Glasgow', letter, *Glasgow Herald* (18 April 1874), 3.
138 'Statue in Glasgow to Dr Livingstone', letter, *Glasgow Herald* (21 August 1874), 4. The writer was quoting Mr John Matheson, who presided over the meeting.

DEATH: LAMENTING LIVINGSTONE

139 Clare Pettitt, *Dr. Livingstone, I Presume? Missionaries, Journalists, Explorers, and Empire* (Cambridge, Mass.: Harvard University Press, 2007), p. 12.
140 Ibid., p. 90.
141 'Acknowledgements and Notes', *Examiner* (6 June 1874), 602.
142 Pettitt, *Dr. Livingstone, I Presume?*, p. 122.
143 Stanley, 'The Life and Labours', p. 213.
144 'Dr. Livingstone', letter, *The Times* (7 April 1874), 5.
145 Pettitt, *Dr. Livingstone, I Presume?*, p. 100.
146 Ibid., pp. 106, 116.
147 'African Exploration', *Birmingham Daily Post* (16 December 1874), 6.
148 Linge, 'Introduction', p. xvi.
149 Driver, *Geography Militant*, p. 22.
150 José Lacerda, *Portuguese African Territories: Reply to Dr. Livingstone's Accusations and Misrepresentations* (London: Edward Stanford, 1865), p. 24.
151 Clare Pettitt notes that Livingstone's story is also that of 'the emergence of a modern notion of celebrity'. His was 'a new kind of fame, and a kind that many in the establishment considered vulgar in its modernity'. See Pettitt, *Dr. Livingstone, I Presume?*, p. 36.
152 The Helmore–Price mission to the Kololo, sent out by the LMS, was established at Linyanti in 1859. The team, consisting of Holloway Helmore, Roger Price, their wives and six children, suffered from malaria and experienced poor relations with the Kololo leader, Sekeletu. Only Roger Price and two of the children would survive. The UMCA had been inspired by Livingstone during his lecture tour of Britain in 1857. This Anglo-Catholic mission sent a party to establish a station at Magomero in the Shire highlands in 1861. The mission became embroiled in local politics, and several of its members, including its leader, Bishop Charles Mackenzie, died of fever. It was soon withdrawn to Zanzibar.
153 Oliver Ransford, *David Livingstone: The Dark Interior* (London: John Murray, 1978), p. 218.
154 Quoted in William Garden Blaikie, *The Personal Life of David Livingstone* (London: John Murray, 1880), p. 295.
155 Ransford, *David Livingstone*, p. 218.
156 If Livingstone's reputation suffered damage after the Zambesi expedition, he was still widely celebrated and remained in the public eye. See John M. MacKenzie, 'David Livingstone – Prophet or Patron Saint of Imperialism in Africa: Myths and Misconceptions', in Justin D. Livingstone (ed.), 'Livingstone Studies: Bicentenary Essays', special issue, *Scottish Geographical Journal*, 129: 3–4 (2013), 282.
157 Judith Listowel, *The Other Livingstone* (New York: Charles Scribner's Sons, 1974), p. 233.
158 Henry Rowley, 'Livingstone', *Cornhill Magazine*, 29: 172 (1874), 420.
159 In another context, Felix Driver has also pointed out that 'the myth-making process was fraught with conflict'. Driver is referring specifically to the way in which Livingstone became the subject of dispute when he was 'found' by H.M. Stanley in 1871. Stanley provoked considerable antagonism by suggesting that 'Livingstone had been virtually abandoned by his official sponsors'. Waller and Kirk, among others, sought to resist his efforts to appropriate Livingstone's reputation. Since Livingstone had taken on the status of a saint, argues Driver, it is no surprise 'that the struggle to represent him was so fierce'. See Driver, *Geography Militant*, p. 131.
160 'Sir Bartle Frere on Livingstone', *The Times* (9 January 1874), p. 7.
161 *Scotsman* (21 April 1874), 4.
162 *Scotsman* (30 July 1874), 4.
163 I refer to the attitude of the Anthropological Society of London in the nineteenth century. Its views sat in opposition to those of the Ethnological Society, which rejected the more extreme forms of scientific racism. The Anthropological Society took a much more pessimistic stance on the issue of African capability.
164 Pettitt, *Dr. Livingstone, I Presume?*, p. 135.

165 Driver, *Geography Militant*, pp. 68–9.
166 Pettitt, *Dr. Livingstone, I Presume?*, p. 134.
167 As Andrew Ross explains, the term 'Johanna men' was 'how the British referred to the porters recruited on Anjoan to work in east Africa'. Livingstone had enlisted ten of these men at Zanzibar. They eventually deserted, returned to Zanzibar and, under the leadership of one called Musa, spread the false rumour that Livingstone had been killed by a group of Ngoni. See Ross, *David Livingstone*, p. 260, 205.
168 'Central Africa and Dr. Livingstone', *The Times* (27 January 1874), 5.
169 Horace Waller, 'The Fate of Dr. Livingstone', letter, *The Times* (12 February 1874), 5.
170 David Leslie, 'Is Dr. Livingstone Dead?', letter, *Glasgow Herald* (23 February 1874), 4.
171 'Dr Livingstone', *Glasgow Herald* (30 January 1874), 5. The paper was reporting a letter that Mott had sent to the *Liverpool Post*. Robert Moffat, Livingstone's father-in-law, placed similar emphasis on the need for Europeans to confirm native testimony. See 'The Reported Death of Dr. Livingstone', *Belfast News-Letter* (19 February 1874), 3. The paper was reporting a comment made in the *Sun*.
172 Fergusson, 'Examination and Verification', p. 566.
173 Dorinda Outram, 'On Being Perseus: New Knowledge, Dislocation, and Enlightenment Exploration', in D.N. Livingstone and C.W.J. Withers (eds), *Geography and Enlightenment* (Chicago: University of Chicago Press, 1999), p. 290.
174 Lieutenant Verney Lovett Cameron was heading a British search and relief party for Livingstone.
175 Clements Markham, 'The Cameron–Livingstone Search Expedition', letter, *The Times* (6 July 1874), 12.
176 The editor's remarks follow Thomas Livingstone's last letter. See T.S. Livingstone, 'The Cameron Livingstone Expedition', letter, *The Times* (10 August 1874), 12.
177 T.S. Livingstone, 'The Cameron–Livingstone Expedition', letter, *The Times* (9 July 1874), 8.
178 Cameron's father, the 'Rev. J.H. Lovett-Cameron, vicar of Shoreham, Kent', had earlier sent extracts of a letter from his son to *The Times*. See 'The Cameron–Livingstone Expedition', letter, *The Times* (6 July 1874), 12.
179 C. Lovett Cameron, 'The Cameron–Livingstone Expedition', letter, *The Times* (18 July 1874), 12.
180 T.S. Livingstone, 'The Cameron Livingstone Expedition', letter, *The Times* (10 August 1874), 12.
181 Leslie, 'Is Dr. Livingstone Dead?', p. 4.
182 Michael Heffernan, '"A Dream as Frail as Those of Ancient Time": The In-Credible Geographies of Timbuctoo', *Environment and Planning D: Society and Space*, 19 (2001), 219.
183 Fergusson, 'Examination and Verification', p. 566.
184 'The Funeral of Dr. Livingstone', *Lloyd's Weekly Newspaper* (19 April 1874), 1.
185 Similarly, the poet W.F.H. wrote: 'We own him by the lion-mark he bore, / The victor sign of many a warfare sore / Fought all alone where quest the noblest led.' See W.F.H., 'David Livingstone', p. 280.
186 Pettitt, *Dr. Livingstone, I Presume?*, p. 126. John M. MacKenzie similarly describes 'the celebrated transportation of the sun-dried body to the coast' as 'a sort of secular resurrection'. See John M. MacKenzie, 'The Iconography of the Exemplary Life: The Case of David Livingstone', in Geoffrey Cubitt and Allen Warren (eds), *Heroic Reputations and Exemplary Lives* (Manchester: Manchester University Press, 2000), p. 86.
187 Noel, *Livingstone in Africa*, p. 114.
188 See Chris Wingfield, 'Remembering David Livingstone 1873–1935: From Celebrity to Saintliness', in Sarah Worden (ed.), *David Livingstone: Man, Myth and Legacy* (Edinburgh: National Museums Scotland, 2012), p. 122. Wingfield follows Livingstone's commemoration in 'the almost continuous circulation and display

of objects' since his death. Specifically, he traces the longstanding fascination with sections of the mvula tree under which Livingstone's heart was buried. These relics, almost like 'splinters of the true cross', came to function 'as objects of spiritual contemplation'. See ibid., pp. 117, 126. He also notes that locations associated with Livingstone became transformed into 'shrines' and sites of 'pilgrimage'. As surprising as it may seem, he argues, the language and practices used to commemorate this Protestant missionary drew on older Christian traditions of saintly veneration. Wooden relics from Livingstone's 'funeral tree' were also the subject of a recent exhibition in Glasgow's Hunterian Museum (20 April–7 May 2012), curated by the Dutch artists Sybren Renema and Timmy van Zoelen. In the accompanying publication, Renema and van Zoelen offer insight into the 'sublime' aura that surrounds such 'secular relics'. See Sybren Renema and Timmy van Zoelen, *You Took the Part that Once Was My Heart* (Glasgow: Sybren Renema and Timmy van Zoelen, 2012), p. 5. As Wingfield's analysis reminds us, however, these objects were not just secular in nature, but often profoundly religious.

189 Debbie Harrison, 'A Pioneer Working on the Frontiers of Western and Tropical Medicine', in Worden (ed.), *David Livingstone*, p. 70.

190 For analysis of another heroic figure who proved able to sustain competing narratives and imaginative significances, see Dawson's study of Sir Henry Havelock: Graham Dawson, *Soldier Heroes: Empire, and the Imagining of Masculinities* (London: Routledge, 1994), pp. 105–13. While he argues for the importance of a 'unified' image of Havelock, deployed to promote national unity during the Indian Rebellion, Dawson recognises that it actually consisted of 'a complex amalgam of many different motifs and meanings'. See also Max Jones, *The Last Great Quest: Captain Scott's Antarctic Sacrifice* (Oxford: Oxford University Press, 2003), pp. 9–11.

191 V., 'David Livingstone', *Derby Mercury* (22 April 1874), 6.

CHAPTER FOUR

Empire: imperial afterlives

> For while Livingstone had his dream, while he had given his life to a cause, there were those of his own country who seemed to be doing things to crush out his high hopes and discount the best promise. Military and commercial imperialism were marching hand in hand to conquer and destroy.
> (Charles Finger, *David Livingstone: Explorer and Prophet*)

> He was like Rhodes in some ways – an imperialist.
> Michael Gelfand, *Livingstone the Doctor*

In the Livingstone biographical tradition it is almost obligatory for authors to commence their work with a prefatory disclaimer justifying their publication. As the Congregational minister Charles Silvester Horne wrote in 1912: 'At first it seemed unnecessary to re-write his life. The task has been so well fulfilled by many sympathetic biographers ... But it is so great a possession that there seemed to be room for yet another attempt to present it to those in our own century who ask for short measure and a clear, simple narrative of facts.'[1] The sheer extent of the discourse that accumulated around Livingstone in the years following his demise meant that such a rhetorical manoeuvre quickly became a prerequisite for putting pen to paper on the subject. Yet prefatory remarks like Horne's tend to beg the question, merely asserting Livingstone's biographical worthiness or the convenience of a more accessible text, without really giving satisfactory justification. The question that inevitably follows, then, is why so many texts purportedly on the same thing should continue over the years to be considered worthy of the press.

We can gesture towards an answer by arguing that, in some sense, all these lives of Livingstone were not really about the same thing at all. As I emphasised in my discussion of his Victorian commemoration, diverse horizons impinged in critical ways upon the manner in which he was constructed; the ideological embeddedness of representative practice led to significantly different posthumous incarnations of Livingstone. These biographies could so easily be churned out not least because of the divergent purposes they served. The *prima facie* similarity of subject masked the multiplicity of agendas busily at work in the texts. It has long been recognised that one enterprise for which Livingstone was routinely marshalled was the British Empire.[2] Imperial endeavours were the ever-present subtext of numerous biographies, whose authors re-presented his life, time and again, in order to have relevance to their particular colonial moment. The aim of this chapter is to interrogate the texts that were responsible for constructing Livingstone as the empire's icon, but to go beyond this very general image and consider a range of specific imperialist concerns for which these biographers employed him.

To date, the most significant examination of Livingstone's changing imperialist reputation has been offered by John M. MacKenzie. His perceptive sketch draws attention to several important phases in which the Livingstone myth was adapted to new circumstances; the earliest biographies were preoccupied with anti-slavery and geographical expansion; in the 1880s they were bound up with the politics of partition; in the early twentieth century they celebrated the course of African progress; and in the 1920s they construed Livingstone as the predecessor of trusteeship.[3] While MacKenzie's account is broadly accurate, and provides a useful touchstone for my discussion, there are several points at which I revise and extend his narrative. Firstly, in what follows I take Livingstone's imperialist legacy temporally further, into the years of imperial decline following the Second World War, and latterly into the period of 'partnership' and the Central African Federation. This chapter, moreover, introduces a degree of competition into the picture, by showing how Livingstone could be contemporaneously constructed in different ways. At the same colonial moment, different authors could envision their subject in conspicuously diverging fashions. For the most part, Livingstone was engaged for triumphalist purposes, yet at the same time he had the capacity to serve as a resource to provide some critique, however limited, of imperial transgressions. Those rare occasions in which Livingstone served an oppositional function are conspicuous enough to be considered counter-hegemonic constructions.

Given that the Livingstone biographies number in the hundreds, it is impossible to devote attention to them all. Inevitably, there will be absences. While the account below surveys numerous biographical portrayals, it is not intended to be exhaustive, and indeed is necessarily selective. In determining texts for analysis, I have pursued what might be called principles of 'direction' and 'difference'. By this I mean that the aim is to convey the general orientation of Livingstone's reputation in a given period, while also seeking those points of conflict, the diverging images at any one time. Consequently, most of the major and popular biographies find a place in my discussion. Yet lesser known works are also incorporated – including biographical sketches, articles and lectures – in order to illustrate a spectrum of representation. Surveying such a range of texts, over a considerable historical period, discloses the polyvalency of Livingstone's posthumous legacy and its political functions. In reciting familiar episodes and drawing on comparable biographical material, Livingstone's 'lives' do repeat the same story time and again, yet underwriting this plot of exterior similarity lies another story of multiplicity and difference.

The genre of empire

Before addressing the specific transformations of Livingstone's imperialist afterlife, it is worth reflecting on the biographical method with which numerous authors approached him. Livingstone certainly lived and died at a time ripe for biographical commemoration. As Juliette Atkinson has argued, while the Victorian period has been described retrospectively as 'the Age of the Novel', for contemporaries it was 'almost as strikingly the Age of Biography'.[4] Biography was an extremely popular – and respectable – literary form, published, sold and read in significant numbers. The period, moreover, as has often been argued, was notable for its inclination to hero-worship. Indeed in classic studies such as Walter Houghton's, 'hero-worship' holds pride of place among the foremost qualities of the Victorian 'frame of mind'.[5] Biographies produced during this time were, unsurprisingly, coloured by this fervent heroic culture. Some critics, finding this distasteful, have been scathing in their estimation of Victorian 'lives and letters'. Nigel Hamilton, for instance, describes them as 'pseudobiography', whose valorisation of 'reputation' and tendency to 'encomia' hindered authentic 'real life' depiction.[6] These comments are too sweeping, and others have justly pointed to the diversity of Victorian life-writing and its considerable expansion of suitable biographical subjects: as Hermione Lee observes, it was not quite as 'monolithic' and 'stolid' as it has sometimes been represented.[7] Nonetheless, for the Victorians biography did perform the function of a 'canonizing tool', and it was undeniably conspicuous for excessive reticence, discretion and veneration.[8]

It was in this climate that the earliest of Livingstone's 'lives' were written. Livingstone therefore quickly became incorporated into the genre of the 'exemplary life'. By 'exemplary life' I mean, following Geoffrey Cubitt, an existence 'valued and admired ... for the moral or ethical or social truths or values which it is perceived to embody and, through force of example, to impress on the minds of others'.[9] While Livingstone was lauded as a unique individual and historical agent, he was also upheld as a model with considerable didactic potential. The discourse of exemplarity has, of course, a venerable history that can be traced at least to Plutarch. The Victorians readily affirmed this, and it was probably this dimension of biography that they valued most highly. As Atkinson puts it, 'exemplary biography was pervasive' and its 'emulative power' was rarely questioned.[10]

The Livingstone biographical industry certainly owes its origin and subsequent pattern to this context. But other cultural developments in the closing decades of the nineteenth century were also of importance in shaping the commemorative process. These years of high imperialism witnessed the expansion of consumer markets that focused on products related to the empire. Significant in these developments and in the diffusion of imperial culture, as John MacKenzie argues, was a 'revolutionary expansion of publishing and popular readership'.[11] One result of this circumstance was a proliferation of 'hero-publishing'. These texts, designed for the growing market of juvenile and popular readers, were often shorter in length and more accessible than conventional biography. As Graham Dawson observes, discussing the memorialisation of Sir Henry Havelock, 'in their selection of episodes, reduction in the volume of detail and employment of a livelier writing style', these books produced 'punchier, more sharply pointed narratives'.[12] From the beginning, then, Livingstone would be the subject not only of lengthy biographies, of the 'life and times' ilk, but also of many shorter, heroic, exemplary lives.

Most of these exemplary texts can fairly be described as 'hagiography', in that they 'represent their subjects in an idealized manner' and 'minimize or altogether ignore their weaknesses'.[13] Certainly, the hagiographic tendency has often been observed in Victorian life-writing. In the late 1920s, Harold Nicolson would describe the biographical literature of the preceding generation in precisely these terms.[14] Likewise, current critics like Lee contend that the period's 'impulses of sympathy and veneration ... often solidified into hagiography'.[15] As Dawson concludes, while the term is normally applied to the lives of saints, it 'catches perfectly the reverential respect' of such celebratory writing.[16] It must be pointed out, however, that the hagiographic impulse is not confined to either medieval or Victorian literature. In fact, what is notable in Livingstone's case is the longevity of his heroic commemoration. While the late nineteenth-century context lay the groundwork for this form of biographical practice, authors consistently distilled Livingstone as an exemplary life and saintly hero well into the twentieth century. Since much of the material studied in the next two chapters can be cast in these terms, it is important to interrogate the logic and tropes of this literary mode. Although addressing only a few of these texts here, the following assortment serves to highlight the way in which authors more generally tended to sanitise the hero's life and project it as a seamless whole.

A good illustrative case can be found in William Garden Blaikie's substantial *Personal Life of David Livingstone* (1880), one of the major Victorian biographies, and one that follows the hagiographic pattern. In writing, Blaikie explained, his method was 'to show the unity and symmetry of [Livingstone's] character'.[17] Driven by a desire to demonstrate the essential integrity of personality and incentive, he was able to present single events in his life as a microcosm of its totality. Rehearsing a scene, later repeated in many biographies, in which a young girl fled her oppressive foster family in order to follow Livingstone, Blaikie suggested that it read:

> like an allegory or a prophecy. In the person of the little maid, oppressed and enslaved Africa comes to the good Doctor for protection; instinctively she knows she may trust him; his heart opens at once, his ingenuity contrives a way of protection and deliverance, and he will never give her up. It is a little picture of Livingstone's life.[18]

The scene served as a metonym for his life's work and purpose; Livingstone was the loving liberator, motivated by hatred of oppression, who stood as a father figure to infant Africa. This sort of trope, whereby a single event comes to signify the whole existence, is a standard device in exemplary biography. As Cubitt notes, 'the essential message to be derived from a life' often tends to be 'encapsulated in a particular dramatic moment'.[19]

The construction of the flawless subject required an authorial method that would tolerate no inconsistency of character or motive.[20] Livingstone must be shown to have, as Blaikie put it, 'such an enamel of purity upon his character that no filth could stick to it'; 'of all his legacies to Africa by far the highest was the spotless name and bright Christian character'.[21] Blaikie's biography was rigorously researched, and it remains one of the most impressive and exhaustive accounts of Livingstone's life and travels. In this respect, it embodies some of the positive dimensions of the best of Victorian biography: attention to detail, a conscientious attitude to sources and an increasing consideration of social context.[22] Yet, in its emphasis on character and its refusal of a critical perspective, it is undeniably indicative of what Nigel Hamilton calls the 'Victorian laundering process' which sought to preserve 'spotless reputations'.[23]

Well beyond the nineteenth century, the vast majority of biographies capitulated to this logic and screened Livingstone from every possible smirch. This may seem surprising, given the changes in biographical practice detectable in the early decades of the twentieth century. Sigmund Freud, for one, had mounted a considerable challenge to reticent and idealised life-writing in his controversial psychoanalytic study of Leonardo da Vinci. Furthermore, modernists such as Virginia Woolf advocated a 'new biography' which would take account of human contradiction, allow for formal experimentation and throw off the moral constraints of the previous era. 'Great men' were increasingly subject to mockery instead of veneration, following Lytton's Strachey's vigorous debunking of such a group in *Eminent Victorians*. Notwithstanding all this, David Churchill Somervell, a teacher in the illustrious Tonbridge School and a prolific historical author, persisted in a protective line of writing. He enthused, in the 1930s, that 'Livingstone's character was as sound as his physique. He was a man of an extraordinary firm, steady, wholesome temperament, a marvel of saintliness but equally a marvel of efficiency.' In these sentiments, Somervell demonstrates that despite prevailing changes in the biographical approach, conventionally heroic works continued to abound.[24] In fact, he actually showed considerable resistance to contemporary patterns of investigation, rejecting the need for psychological perspectives. 'Never was there a hero less in need of the attentions of a psycho-analyst' than David Livingstone, he argued. 'Such a man does not flatter his biographer. There are no weaknesses to probe, no secrets to explore.'[25] This forceful assertion, of course, signals Somervell's apprehension over psychological investigation and his desire to protect the integrity of the hero. Such a response was not an uncommon reaction to the uncomfortable intellectual developments of Freudian analysis and critical biography.

Those hagiographers who wanted to retain an unambiguous idol adopted certain rhetorical strategies. Somervell's tendency was merely to brush aside criticisms and disperse all hint of misconduct. So in dealing with those casting aspersions on Livingstone's role as husband and father, he gave no censure but rather dismissed them as the fault-finding grievances of 'those who dislike missionaries in general'.[26] Other hagiographers had more sophisticated tactics to counteract animadversion. James I. Macnair, the first Director of the Scottish National Memorial to David Livingstone in Blantyre, strived fairly systematically to reinterpret personality defects and unsavoury incidents in his 1940 biography.[27] While Macnair conceded, more than Somervell, that there might be some justice in the charge that Livingstone mistreated his family, he rather unconvincingly suggested that 'it is only fair to remember that in suitable places and in good weather, travel by bullock wagons was like a holiday, a substitute for a trip to the Hills or to the Coast'. Livingstone's decision to drive his children and heavily pregnant wife across the Kalahari became reduced to a mere holiday outing. Macnair passed swiftly over the question of Livingstone's responsibility for the premature death of his newborn infant and his wife's facial paralysis, focusing instead on his hero's ability to transcend such misfortune. 'Few are the men who would not have accepted this defeat as evidence that they had done enough ... Not so this man of steel. Every rebuff heightened his resolve.'[28] The Kalahari crossing became significant, not for its questionable judgement, but for its demonstration of steadfast purpose.

Macnair continued to trade in gloss and reinterpretation. Livingstone's strained relationship with the LMS, for instance, was not read as evidence of any character defect but rather as a symptom of powerful vigour. 'Obviously a man of such iron will could hardly be expected to be an easy colleague, still less a satisfactory agent ...'. Macnair further insulated Livingstone from censure by unveiling a fundamental irony that both his successes and seeming failures shared a common source in his robust character. Livingstone's ineffective leadership on the Zambesi expedition became emblematic of sturdy individualism: 'he was not a good "mixer". In this respect his very strength of character was his weakness': 'He had, in short, the defects of his high qualities.' Even his reluctance to relinquish grievances against his one-time colleagues Norman Bedingfeld and Thomas Baines was transmuted into 'a by product of that inflexible rigidity of mind that was one secret of his power'.[29] Every flaw and foible became subordinated to strength and success: under the logic of the seamless life Livingstone was permitted to defy conventional categories of judgement.

Given that Livingstone was so often shaped into a heroic and exemplary life, the task is to evaluate the effect that such hagiographic constructions might have for his legacy as an imperialist. Alan Neely has made the perceptive point that 'missionary hagiography' contains many of the key elements of the folktale: the protagonist departs from the family home and journeys to a mystical land of adventure, and a sequence of struggles and 'multiple reversals' of fortune ensues until the hero ultimately proves victorious, in either life or death.[30] It is important, however, to press this further and consider the ramifications of deploying the folktale – or, better put, the romance narrative – in order to construct a plot based on the experience of cultural encounter. Leon de Kock has addressed this in the context of missionary writing, which, he argues, often adopted the conventions of the individualistic romantic quest.³¹ The romance formula allowed Robert Moffat, for instance, to represent himself as a crusading hero, sacrificially labouring among the perishing masses. Patrick Brantlinger adopts a similar stance towards explorers' travelogues, suggesting that they are best thought of as 'nonfictional quest romances'.³² In both cases the interest lies in the deployment of a literary narrative in which, as Northrop Frye famously argued, heroes and villains exist 'to symbolize a contrast between the two worlds, one above the level of ordinary experience, the other below it.' ³³ In this 'mental landscape', notes de Kock, 'The upper world is idyllic, while the lower world, associated with exciting adventures ... is a "demonic or night world".'³⁴ Applied to a missionary or exploratory context, such romance conventions have the effect of mapping racial relations onto a Manichean dichotomy in which the white subject is elevated to a conquering champion while the indigenous are reduced to an indiscriminate mass. The valiant hero must descend into this underworld – the realm of African ignorance and superstition – with the task of shedding light. As de Kock puts it, 'the sentimental romance-version of the missionary's quest brings to prominence the individual hero's battle with evil and unreason'.³⁵ Or as Brantlinger puts it, the explorer-heroes 'struggle through enchanted, bedevilled lands', encountering 'no other characters of equal stature, only bewitched or demonic savages'.³⁶ As my earlier critical analysis of *Missionary Travels* should make clear, such a pattern does not hold in any simple way for Livingstone's own self-representation in what is a deeply ambivalent text. However, it was certainly the way in which his African experiences were represented in the hagiographical tradition. Ignoring the complex cultural encounters that appear in his own writings, many biographers plotted him in a romance narrative in which Africa was the 'dark continent' and Livingstone its 'obverse', a 'Promethean' figure and 'saintly bestower of light'.³⁷

One of the best-known biographies, Basil Mathews's 1912 *Livingstone the Pathfinder*, is among the most conspicuous to ply the romance form. From the beginning Livingstone appears as an individualistic questing figure, seeking a path into the heart of Africa (see Figs. 6 and 7).³⁸ He enters the savage domain, living 'among men who are by nature filthy-mouthed, quarrelsome, vain and violent', yet he retains his calling, remaining 'clean, strong and most powerfully peaceful, guiding his walk and that of his wild companions by a Book which is to him the Pathfinder's manual – his Bible'.³⁹ But the text most firmly situates Livingstone in the individualist romance mode by an intriguing rhetorical manoeuvre in which he is interpreted through medieval chivalric literature. Most chapters begin with epigraphs from Malory's *Le morte d'Arthur* which effectively transpose the events of travel into

6. Ernest Prater, front cover of Basil Mathews, *Livingstone the Pathfinder* (London: Oxford University Press, 1912).

7. Ernest Prater, 'Livingstone Preaching to the Makololo'.
In Basil Mathews, *Livingstone the Pathfinder* (London: Oxford University Press, 1912), p. 80

a tale of knightly virtue.⁴⁰ The sundry details of Livingstone's early life are framed by this fragment:

> Damosel, I pray you suffer me as well to assay (to pull the sword out of the sheath); though I be so poorly clothed meseemeth in my heart to speed right well. The Damosel beheld the Knight, but because of his poor clothes she thought he should be of no worship. 'Ah! Fair Damosel;' said Balin, 'worthiness and good qualities and good deeds, are not only in clothes, but manhood and worship is hid within man's person, and many a worshipful knight is not known unto all people'. Then Balin took the sword and drew it out easily.⁴¹

Livingstone was accordingly configured as a knightly figure in peasant attire. The inner worth of the hero might be disguised to the outside world because of the humble circumstances of his upbringing, but ultimately he would prove to be a true knight. Livingstone's departure from home was similarly likened to the farewell of Sir Galahad on beginning his quest: 'Then he went to his father and kissed him sweetly and said: Fair sweet father, I wot not when I shall see you more till I see the body of Jesus Christ.' Again, his famous struggle with a lion was equated with the courage of Percivale, a knight who was committed to 'Christ, the best Man in the world', and who confidently declared that 'in His service He will not suffer me to die'.⁴² Such comparisons are of significance since, as Stephanie L. Barczewski has argued, King Arthur, his knights and the grail quest have often acted as an analogue for the British imperial mission. The legend's trajectory is of course 'inherently imperial'; the concept of the Knights of the Round Table dispersing 'their ostensibly superior civilisation' to the less fortunate resonated with Britain's colonial ideal.⁴³ Certainly, from the later part of the nineteenth century, it was not uncommon for imperial heroes to be directly likened to medieval knights. As in Livingstone's case, the most frequently invoked were Percival and Galahad, 'the only members of Arthur's retinue sufficiently pure to achieve the quest for the Holy Grail'.⁴⁴ The supposed similitude of colonial servants and Arthurian heroes helped to certify the idea that imperialism was underwritten by a chivalric and moral prerogative. Thus in Mathews, the knightly Livingstone appears as one such pure and courageous embodiment of righteous imperialism.

While Mathews found numerous correspondences between Livingstone and medieval chevaliers, the quotation prefacing the chapter 'On the Slave Trail' most clearly reveals the imperial resonance of his hermeneutic of chivalry. It is a scene in which noble Sir Launcelot rescues a 'damosel' from the clutches of Sir Breuse the Pityless: 'Then when Sir Launcelot saw Sir Breuse the Pityless,

Sir Launcelot cried unto him, and said: False knight, destroyer of ladies and damosels, now thy last days be come'.[45] Since this foregrounds Livingstone's experience of the Zanzibari slave market and inland trade, the extract aims to forge an analogy in which Sir Breuse the tyrant represents slavery and the 'damosel' symbolises both Africa and Africans. In consequence, Livingstone becomes a heroic knight-errant who would vanquish the false-knight slavery and emancipate a female and defenceless continent.[46]

In surveying these panegyrics it is conspicuous that the translation of the missionary encounter into a romance narrative can easily become an act of textual domestication. Indeed, it would be difficult for romanticised hagiography to be anything other than an imperialist mode of writing in this context, since the intensity of focus on an individual missionary must, in the words of James Rohrer, 'invariably reduce the converts to background scenery'. A story that pivots around the nucleus of one dominant 'personality' runs the risk of effacing the individuality of encountered peoples. In such literature, 'The intrinsically *relational* dynamic of the missionary encounter is lost, with the indigenous host either ignored or lumped together into an amorphous collectivity.'[47] For James I. Macnair, Livingstone's life was certainly the tale of a 'dynamic personality', one 'so powerful that he could not but lead in whatever company he found himself'. Against the vigour of this 'overwhelming personality', which Macnair calls 'daemonic', Africans are reduced to part of the *mise en scène*. Indeed, it was his charismatic 'daemonic force that by a flash from his masterful eyes could subdue crowds of excited savages'.[48] In D.C. Somervell too, indigenous cooperation becomes subordinated to Livingstone's 'wonderful ascendancy over the African mind'.[49] In other words, the very genre in which Livingstone was represented itself emitted a symbolic message about its subject. Romantic hagiography, with its reliance upon a narrative schema in which personality and individual heroism loomed large, almost unavoidably transformed the ambivalent moment of encounter into a series of triumphalist victories. Of course the conventions of romance are not followed slavishly in every Livingstone biography, but its resonance can be felt wherever he is constituted unambiguously as a hero.

At this point, it is important to remember that Livingstone has not altogether avoided criticism. In fact, today it is probably more fashionable to debunk heroes than to valorise them. This sort of approach – an inversion of hagiography that can be characterised as 'pathography' – will be explored at length in the final chapter, but in Livingstone's case it is striking that a robust critical perspective took so long to appear.[50] While an author like R.J. Campbell, whose 1929 biography is discussed below, might distance himself from earlier writers like Blaikie – whose book 'inferentially represents [Livingstone] as flawlessly wise and good ... never descending from the loftiest pedestal of motive' – substantive revision would not truly emerge until around the 1970s.[51] The fact that many of the biographies were written by clergy, or sponsored by missionary societies, no doubt helped to perpetuate his heroic integrity. And given Livingstone's utility in the service of empire, moreover, it is likely that he was he was too valuable an icon to dismantle prior to decolonisation. Yet, for our discussion of romantic hagiography here, what is important is not that later authors eventually rejected the approach, but rather that such constructions continue to be produced. Even contemporary biography, as Hermione Lee observes, can involve occasional 'acts of piety'.[52] Martin Dugard's *Into Africa: The Dramatic Retelling of the Stanley–Livingstone Story* (2003), for instance, is an example of the continued penchant for celebration.[53] The text is primarily an adventure narrative and once again underwritten by romance logic. Indeed in *Into Africa* Livingstone appears in familiar garb, as a figure of heroic mettle journeying through the obstacle-ridden African terrain. Dugard traces his battle with a hostile environment until broken and 'skeletal': 'the continent in which he felt most content whittled the world's greatest explorer down to a nub'. Dugard is markedly preoccupied with Livingstone's bodily capacity, noting that his 'pain threshold was incredible and his endurance remarkable'.[54] He survived a lion attack 'with a preternatural calm' and 'set the bone and sutured the eleven puncture wounds himself, without anaesthetic'. A paradigm of fortitude, Livingstone left writings that 'were often flecked with blood or stained by drops of sweat'.[55] Such an emphasis clearly harks back to Victorian and Edwardian commemoration, in which, as Driver points out, 'Livingstone's body was integral to his reputation'. At that time, his physical frame 'was represented in the field as being in perpetual motion, warring with the elements, scarred by the battle with Africa, yet resilient to the last'.[56] In returning to such a narrative, Dugard's text inscribes the African continent as a particular kind of space. It appears, in colonial fashion, as a pestilential domain, or an underworld in which the explorer's heroism is tried and tested. In this respect, we can detect in Dugard what Derek Gregory calls 'colonial nostalgia', a version of history wistful for the imperial era, for its 'aggrandizing swagger ... its privileges and powers'.[57] In Dugard's *Into Africa*, the colonial past is romanticised and its vision of Africa is frozen in a sort of 'cultural cryonics'. Even contemporary biographies, then, if they rely on the heroic tale of man versus environment and a hagiographical romance trajectory, run the risk of repeating a colonial narrative.[58]

Imperial constructions:
Livingstone and the scramble for Africa

The hagiographical tradition dominated representations of Livingstone from the late nineteenth century to the mid-twentieth century, and indeed it has not been entirely extinguished. Such a heroic cult, as MacKenzie points out, must have required 'a mediator figure, in effect a priest who constructed, developed and interpreted the myth'.[59] In Livingstone's case there are a variety of candidates, the most notable being H.M. Stanley and Horace Waller. Clare Pettitt, for instance, has argued that 'Without Stanley and the famous meeting, we would probably not remember Livingstone.' Their encounter, which successfully 're-established Livingstone's celebrity', was 'one of the greatest newspaper stunts ever' and was made possible by the newly laid Atlantic cable which permitted rapid communication across the Anglophone world.[60] Others have suggested too that Stanley's 'eulogistic descriptions' helped to form 'the basis of the hagiography which has ever since mantled Livingstone's figure'.[61] Similarly, Horace Waller has received his fair share of critical attention. Dorothy O. Helly has explored at length his capacity in editing Livingstone's *Last Journals*, and the meticulous censorship he pursued in order to protect Livingstone's public image and confirm his saintly stature in the national imagination. Waller's governing logic was 'less the exact reproduction of the journals ... than the overall impact of the work in establishing Livingstone's reputation'.[62] Yet, while these two figures clearly played vital roles in the Livingstone legend, they have generated such substantial critical attention that it seems unnecessary to elaborate on them further here.[63] Moreover, it is possible to overemphasise the roles of these 'high priests', for even while their contributions were weighty, subsequent hagiographers would stage-manage their material differently in order to fit all the diverse motivations that could prompt the mobilisation of a valiant life.

It is precisely this issue of difference that I want to highlight here: not the important role of a select few, but rather the malleability of Livingstone's reputation for a range of imperial purposes. Beyond the implicit semiotics of genre that have occupied my attention thus far, I now want to turn to consider the way in which many biographies sought in an explicit manner to intervene in empire. In a sense, this is unsurprising, for it is well known that Livingstone made a significant impact on Britain's imperial future in Africa. His death fuelled a flurry of overseas missionary activity, which aimed to radiate the twin influences of commerce and Christianity. The remainder of this chapter, however, is less concerned with the diffuse influence he had on future imperialism than with concrete biographical constructions. By engaging with specific representations of Livingstone in some detail, it becomes clear that a new socio-political moment in empire would often result in the remobilisation of his life. Since multiple moulds of Livingstone emerge from a changing imperial framework, these circumstances immediately caution us against speaking in any singular terms of Livingstone's imperial legacy. And the story is yet more complex: even at the same moment in history, competing imperialist representations of Livingstone can be found jostling cheek by jowl with one another. Imperialism was of course no unitary phenomenon but a conflicting process subject to diverging conceptions. This complexity was mirrored in Livingstone's afterlife: competing imperialisms would result in competing portraits of the hero.

Livingstone was already being published on during his lifetime, and he even received mention in Samuel Smiles's famous collective biography, *Self-Help*. The first wave with significant imperialist purpose, however, emerged in the 1880s, during which time, as MacKenzie has argued, he was often interpreted as a harbinger of African partition.[64] To commence my study of Livingstone's changing imperial afterlife, then, attention must first be devoted to those biographies embedded in the political concerns of the scramble. While my discussion ranges across a number of texts, particular attention is given to two works by well-known figures, Harry H. Johnston and Thomas Hughes. As texts written, respectively, by the first Commissioner of British Central Africa and by the celebrated author of *Tom Brown's Schooldays*, both were widely read. And, taken together, they indicate some of the commonalities and important differences in contemporary uses of Livingstone.

Of all the regions in which Livingstone's name had colonial cachet, central Africa and particularly Nyasaland take centre stage. It was there that the missions most directly inspired by Livingstone, those of the Free Church and the Church of Scotland, had established themselves. Indeed, it was due in part to the settlements at Livingstonia and Blantyre and to the remembrance of Livingstone that Nyasaland came under the British sphere of influence and subsequently took on protectorate status. In the late 1880s the area was subject to territorial dispute between Britain and its rival Portugal, which claimed a longstanding historical presence and aspired to create a 'Rose Coloured Map' linking Mozambique and Angola through the Zambesi basin.[65] When news became known of a possible treaty with Portugal, which would concede the Shire highlands and part of the western shore of Lake Nyasa for the price of a British corridor running north to south, it was resisted with considerable public force. This was particularly the case in Scotland, where a memorial protesting the abandonment of Dr Livingstone's land was signed by over 11,000 clergy and church elders. As Brian Stanley argues, the Scottish churches pressurised Lord Salisbury's government to protect British subjects and interests in Nyasaland.[66] When Portugal sought to establish domination of the southern highlands, in a military advance led by Colonel Serpa Pinto, the British government delivered an ultimatum that instructed his forces to withdraw. While there were of course a litany of factors involved in leading Britain to so forcefully defy Portuguese claims in the Zambesi basin, historians like David Birmingham have pointed to the importance of 'the emotional heritage of Livingstone in the pious politics' of Victorian Britain.[67]

In the wake of these events, it became common for biographers to find legitimacy in Livingstone for the establishment of the protectorate. This endeavour was certainly the aim of the life sketched by Sir Harry H. Johnston in 1891. Writing his book at around the time when he accepted the appointment of Commissioner in British Central Africa, Johnston sought to present Livingstone as a forerunner to his own political work and so provide himself with a powerful precedent. In order to achieve this, he ensured that Livingstone was constituted as the conscious agent of British expansion who laid the foundation for later imperial influence. He argued that:

> In Zambezia and Nyasaland especially – in what will soon be called 'British Central Africa' – Livingstone's work is rapidly nearing the fruition he longed for under the flag he loved. Almost in the centre of this newest addition to the Queen's vast Empire, near the southern shores of Lake Bangweolo, the heart and entrails of Livingstone were buried.[68]

Livingstone was foremost a patriot, an imperial pioneer, the spiritual founder of the political formation where the new commissioner would follow in his footsteps. Johnston was not of course alone in connecting Livingstone to British Central Africa. Horace Waller had publicised the same narrative in his 1887 pamphlet *Title Deeds to Nyassa-Land*. As Helly points out, Waller drew upon both Livingstone and General Gordon in order that Britain might demonstrate its 'title deeds' to contested regions; he aimed to use Livingstone's 'legacy to undergird the structure of imperial arrangements'.[69]

In providing rationale for British influence in central Africa via Livingstone, it was necessary to put him to work in the international colonial competition with Portugal. Johnston made Livingstone the terrain on which to mount such a challenge by unfavourably contrasting the unspectacular exploratory history of the Portuguese in Africa with Livingstone's heroic achievements. What he found most conspicuous about his continental rivals was 'not what they discovered, but what they missed. They picked their way among great lakes, and saw none of them.'[70] Portuguese claims in central Africa were deemed undeserving, their explorers having merely played at the game of discovery at which Livingstone was master. In fact, his surpassing explorations were deemed to lend Britain its entitlement, despite Portugal's lengthier historical presence and what Lord Salisbury derisively called their 'archaeological arguments'.[71] Portuguese claims, argued another biographer named T. Banks Maclachlan, were grounded on 'perfunctory explorations' alleged to have taken place in previous centuries, but they had notably failed to attempt 'effective occupation'. British title, in contrast, was 'based upon the fact that a British explorer, David Livingstone to wit, had discovered Nyasaland and traversed it in all directions'.[72] Arthur Montefiore Brice, a fellow of the Royal Geographical Society, was among the most vociferously hostile to the Portuguese. 'Portugal was first on the Zambesi, that is true', he conceded, 'but Livingstone showed most conspicuously that she never utilized her position by Christianizing the natives, or in any way opening up the country.' Britain's rival was a second-rate power with 'neither men, nor money, nor commercial genius to develop one-quarter of the country she claims'.[73] In this instance of partition, Livingstone offered an arena in which Portuguese interests could be contested and those of the British secured. He provided a narrative to simply and effectively justify the imperial present.

Colonial competition with Germany, under the leadership of Otto von Bismarck, also impinged on the early Livingstone texts. Arthur Montefiore Brice praised the British East Africa Company for spreading civilisation from the east coast to Victoria Nyanza, but he warned that the Germans were 'showing the world how not to do it between Zanzibar and Unyamwezi'.[74] In Thomas Hughes's 1889 work, which Pettitt describes as one of the classic nineteenth-century Livingstone biographies, the same colonial horizon rears its head.[75] In the recent German presence in east Africa, Hughes sensed a newly present threat to Livingstone's land emerging from 'an unexpected quarter'.[76] Imperial rivalry between Britain and Germany was intensifying at this time. As D.M. Schreuder observes, Bismarck's annexation of Angra Pequena in south-west Africa in 1884 had lent urgency to the scramble for land. The new creation of a German colony had duly troubled the vision of a British South Africa from the Cape to the Zambesi. From this point, 'the nebulous fear of sudden German forward actions', particularly on the south-east coast, steadily began to mount.[77] In Hughes's biography, the immediate threat was the recently laid foundation of the German East African Protectorate. He complained that certain sections of the 'East coast, including the Rovuma and Usumbara districts', had passed to Britain's rivals. Bemoaning the inexperience and inefficiency of the protectorate's administration, he complained: 'Utterly unused to such work, without settlements or stations in the country and with no sympathy for the natives ... the German African Company have made a complete failure.' Since Bismarck himself had declared that he 'never was a man for the colonies', Hughes had 'grave apprehensions as to this African adventure'. While he urged the two nations to be 'wedded' in policy, Hughes was eminently anxious, warning his readers that it was imperative not to abandon 'Livingstone's principles and methods with the natives'.[78] He clearly deemed the retelling of Livingstone's life to be pertinent in a moment of colonial uncertainty when the future of east Africa hung in the balance.

In the period of partition, Livingstone provided his biographers with a resource to engage in colonial competition. Yet apprehensions of a different sort ran alongside intra-European rivalry. As Brice wrote, central Africa was 'under a reign of terror – the reign of the Arabs' – which had spread from Zanzibar 'like a hideous leprous blotch'. 'Now, as in the days of Livingstone, the great question' of the best way to meet this challenge remained pressing: 'How can we benefit the African and not benefit the Arab?'[79] Hughes gave voice to similar trepidations. A 'great change in the situation has occurred during the last year' in the 'scene of Livingstone's labours', which had thrown the fruits of the British mission into jeopardy. The region had been cast into a 'controversy between cross and crescent, the slave-trade and free industry'. For Hughes, the future of central Africa was held in a fine balance, uncertainly caught between warring faiths, Islam and Christianity. In his version of history, the collapse of the Congo Free State had fuelled the internal slave trade, leading to Arab dominance on the upper Congo and in the country west and south of Lake Tanganyika. This Arab 'wave' 'swept' eastwards to crash upon the stations of the Scottish churches in 1887. While this invasion down the Stevenson Road was successfully beaten back, the threat ominously remained. Furthermore, he warned, with a recent revolution in Uganda, Arabs were becoming supreme in yet another vast region.[80]

In his disquietude over Islam, Hughes was very much a child of his time. Certainly, trepidation over the Islamic presence in Nyasaland had been heightened by Lugard's reportage of the Arab–Swahili wars and the threat to the missions on Lake Malawi.[81] Yet the anxieties in Hughes, and Brice too, were on a scale larger than local. As the imperial historian Andrew N. Porter points out, Britain emerged in the nineteenth century as the single largest ruler of Muslims.[82] This became most conspicuous, argues Stewart J. Brown, after the British invaded Egypt in 1882 to protect their investments in the Suez Canal.

The addition of millions of Egyptian Muslims to the forty or so million already in India 'profoundly changed the religious nature of Britain's empire'.[83] The subsequent rebellion in the Sudan, which led to the deployment and death of the celebrated General Gordon, exacerbated the deepening unease about Muslim resurgence. Even before this, the historical stereotype of excessive Islamic cruelty had been fuelled by the infamous 'Bulgarian atrocities', in which thousands of Orthodox Christians rebelling against the Ottoman Empire had been brutally slaughtered. Hughes's sense of competing faiths, pitched in a battle for Africa, thus corresponded to the broader contemporary dread of so-called 'pan-Islamic fanaticism'.[84] His biography of Livingstone was an effort to marshal his legacy against a rising tide of Muslims; it was an intervention in a spiritual battle that he felt was being performed on the world stage.

From this survey, we can establish that Livingstone was mapped onto a range of issues facing British imperialism in Africa. His various biographers used his clout against Portuguese and German colonial aspirations and to lend voice to increasing concerns over Islam; there were no doubt other affairs too which Livingstone's powerful iconic status was mobilised to serve. Lessons were sought in Livingstone as colonial issues arose, but these readily became redundant as developments took their course. As MacKenzie puts it, the fast-changing nature of the African scene 'ensured that each biography had a tendency to obsolescence'.[85] Yet what is of particular interest in the early biographies is not merely that Livingstone served a range of imperial purposes, but that he actually served a range of different imperialisms. The imperialism that Harry Johnston cultivated in his life of Livingstone, for instance, was rather different from the *modus operandi* of the missionaries at Blantyre. And it was certainly different too from the exemplary colonial character that Livingstone was called on to represent by the Christian socialist Thomas Hughes.

Harry H. Johnston was an imperialist of the more militant caste. Roland Oliver suggests that, in the period of partition, he 'emerges, if not as a titan, at least as a ubiquitous and always significant personality'. From any early stage, he was 'one of the very small company of people who were thinking of the coming partition of Africa on a continental scale'.[86] In the 1880s, he had been at the centre of a failed attempt to colonise Kilimanjaro, and later, when appointed to the double vice-consulship of the Oil Rivers District and the Cameroons, he had engaged in a prolonged and hostile dispute with an African merchant operating on the Niger coast. In both contexts Johnston proved his militaristic bent. His imperialism was always expansionist, 'intellectual and opportunist, not congenital or romantic'. Sir Harry was also an obsessive colonial strategist. During his spell as Consul in Mozambique in the late 1880s, he had busily involved himself in securing conditional treaties in order to help define the British sphere of influence. There is even evidence to suggest that his was the mind behind the infamous 'Cape to Cairo' scheme more commonly associated with Cecil Rhodes.[87]

When it came to writing a life of Livingstone, Johnston ensured that his subject buttressed his own brand of imperialism. These mechanics of representation are first conspicuous in the way he constituted the dynamic between Livingstone and his indigenous auxiliaries. Johnston's stratagem was to magnify the moments in which the man so often advertised as the exemplary racial liberal adopted a heavy hand. He recounted how Livingstone once threatened his men, reminding them in no uncertain terms that 'they must remember that I was master and not they'. To Johnston this proved that 'Livingstone was no fool. No one had a greater sympathy or a more indulgent regard for the black people than he, and even he knew that they are only grown-up children, that ... as a last resort force must be used to compel them to do as they are told.' Johnston set about reclaiming Livingstone from the liberal camp, remoulding his subject in a more supremacist mode so as to extrapolate on his ideal form of inter-ethnic interaction. 'Livingstone never forgot that we stand to the negro *in loco parentis*', he argued. Developing this parental metaphor, he told his reader to remember that 'when verbal persuasion is of no use and the naughty child absolutely refuses to obey, then even the kindest of fathers is compelled to resort to a gentle smacking'.[88] Through Livingstone, Johnston projected a normative paternalism that was not prepared to spare the rod. His subject provided him with a didactic resource through which he could advocate his own racial convictions.

Underlying Johnston's attitude was the scientific racism that emerged out of the extremist anthropology of the middle decades of the nineteenth century. As Edward Beasley points out, it was at this time that the idea of 'race' as biological and heritable, carrying indelible characteristics, began to become established.[89] Johnston's was a worldview in which the various human races occupied different levels on the evolutionary trajectory, and he made this clear by commencing his biography with a lengthy ethno-scientific preamble on the history of racial development. In humanity's original 'Asiatic home', he wrote, 'there soon sprang up two distinct variations from the primal stock – the men with short, curly hair, and the men with long, coarse, straight hair'. The latter of these 'in long ages differentiated into the red American, the yellow Mongol, and the white European'. In the former group, however, lay the origins of the 'Negritic stock', which could be subdivided into 'three leading types – the ascending Hamite and Semite, and the somewhat retrograding Negroes and Hottentot Bushmen'. While the 'Hamite' and 'Semite' might have had the potential to progress, those others, who had occupied the bulk of Africa, either 'remained stationary' or 'retrogressed'.[90] The diverging evolutionary pathways that Johnston was at pains to trace resulted not just in racial difference, but in a rigidly hierarchical ethnic map.

In pursuit of his ideal imperial image, Johnston also purged Livingstone of some of the dross that surrounded him. As an avowed atheist, Johnston faced the difficulty of celebrating a hero who had close associations with the evangelical movement. So he set out to secularise Livingstone, to distance him from religious conservatism and indeed to reduce his religious impulses to his social and historical moment. One could see, wrote Johnston, that Livingstone was 'not naturally disposed to concern himself much with supra-mundane questions'. However, 'the desire to feel as those around him felt, or affected to feel, and the real, earnest goodness in the lad, which regretted that it could not find orthodox expression in conformity with the sectarian bigotry of his parents, pastors, and masters' led him 'through the stereotyped course of religious development'. Approaching religious belief as a social phenomenon, with a strictly mundane explanation, Johnston could be scathing. As though possessing an Archimedean vantage point, he made the unsubstantiated claim that Livingstone '*imagined*, after an intervening period of callousness, that he had attained "grace"' (emphasis added). Really it was all a product of environment, 'a faint, unconscious simulation of the religious hysteria of those around him'.[91]

Having debunked the foundation of Livingstone's conviction, Johnston routinely sought to distance him from the faintest aroma of religious zealotry. Livingstone's self-reflexive dialogue with the rain doctor thus served to show a 'kindly tolerance rare in those days amongst the usually bigoted missionaries'. His writing too was utterly free from the 'falsification of reports which is so striking a blemish in the publications of most Christian missionary societies'.[92] Yet all this is not to say that Johnston saw no value in missionaries. In fact, Roland Oliver argues that while Johnston was the 'most self-advertised of unbelievers' he was an 'unqualified advocate of Christian missions'.[93] He supported them, however, in a sense that firmly domesticated them to the purposes of empire. They were useful first and foremost as civilising agents. As he argued in the *Nineteenth Century*, by living with European standards among Africans, missionaries might 'open the eyes of the brutish savages, to the existence of a higher state of culture, and prepare them for the approach of civilisation'. They played an important role as 'mediator between the barbarian native and the invading race of rulers'.[94] Missionaries were the frontmen of empire, forerunners of the colonial presence, valuable as cultural rather than as religious agents. In fact, Johnston would have preferred missions to give up on preaching, but he felt that they should be permitted to 'dogmatise without let or hindrance, on account of the education and civilisation which they laterally introduce'.[95] For Johnston, an ideal missionary would be one without the Christianity. Sermonising, while fruitless in itself, was to be tolerated in the name of civilisation, that convenient by-product of the Christianising impulse. While Johnston was drawn to Livingstone, a missionary, it was clearly not his spiritual credentials that attracted him. In distancing him from religiosity he created an icon that an atheist could support, a secular figurehead for his brand of imperialism.

This controversial version of Livingstone, largely stripped of religious trappings, would be rejected by many later biographers. And it departed significantly too from the model in whose name the Scottish churches established their missions. These same missionaries, however, as I observed earlier, had been crucial in winning Nyasaland to the British Empire in the first place. Nevertheless, as Brian Stanley points out, even though they had fulfilled their objective of thwarting the Portuguese, the missionary perspective was quite divided on the British South Africa Company, which had won a government charter to promote its concerns in the region. The relationship between Johnston, the company-appointed commissioner, and the missionaries was not always smooth. While the Free Church agents were for the most part positive, those of the Church of Scotland mission tended to be much harsher critics. According to Stanley, David Clement Scott, the leader at Blantyre, was antipathetic to the commissioner, whom he saw as a representative of the unsavoury aspects of Western civilisation and who seemed intent on destroying African political powers. It was Scott's hope that full protectorate status, 'founded on respect for indigenous authority', would replace the heavy-handed company rule.[96]

Yet of course, like Johnston, the Blantyre mission equally claimed to be Livingstone's legatee. And so a pair of rivals, Johnston and Scott, both claimed to be continuing Livingstone's work. In 1901, when asked to give a lecture on the history of Blantyre, Scott adopted the symbolic title '"Living-Stones": Sermon upon the Church of Scotland Blantyre Mission, British Central Africa'. The motif that governed the essay was taken from 1 Peter, where Christ is described as the 'capstone' and the 'living Stone' of the Church. The individuals making up the unity of the Church too are 'living stones', 'being built into a spiritual house' (1 Peter 2.4–7). The sermon thus naturally concerned itself with the heroic personages who lay behind Blantyre's foundation. The foremost of these was of course David Livingstone, and the pun was certainly intended: 'I dare the play upon words', wrote Scott.[97] In his spiritual history of Blantyre, the work of Christ – the 'Living Stone' – was begun by David 'Livingstone' and continued by other 'living stones'.

In this sermon, David Clement Scott did not directly criticise Harry Johnston, although he certainly did so elsewhere. And strange as it might seem, for one so opposed to the colonial authority, the pamphlet explicitly endorses empire. The point, however, is that imperialism was no unitary phenomenon. As David Lambert and Alan Lester observe, a body of 'new' imperial history has developed this idea, urging attention to the 'multiple, and often contestatory "projects" of colonialism' that co-existed uneasily.[98] The conflict between Scott and Johnston was a clash between diverging logics of empire, and each claimed Livingstone in the name of his own version.

Much of Scott's sermon addressed the Old Testament prophecy that Ham, the son of Noah, was destined for a life of service. He rejected some of the racial interpretations that have historically surrounded this 'curse of Ham' text and argued that the African was no more fitted for the role of servant than any other ethnic group. Scott did observe that in ways Africa was indeed a continent 'girded for service'. In doing so, however, he aimed to subvert a conventional conception of service: 'But it is the servant who *possesses* the beautiful land, served by the hierarchy of the Powers; and our Church Diaconate is a *golden sunny Kaffirdom*, served by the hierarchy of apostles, prophets, evangelists, pastors, and teachers.' Here, in keeping with the Christian ethic, the servants became the served. The 'hierarchy of government and hierarchy of Church power, serves the Kaffir diaconate', Scott argued. This, he wrote, was his 'plea for an inspired Imperialism'.[99] Scott's imperialism, while firmly paternalistic, was inflected with humanitarian ideals and departed significantly from Johnston's harsh politics of power.

For all that, Clement Scott continued to maintain a rather triumphalist interpretation of the British presence. Despite his problems with Johnston and colonial abuses, he was able to say that 'We came in the nick or notch of time – *i.e.*, in God's time – to help and to save' Africa from Arab abuses. It was up to Britain to lead the 'CO-IMPERIALISM OF EUROPE' in its 'march' toward 'the throne of God!'[100] The British Empire here became the agent of God's will and the world's Christianisation. In contrast to Johnston's secular scientific basis for superiority, Scott presented an imperialism based on a notion of providential purpose. And of course Livingstone, 'the Le Verrier who brought [Africa] to light', remained its patron saint.[101] Stewart J. Brown has recently pointed out the importance and persistence of the relationship between the empire and ideas of providence. In the nineteenth and early twentieth centuries, much of British religious life was infused with a 'vital religion' that had the power to inspire believers with a sense of divine purpose.[102] Many became convinced that the United Kingdom and its empire were God's chosen instruments to spread his Kingdom purposes. It is thus to be expected that a significant number of hagiographies would reflect this theology, portraying Livingstone as God's ordained agent forerunning his empire in Africa.

It was in these terms that Thomas Hughes sketched his biography. Norman Vance observes, in his analysis of 'Christian manliness', that Hughes had derived a divine interpretation of history from Thomas Carlyle and Thomas Arnold.[103] Certainly, to Hughes, Livingstone and Britain were the tools with which God had been shaping the African continent. He devoted the final chapter of his biography to exploring 'the fruit' that Livingstone's 'grain of martyr-wheat has borne in the last sixteen years'. The 'devotion and energy' of Britain's response to his African labours moved Hughes to pronounce that 'it stands on the face of recent history that this burthen is one which in God's providence we have to bear'. The legacy bequeathed by Livingstone's death became a divinely ordained responsibility. That 'noble band of Englishmen', who so faithfully continued to tread his path in east Africa, should recognise their work as the 'present duty which God who has called them to this mighty and beneficent task now requires of them'.[104]

Hughes's understanding of empire was clearly built on different foundations from Johnston's. And this difference is most conspicuous in the nature of the imperial character that he fashioned in Livingstone. In his personality and disposition, Hughes shaped Livingstone to embody the ethos that he felt should underlie the praxis of empire. Out of his text emerged a muscular Christian, bearing the mixed bag of qualities that would prove a good fit 'to the needs of colonial administration'.[105] It was this character, with its amalgam of chivalry and service, physical and moral manliness, that Hughes had already cultivated in his bestselling *Tom Brown* novels. As Jeffrey Richards argues, the 'fighting spirit, clannishness, quixotic temper and optimism' of its protagonist were 'exactly the qualities needed to run an empire. All this struck the right chords later in the century when imperialism had become the dominant ideology.'[105]

Much of Livingstone's appeal as an imperial paragon obviously resided in his rude strength. Hughes relished his hero's robust sturdiness, quoting with obvious pleasure Livingstone's encomium on the rugged life: 'The mere animal pleasure of travelling in a wild unexplored country is very great … the muscles grow as hard as boards.'

Livingstone proved resilient through illness and hardship: 'no suffering is allowed to interfere with discipline'.[107] In selecting material for his biography, Hughes focused in on those episodes that most conspicuously paraded Livingstone's implacable courage. Borrowing from H.M. Stanley's report of his time with the famous explorer, Hughes recounted a confrontation of 'considerable animus', in which 'a naked young man ... storming away like a madman' provoked the American journalist to reach for his trusty Winchester. Livingstone, who arrived in the nick of time, was cool by contrast and merely 'asked calmly what was the matter' before diffusing the tension. Hughes heightened his dauntless spirit by comparing the divergent reports of the encounter as they emerged from the respective pens of Stanley and Livingstone. While the former granted it considerable textual space, the latter quickly skimmed over it in his journal: 'Some men were drunk and troublesome', he wrote, with both a humility and a confidence born from experience.[108]

Norman Vance, however, reminds us that Christian manliness was not concerned with brute muscularity alone, but also with moral manhood. As he points out, *Tom Brown's School Days* tells a tale of maturation, a progression beyond the primitive yet wholesome manliness of pluck into a more specifically Christian ethic.[109] Livingstone's early life was similarly one of boyish toughness, and it served as a promissory note for the later fruition of true Christian manliness. From the beginning he was 'a boy of remarkable powers, physical and intellectual'. While he was certainly studious, 'It must not be inferred,' Hughes assured his readers, 'that Davie was a mere precocious bookworm ... On the contrary, he delighted in rough play.' But just as Tom Brown evolved beyond his youthful roughness and learnt the power of gentle goodness, so did Livingstone. Hughes unashamedly divulged his hero's manly emotion when he heard of the withdrawal of the UMCA from the African interior: although he 'could hardly write of it' and 'felt more inclined to sit down and cry' his tears suggested no womanish weakness but spoke volumes about stalwart commitment.[110]

In formulating Christian manliness, a major concern of Hughes was the proper exercise of manly strength. As Vance writes, he believed 'that chivalry and service are required of the strong man, "the protection of the weak, the advancement of all righteous causes ..."'. In fact, in Hughes's book *The Manliness of Christ*, it was Jesus' self-sacrifice and moral courage that most fully demonstrated his true masculinity. Likewise, Livingstone's manliness found its truest expression in his sacrificial journeys and ultimate martyrdom. His masculinity, once Christianised, was directed to the greater good. Physicality, then, was necessary but not sufficient for true manfulness. As Vance succinctly writes, 'Sturdy manliness leads on to and in a sense becomes a metaphor for unflinching moral resolution.'[111]

In all this, Livingstone was invested with the combination of fortitude and faith, physical prowess and moral resolution, that seemed to Hughes the best foundation for colonial service. And in pursuing the manly Christian temperament Hughes ended up, as Mary Angela Schwer puts it, 'interpret[ing] the missionary-explorer as though he were a public-school product'.[112] Even though Livingstone did not share this background of privilege, Hughes took pains to trace in him the flourishing of essentially the same character. As Jeffrey Richards has argued, the wider colonial milieu certainly made its presence felt throughout the pages of *Tom Brown*. At the very end of the text, when the youthful Harry East departs to serve in an Indian regiment, the schoolmaster tells Tom: 'Perhaps ours is the only little corner of the British Empire which is thoroughly, wisely and strongly ruled just now.'[113] To some degree, then, Christian manliness and the relationships between teachers, prefects and fags are cast as a paradigm for imperial leadership. It is this paradigm that Hughes's Livingstone is seen to enact with his indigenous carriers. As Schwer argues, he appears ever the master of the situation among rowdy African 'schoolboys', able to tame their energy because he has matured well beyond them.[114] Livingstone transmitted the same order of colonial relations to Stanley, who 'above all ... received and mastered a noble lesson in the treatment of the natives'. Indeed, the two men were in something of a prefect–fag relationship themselves, the younger gaining 'that most precious of all experiences ... intimate contact with a thoroughly noble and pious life'.[115]

The character that Hughes established was pounced upon by a subsequent generation of empire-builders. But the nuances of his Christian manliness were blunted by this later jingoistic cult; increasingly, the 'pronounced religious element' was 'downgraded in favour of the games-playing' ethic.[115] Some aspects of the character that Hughes strived to form proved more useful than others to the cult of imperialism. His own ethos of empire, however, to be distinguished from its later appropriation, had as its ideal figurehead one in whom might and morality were wed.

By casting an eye across a range of biographical representations, and by focusing in detail on a few, it has become clear that in the period of high imperialism Livingstone was routinely mobilised for his relevance to contemporary problematics – including colonial competition with Portugal and Germany, and concerns about the rise of Islam. At the same time, he was also used to underwrite diverging imperial logics. For Harry H. Johnston, Livingstone proved useful to support a discourse of mastery, based on a racialist ethno-science, while for David Clement Scott and Thomas Hughes, he seemed a paternalistic servant of the providential empire. Livingstone found himself secularised and spiritualised in order to meet the needs of the hagiographer: in fact he was himself a colonised space, a site of competing representations.

Livingstone and the Edwardian empire

In ways, the Edwardian biographies of Livingstone perpetuated the pattern of colonial implementation established by the Victorians. Imperial contest remained patent, and he continued to be mobilised in defence of British interests against those of the nation's rivals. John Marshall Pryde, winner of an essay prize at the University of Glasgow, followed earlier authors in disparaging Portugal in his 1902 pamphlet *Livingstone and the Slave Trade*. While Portuguese explorers had visited central Africa before Livingstone, all 'they *saw* was merely a country with lakes, and rivers, hills and valleys'. In contrast, 'What Livingstone *discovered* was a land as productive as any, with admirable water-ways, with rich gold veins.'[117] Likewise, a 1904 biography by Edward Hume confidently asserted that Livingstone would have been relieved that so vast a region of central Africa 'would fall under the control, not of Portugal or Germany, but of his own countrymen'.[118] As this implies, the narrative connecting Livingstone to the formal empire in British Central Africa still circulated in the early twentieth century. Pryde, for instance, suggested that he had 'formed the germ of the magnificent British Protectorate of Central Africa', while J. W. Gregory, a professor of geology at Glasgow, insisted in 1913 that the Zambesi expedition 'led to the foundation of the British Protectorate of Nyasaland'.[119] As in Victorian biography, then, Livingstone continued to be represented as the herald of the African scramble who had ushered in a new colonial era. Britain had been politically faithful to his legacy 'in the sharp struggle of the eighties', argued Hume, by taking 'vast tracts of country within her protection and sphere of influence'. Or as Gregory rather grandly put it, 'The revolution in the condition of Africa was mainly due to the great Scottish explorer.'[120]

Despite such continuities, the Edwardian biographies do manifest a shift in tone. John M. MacKenzie touches on this when he argues that the early twentieth-century 'lives' were preoccupied with the 'balance sheet of empire', itemising the colonial achievements that had followed in Livingstone's wake.[121] These works tracked the successes of modernisation in Africa and the progressive transformation of the continent. Indeed, I would suggest that, in the aftermath of partition, they lacked the urgency evident in earlier texts and instead manifested – at least on the face of things – a more celebratory quality. A biography published by the LMS in 1908, authored by William A. Elliott, is indicative of this trend. Setting up triumphal oppositions between past and present, Elliott wrote, 'In 1841 there were no missions to Central Africa, no Christians there! To-day there are over 60,000 native church members, with 2,000 church and school buildings.' The region, moreover, had experienced commercial as well as religious revolution. While 'In 1873 there was practically no legitimate commerce' in North-Western and North-Eastern Rhodesia, impressive trading profits in 1906 could be considered 'The first-fruits of Livingstone's sowing'.[122] The same exultant parade of the benefits of imperial intervention is also evident in Hume. 'Nearly half a century has passed, and time has proved the justness of Livingstone's contentions', he reflected. 'Missionary stations have been established and have flourished. Commerce has developed to an extent which even he hardly anticipated.' Under 'Pax Britannica', he mused, the 'Old Order' would 'give place to the New'.[123]

If the Victorian biographies sought, broadly speaking, to galvanise imperial intervention, the Edwardian biographies were more reflective in character. Nevertheless these texts were as intimately bound to the present as their predecessors were. To appreciate this, it is important to recognise that the first decade of the twentieth century is generally considered to have been a time of colonial anxiety.[124] The closing decades of the 1800s had been the heyday of British imperialism, but as the new century dawned the empire was no longer expanding and confidence began to falter. As Bernard Porter puts it, a 'new imperial mood' was palpable. As Germany and the United States became more prominent on the world stage, Britain's position seemed increasingly vulnerable. The Boer War, moreover, fought between 1899 and 1902, had been a deeply troubling experience.[125] While Britain was ultimately victorious, its poor performance against a much smaller and weaker opponent revealed the nation's military insufficiency and the inadequacy of its soldiers. The condition of the troops also raised questions concerning the 'physical deterioration' of the populace and fuelled prognostications of national decline. Social challenges, such as the women's suffrage movement, coalesced with concerns over the 'decadence' of the elite classes into fears about the degeneration of the imperial centre. As Max Jones argues, in the run-up to the First World War an 'array of Victorian shibboleths' were called into question and discussions about 'the health of the nation' gained momentum.[126]

The Edwardian Livingstone biographies can be read in the light of this unease. In the midst of proliferating concern over national security and vitality, the recitation of imperial successes was undoubtedly comforting. Citing post-Livingstone imperial achievements, as these biographies constantly did, served an ameliorative function by reminding readers that theirs was still an empire of progress and activity. The most conspicuous issue to emerge in these texts, however, in response to Edwardian concerns, was that of imperial masculinity. To a considerable degree, the complaint over national degeneracy articulated a crisis in British manhood and virility. As Graham Dawson puts it, official fears about the decay of the imperial race 'became focused on the condition of the manly body ... as its most visible sign'.[127] Livingstone had of course long served as an icon of exemplary masculinity, as can be seen in Thomas Hughes's distinctively muscular Christian construction. Thus, retelling Livingstone's story in the Edwardian period served to rearticulate a vision of robust manhood. Jones, discussing the Antarctic travels of Robert Falcon Scott, notes how tales of exploration in the early twentieth century provided a 'hymn of traditional manliness', 'a reassuring example of heroic character' that could assuage fears of decline. Those concerned by the state of British manhood valorised just this sort of masculinity, a version composed of 'virility, courage, endurance, hardihood, and duty' and defined against 'the effete, the flaccid, the luxurious, the materialistic, the nerve-ridden'.[128]

The Livingstone story inherited from the Victorians fitted this discourse well. However, since the Edwardian antidote to the masculine crisis involved a new attention to 'physical hardship', his biographers increasingly stressed his bodily capacity and endurance.[129] Arthur Lincoln, for instance, writing in 1907, contended that Livingstone's years of 'hard labour' had been a 'Spartan training' of 'inestimable value'. This had the effect of 'inuring his body to hardship and privation', thereby enabling him to endure 'those long, toilsome marches'.[130] This sort of construction is at its clearest in Basil Mathews's 1913 *Livingstone the Pathfinder*, examined earlier for its use of the romance structure. In Mathews's biography, Livingstone is pictured 'in ceaseless trudging' through countless 'miles of blistering plain and tangled forest'. Nothing, 'whether beast, savage men, marsh, fever, or the yearning for home', was able to deter him (see Fig. 8).[131] As Felix Driver observes, Mathews represents Livingstone's 'body as a tool of conquest' and in so doing reflects the Edwardian enthusiasm for 'physical fitness'.[132] Bearing this in mind, it is significant that Mathews repeatedly describes Livingstone as a 'scout'. He refers to 'the old scouting walks on the Scottish hills' that prepared the explorer for African travel, and assures his readers that 'The heart of the scout and pathfinder was as lively in Livingstone' as an older man as it was when he was a boy: nothing could stop this 'hero-scout'.[133] When Mathews was writing, Robert Baden-Powell's Boy Scout movement was in its infancy, having been in existence for only five years: it was, however,

8. Ernest Prater, 'A Large Spear Grazed Livingstone's Back'. In Basil Mathews, *Livingstone the Pathfinder* (London: Oxford University Press, 1912), p. 178

already international and astonishingly popular. The Scouts were in some ways a distinctly Edwardian phenomenon, since they had partly been established in response to worries about the 'deteriorating health' of Britain's youth.[134] As Elleke Boehmer argues, the early success of the movement – and of Baden-Powell's *Scouting for Boys* – lay in its ability to 'respond powerfully to British national anxieties' in a 'period of wavering imperial self-confidence'. At a time when the 'failing strength of the nation was mirrored in the alleged deterioration of the male physique' the Scouts' prescription of 'physical training' for moral improvement had considerable appeal.[135]

In connecting Livingstone to the scouting movement, Mathews sought to use him as part of the remedy for the crisis in British imperial masculinity. He held up his subject as a paragon of the manly physical and moral virtues felt to be desirable in British youth, and which his young readers might emulate. In fact the title of his book, *Livingstone the Pathfinder*, is borrowed from scouting discourse. In *Scouting for Boys*, Baden-Powell devoted attention to the character of the 'Pathfinder', a term of 'great honour' used by 'the Red Indian scouts' to describe 'the man who was good at finding his way in a strange country'. He encouraged his British Boy Scouts to develop such an 'eye for the country' and included a section in his book entitled 'Games in Pathfinding' to help hone these skills.[136] Other authors, alongside Mathews, likewise portrayed Livingstone in scouting terms. For instance, a 1913 centenary article in *The Boys' Own Paper*, while primarily celebrating Livingstone's missionary efforts, nonetheless reminded its readers that he 'ranks high in the list of explorers and *path-finders*' (my emphasis).[137] William A. Elliott similarly described Livingstone as 'an advance scout' of the missionary movement, 'a missionary-scout feeling his way into the heart of the enemy's country'.[138] In fact, Baden-Powell had himself included Livingstone in *Scouting for Boys* as evidence of how important it was to 'know something about doctoring'. Livingstone was one of the great 'peace scouts', who put all the military-style skills of scouting into practice in a situation of non-conflict.[139] By capitalising on this connection, the authors who portrayed Livingstone as a scout aimed their book at boy readers. They directed these youths – the imperialists of tomorrow – towards an exemplar of the kind of masculinity that was felt to be needed to stall decline and to reinvigorate the empire.

Even biographers who were not imperial enthusiasts saw in Livingstone a productive version of manhood. Charles Silvester Horne, a nonconformist minister, sometime Chairman of the Congregational Union of England and Wales and in 1913–14 the National President of the Brotherhood Movement, was one of those liberals who considered himself opposed to imperialism.[140] To understand such an attitude, as Clyde Binfield points out, it is important to recognise that a distinction was drawn between imperialism and the empire, with the former rather than the latter being deemed problematic.[141] Indeed despite his hesitancies over imperialism, Horne considered Livingstone – one of the empire's great heroes – to possess the resources necessary to meet the future. As he put it in the preface of his 1912 biography, 'whatever our views on African problems may be, we may all agree that her white population may well pray for a double portion of his spirit'.[142] Throughout the book Horne devoted considerable attention to the qualities that made Livingstone great, even concluding with a didactic chapter entitled 'Characteristics', designed to reinforce a clear impression of 'the personality of the man'. Much of the biography focused on his Christian character, and Horne quoted numerous passages from Livingstone's journals that gave voice to his religious convictions. But what is particularly notable is the considerable emphasis on Livingstone's persistence in the face of suffering. '[E]ven in the hour of despair', wrote Horne, 'he searches for some support for optimism.'[143] While 'almost beaten' in the battle with the slave trade he was never fully vanquished: 'almost, but never quite'. It was 'the great leader's fortitude' that was among his most striking qualities.[144] As Jones argues, 'self-control' was at 'the core of the Edwardian heroic ideal', and there was fairly wide acceptance that 'adversity offered the truest test of character'.[145] In parading Livingstone's resilience in the face of extraordinary hardship, Horne clearly worked to construe him as an exemplar of that particular value system.

Against a backdrop of decline, Horne's Livingstone stood as a beacon of heroism and selflessness, and one that clearly had didactic value for the present. In his concluding chapter on 'Characteristics', Horne presented Livingstone as an alternative to the prevailing contemporary moral character. The Edwardian preoccupation with physical hardiness is present to an extent: readers are reminded that Livingstone had a 'strong, rugged face', 'the broad chest and shoulders of a man specially built to endure exceptional fatigue'.[146] But what is more striking is that when concerns about moral 'degeneracy' were at high pitch, Horne should choose to foreground 'Livingstone's Puritan soul'; Livingstone had, he argued, 'a Puritan disposition towards restraint and reserve'. Even his language was 'plain and truthful', for he 'hated the vulgarity of useless or tawdry rhetoric', opting instead for 'the refinement of simplicity'.[147] Horne illustrated Livingstone's difference to contemporary mores by relating an anecdote about his behaviour in high society. When one 'society lady' was apparently 'injudicious enough to indulge in some very highly coloured compliments of his achievements', Livingstone retreated to a darkened room because 'he could not endure to be praised to his face'. For Horne, such an action displayed the 'humility and sincerity of his Christian faith and character' and demonstrated that 'He was the least vain and most unspoiled of any man who was ever lionised.'[148] If we recall that the run-up to the First World War was, as Bernard Porter puts it, notable for its inordinate 'talk of national decadence', this version of Livingstone takes on added significance.[149] Horne's biography presents us with a character who could not have been further from the decadence and degeneracy supposedly at large. In a context where concerns about the state of masculinity and the imperial and social health of the nation abounded, Livingstone provided Horne with a positive moral paradigm and a means to counteract anxieties.

In the first decade and a half of the twentieth century, the Livingstone biographical industry did not slacken. Events such as the Boer War at the start of the period, and the World Missionary Conference (1910) and the centenary of Livingstone's birth (1913) at the end, undoubtedly helped to fuel interest. The texts that appeared in these years continued to promote aspects of the Victorian narrative, by using him in colonial competition and by grounding the British Central African Protectorate – and the project of partition more broadly – in his legacy. Nonetheless, they also bear the distinctive imprint of their specific context. While earlier texts were more intimately involved in the machinations of the scramble, the Edwardian biographies tended to celebrate the course of events in Africa since Livingstone. On the one hand, then, they were retrospective in quality, yet on the other they simultaneously looked forward to the future modernisation of the continent. At a time when imperial confidence was not at its zenith, these texts worked to project an empire of purpose and direction. Indeed, it is the climate of imperial anxiety that lends the Edwardian biographies their particular character. While questions about the health of the empire and nation were being connected to issues surrounding British masculinity, Livingstone was used to provide a model of manliness. The way in which authors did this was not necessarily uniform; Basil Mathews's pathfinding 'scout' and Charles Silvester Horne's 'Puritan soul' are quite different constructions. Yet in their contrasting ways they both employed their subject as an exemplar of the kind of manliness felt to be apposite in the midst of decline.

Livingstone and trusteeship

If the Livingstone mythology continued unabated in the early decades of the twentieth century, it also managed to withstand the First World War. In some ways this might seem surprising, given that it has often been argued 'that nineteenth-century ideals of duty, honour, and sacrifice were buried with the corpses of the Western Front'.[150] Livingstone, however, was perhaps sufficiently a hero of peace to remain relatively insulated from post-war disillusionment. It has been suggested that while the unprecedented suffering of the conflict problematised military icons, explorers like Scott and Livingstone were able to offer a palatable 'epic of heroism for a generation tired of war'.[151] Some biographers like R.B. Dawson, however, did try to directly connect Livingstone with the recent conflict, and he advertised his 1918 biography on the grounds that it was the first to be written since the First World War. While he did not explicitly militarise Livingstone, Dawson did try to convince his readers that both he and the Entente powers shared as their 'great Cause' the same 'fight for justice and liberty at whatever cost' (see Fig. 9).[152]

Such a pattern of interpretation was undoubtedly rare. Nevertheless, the First World War made an impact on Livingstone's reputation in other ways. As the empire altered in its aftermath and as imperialism was subjected to re-theorisation, Livingstone was re-packaged for the new socio-political climate. Following the war the idea of 'trusteeship' became increasingly prominent in international discourse, thanks to the mandate system established by the League of Nations. The

9. Front cover of R.B. Dawson, *Livingstone the Hero of Africa* (London: Seeley, Service, 1918)

fundamental principle was that non-European territories administered by European powers were to be held in 'trust', with a responsibility to develop a country to the advantage of its inhabitants.[153] Trusteeship, of course, was by no means a new notion. The idea that political power should be used to benefit those subject to it had a heritage that stretched back to Edmund Burke.[154] During the notorious imperial conferences of the 1880s, at Berlin and Brussels, the discourse of trusteeship could be readily detected. As William Bain has pointed out, while the delegates evidently sought to consolidate their own prosperity and international position, there was a considerable attempt to 'establish principles of conduct' and promote African 'advancement'. By making indigenous populations a point of focus, the conferences actually 'institutionalised the idea of trusteeship' in international law.[155] Yet, as Bain argues, if the imperial conferences institutionalised the principle, the post-war League of Nations internationalised it by establishing a number of 'procedures of international supervision'. Owing in large part to pressure from the United States, and its opposition to 'territorial aggrandizement', the trusteeship of the League of Nations covenant went considerably beyond its earlier articulation at the conferences. Now it not only would be considered an important principle of conduct, but would be upheld in considerable 'international machinery'.[156]

In the aftermath of the First World War and the covenant of the League of Nations, trusteeship achieved greater prominence in articulations of British colonial policy. As Ronald Hyam observes, from the mid-1920s this was dominated by the idea of indirect rule, composed by Frederick D. Lugard in his volume *The Dual Mandate in British Tropical Africa*. Indirect rule, which was rapidly accorded 'guru-like respect', meant 'ruling native peoples on native lines', using power structures already in place in order to 'develop all that is best in indigenous methods and institutions'. With Britain experiencing an unprecedented decline in strength and with ever-mounting challenges to imperial rationale, indirect rule seemed an economic, moral and plausible way forward. It was a formulation, moreover, in which 'trusteeship' and the 'dual responsibilities and reciprocal benefits' of the imperial relationship were preeminent.[157] Indeed, it is important to note that while Americans primarily understood trusteeship as an alternative to empire, the British tended to interpret it as part of an historic imperial tradition and as a standard by which to judge colonial governance.[158] In the British context, then, the new valorisation of trusteeship provided 'a sop to the liberal conscience and a prod to the wavering imperialists'.[159] It was a remodelled imperialism that suited a changing world.

Livingstone biographers at this time moulded their subject to cohere with the *modus operandi* of empire. W.P. Livingstone, whom

MacKenzie calls that 'most prolific of missionary authors', is illustrative of this process.¹⁶⁰ In his 1929 biography he argued that 'the mandate system under the League of Nations' was established on 'Livingstone's principle; "that the well-being and development of native peoples form a sacred trust of civilization"'.¹⁶¹ Yet while he was deemed to be the pioneer of imperialism's new principles, Livingstone was not mapped in any simple way onto the new formula. By focusing on two biographies – one by D.C. Somervell, discussed briefly earlier, and another by Reginald John Campbell, a Congregationalist theologian – we can see that Livingstone provided a means to engage in dialogue with the colonial context. Under the umbrella of trusteeship, as in earlier periods, diverging images of Livingstone continued to jostle against one another.

In the early years of the twentieth century, R.J. Campbell had been a leading light in public Christian life and a celebrated preacher at the nonconformist City Temple in London. He was perhaps best known as the central figure in the controversial 'New Theology' of 1907, a movement that essentially advocated 'a mystical version of Christianity' and emphasised divine immanence over and against transcendence.¹⁶² In directing focus towards God's presence in the world, rather than his presence above it, Campbell engaged in critique of what he perceived to be a failure in traditional theology. Although he later distanced himself from his more contentious views and returned to the fold of the Church of England in 1915, there is no doubt that part of Campbell's attraction to Livingstone lay in his experience of religious faith. Livingstone's formal theological views were more conservative and evangelical than his own, but Campbell was struck by his 'solitary communings with God', and his 'sublime' faith that he 'was a chosen instrument'; in Livingstone, Campbell found one who was attuned to an immanent spirit, who 'dwelt in the presence of God and breathed the air of devotion'.¹⁶³ While Campbell was attracted to Livingstone's spiritual formation, what is of more significance here is his conviction that Livingstone was the true mastermind behind contemporary colonial policy. As he put it in his 1929 biography, 'it may with truth be said that it was chiefly he who made possible the moral trusteeship of the advanced over the backward races which is now a principle of the League of Nations'. Campbell went on: 'The British imperial Government has frankly admitted and applied the principle of trusteeship to all its dealings ... this was Livingstone's vision.'¹⁶⁴ By forging an imaginative link to the now consecrated formula, Campbell produced an appropriate hero for the new colonial present. The connection of course was one of reciprocal benefit, the mechanism of trusteeship standing only to profit by the certification of Livingstone's powerful name.

For Campbell, the way Livingstone foreshadowed trusteeship was expressed first and foremost in his dealings with indigenous populations. His life was one that 'broke down stubborn barriers of prejudice'. 'The African', wrote Campbell, 'has unjustly been looked down upon by his white masters as an inferior type ... This mistaken view, against which Livingstone was among the first to protest, is at length giving way before the evidence of sociological facts.'[165] In this sense, Campbell yoked Livingstone to what was best about trusteeship. Certainly, one of its strengths was that it heralded the decline of what Sir Arthur Grimble called 'the Heaven-born Big-White-Master theory of colonial administration'.[166] Yet for all that trusteeship signalled greater attention to local inhabitants, it was underpinned by a fundamentally 'gradualist' assumption about the course of African 'advancement'.[167] So even while Campbell claimed that Livingstone was among the first to envisage white–black relations 'in other terms than those of master and servant', he continued to assert the necessity of the British moral presence to uplift Africans. Even at his most radical, Campbell could only write that 'the educated negro is showing himself able to do *most* that his white contemporary can do' (emphasis added).[168] His attitude remained paternalistic; the 'negro' significantly fell short of doing all. In fact, for Campbell's Livingstone, 'all-round demoralisation must inevitably proceed from the habitual intercourse of white and black races which recognised no moral obligation on the part of the former to raise the status of the latter'.[169] A moral hierarchy that naturalised European authority as 'trustees' and that positioned Africans as a potentially degenerating influence remained intact. While Campbell moved away from the master–servant discourse on the one hand, he re-inscribed it on another.

By the time D.C. Somervell wrote his Livingstone biography in 1936, he had already published extensively on historical, political and imperialist matters. According to his obituary in *The Times*, his *English Thought in the Nineteenth Century* (1920) and *The British Empire* (1930) were examples of 'well-ordered, clear and balanced exposition', and they earned him a 'national reputation' for 'useful and reliable' popular history.[170] Like Campbell's, Somervell's biography of Livingstone was imbued with political import, and he similarly offered his subject's interracial relations as a microcosm of colonial order. In so doing, however, he revealed the starker face of his imperialism by putting considerably less emphasis than Campbell on the possibilities of racial progress. Livingstone was such an ideal leader of Africans, he wrote, 'because of the infinite gulf between them and him'. The master–servant dichotomy, which Campbell could not quite escape, was much less restrained in Somervell: Livingstone's men 'were to him as children, and he was to them as God'. Less confident too in the possibilities of the civilising mission, he described how Livingstone's beloved Makololo, his 'chosen comrades' from 'what he believed to be the noblest of African races', enjoyed the 'flesh-pots' of Tette and subsequently engaged in systematic plundering. From this, Somervell deduced that 'The task of civilising the African has its discouraging side.'[171] In fact, he asserted that Livingstone's writings offered 'a truly formidable array of what he regarded as absolutely damning evidence against the African character and in favour of those who hold that the African is fit for nothing better than either the savagery that must be his lot in isolation, or a life of brutish labour in the service of his betters'. Somervell qualified his pessimistic statement by writing, 'Such evidence was never regarded as damning by the man who so candidly compiled it. Livingstone never stooped to whitewash the black man, but he never lost his faith in him.'[172] Despite this postscript gesture, he left the reader in little doubt that Livingstone's optimistic attitude to indigenous improvement was very much against the odds. His imperial paradigm resembled Johnston's more than Campbell's in its effort to inscribe a colonial relationship in which the distance between white and black showed little sign of diminishing.

But like Campbell, Somervell did make direct connections to colonial policy currently in vogue. He explicitly yoked Livingstone to F. D. Lugard, author of *The Dual Mandate*, who had argued that Europe had a twofold duty 'to secure for the benefit of the world at large the fullest development of Africa's contribution to its resources, and to secure for the peoples of Africa the fullest participation in world civilisation'. For Somervell, these principles of trusteeship were really nothing more than 'a sophisticated and polysyllabic version of Livingstone's "Christianity and commerce"'. A striking feature of Somervell's representation, however, is that he chose to connect Livingstone to Lugard in his most military fashion. The famed colonial administrator became 'the representative of the Livingstonian tradition in its third generation' because 'At decisive moments he saved the situation, first in Nyasaland and afterwards in Uganda. A few years later, on the other side of Africa, he led the expedition which conquered the slave-raiding Emirates of Northern Nigeria.'[173] In fact, it was less Lugard's formulation of trusteeship than his martial achievements that appealed to Somervell. It was in his vigorous guise that he was heir to Livingstone's legacy, as much for his military activity as for his colonial theory.

Somervell reinforced his aggressively imperialist image of Livingstone by coupling him with the most infamous titan of colonial advance. 'Strange as it may seem', he wrote, 'Livingstone was the forerunner of Cecil Rhodes.' 'Both alike, starting from a base in Cape

Colony, thought in terms of continents.' In Somervell's account, the two men were united as bearers of the selfsame expansionist logic: 'To both the barren wastes of Bechuanaland were the key to the future. Forty years before Rhodes described that country as the Suez canal to the North, Livingstone was extending by hundreds of miles what in his day was called the Missionaries' Road.'[174] The implication was that Livingstone's explorations and Rhodes's exploits belonged in the same category as exercises in the extension of empire's territory. Perhaps Somervell aspired to encourage a more vigorous imperialism at a time when foreign policy was less than enterprising. Hyam points out that the 1930s were a decade lacking in a forward-looking colonial programme. For around ten years from 1929 foreign policy often diminished to a 'vague reliance' on the League of Nations.[175] Somervell's representation of Livingstone as an active colonial agent might consequently be read as an effort to lend impetus to what may have seemed like a stagnating imperialism.

One of the most conspicuous features of Somervell's biography was his implementation of Livingstone to engage in a celebratory interpretation of the British presence in Africa. After the ravages of the slave trade, he argued, Europe was busily paying 'reparations', making instalments on a debt 'far too weighty to be paid in money' but which rather conveniently 'could only be paid in terms of moral values'. For Somervell, the scramble for Africa was part of this endeavour, and he connected it seamlessly to Livingstone: in his efforts to suppress slavery and promote legitimate commerce, he could be said, 'without exaggeration', to have laid 'the policy which, forty years later, made what is called the "scramble for Africa"'.[176] Through this reductive historiography, which causally connected Livingstone to later events, Somervell strove to deflect denunciations of the imperial past and so shore up the imperial present. While he did concede that the scramble engendered 'many unseemly incidents', he sought to forcefully combat the anti-colonial 'cynic': 'only one who has not read the records – and the cynic very seldom has – will dispute the fact that most of those who led and guided these imperial ventures were convinced that what was being done would accrue to the benefit of the African peoples'.[177] The latent aggression in his defensive efforts and his scorn for those doubting cynics expose his unrestrained enthusiasm for aggressive imperialism. Livingstone provided the means by which he could clothe the scramble in philanthropy and spur his nation on to more active imperial engagement.

Campbell also relied on Livingstone as a hermeneutic tool to comment on colonial history. While he made little comment on African partition, he at least showed a healthier scepticism than Somervell, who so facilely celebrated 'philanthropy and five per cent'.[178] Indeed,

Campbell questioned Livingstone's somewhat 'naïve belief in the ameliorating effects of civilisation': 'We are not so sure now as the early Victorians were that civilisation is to be trusted.' He regretted that Livingstone's explorations had been abused: 'advantage was taken of his discoveries by Europeans in many instances to render the state of the untaught African worse instead of better'.[179] But these questioning moments are quiet notes in the text. The major historical imperial concern to intrude on Campbell's biography was the South African War, of which he was an enthusiastic supporter. According to Keith Robbins, his zeal 'caused unease in more than one section of the Liberal Party'. He sat on the imperialist Liberal League and 'saw no contradiction between Imperialism, progressive Liberalism and militant nonconformity: a view not universally shared'.[180] However, as Donal Lowry points out, nonconformity did for the most part rally behind the British cause at the turn of the century. 'There can be little doubt', he writes, that it 'sanctified military involvement in the war against the Boers.'[181] While Campbell had originally opposed 'the motive of this war', instigated by the 'filibustering' Jameson Raid, his broader commitment to the empire allowed him to be quickly swayed.[182]

Twenty-seven years later, Campbell would marshal David Livingstone in order to reiterate the justice of British action. He mounted a case against the Boers by reminding his readers of their unruly exploits in Livingstone's day. 'Like the southern planter in the grimly humorous gibe, the Boer trekker sought for liberty "to whop his own nigger in peace"'. For Campbell, this significant fact had from 1900 been forgotten by the 'pro-Boer' party, who had waged 'wordy warfare' 'against the supposed tyranny of annexing two free self-governing Dutch communities to the British Commonwealth of nations'. In contrast to this history of racism, 'British imperial policy stood for fair play for the native', at least from 1833.[183] Campbell took Livingstone's notorious struggle with the Boers and translated it into unambiguous support for British military action. Livingstone, he wrote, 'believed in the moral use of physical force to restrain the predatory and homicidal proclivities of the unruly ... There is no doubt that he would have coerced the Boers by British military force.'[184] In this narrative Livingstone provided the historical precedent for martial engagement: he became, years after the fact, the standard-bearer for the South African War.

Livingstone also provided a standard by which Campbell could judge British passivity and imperial insufficiency. It became a theme in his work that by listening more attentively to Livingstone, the British might have avoided many later colonial problems. He rebuked the government for allowing his pleas on behalf of the indigenous, and for military intervention, to fall on deaf ears. While Livingstone and the Bakwains were victimised by Boer aggression, 'It was useless to protest; the British authorities would not listen.' But if the government had engaged in armed response, as Livingstone had urged, 'much subsequent trouble and bloodshed would have been saved in South Africa'.[185] Campbell, following William M. Macmillan, maintained that the entire racial tangle of the twentieth century could be traced back to imperial indecision and the failure to shoulder the burden of the 'native problem' at the opportune moment. In 1910, during the formation of the Union of South Africa, the contention that only a united government could deal effectively with racial tensions held considerable weight. But, for Campbell, the need for this unity of control had been yet more pertinent in the 1840s and 1850s, when Britain failed to take responsibility and ignored Livingstone's pleas.[186] To his mind, Britain had been soft on response and had failed to be sufficiently imperialist.

Campbell's picture of the South African War, then, was one of tardy but justified action. While Britain should have engaged earlier, Campbell left the reader in no doubt that South Africa was a better place because of British intervention. After a history of Afrikaner racism, Campbell now felt able to write, 'British and Dutch statesmen to-day in the vast South African Federation are at one in the endeavour to find a permanent solution of the complicated problem of white and coloured peoples dwelling side by side without placing the weaker in a position of chattel to the stronger.'[187] In this sentiment, Campbell reflected some of the optimism following the Balfour Declaration of 1926, which defined the status of the dominions of the Commonwealth as 'autonomous communities ... equal in status ... though united by a common allegiance to the Crown'.[188] As John Darwin puts it, the declaration was accepted in 'a sunburst of good will', and it opened the way for substantial idealising of the Commonwealth.[189] Thanks to Livingstone, and the eventual British response, South Africa seemed for Campbell to present a more hopeful future. But his optimism was wary. Was he truly convinced that the 'cleavage of opinion' over race relations, between Brits and Boers, had ceased?[190] His vigorous recitation of Afrikaner racism, his triumphalist account of the South African War and his construction of Livingstone as its harbinger insinuated that his hero's legacy should be kept in mind in contemporary dealings with South Africa.

Both Somervell and Campbell undoubtedly remade Livingstone for a changing empire with new mechanisms of imperial power. Following the covenant of the League of Nations and the publication of *The Dual Mandate*, Livingstone was seen to prefigure trusteeship, the now prevailing colonial credo. But Livingstone was not constructed in any simplistic way out of the contemporary scene; he was rather produced in dialogue with it. Our two biographers thus forged the important link quite differently; one sought to fortify trusteeship while the other made the connection in order to foster a more militant imperialism. Livingstone also provided a resource to interpret the British colonial past. Somervell was preoccupied with celebrating the scramble, thereby shoring up public opinion against the 'cynics' at a time when public interest in overseas was perhaps waning a little. Campbell, on the other hand, aimed to vindicate the British role in the South African War, an attempt made at a critical juncture in Commonwealth history and when racial tensions in South Africa were far from resolved. In other words, Livingstone served as a malleable historiographical tool, deployed to interpret the past in order to comment on the present.

Livingstone and the declining empire

In 1945 the imperialist historian and holder of Oxford's Beit chair, Sir Reginald Coupland, went to press with his tome-length study of *Livingstone's Last Journey* – certainly the major Livingstone work of the decade. Described by A.L. Rowse as perhaps 'the most distinguished historian among the Empire and Commonwealth group at Oxford', Coupland was truly original in his research on east Africa and successfully laid the foundations for future historical study.[191] But as significant as much of Coupland's work undoubtedly was, his biography of Livingstone was part of a monumental effort to interpret imperialism as a history of philanthropic intervention. His text emerged at the close of the Second World War, that collision of world powers that had such cataclysmic implications for the future of the declining empire. As imperialism was re-evaluated in a new world climate, Reginald Coupland chose to reassert and remould Livingstone's life.

For the historian Richard Drayton, Coupland was an important figure in the history of imperial apologia. His very appointment to the Beit chair in 1920 occurred at a moment of imperial unrest, following anticolonial stirrings across Ireland, Egypt, Trinidad and India. In such a context, Coupland's confidence in British moral courage and in empire as a vehicle of justice was reassuring. Indeed, as Drayton points out, British imperial history as a discipline actually began as 'a patriotic enterprise, where the past was ordered in ideological defence of contemporary British expansion'. Following Seeley, it applied the 'Whig narrative of the nation, the idea that British history was the story of the progressive expansion of liberty', to imperial development.[192] This disciplinary investment in a 'humanitarian' historical narrative proved to be remarkably persistent. Coupland's endeavours were contributions to 'a scholarly industry' that largely remained intact until the 1970s.[193]

Coupland thus broached Livingstone with the celebratory tone he inherited from his discipline. In *Livingstone's Last Journey* he hoped to show the true humanitarian impulse coursing through the imperial veins. As he wrote: 'Anyone who has had the patience to peruse the dusty files of official correspondence is aware that the one subject in which the British Government was really interested ... was the abolition of the Arab Slave Trade.'[194] The primary agenda of Coupland's text was actually less a mere celebration of Livingstone than a revisionist revelation of what he saw as a tireless anti-slavery network, a crusading 'triple alliance', operating for the freedom of east Africa: 'Livingstone, its spearhead, penetrating the black veil ... Kirk, his tried and trusted Lieutenant ... Waller ... with his hand on all the strings of the humanitarian movement'.[195]

As one fork of this triple-pronged-alliance, Coupland ensured that Livingstone was fixed on an anti-slavery trajectory. As his narrative took shape, it became a story of a man's loss of purpose and subsequent return to his fundamental convictions. In the book's middle section, Coupland was preoccupied with a 'mysticism' or 'fatalism' that allowed Livingstone 'to be diverted and obstructed as he never did in the old days'. With this loss of fervour, and with his all-consuming quest for the Nile, he even 'allowed his movements to be more or less decided by [his] Arab associates'.[196] The horrifying massacre of a local market in Nyangwe, by a group of these traders, was a turning point – it 'bit indelibly into his soul ... it was a vision like Gehena' – and drove him back to his original purpose.[197] Discovery, he realised, was of worth only for the political platform it would grant him in opposing slavery: 'the "geographical feat", whatever it may prove to be, is not an end in itself'. For dramatic appeal, Coupland's Livingstone lost his way in order that he might regain it, and in the overarching scheme he emerged with integrity of motive. Coupland concluded his book by attending to the 'historical coincidence' that on the very day Livingstone died 'the first blow was struck in a campaign which in three short years brought to its final triumph the cause to which he had given his life'. Thanks to John Kirk's efforts with the Sultan of Zanzibar, 'the Arab Slave Trade ... received a mortal blow'.[198] The government and Livingstone were represented on the same plane, at one in motive and spirit. For Coupland, Livingstone's crusade for justice found its ultimate consummation in the subsequent efforts of the British Empire to curb the east African slave trade.

But strangely, for a book with only Livingstone's name in the title, another member of the abolitionist trio received nearly as much attention. One of Coupland's most explicit intentions was actually to redeem Kirk from historical condemnation, and he devoted over fifty pages to the task. Kirk, he argued, had often been accused of abandoning Livingstone in his hour of need by failing to send him sufficient aid from Zanzibar. No biography, protested Coupland, had cleared his name from this unjust accusation; it was now time to debunk the 'legend of Kirk's lethargy'.[199] Coupland thus went to considerable effort to demonstrate that he was in no breach of duty: Unyanyembe and Ujiji, where Livingstone would return for provisions, were among the most difficult places to supply from Zanzibar. And according to Coupland, Kirk had to battle additionally against an outbreak of cholera that was sweeping the Ujiji road.[200]

The issue of Kirk's unjust reputation, however, really boiled down to Stanley, who had damned him in the eyes of the public. Yet Stanley, argued Coupland, seemed to have been somehow prejudiced against Kirk even before their first encounter, which compounded the natural antipathy between 'sober' Scot and 'self-confident' American.[201] He speculated that blame lay with the morally dubious Captain H. C. Fraser, who had likely slandered the British representative. Despite the Act of 1843 which forbade British subjects from purchasing slaves, Fraser continued to secure them on hire from Zanzibari merchants. When his nefarious practices were curtailed, he fled from the island, bankrupt and disgraced. Surely, Coupland surmised, Fraser's going sour on Kirk and Britain must have led him to prejudice H.M. Stanley.[202] The truth of Coupland's speculative explanation is of little importance here. More significant is the insinuation that it was Kirk's staunch opposition to exploitative practices that ironically resulted in his undeserved reputation as a traitor to Livingstone. Stanley of course deserved his share of culpability too. He had set out to appropriate Livingstone 'and all the credit of befriending him' in Britain. And by wildly castigating Kirk, he had jeopardised his crucial anti-slavery capacity at its hub in Zanzibar; Stanley had threatened to 'break up the triple alliance'. Coupland hoped to clear the mire from Kirk's name and re-polish imperial history: 'it was time', he wrote, 'that the memory of a great servant of the British Empire and the humanitarian cause should be cleansed'.[203]

Coupland's moral triumphalism and explanation by celebration shone brightly across his text. Yet for what ends did he seek to emplot the 'triple alliance' and create a tapestry of empire as humanitarian history? While Coupland was writing, Britain's world role was beginning to diminish and its empire to decline. As Ronald Hyam points out, the global conflict of the Second World War struck a powerful blow to the prestige of white authority. The whole milieu of empire shifted when it was realised across the colonial world that whites were capable of warring on other whites. Furthermore, Europe's battle against Hitler's domination seemed to legitimate colonial peoples' own struggles against alien forces.[204] This new geo-political climate required a new vision for empire in order for it to have any future place in world affairs at all. Clement Attlee famously said in 1942 that Britain must 'set aside sentimental imperialism and take a realist view of our problems': the colonial predicament would not be solved by fantasising about re-creating the past.[205] This, however, was precisely Coupland's project. While there was growing recognition that empire must be revised to survive, he recited the old narrative of its glorious history. Coupland's deployment of Livingstone and his heroic historiography of the 'triple alliance' were a conservative endeavour against the liberalisation of colonial policy and a prevailing political perception of the need for change. It perhaps also revealed an anxiety over the developing nationalist movements in the colonial world. Indeed, Coupland was known to have lectured Gandhi when he visited Cambridge on India's need to exhibit patience in waiting for self-government, and before his death he had embarked on a comprehensive study of nationalism.[206] *Livingstone's Last Journey* can thus be read as an attempt to intervene at a key imperial moment, to buttress the integrity of the empire's achievement against the backdrop of British decline and the rising tide of anti-colonial sentiment.

Livingstone, partnership and the Central African Federation

While imperialism was on the decline, the empire was far from finished. If the Labour Party *Speaker's Handbook* of 1948–49 publicised the slogan 'Imperialism is dead', it could also declare, without irony, that 'the Empire has been given new life'.[207] As Hyam points out, it is mistaken to characterise colonial policy after the war as one of determined decolonisation.[208] Rather, it was felt that while the old style of imperialism might have died, there was much productive work remaining for a world power to engage in. In order to meet the empire's changing realities, emphasis was now laid on 'political advancement'. A 'rhetoric of new beginnings' came to flourish, argues Stephen Howe, in which the old form of 'capitalist imperialism' was declared to have been relegated to the past.[209] In this context 'partnership' became the new byword; paternalism was to have been abandoned and collaboration adopted. The notion of 'partnership' certainly redefined relationships in the British Empire, yet at the same time it belonged in the longer tradition of imperial trusteeship. It is best understood, as William Bain suggests, as 'a refined and elaborated' version of trusteeship which moved beyond the permanence that word implied.[201] The Colonial Secretary, Oliver Stanley, described the term 'trustee' as 'too static in connotation' and suggested that it would be better to 'combine with the status of the trustee the position also of partner'.[211] It thus implied 'a dynamic and ever changing empire' and the potential for colonial states to progress to self-government. Of course, the partnership ideology was not simply embraced for the benefit of the colonised; it was a timely attempt to remodel the empire in response to its weakened condition. As John Darwin points out, the new programme was 'Reassuring and flexible'. It had the capacity to 'cover a multitude of colonial sins' while offering 'firm reassurance that what was good for Britain ... was also an act of imperial benevolence'.[212]

One of the most infamous experiments to emerge in this environment, in the 1950s, was the Central African Federation, which brought Nyasaland and the two Rhodesias together into one body. This union had long been on the agenda of European settlers who lobbied the British government to permit amalgamation.[213] Advocates of the federal system appealed to the comparative economic advantage of conjoining the territories. It was also proposed that a strong central Africa would diminish the chance of Afrikaner nationalism spreading from the south. The Central African Federation was important too for the British government's plans for the continent. It carried, as Darwin observes, its hopes for the realisation 'of a racial partnership between whites and blacks in a dynamic economy'.[214] Yet no partnership in any real sense was achieved, for in actuality Nyasaland represented a massive labour reserve for the much wealthier Rhodesias. The whole endeavour was carried out despite considerable opposition in Nyasaland from indigenous communities, who objected to union with Southern Rhodesia where the insidious 'parallel development' policy was already at work.[215] From this perspective, the federation was a union that not only would fail to resist, but would actually promote discrimination.

Yet again Livingstone's life was remoulded and re-conscripted for the empire's concerns. In Cecil Northcott's biography of 1957, Livingstone was seen to foreshadow the contemporary colonial zeitgeist: 'the growth of the idea of partnership between the races', he argued, was 'truly Livingstonian'. '[T]he gradual advancement of Africans into positions of authority in government and industry' was in keeping with what he called 'The Livingstone Tradition'. In Northcott's view, Livingstone was a clear forerunner to the current emphasis on partnership. But he did more than anticipate contemporary logic; he also had direct relevance to Africa's newest political formation. The remembrance of Livingstone and 'the intangible fields of "goodwill"' he left behind, Northcott suggested, would provide 'a practical asset, particularly in the life of the Federation'.[216] In his view, Livingstone's spirit was conducive to helping the federation function.

Northcott was not of course the only author to link Livingstone to the federal arrangement, although authors did not all follow him to the same extent in emphasising partnership. As Timothy Holmes has observed, the 1950s actually witnessed the publication of a number of substantial biographies.[217] Several of these made clear attempts to certify the ill-conceived imperial endeavour, which was destined for failure within a decade. Nevertheless, Livingstone's implementation in the Central African Federation was not entirely uncomplicated. In fact, while some authors employed him on its behalf, there was another quiet line of thought that used him in a critical capacity to demonstrate the federation's failings.

One of the works pertinent to this colonial experiment, *The Way to Ilala: David Livingstone's Pilgrimage*, by Frank Debenham, was in the first place a significant analysis of Livingstone's contribution as a geographer. Having been a member of Robert Falcon Scott's *Terra Nova* expedition to the Antarctic and the first Professor of Geography at Cambridge, and having travelled extensively in central Africa, Debenham was well suited to interrogating his subject in this respect.[218] The work's scholarly parameters aside, however, imperial concerns were writ large on Debenham's pages. The fact that its prefatory note was penned by Sir Arthur Benson, the Governor of Northern Rhodesia, announced its relevance to the federation. As Benson wrote, 'We whose lives are now spent in Northern Rhodesia owe to Livingstone, more than to any other man, the fact that our fathers were received here with friendship, and were so enabled to remain here to repay that friendly welcome a thousandfold.'[219] From the outset of the book, then, it was clear that the image of Livingstone it contained received the approbation of the colonial administration. Throughout the text, Debenham followed the author of the postscript by periodically linking Livingstone to central and south-east African imperial affairs. At one point he suggested that it was germane in the present to remember that 'Nyasaland owes its establishment of a Crown Colony even more definitely than most historians suppose, to the dream of David Livingstone'. While he was not making any original point here, Debenham found it useful to reassert the familiar genealogy in which the missionary-explorer was the prime mover behind the protectorate. He returned to this later in the text. Since settlement in the Shire highlands was the happy result of Livingstone's so-called failed Zambesi expedition, Debenham argued that the journey had actually 'made Nyasaland the most advanced and contented of all our mid-African protectorates'.[220] Given the strength of contemporary opposition to the federation, from the indigenous in Nyasaland as well as the Scottish missionaries, it is possible to see Livingstone functioning here as a cloak to veil discontent.[221]

While the concerns of the federation are eminently detectable in Debenham's work, they take on more explicit proportions in Michael Gelfand's *Livingstone the Doctor*. Gelfand was himself a prestigious physician, Professor of Medicine at the University of Rhodesia and founding editor of the *Central African Journal of Medicine*.[222] Consequently, as the title of his book indicates, his interest in Livingstone lay in his career as a practitioner, a context that had formerly received scant attention. But Gelfand made it clear that as much as his physician's vocation, it was Livingstone's critical relevance to the African political situation that made him worth writing about: 'Never has it been more necessary than at the present time in the history of Rhodesia and Nyasaland that we should try to understand the origins of this new state, for once we understand its beginning, we can prepare ourselves for the best way in which to ensure its welfare.'[223] By creating a narrative in which Livingstone became the originator of the federation, Gelfand, like so many others, sought to probe history in order to equip the present:

> His influence, after he had died, was the driving force which led other men, imbued with the missionary spirit, to seek the Central African field. They became the nucleus of white colonization and were the first bulwarks of European civilization as well as the forerunners of the Central African Federation.

Gelfand turned Livingstone into a spiritual father whose vital force would become embodied in the future state. With his Christian ideal and missionary vocation, Livingstone's ultimate 'goal was the settlement in Africa of English Colonists'. His outlook gained hold, argued Gelfand, 'and it is not hard to see that the birth of the new Federation of Central Africa owes its existence to this early influence'.[224] The federation, as the logical outworking of Livingstone's endeavours, was thus conceived as a magnanimous creation. The man and the state were woven together in a seamless tapestry of civilising benevolence: Livingstone provided a founding narrative for a foundering state.

In addition to this explicit effort to consolidate the federation, Gelfand used Livingstone in another way to more tacitly nurture the imperial cause. As Diana Wylie reminds us, scholars have now 'begun to examine how power was exercised through skills and disciplines which were once thought to be "apolitical", such as medicine'. They point out that, for a considerable period, historians paid little attention to the 'imperial contexts in which Western medicine had come to operate, or to the ideas and activities of patients'.[225] As a piece of imperialist medical history, Gelfand's narrative is indicative of this longstanding tendency. He may have pointed to Livingstone's 'complete open-mindedness in medicine', his absence of 'bias or prejudice', but this hint of relativism was quickly erased, for Gelfand noted that he 'concluded that ... his own methods were just as good, if not better'.[226] To give credit to Gelfand, his own classic work, *The Sick African*, has been described as one of 'the first "local" textbooks of medicine written from the perspective of local experience'.[227] Moreover, he was profoundly interested in the beliefs of his African patients, a leading authority on Shona religious rites and – according to one of his obituarists – without trace of 'race-consciousness or prejudice'.[228] Despite this, it remains the case that in Gelfand's work Western medicine is, for the most part, uncritically endorsed. Indeed, Wylie finds his medical corpus to be exemplary of a genre in which colonial subjects are represented 'as fortunate recipients of cures discovered in the medical laboratories of Britain'. His work is part of a literature that 'emphasized the power of Western medical intervention' and assumed that its practitioners were 'benign and progressive'.[229] For Gelfand, Livingstone represented the selfless doctor, one for whom 'medicine was an integral part of the Christian faith'. And he showed the indigenous gratefully receiving the remedies he offered. In fact, Gelfand made a strong causal link between Livingstone's success and the efficacy of his treatments: 'To the Natives his medicine was of supreme importance'; his 'popularity was also the greater because of his reputation as a doctor'.[230] The image of the altruistic physician, blessing the eager native, consolidated Gelfand's founding narrative for central Africa in which imperialism was carried on in pure beneficence, following in Livingstone's footsteps.

Livingstone was clearly widely wielded on behalf of the federation. But if he was exercised to provide a legitimising context, there were others who used him for an antithetical purpose. At the same time as he was being conscripted to bolster an imperial project, he was also deployed in oppositional capacity to critique the Federal structure and its failure to deliver democratic representation to the African populace. Such a perspective was offered in James Griffiths's *Livingstone's Africa: Yesterday and Today*, which took as its subject the '"agonizing and complex issue" of black and white relations'.[231] The author, a founding member of the Independent Labour Party and a driving force behind the construction of the welfare state, had in 1950 been appointed as Secretary of State for the Colonies.[232] Originally Griffiths supported the proposal for the Central African Federation, deeming it to offer political and economic advantages. His position, according to

J. Beverley Smith, was one of 'conditional commitment', contingent on its realisation of genuine racial partnership.[233] However, on attending a conference at Victoria Falls in 1951 he encountered the intensity of black opposition and revised his opinion. From this point, argues Kenneth O. Morgan, Griffiths campaigned against the federal plans being pushed through.[234]

Griffiths wrote his book on central African race relations in 1958, about half-way through the duration of the federation. He began by distinguishing three major strands of influence in the history of British colonial policy: 'David Livingstone the liberator, Cecil Rhodes the Empire builder, and Lord Lugard the administrator'. Livingstone and Rhodes, liberator and conqueror, were deemed to be oppositional forces in its history. In distilling these traditions he was by no means sparing in his criticism of the empire's past. He argued that in Africa, Britain had 'transformed millions of peasants into plantation workers, miners, and factory hands and ha[d] created a black proletariat'.[235] He condemned the acquisitive rush of the African scramble, bemoaning that 'In our desire for Empire and glory and gain, all had to be sacrificed.' To some extent, Griffiths intimated responsibility on Livingstone's part, for the revolution in Africa followed in his wake. It is clear, though, that he considered culpability to lie primarily with the Rhodes tradition. Indeed, for Griffiths, 'the great drama of the clash of race and colour and culture' in central and east Africa could be conceptualised in terms of these same two competing impulses: 'here the two names are familiar and the two traditions meet, mingle, and clash'. The Livingstone tradition more or less appears to be one that takes the part of the indigenous: Livingstone treated Africans 'as fellow human creatures to be cherished and befriended'.[236] In contrast, Rhodes was a 'racialist' who aspired to the 'Anglo-Saxon absorption of the world'; the Southern Rhodesian parliament and government, which were both 'exclusively European', clearly followed this tradition.[237]

For Griffiths, central and east Africa faced competing forces, 'Black African Nationalism and White Racialism'.[238] While he showed some degree of understanding of the white minority, who feared losing European standards of justice, his sympathies lay with the oppressed majority: it was 'imperative we should endeavour to understand the black man's agonies'.[239] Griffiths argued explicitly that '*In our policy there can be no place for the doctrine of racial superiority.*' He conceded some ground to the white community by saying that the 'black man still needs your guidance', but he challenged it with the need to 'learn to live together'. '"Together". This is the key word', wrote Griffiths, appealing to the notion of racial partnership that was so obviously failing in the federation.[240] The under-representation of black

Africans in central Africa motivated him to advocate a move to full democracy. It also encouraged him to resist proposals for the further amalgamation of the federal nations, unless the decision was reached by 'the inhabitants – all the inhabitants – of the three countries'. Any decision to merge made under the current political structure, with its predominantly European electorate, would be undemocratic. Griffiths also appealed for 'the disparities in wealth and opportunity between the races' to be addressed; for him this was a major problem in the area that he dubbed 'Livingstone's Africa'.[241] Indeed, by continually giving central and east Africa the appellation 'Livingstone's Africa', Griffiths implied that it was this tradition that bore his allegiance. His critique of the federation and his appeal for genuine togetherness and the eradication of inequality were made possible by the Livingstone tradition. This was most explicit towards the end of his book, where he reminded his readers that the occasion for his authorship was the centenary of Livingstone's famous appeal, made in Cambridge in 1857, for greater attention to Africa. The ideal means 'of commemorating the centenary of Livingstone's call', he suggested, would be to remove the colour bar in schools. A move to combat racial discrimination was Griffiths's ideal memorial to his conception of Livingstone. The best way to face the federation's ethnic relations, and the question of racial injustice, was with his 'spirit and dedicated purpose'.[242]

In mobilising Livingstone to critique the federation, Griffiths departed from the prevailing representation: to this extent, his image of the missionary-explorer can be considered counter-hegemonic. But while Griffiths may have been alone in engaging Livingstone critically with the central African political arrangement, there were others who similarly resisted the norm by presenting a radical vision of the explorer. The eminent imperial and domestic historian Jack Simmons, for instance, found Livingstone to be a remarkably progressive figure in his 1955 biography.[243] While Simmons followed contemporaries by connecting 'the inspiration [Livingstone] left behind him' to 'the new Central African Federation', his representation actually marks an interesting departure. He argued that Livingstone had quickly differentiated himself from his roots in a 'narrow evangelical tradition' that had persisted in judging Africans with a 'ready-made code' and unrelenting rigidity.[244] Livingstone, as Simmons put it, 'made it his business to try and understand their religion too'; he 'wanted first to *know*, not to judge or condemn'. In fact, for the most part 'what he has to say is hardly different in spirit from the verdict of a modern anthropologist'. In *Missionary Travels*, Simmons found evidence to argue that Livingstone aspired to deep cultural understanding and strove to disrupt sedimented patterns of thinking about

Africa. This vision, he wrote, was only 'very dimly' understood by Livingstone's contemporaries.[245]

The renowned anthropologist and expert in comparative jurisprudence Max Gluckman likewise queried the mainstream understanding. He agreed that Livingstone manifested an 'absence of prejudice' but felt that Simmons had not pressed this argument far enough. In a short but significant article for the magazine *The Listener*, Gluckman fastened onto one important quotation from *Missionary Travels* in which Livingstone declared that Africans 'are just such a strange mixture of good and evil as men are everywhere else'. This statement, he argued, and Livingstone's writings as a whole, demonstrated that he 'brought to his observations of African life and society a balanced, open mind'. Indeed, the theme 'that the observer must carefully count and compare his facts runs through all Livingstone's writings'.[246] In his unprejudiced enquiry, Gluckman detected an observer who foreshadowed the anthropologist's methodology. Yet he noted that, unfortunately, 'the passages showing these qualities are often neglected' by Livingstone's biographers. The explanation, he suggested, was that many authors became caught up in the '*mystique*' of personality and 'savage' encounter. They were set on portraying Africans like 'painted figures on a backdrop, savage, warlike', and so overlooked the 'vividness' and sensitive individuality with which Livingstone had portrayed Africans himself.[247] By fixating on those moments where he appeared as a 'dauntless man of courage', they tended to ignore that 'his own writings show that he was only very rarely in danger from the weapons of Africans'.[248] In suggesting that recent biographies, like those by Coupland and Debenham, had fallen into this trap, Gluckman demonstrated the difference between the orthodox conception of Livingstone and his own. It was not Livingstone's heroic fortitude that made him a hero, but rather what the Makololo called '*butu*, his sense of human kindness'.[249] While Gluckman may not have used Livingstone in direct critique of any political formation, his anti-colonial views revealed themselves in the extent to which he rejected the heroic and paternalist construction and instead valorised his subject as one sensitively attuned to cultural difference.

In the 1950s, during the period of 'partnership' and the Central African Federation, Livingstone was again a site of different interpretations. For some authors, he provided a narrative of origin to justify the federal state's existence. At the same time, Livingstone also offered a means to engage in critique of its discriminatory political structure and to reflect critically on the empire's history in Africa. While Livingstone may not have been used to challenge the existence of the federation altogether, he was certainly employed at the least to advocate essential reform. In this period too, with the rise of cultural relativism and anti-colonial sentiment, there were those who saw Livingstone less as one who justified a colonial mentality than as one who pioneered principles of sympathetic cultural engagement.

It has often been suggested that Livingstone was a hero not only in Britain but in African traditions too. When in the 1970s Bridglal Pachai asked the question, 'What did Africans themselves think of Livingstone?', he concluded that, in Malawi at least, local communities remembered him favourably.[250] Others have gone further, arguing that this icon of empire even came to sustain a rival legacy as a patron saint of African nationalism.[251] After independence, for instance, place-names associated with him remained intact, and during the centenary of his death a number of countries issued Livingstone-themed stamps in commemoration.[252] The former president of Zambia Kenneth Kaunda even characterised him as the first 'freedom fighter' for Africans.[253] Yet, while Livingstone has retained heroic proportions in parts of the postcolonial continent – and while he helps to sustain a tourist trade – his remembrance in Africa requires much closer attention than it has hitherto been given. In fact, there is evidence to suggest that his name has been the subject of geographical dispute. In 2001 at a congress of the ruling party, a group of Zimbabwean veterans began to stone the large bronze Livingstone statue that overlooks Victoria Falls, demanding that it be replaced with effigies of the heroes of black liberation. Under the influence of Mugabeism, Livingstone was seen not as a forerunner of nationalism but as a symbol of the colonial past and white racism. His perception on the other side of the falls, however, was rather different. In 2004, Donald Chikumbi, the Director of the Zambian National Heritage Conservation Commission, requested that the Zimbabwean government transfer custody of the statue to Zambia. Commenting on the petition, Chief Silha Mukuni of the Leya said that 'The Zambians have a great deal of affection for Livingstone's memory, unlike the Zimbabweans ... We have changed a great many of our colonial place names since independence, but we have kept the name of Livingstone out of a deep respect.'[254] The petition was refused and the statue continues to attract occasional vilification. As recently as 2010, Cain Mathema, the ZANU-PF Governor of Bulawayo, demanded that the body of Cecil Rhodes be exhumed and the Livingstone statue pulled down. For Mathema, they were 'symbols that persecuted our people and took away our freedom and wealth'.[255]

To fully evaluate Livingstone's legacy in Africa, then, would demand attention to intranational and supranational differences in remembrance, and a consideration across geographical space of commercial tourism, economic histories and different experiences of colonial rule.[256] It would, moreover, require anthropological and sociological investigation within local communities – something that exceeds the parameters of this project's textual focus. Nevertheless, even this brief glimpse into Livingstone's African remembrance since decolonisation undermines any simplistic account of his imperialist legacy. A narrative that fails to recognise that he was simultaneously castigated as empire's prophet and hailed as proto-nationalist sells its real complexity short. We are reminded too that Livingstone's meaning is a shared commodity; it does not belong solely to his many biographers or even to contemporary academics.

Nevertheless, as we have seen in the course of this chapter, the printed texts themselves tell no monolithic story. Tracking Livingstone's politicised construction as colonial pioneer, I have followed the ways in which he was marshalled for the empire's forward motion and remade to fit the changing face of the imperial present. From the scramble to the Edwardian empire, from 'trusteeship' to post-war imperial decline, and from 'partnership' to the federal experiment in central Africa, Livingstone was constructed in dialogue with the needs of the moment. But while his empire image varied across socio-political time, the argument of this chapter goes beyond chronology. Even at the same colonial instant Livingstone could be constructed in significantly different ways, according to deviating colonial needs and logics. In other words, contrasting Livingstones emerged out of a range of competing imperialisms. While the spectrum of meanings that he could accommodate was by no means infinite, it would perhaps be better to speak of his imperial legacies. We need to make space too for constructions of Livingstone that countervail the norm and even employ him for purposes of critique; the heterogeneity of his posthumous legacy is such that counter-hegemonic constructions must be taken into account. It is notable that the divergent readings of Livingstone often drew on the same source material, and particularly on *Missionary Travels*. That the text could sustain the rival readings of Johnston and Hughes, Somervell and Gluckman, points to its fundamentally ambivalent nature. This also reveals, moreover, the located nature of the biographers and their reading practices, the inescapable impact of the individual's ideological and historical horizons.

The majority of the authors who participated in using Livingstone for the ends of empire relied on the hagiographical genre. Although a number were historically rigorous and some went so far as to tentatively criticise their subject, they cultivated him for the most part as an exemplary life and unambiguous hero. By projecting Livingstone's life onto a seamless narrative of near-perfection of character, with motives of the utmost purity, these authors consolidated their own imperial purposes. I also contended that in a context of racial encounter, hagiography, with its reliance on the romance structure, was almost always an imperialist mode of writing. The image of the hero entering the chthonic darkness and emerging in splendid victory (even in death) routinely had imperialist overtones when mapped onto the missionary and exploratory experience. Indeed, the intense focus on one individual radically simplified the complex moment of exchange and the reflexivity involved in cultural encounter. The centrality of the hero often led to the effacement of the indigenous and the reduction of subjectivities to mere types – either the 'faithfuls' or the opposition. The hagiographical and romance narrative thus emerged as a convenient medium for those who wished to project Livingstone as empire's servant. It was a cultural imperialist text that best served those authors who sought to employ their subject for political imperialist ends.

Notes

1 Charles Silvester Horne, *David Livingstone* (London: Macmillan, 1912), p. vi.
2 Given Livingstone's political utility in empire, the more recent debate over his imperial status has hinged on the extent to which the subsequent history of British intervention in Africa was or was not a logical consequence of his endeavours. For Tim Jeal, the empire in Africa largely followed Livingstone's ideal. He argues that Livingstone strongly advocated colonisation, 'on the pattern of a minority of whites ruling, albeit philanthropically, a vast majority of blacks'. The 'coupling of moral fervour with the right to power was implicit in much of what Livingstone had written about Britain's special duty', a sentiment which Chamberlain's evocation of Britain's 'manifest destiny' would later echo. See Tim Jeal, *Livingstone* (New Haven: Yale University Press, 2001), pp. 374, 382. But other critics, like Andrew Ross, have resisted Jeal's account, insisting that Livingstone had this 'mythic status' of arch-imperialist thrust upon him; the leading politicians of Europe conveniently appropriated his popularity, using him to morally glorify the empire. Colonialism as it later took shape, Ross argues, was foreign to Livingstone's conception of the word. See Andrew Ross, *David Livingstone: Mission and Empire* (London: Hambledon and London, 2002), pp. 243, 239.
3 John M. MacKenzie, 'David Livingstone: The Construction of the Myth', in Graham Walker and Tom Gallagher (eds), *Sermons and Battle Hymns* (Edinburgh: Edinburgh University Press, 1990), pp. 33–4.
4 Juliette Atkinson, *Victorian Biography Reconsidered: A Study of Nineteenth-Century 'Hidden' Lives* (Oxford: Oxford University Press, 2010), p. 14.
5 Walter E. Houghton,*The Victorian Frame of Mind, 1830–1870* (New Haven: Yale University Press), pp. 305–40. Quoted in Atkinson, *Victorian Biography*, p. 46.
6 Nigel Hamilton, *Biography: A Brief History* (Cambridge, Mass.: Harvard University Press, 2007), pp. 105, 109–10, 112.
7 Hermione Lee, *Biography: A Very Short Introduction* (Oxford: Oxford University Press, 2009), p. 73.
8 Atkinson, *Victorian Biography*, p. 22.
9 Geoffrey Cubitt, 'Introduction: Heroic Reputations and Exemplary Lives', in Geoffrey Cubitt and Allen Warren (eds), *Heroic Reputations and Exemplary Lives* (Manchester: Manchester University Press, 2000), p. 2.

10 Atkinson, *Victorian Biography*, p. 25.
11 John M. MacKenzie, *Propaganda and Empire: The Manipulation of British Public Opinion, 1880–1960* (Manchester: Manchester University Press, 1984), p. 199.
12 Graham Dawson, *Soldier Heroes: British Adventure, Empire, and the Imagining of Masculinities* (London: Routledge, 1994), p. 149.
13 James Rohrer, 'Biography to Missiology: A Reflection upon the Writing of Missionary Lives', *Taiwan Journal of Theology*, 28 (2006), 196.
14 Quoted in Hamilton, *Biography*, p. 109.
15 Lee, *Biography*, p. 57.
16 Dawson, *Soldier Heroes*, p. 125.
17 Blaikie's biography was popular enough to reach its sixth edition by 1910. William Garden Blaikie, *The Personal Life of David Livingstone* (London: John Murray, 1880), pp. iii–iv.
18 Ibid., p. 45.
19 Cubitt, 'Introduction', p. 13.
20 Hamilton points out that Victorian evangelicalism discouraged the revelation of any impropriety in biography and encouraged encomia for moral improvement. See Hamilton, *Biography*, p. 110. Furthermore, Hermione Lee argues that nineteenth-century hagiographical veneration had much to do with 'consolidating a national story'. See Lee, *Biography*, p. 63.
21 Blaikie, *The Personal Life*, p. 471.
22 See Atkinson, *Victorian Biography*, p. 20.
23 Hamilton, *Biography*, pp. 118, 115.
24 It is important not to over-simplify the cultural shift at the turn of the century. Despite the rise of the 'new biography', Lee argues, 'protective, decorous biographies went on being written'. See Lee, *Biography*, p. 73.
25 David Churchill Somervell, *Livingstone* (London: Duckworth, 1936), p. 139.
26 Ibid., p. 29.
27 Both Macnair's writings and the Scottish National Memorial to David Livingstone will be discussed in more detail in the next chapter.
28 James Irvine Macnair, *Livingstone the Liberator: A Study of a Dynamic Personality* (London: Collins, 1940), pp. 113, 121.
29 Ibid., pp. 113, 218, 327.
30 Alan Neely, 'Saints who Sometimes Were: Utilizing Missionary Hagiography', *Missiology: An International Review*, 27: 4 (1999), 443.
31 Leon de Kock, *Civilising Barbarians: Missionary Narrative and African Textual Response in Nineteenth-Century South Africa* (Johannesburg: Witwatersrand University Press, 1996), p. 145.
32 Patrick Brantlinger, *Rule of Darkness: British Literature and Imperialism, 1830–1914* (New York: Cornell University Press, 1988), p. 180.
33 Northop Frye, *The Secular Scripture: A Study of the Structure of Romance* (Cambridge, Mass.: Harvard University Press, 1976), p. 53.
34 de Kock, *Civilising Barbarians*, p. 145.
35 Ibid., pp. 166–7.
36 Brantlinger, *Rule of Darkness*, pp. 180–1.
37 Ibid., p. 180.
38 Basil Mathews, *Livingstone the Pathfinder* (London: Oxford University Press, 1912), p. 6. *Livingstone the Pathfinder* was still in print as late as 1960. It was even translated into Tamil for the Christian Literature Society for India by the Rev. N. Devasahayam.
39 Ibid., p. 95.
40 As Inga Bryden argues, throughout the Victorian and Edwardian periods Malory served as 'a reference book for the "modern knight"', an important guide to gentlemanly behaviour. See Inga Bryden, *Reinventing King Arthur: The Arthurian Legends in Victorian Culture* (Aldershot: Ashgate, 2005), p. 74.
41 Mathews, *Livingstone the Pathfinder*, p. 10.
42 Ibid., pp. 20, 32.

43 Stephanie L. Barczewski, *Myth and National Identity in Nineteenth-Century Britain: The Legends of King Arthur and Robin Hood* (Oxford: Oxford University Press, 2000), pp. 10, 214.
44 Ibid., p. 220.
45 Mathews, *Livingstone the Pathfinder*, p. 158.
46 More scholarly biographies could also rely on romance logic. For instance, Frank Debenham's 1955 biography is tellingly entitled *The Way to Ilala: David Livingstone's Pilgrimage*. Like Mathews, Debenham provides a textual key for the interpretation of his subject. Drawing upon John Bunyan's *Pilgrim's Progress*, he portrays Livingstone as a pilgrim whose ultimate destination is Ilala, his place of death. His life is transformed into allegory – a path of rises, falls, struggles and ultimate victory.
47 Rohrer, 'Biography to Missiology', p. 206.
48 Macnair, *Livingstone the Liberator*, pp. 22, 137–8, 298.
49 Somervell, *Livingstone*, p. 49.
50 The term 'pathography' was coined by Joyce Carol Oates. See 'Adventures in Abandonment', *New York Times* (28 August 1988), www.nytimes.com/1988/08/28/books/adventures-in-abandonment.html?pagewanted=all&src=pm (accessed 7 November 2012).
51 Reginald John Campbell, *Livingstone* (London: E. Benn, 1929), pp. 8–9.
52 Lee, *Biography*, p. 92.
53 Rob Mackenzie's explicitly Christian narrative, *David Livingstone: The Truth behind the Legend*, is also largely celebratory. It is essentially an exemplary life, upholding Livingstone as one of 'the world's spiritual pioneers'. Rob Mackenzie, *David Livingstone: The Truth behind the Legend* (Fearn, Ross-shire: Christian Focus, 2000), p. 366.
54 Martin Dugard, *Into Africa: The Dramatic Retelling of the Stanley–Livingstone Story* (London: Bantam, 2003), pp. 346, 312.
55 Ibid., pp. 19, 17.
56 Felix Driver, *Geography Militant: Cultures of Exploration and Empire* (Oxford: Blackwell, 2001), p. 70.
57 Derek Gregory, *The Colonial Present: Afghanistan, Palestine, Iraq* (Oxford: Blackwell, 2004), p. 10. This is to be distinguished from Renato Rosaldo's understanding of 'imperialist nostalgia', which signifies a desire on the part of colonial agents 'for the very cultures that had been destroyed by their encroachments'. See Derek Gregory, 'Colonial Nostalgia', in Nezar AlSayyad (ed.), *Consuming Tradition, Manufacturing Heritage: Global Norms and Urban Forms in the Age of Tourism* (London: Routledge, 2001), p. 140.
58 This raises questions about the ethics of life-writing and how one might responsibly write about 'great men'. Some authors choose, of course, to move away from celebrated figures and instead tell the life stories of the marginalised (see, for instance, my discussion of Mary Livingstone's biographers in Chapter 7). However, if one continues to address the biographies of renowned subjects, one option, as Miles Ogborn points out, is to give less priority to 'individual motivation' and instead to pursue 'careful anthropological contextualisation'. See Miles Ogborn, *Global Lives: Britain and the World 1550–1800* (Cambridge: Cambridge University Press, 2008), p. 9. Similarly, as David Lambert and Alan Lester suggest, authors might follow James Clifford in seeking a 'less centred biography', which would bring the background to a life into the foreground and present the biographee as the focal point of a range of influences. See David Lambert and Alan Lester, *Colonial Lives across the British Empire: Imperial Careering in the Long Nineteenth Century* (Cambridge: Cambridge University Press, 2006), p. 20. Various authors writing on Livingstone have, to some extent, adopted such approaches. For instance, Roy Bridges's edition of Jacob Wainwright's diary is an example of scholarly retrieval, an effort to recover the experience of one of the Africans who accompanied Livingstone. See Herbert K. Beals et al. (eds), *Four Travel Journals: The Americas, Antarctica and Africa, 1775–1874* (Aldershot: Ashgate, 2007).

Andrew Ross's biography, while retaining Livingstone as the primary subject, goes some way towards a more Afrocentric evaluation of his explorations. Lawrence Dritsas's recent book likewise pays close attention to local context, while also seeking to decentre the Zambesi expedition from Livingstone; instead he understands the expedition 'as an aggregate of projects unified by goals, relationships, and responsiblities'. See Lawrence Dritsas, *Zambesi: David Livingstone and Expeditionary Science in Africa* (London: I.B. Tauris, 2010), p. 3.

59 John M. MacKenzie, 'Heroic Myths of Empire', in John M. MacKenzie (ed.), *Popular Imperialism and the Military* (Manchester: Manchester University Press, 1992), p. 115.
60 Clare Pettitt, *Dr. Livingstone, I Presume? Missionaries, Journalists, Explorers, and Empire* (Cambridge, Mass.: Harvard University Press, 2007), pp. 11, 48–9.
61 Oliver Ransford, *David Livingstone: The Dark Interior* (London: John Murray, 1978), p. 283.
62 Dorothy O. Helly, *Livingstone's Legacy: Horace Waller and Victorian Mythmaking* (Athens, O.: Ohio University Press, 1987), p. 124.
63 Another important 'high priest' was of course Roderick Murchison, President of the RGS. Perhaps we can also extend the list to include William Garden Blaikie, since his biography provided much of the source material for the later, and more derivative, texts that followed in its wake.
64 MacKenzie, 'David Livingstone: The Construction of the Myth', p. 33.
65 For discussion of this political contest, see David Birmingham, *Portugal and Africa* (Basingstoke: Macmillan, 1999), pp. 110–21.
66 Brian Stanley, *The Bible and the Flag: Protestant Missions and British Imperialism in the Nineteenth and Twentieth Centuries* (Leicester: Apollos, 1990), p. 125.
67 Birmingham, *Portugal and Africa*, p. 111.
68 Harry Hamilton Johnston, *Livingstone and the Exploration of Central Africa* (London: George Philip & Son, 1891), p. 367.
69 Helly, *Livingstone's Legacy*, p. 325.
70 Johnston, *Livingstone*, p. 39.
71 Quoted in Birmingham, *Portugal and Africa*, p. 112.
72 T. Banks Maclachlan, *David Livingstone: The Factory Lad who Became Africa's Greatest Missionary* (Kilmarnock: John Ritchie, 1900), p. 144.
73 Arthur J.H. Montefiore Brice, *David Livingstone: his Labours and his Legacy* (London: S.W. Partridge, 1890), pp. 160, 158.
74 Ibid., p. 156.
75 Pettitt, *Dr. Livingstone, I Presume?*, p. 211.
76 Thomas Hughes, *David Livingstone* (London: Macmillan, 1889), p. 206.
77 Deryck Schreuder, *The Scramble for Southern Africa, 1877–1895: The Politics of Partition Reappraised* (Cambridge: Cambridge University Press, 1980), pp. 115, 142.
78 Hughes, *David Livingstone*, p. 206.
79 Brice, *David Livingstone*, pp. 151, 94.
80 Hughes, *David Livingstone*, pp. 203, 205.
81 Helly, *Livingstone's Legacy*, p. 331.
82 Andrew N. Porter, *Religion versus Empire? British Protestant Missionaries and Overseas Expansion, 1700–1914* (Manchester: Manchester University Press, 2004), p. 211.
83 Stewart J. Brown, *Providence and Empire: Religion, Politics and Society in the United Kingdom, 1815–1914* (Harlow: Pearson Longman, 2008), p. 302.
84 Porter, *Religion versus Empire?*, pp. 219, 213. This concern did not disappear quickly and can be felt in later 'lives' of Livingstone too. In 1920 John Alfred Sharp concluded his biography by asking: 'What is to be the future of the great Continent for which Livingstone gave his life, his all? Who is to be king of this vast territory, Christ or Mahomet?' Reacting to 'the rise of the pan-Islam movement', he called for resistance to this 'terrible external foe' that had invaded an area of 'Christ's heritage'. His biography was a platform for anti-Islamic sentiment, and he used his subject to bolster it directly: 'The Mahommedan is a lower type of civilization than

the Christian: David Livingstone was under no delusion in regard to this.' See John Alfred Sharp, *David Livingstone: Missionary and Explorer* (London: Epworth Press, 1920), pp. 223, 225, 227, 231–2.
85 MacKenzie, 'David Livingstone: The Construction of the Myth', p. 33.
86 Roland Oliver, *Sir Harry Johnston and the Scramble for Africa* (London: Chatto & Windus, 1957), pp. vii, 99.
87 Ibid., pp. 17, 144–8, 142.
88 Johnston, *Livingstone*, p. 162.
89 Edward Beasley, *The Victorian Reinvention of Race: New Racisms and the Problem of Grouping in the Human Sciences* (London: Routledge, 2010), p 1.
90 Johnston, *Livingstone*, pp. 18, 20.
91 Ibid., pp. 58–9.
92 Johnston, *Livingstone*, pp. 75, 93.
93 Oliver, *Sir Harry Johnston*, p. 6.
94 H.H. Johnston, 'British Missions and Missionaries in Africa', *The Nineteenth Century: A Monthly Review*, 22: 129 (1887), 723.
95 Quoted in H.H. Johnston, 'Are Foreign Missions a Success?', *Fortnightly Review*, 45: 268 (1889), 489.
96 Stanley, *The Bible and the Flag*, p. 125.
97 David Clement Scott, *'Living-Stones': Sermon upon the Church of Scotland Blantyre Mission, British Central Africa* (Edinburgh: William Blackwood, 1901), p. 11.
98 This 'new' imperial history recognises that 'there was never a single European colonial project', 'a single colonial discourse, or a set of representations' (Lambert and Lester, *Colonial Lives*, pp. 6, 9). See, for example, N.J. Thomas, *Colonialism's Culture: Anthropology, Travel and Government* (Cambridge: Polity, 1994). Likewise, Ann Laura Stoler and Frederick Cooper contest the idea that imperialism was ever cohesive, and direct research to the 'competing visions' and 'tensions of empire'. See F. Cooper and A. Stoler, 'Introduction: Tensions of Empire: Colonial Control and Visions of Rule', *American Ethnologist*, 16: 4 (1989), 609.
99 Scott, *'Living-Stones'*, p. 8.
100 Ibid., pp. 9, 30–1.
101 Ibid., p. 9.
102 Brown, *Providence and Empire*, p. 2.
103 Norman Vance, *The Sinews of the Spirit: The Ideal of Christian Manliness in Victorian Literature and Religious Thought* (Cambridge: Cambridge University Press, 1985), p. 76.
104 Hughes, *David Livingstone*, pp. 196, 206.
105 Mary Angela Schwer, 'Imperial Muscular Christianity: Thomas Hughes's Biography of David Livingstone', in Gary Day (ed.), *Varieties of Victorianism: The Uses of a Past* (Basingstoke: Macmillan, 1998), p. 25.
106 Jeffrey Richards, *Happiest Days: The Public Schools in English Fiction* (Manchester: Manchester University Press, 1988), p. 50.
107 Hughes, *David Livingstone*, pp. 120, 181.
108 Ibid., p. 150.
109 Vance, *The Sinews of the Spirit*, p. 145.
110 Hughes, *David Livingstone*, pp. 2, 112–13.
111 Vance, *The Sinews of the Spirit*, pp. 158, 146.
112 Schwer, 'Imperial Muscular Christianity', p. 29.
113 Quoted in Richards, *Happiest Days*, p. 50.
114 Schwer, 'Imperial Muscular Christianity', pp. 131–2.
115 Hughes, *David Livingstone*, pp. 153, 152.
116 Richards, *Happiest Days*, p. 24.
117 John Marshall Pryde, *Livingstone and the Slave Trade, or, The Opening Up of Central Africa* (Glasgow: Oppenheim & Langman, 1902), p. 14.
118 Edward Hume, *David Livingstone: The Man, the Missionary, and the Explorer* (London: Sunday School Union, 1904), p. 145.

119 Pryde, *Livingstone*, p. 33; John Walter Gregory, *Livingstone as an Explorer* (Glasgow: University of Glasgow, 1913), p. 21.
120 Hume, *David Livingstone*, p. 235. Gregory, *Livingstone as an Explorer*, p. 34.
121 MacKenzie, 'David Livingstone: The Construction of the Myth', p. 33.
122 William A. Elliott, *'Nyaka' the Doctor: The Story of David Livingstone* (London: London Missionary Society, 1908), p. 95.
123 Hume, *David Livingstone*, pp. 108, 102–3.
124 While this is true for the most part, John Darwin has recently suggested that Edwardian imperial problems have sometimes been overstated. While the period was certainly one of increased international vulnerability, and while Britain's share of global trade did reduce, the nation still remained the world's greatest trader. British banks also generated significant income as the 'supplier of capital'. See John Darwin, *The Empire Project: The Rise and Fall of the British World-System, 1830–1970* (Cambridge: Cambridge University Press, 2009), pp. 274, 278.
125 Bernard Porter, 'The Edwardians and their Empire', in Donald Read (ed.), *Edwardian England* (London: Historical Association, 1982), pp. 128–9.
126 Max Jones, *The Last Great Quest: Captain Scott's Antarctic Sacrifice* (Oxford: Oxford University Press, 2003), pp. 162, 197.
127 Graham Dawson, *Soldier Heroes: British Adventure, Empire, and the Imagining of Maculinities* (London: Routledge, 1994), p. 148.
128 Jones, *The Last Great Quest*, pp. 163, 199.
129 See ibid., p. 250.
130 Arthur Lincoln, *David Livingstone: Missionary, Explorer, and Philanthropist* (London: A. Melrose, 1907), p. 8.
131 Mathews, *Livingstone the Pathfinder*, pp. 108, 86.
132 Driver, *Geography Militant*, p. 70.
133 Mathews, *Livingstone the Pathfinder*, pp. 41, 169, 6.
134 Jones, *The Last Great Quest*, p. 203.
135 Elleke Boehmer, 'Introduction', in Robert Baden-Powell, *Scouting for Boys* (Oxford: Oxford University Press, 2004), p. xii.
136 Baden-Powell, *Scouting for Boys*, pp. 162, 172.
137 A.L. Haydon, 'From Weaver-Boy to Missionary-Explorer', *Boy's Own Paper*, 25: 35 (March 1913), 410.
138 Elliott, *'Nyaka'*, pp. 15–16. The notion of Livingstone as a scout, while clearly meeting British needs, was not confined only to British soil. In 1913, the Boy Scouts of America published an article entitled 'David Livingstone, the Hero-Scout of Africa' in its monthly magazine, *Boys' Life*. For its author, Livingstone spent his life 'blazing his scout trail in unknown Africa': his was 'one of the greatest scouting stories in the world'. See B. Burgoyne Chapman, 'David Livingstone, the Hero-Scout of Africa', *Boys' Life: The Boy Scouts' Magazine*, 12: 2 (Feburary 1913), 8–9.
139 Baden-Powell, *Scouting for Boys*, p. 195.
140 See Clyde Binfield, 'Horne, (Charles) Silvester (1865–1914)', in *Oxford Dictionary of National Biography* (2004), www.oxforddnb.com/view/article/37569 (accessed 8 November 2012).
141 Clyde Binfield, *So Down to Prayers: Studies in English Nonconformity, 1780–1920* (London: Dent Totowa, 1977), p. 214.
142 Charles Silvester Horne, *David Livingstone* (London: Macmillan, 1912), p. vi.
143 Ibid., pp. 229, 149–50.
144 Ibid., pp. 163, 213.
145 Jones, *The Last Great Quest*, pp. 244, 249.
146 Ibid., pp. 229, 231.
147 Ibid., pp. 237, 233, 232.
148 Ibid., pp. 234–5.
149 Porter, 'The Edwardians', p. 133.
150 Jones, *The Last Great Quest*, p. 262.

151 Ibid., p. 269.
152 R.B. Dawson, *Livingstone the Hero of Africa* (London: Seeley, Service, 1918), pp. 25, 245.
153 William Bain, *Between Anarchy and Society: Trusteeship and the Obligations of Power* (Oxford: Oxford University Press, 2003), p. 99.
154 Ibid., p. 107.
155 Ibid., pp. 67–8. In fact, when the horrors of Leopold's Congo experiment became known, it was by the standard of trusteeship that they were condemned.
156 Ibid., pp. 78, 102.
157 Ronald Hyam, *Britain's Declining Empire: The Road to Decolonisation, 1918–1968* (Cambridge: Cambridge University Press, 2006), p. 13. See F.D. Lugard, *The Dual Mandate in British Tropical Africa* (Edinburgh and London: W. Blackwood and Sons, 1992).
158 Bain, *Between Anarchy and Society*, p. 108.
159 Hyam, *Britain's Declining Empire*, p. 13.
160 John M. MacKenzie, 'Missionaries, Science, and the Environment in Nineteenth-Century Africa', in Andrew N. Porter (ed.), *Imperial Horizons of British Protestant Missions, 1880–1914* (Grand Rapids: Eerdmans, 2003), p. 111.
161 William Pringle Livingstone, *Story of David Livingstone* (London: Livingstone, 1929), p. 124. While trusteeship is particularly emphasised in biographies written after the First World War, its presence is detectable in some earlier works. Edward Hume, for instance, referred to 'the trust committed to us by David Livingstone' in Africa. See Hume, *David Livingstone*, p. 242.
162 Brown, *Providence and Empire*, p. 293. For information on Campbell and the 'New Theology', see Keith W. Clements, *Lovers of Discord: Twentieth Century Theological Controversies in England* (London: SPCK, 1988), pp. 20–43. See also Keith Robbins, *History, Religion and Identity in Modern Britain* (London: Hambledon Press, 1993), pp. 133–48.
163 Campbell, *Livingstone*, pp. 251, 317, 352.
164 Ibid., p. 20.
165 Ibid., pp. 21, 19.
166 Quoted in Hyam, *Britain's Declining Empire*, p. 13.
167 Bain, *Between Anarchy and Society*, pp. 62, 107. The legitimacy of the discourse of trusteeship would eventually be undermined in two ways. Firstly, for those who experienced colonial rule, it was evident that European powers had failed to live up to their self-designated role as 'trustees'. Secondly, the ascendancy of the idea of self-determination altered the terms of the debate. It brought about a 'normative shift' whereby independence became acknowledged as a fundamental human right. See ibid., pp. 129–39.
168 Campbell, *Livingstone*, pp. 75, 19.
169 Ibid., pp. 199–200.
170 'Mr. D.C. Somervell', *The Times* (25 January 1965), 12.
171 Somervell, *Livingstone*, pp. 85, 93.
172 Ibid., pp. 130–1.
173 Ibid., p. 137.
174 Ibid., pp. 21–2.
175 Hyam, *Britain's Declining Empire*, pp. 79, 76.
176 Somervell, *Livingstone*, pp. 23–4, 25.
177 Ibid., p. 136.
178 Ibid., p. 25.
179 Campbell, *Livingstone*, pp. 79, 125.
180 Robbins, *History*, pp. 139–40.
181 Donal Lowry, *The South African War Reappraised* (Manchester: Manchester University Press, 2000), p. 170.
182 Quoted in ibid., p. 175.
183 Campbell, *Livingstone*, p. 111.
184 Ibid., p. 148.

185 Ibid., pp. 152, 148.
186 Ibid., p. 152.
187 Ibid, p. 111.
188 Quoted in Charles Arnold-Baker, *The Companion to British History* (London: Routledge, 2001), p. 187.
189 Darwin, *The Empire Project*, p. 407. In this Commonwealth spirit, Livingstone was used as a reconciling figure between Britain and South Africa by General J.C. Smuts in a lecture before the Royal Scottish Geographical Society in November 1929. Livingstone's bad relations with the Transvaal Boers had always been 'a source of regret' to him. Smuts told his audience that he had recently made 'small amends' for the 'rough treatment' that Livingstone received at their hands by restoring the remains of his mission station at Mabotsa as far as possible when he was a Transvaal minister. 'After that small attention and this lecture', he wrote, 'I hope his impacable spirit against my people will at last relent.' See Jan C. Smuts, *Africa and Some World Problems* (Oxford: Clarendon Press, 1930), p. 6.
190 Campbell, *Livingstone*, p. 111.
191 A.L. Rowse, *Historians I have Known* (London: Duckworth, 1995), p. 170.
192 Richard Drayton, 'Where Does the World Historian Write From? Objectivity, Moral Conscience and the Past and Present of Imperialism', *Journal of Contemporary History*, 46: 3 (2011), 675.
193 Ibid., p. 677.
194 Reginald Coupland, *Livingstone's Last Journey* (London: Collins, 1945), p. 147.
195 Ibid., p. 32.
196 Ibid., pp. 56–7.
197 Ibid., pp. 123–4. For information on Nyangwe, an important depot in the Arab-African trading network throughout east Africa, see Adrian S. Wisnicki, 'Livingstone in 1871', *The David Livingstone Spectral Imaging Project*, Livingstone Online and the UCLA Digital Library Program (November 2011), http://livingstone.library.ucla.edu/1871diary/livingstone1.htm (accessed 5 November 2012). See also Adrian S. Wisnicki, 'Victorian Field Notes from the Lualaba River, Congo', in Justin D. Livingstone (ed.), 'Livingstone Studies: Bicentenary Essays', special issue, *Scottish Geographical Journal*, 129: 3–4 (2013), 210–39.
198 Coupland, *Livingstone's Last Journey*, pp. 222, 254.
199 Ibid., p. 216.
200 Ibid., pp. 93–4.
201 Ibid., p. 147.
202 Ibid., pp. 151–2.
203 Ibid., pp. 182, 199, 216.
204 Hyam, *Britain's Declining Empire*, p. 91.
205 Quoted in ibid., p. 94.
206 Alex May, 'Coupland, Sir Reginald (1884–1952)', in *Oxford Dictionary of National Biography* (2004), www.oxforddnb.com/view/article/32585 (accessed 6 September 2010).
207 Quoted in Stephen Howe, *Anticolonialism in British Politics: The Left and the End of Empire, 1918–1964* (Oxford: Clarendon Press, 1993), p. 144.
208 Hyam, *Britain's Declining Empire*, p. 94.
209 Howe, *Anticolonialism*, p. 144.
210 Bain, *Between Anarchy and Society*, p. 116.
211 Quoted in ibid.
212 Darwin, *The Empire Project*, p. 546.
213 Harvey J. Sindima, *Malawi's First Republic: An Economic and Political Analysis* (Lanham, Md.: University Press of America, 2002), p. 44.
214 Darwin, *The Empire Project*, p. 619.
215 Sindima, *Malawi's First Republic*, pp. 44, 47.
216 Cecil Northcott, *Livingstone in Africa* (London: Lutterworth, 1957), pp. 79, 77.
217 Timothy Holmes, *Journey to Livingstone: Exploration of an Imperial Myth* (Edinburgh: Canongate, 1993), p. 349.

218 J.A. Steers, 'Debenham, Frank (1883–1965)', in *Oxford Dictionary of National Biography* (2004), www.oxforddnb.com/view/article/32764?docPos=2 (accessed 6 September 2010).
219 Arthur Benson, foreword, in Frank Debenham, *The Way to Ilala: David Livingstone's Pilgrimage* (London: Longmans, 1955), p. 5.
220 Debenham, *The Way to Ilala*, pp. 130, 213.
221 Debenham also had colonial concerns aside from the federation. Like Campbell, he enlisted Livingstone against South Africa, which he felt to be a predatory nation. Discussing Bechuanaland, he outlined its political lineage: it was 'just over a century since Livingstone first put it on the map. It remained a no-man's-land for many years and was ultimately saved by Chief Khama from being either annexed by the Transvaal republic or attached to Cecil Rhodes's South Africa Company.' For Debenham it was fortunate that Britain followed Livingstone's discovery by making Bechuanaland a protectorate in 1885, thereby rescuing it from others' grasping clutches. Debenham quickly moved on from this history to consider the uncertainty of the protectorate's political future: 'It would not be hard to imagine what would be Livingstone's comments on the present situation, with the Union of South Africa claiming the Protectorate.' Livingstone was thus called in to negotiate, and defy, claims to a territory jeopardised by the expansionist nature of the Union of South Africa. See Debenham, *The Way to Ilala*, pp. 66, 68.
222 See D.M.K., 'Michael Gelfand CBE, MD Cape Town, FRCP', *Lancet*, 326: 8452 (August 1985), 458. See also R.H., 'Prof Michael Gelfand', *Lancet*, 326: 8453 (August 1985), 512.
223 Michael Gelfand, *Livingstone the Doctor: His Life and Travels. A Study in Medical History* (Oxford: Blackwell, 1957), p. xii. Gelfand's work, like Debenham's, received colonial certification in the foreword, for his was written by C. Hely-Hutchinson, President of the British South Africa Company.
224 Ibid., pp. 13–14.
225 Diana Wylie, 'Disease, Diet, and Gender: Late Twentieth-Century Perspectives on Empire', in Robert W. Winks (ed.), *The Oxford History of the British Empire*, vol. 5: *Historiography* (Oxford: Oxford University Press, 1999), pp. 277–8.
226 Gelfand, *Livingstone the Doctor*, pp. 63–4.
227 D.M.K., 'Michael Gelfand', p. 458.
228 R.H., 'Prof Michael Gelfand', p. 512.
229 Wylie, 'Disease, Diet, and Gender', p. 278.
230 Gelfand, *Livingstone the Doctor*, pp. xi, 66.
231 James Griffiths, *Livingstone's Africa: Yesterday and Today* (London: Epworth, 1958), p. 27. The book is an expanded version of 'The Beckly Social Service Lecture', which Griffiths delivered at Central Methodist Church, Newcastle, on 8 July 1958.
232 J. Beverley Smith, *James Griffiths and his Times* (Ferndale, Wales: W.T. Maddock, 1976), pp. 89–90.
233 Ibid., p. 94.
234 Kenneth O Morgan, 'Griffiths, Jeremiah [James] (1890–1975)', in *Oxford Dictionary of National Biography* (2004), www.oxforddnb.com/view/article/31175 (accessed 25 July 2011).
235 Griffiths, *Livingstone's Africa*, pp. 13, 21.
236 Ibid., pp. 27, 13.
237 Ibid., pp. 17, 30.
238 Ibid., p. 37.
239 Ibid., pp. 39–41, 41.
240 Ibid., pp. 53, 58.
241 Ibid., pp. 69, 83.
242 Ibid., p. 94.
243 See G.H. Martin, 'Simmons, Jack', in *Oxford Dictionary of National Biography* (2004), www.oxforddnb.com/view/article/74629 (accessed 28 October 2010).

See also Michael Robbins, 'Jack Simmons: The Making of an Historian', in A.K.B. Evans and J.V. Gough (eds), *The Impact of the Railway on Society in Britain: Essays in Honour of Jack Simmons* (Aldershot: Ashgate, 2003), pp. 1–7.
244 Jack Simmons, *Livingstone and Africa* (London: English Universities Press, 1955), pp. 163, 16.
245 Ibid., pp. 165–6.
246 Max Gluckman, 'As Men are Everywhere Else', *Listener* (22 September 1955), 459.
247 Ibid., p. 460.
248 Ibid., p. 459.
249 Ibid., p. 461.
250 Bridglal Pachai, 'Introduction', in Bridglal Pachai (ed.), *Livingstone, Man of Africa: Memorial Essays, 1873–1973* (London: Longman, 1973), p. 3.
251 See Ross, *David Livingstone*, p. 239; MacKenzie, 'David Livingstone: The Construction of the Myth', p. 32.
252 Pettitt, *Dr Livingstone I Presume?*, p. 65.
253 Ross, *David Livingstone*, p. 239.
254 The dispute over the Livingstone statue is discussed in Dana L. Robert, *Christian Mission: How Christianity Became a World Religion* (Malden, Mass.: Wiley Blackwell, 2009), pp. 85–6. See also Angus Howart, 'Diplomatic Tussle over Scot's Statue', *Scotsman* (26 July 2004), http://news.scotsman.com/scotland/Diplomatic-tussle-over-Scots-statue.2548987.jp (accessed 20 May 2011); Jane Flanagan, 'Dr Livingstone's Statue is Ours, we Presume, Zambia Informs Mugabe', *Telegraph* (1 August 2004), www.telegraph.co.uk/news/worldnews/africaandindianocean/zambia/1468390/Dr-Livingstones-statue-is-ours-we-presume-Zambia-informs-Mugabe.html (accessed 20 May 2011).
255 Lunga Sibanda, 'Governor Wants Rhodes Exhumed', *New Zimbabwe* (15 December 2010), www.newzimbabwe.com/news-4051Governor%20wants%20Rhodes%20exhumed/news.aspx (accessed 20 May 2011).
256 Friday Mufuzi has recently gone some way in this direction, by offering an account of the complexities involved in Livingstone's remembrance by both white and black communities in Zambia before and after independence. See Friday Mufuzi, 'The Livingstone Museum and the Memorialisation of David Livingstone in Colonial and Postcolonial Zambia, 1934–2005', in Sarah Worden (ed.), *David Livingstone: Man, Myth and Legacy* (Edinburgh: National Museums Scotland, 2012), pp. 131–53.

CHAPTER FIVE

Nation: Scotland's son

> On the north side of George Square stands a monument which I seldom pass without lifting my hat and greeting with, 'Hail, Scotia's noblest son'. It is erected to the memory of humble, devoted, yet immortal David Livingstone.
> (Henry Y. Pickering, *Scotia's Noblest Son*)

If Livingstone has been hailed as a great British and imperial icon, he has also been upheld as the national hero of his country of birth. He is, it has been claimed, 'Scotia's noblest son' and one of the north's many determined 'sons of toil'.[1] Indeed, a considerable body of the modern Livingstone scholarship has rightly contended that any serious study must not fail to take account of his 'Scottishness'. George Shepperson's 1960 article 'David Livingstone the Scot' took a major step in this direction. He argued that Livingstone was fundamentally shaped both by his perception of his Highland ancestry and by the 'democratic influence' of his Lanarkshire upbringing, which may well, he speculated, have owed something to the cooperative philosophy of Robert Owen, 'whose New Lanark experiments took place only a few miles away'.[2] While in many ways Shepperson was reasserting older suggestions in more cogent form, he took the opportunity to appeal for sustained attention to Livingstone's position in the Scottish intellectual tradition, in areas ranging from evolution to economics, and from abolition to emigration. More recent academics have followed Shepperson in discussing the specifically Scottish forces responsible for shaping Livingstone. For Angus Calder, for instance, he 'should be seen primarily as momentously a self-improving Lowland Scot' who imbibed the 'ingrained traditions of dour stubbornness and wilful self-sacrifice' that abounded locally.[3] Andrew Ross, in contrast, puts emphasis on Livingstone's status as a 'displaced Gael':[4] since his grandfather had resided in the isle of Ulva before migrating to Blantyre, Livingstone was 'in living connection as he grew up with those in his family who themselves were a living connection with pre-1746 tribal Gaeldom'.[5] His Scottish background is seen now, by many scholars, to have explanatory value, casting light on the man and his mentality. Indeed, as Clare Pettitt puts it, 'one of the most crucial things – perhaps *the* most crucial – to remember about Livingstone's identity is that he was definitely Scottish and not English'.[6] In recent criticism, then, Livingstone's distinctiveness as a Scot is granted an integral, or even paramount, position.

In keeping with the current critical inclination, this chapter takes 'Scottishness' as its theme – yet it pursues quite a different approach in so doing. Rather than exploring the formative influence of Livingstone's early environment or the identifiably Scottish features of his social and philosophical outlook, the aim here is to explore a vital dimension of Livingstone's posthumous legacy by asking both how his Scottishness has been represented and, more specifically, how he has been represented by Scots. Those scholars who have studied Livingstone's legacy have passed comment on this dimension of his reputation before. John MacKenzie, for one, attaches special significance to the 1920s, in which the hero took shape as a specifically national icon with the opening of the Scottish National Memorial to Livingstone at his birthplace.[7] It is certainly correct to emphasise the importance of this decade in re-forming Livingstone, but here I take a considerably longer view. While the period does represent the apotheosis of his Scottishness, this strand of his legacy had long existed, if in more subdued form, before eventually coming to greater prominence. MacKenzie recognises this, pointing to the Livingstone statues erected in Edinburgh in 1876 and Glasgow in 1879, the establishment of a memorial church in Blantyre in 1877 and the Livingstone centenary exhibition at the Royal Scottish Museum in 1913.[8] Likewise, Ross has gestured in this direction by casting back to the 1880s, when the Scottish public put pressure on the British government to save Nyasaland – the heartland of Livingstone terrain – from Portuguese intrusion.[9] Nevertheless, Livingstone's posthumous Scottish identity, particularly as it appears in the biographies, has not received detailed assessment in the existing scholarship, and it remains for this chapter to sketch out its longer history in fuller form. This dimension of his reputation has by no means been unified in the century and a half since his death, and so the aim here is to trace its lineage and situate its historical development in the context of an evolving political climate.

Englishness and Anglo-Saxonism

Some authors, of course, have not been particularly interested in Scottish identity at all. This was certainly the case with Henry

Morton Stanley, whose *How I Found Livingstone* barely acknowledges Livingstone's nationality aside from a fleeting reference to his birth 'near Glasgow'.[10] Others followed suit, and in several 'lives' of Livingstone written in the late Victorian and Edwardian periods, Scottishness is conspicuous only by its absence. The children's author William H.G. Kingston, for instance, almost entirely eradicated the trace of the explorer's Alban roots from his biography. Passing over the specifics of Livingstone's upbringing, he readily described his subject as an 'Englishman'.[11] Anne Manning, another prominent writer, better known to contemporaries as 'the author of Mary Powell', was similar in her approach. She rhapsodised over Englishness, offering her readers a hymn to a national character of which Livingstone was a sterling representative: 'There is a race of men – of Englishmen – distinguished beyond almost all the world besides ... Who would not be one of them?'[12] In Manning's biography, Livingstone is less a Scot than a 'solitary, energetic Englishman'.[13] This approach was not entirely uncommon: Robert Cochrane was able to canonise Livingstone in his book *The English Explorers*, without irony, alongside his fellow Scots James Bruce and Mungo Park. All that Livingstone had accomplished was 'to the lasting glory of the English name'.[14]

It is not the case of course that these biographers were attempting, in calculated fashion, to efface the vestiges of Livingstone's Scottishness. Instead, they were following a broader pattern in late nineteenth-century historiography. Stephanie L. Barczewski points out the growing tendency by the end of the century to speak of 'Englishness' in place of, and to indicate, 'Britishness'.[15] While this trend is not reducible to the dominance of the English 'centre', and was met with considerable opposition by some Scots, Welsh and Irish, it certainly reflects this to some degree. As Barczewski notes, the same period saw the rise of histories of Britain, engaged in constructing a national narrative, which were 'conceived, written and marketed specifically as histories of *England*'.[16] The historiography of the period was thus caught in an Anglocentrism that told a triumphal story of English expansion and English institutions, but paid little attention to the other identities of Britain. Manning, born into a southern family with considerable legal connections, and Kingston, the son of a London wine merchant and the grandson of a Justice of the Common Pleas, both reflect this historiographical tendency by happily enmeshing Livingstone within an English framework. As Peter Mandler writes, at this time 'it was now possible unselfconsciously to talk about "England" and mean "Britain"'.[17]

By the mid nineteenth century, the notion of Anglo-Saxon superiority was firmly established in England. Some variety of the myth had existed since at least the 1500s. It had focused, as Reginald Horsman points out, on the superiority of those institutions which were supposedly inherited from the Anglo-Saxon past. In the nineteenth century, however, it was now argued that such superiority 'lay not in the institutions but in the innate characteristics of the race'.[18] This new dimension of the myth reflects a more general nineteenth-century preoccupation with race. From the 1850s, Robert Knox, the anatomist infamous for buying cadavers fresh from Burke and Hare, was proclaiming that 'Race is everything: literature, science, art, in a word, civilization depends on it.'[19] While Knox and his cohorts were considered extremists by their contemporaries, Edward Beasley argues that more mainstream thinkers, from Walter Bagehot to Charles Darwin, helped to foster the idea of race as a biologically determined and inheritable category, which brought with it inherent 'mental and moral characters'.[20]

Few of the authors who wrote about Livingstone would have endorsed this hyper-racialised worldview. A too rigid conception of racial hierarchy would have troubled these often evangelical authors, who held onto the notion of the potential salvability of all humankind. Furthermore, Livingstone had Gaelic ancestry, and so to envelop him in a strongly racial version of the Anglo-Saxon mythos would have been difficult. Yet as Horsman points out, there also existed a more 'pious' and 'vague' counterpart, which valorised the Saxon love of liberty and equality without the same degree of racial vehemence.[21] It was under this version of the myth that Basil Mathews, editor of the LMS's publications, incorporated Livingstone in his biography of 1912. Even while describing Livingstone's Highland ancestry, he gives more emphasis to his embodiment of Anglo-Saxon character. Mathews recounts a scene where Livingstone is recognised at Mpende's village as a member 'of that tribe that has heart to [loves] the black men'. He goes on to write that it gladdened Livingstone 'to think that even in the heart of Africa the people had heard that white men of the Anglo-Saxon race "had heart to" them'.[22] On another occasion, Mathews describes a confrontation with a group of slavers. When Livingstone informed the leaders of the cartel 'that they were Anglo-Saxons the men were afraid' and fled during the night.[23] Throughout the book, Livingstone thus becomes the representative of the Anglo-Saxon race. The biography actually concludes by placing him at the end of a long line of celebrated Saxons. When still a student, Mathews writes, Livingstone had entered Westminster Abbey 'with bared head before the monuments of the heroes and kings, soldiers and saints, of the Anglo-Saxon race'. Thirty-five years later this man, who was 'among the greatest of the "race of hero spirits"', would join the illustrious group in his own Westminster interment.[24]

As Barczewski argues, Anglo-Saxonism asserted an ethnically exclusive identity in a country whose genetic origins were too diverse to sustain such a monolithic narrative.[25] As it operated in the United Kingdom, Anglo-Saxonism was an Anglocentric myth which sought to severely limit the other 'bloodlines' that also claimed to have contributed to the mix of peoples forming Britain. Mathews's biography perhaps represents an uncritical acceptance of this mythology. He is able to tell his readers about Livingstone's Highland descent and the exploits of his ancestors at Culloden, while blithely representing him as a foremost Anglo-Saxon. Tellingly, throughout the book Mathews altogether avoids the words 'Celt' and 'Gael', which would have troubled the image he was trying to project. Even while Livingstone had 'Highland blood', this was less significant than the Anglo-Saxon qualities he embodied.[26] In casting his subject in this way, Mathews implicitly follows a line of construction owing its early genesis to H.M. Stanley, who was prepared to suppress both his own Welsh background and the traces of Livingstone's 'Celtic inheritance' in order to use their African encounter in the service of 'a redolent myth of an exclusively Anglo-Saxon empire'.[27]

Livingstone and the Celtic revival

The highpoint of British Anglo-Saxonism was also the period of a very different intellectual and cultural development: the 'Celtic revival'. As Richard Zumkhawala-Cook observes, this consisted of a major investigation by historians, folklorists and anthropologists into the Gaelic traditions of the Highlands.[28] David Livingstone became enmeshed in this movement as an assortment of researchers took it upon themselves to delve into his Highland lineage and connect Scotland's hero with the heritage of the Celtic regions.[29] In contrast to those who rendered Livingstone an Anglo-Saxon, these authors portrayed him as representative of Gaelic culture and character.

Most attention was paid perhaps to the traditions of his family's involvement in the battle of Culloden. An article published across three issues of the *Celtic Monthly* in 1896 was among the first to connect Livingstone with specific exploits of the famous last stand of the '45. Its author, Duncan Livingstone, who asserted a familiar and romantic image of Culloden, was specifically engaged in tracing the role of 'Domhnuill Mac an Liegh' in the conflict, 'or, as he would be called in English, Donald Livingstone'.[30] He came from a family who had anciently been tenants of the Stewarts in Lismore, and who also followed them into war. It was Donald's distinction, notes Duncan, to have saved the 'colours' of the Stewarts of Appin when the Scottish clans were defeated by Cumberland: he thereby spared their banner the fate of the twelve that were publicly burned in the aftermath of the battle.[31] In telling the story, Duncan emphasises Donald's heroism. He did not simply take up the flag when the standard-bearer fell, and tear it from the staff. Rather, he 'turned back, under fire, to where it lay ... The banner itself indicates that it was *cut*, not *torn*, from the staff.' Furthermore, since 'the flag was cumbersome, heavy and difficult to carry', Donald was 'incommoded' and vulnerable to assault.[32] Neither did his heroism end with the battle of Culloden. On his return journey to Appin he was apparently accosted by an English officer, but he drew his dirk, and 'tradition says there was one less soldier in the army of king George'.[33]

While David Livingstone is not the primary focus of the article, Duncan makes sure to connect him to the heroic story he had unearthed. He points out that the family of Livingstones to which Donald belonged was also known as 'the Barons of Bachuil'; 'At Culloden four of the name were killed and one wounded. David Livingstone was of this race, and some of his relations still reside in Appin.'[34] At the close of his series Duncan once again reminds his readers of the same connection. 'There are lineal descendants of the Livingstones still surviving. Dr. Livingstone, the traveller, was related to him.'[35] The article thus works to bind the explorer to a heroic Culloden legend surviving in oral tradition. Under the auspices of the Celtic revival, with its part recovery and part construction of Highland tradition, Livingstone was endowed with a romanticised Gaelic and Jacobite inheritance.

Over time the story of Livingstone's ancestor, Donald, would take on more epic proportions. In her 1925 book, *Myth, Tradition and Story from Western Argyll*, K.W. Grant recounts a version of the same legend yet more rich in heroics. According to Grant, before the battle of Culloden an elderly woman had foretold that eight men by the name of Donald would fall while flying the banner of the Stewarts, each one 'seizing the coveted ensign' as his predecessor perished.[36] The woman's second sight proved *bona fide*, and one after another was killed in the conflict. But according to Grant's tradition, after the eighth fell, it was another Donald, this time Donald Livingstone, who took up the flag. As he fled the scene with the Stewart colours, a 'spent ball' struck him full in the chest. The banner took the force from the bullet so that he was only knocked unconscious. When he awoke, he laid eyes on his horse, 'grasped the bridle of the flying steed, swung himself into the saddle and sped away'. Immediately, two English troopers were in hot pursuit, so he 'was compelled to stop and face them. The first to reach him was met with a blow so fierce that his head was clove to the chin.'[37] Eventually, 'After many marvellous escapes', Donald managed to deliver the banner to the old chief at Ardshiel.[38]

The connection between Livingstone's family and Culloden, which he had himself mentioned in passing in *Missionary Travels*, was thus capitalised on by Celtic enthusiasts. But connections were also forged with other famous Highland traditions. One author involved in this, Alexander Carmichael, was among the most significant figures in the Celtic revival. As Ian Bradley observes, he travelled around the Highland regions of Scotland between 1855 and 1899 assiduously gathering 'prayers, poems, chants and incantations'.[39] His day job as an exciseman, with the duty of checking on illicit whisky distilleries, offered him the opportunity to travel to the furthest reaches of the Gaelic regions. The product of his researches was published in a multi-volume work, the *Carmina Gadelica*, which has subsequently served as a treasure trove for those with an interest in Celtic Christianity.

In the second volume of his work, Carmichael offered some comments on the ancestry of David Livingstone. Like Duncan Livingstone, he connected the explorer to the 'Barons Livingstone of Bachuill', 'almoners to the church of St Moluag in Lismore'.[40] But Carmichael went beyond this, by further positioning the Barons of Bachuill in an illustrious lineage that could be traced back to the famous Gaelic family of physicians, the Beatons, 'who are said to have come down from Beatan, the medical missionary of the Columban Church'. 'These Beatons', wrote Carmichael, 'produced many eminent men, among them ... the Barons Livingstone of Bachuill, Lismore, David Livingstone, physician, missionary, traveller, and explorer.'[41] Carmichael was clearly building on the notion that the name Livingstone was an Anglicised version of the Gaelic name 'McLeay', which according to one derivation meant 'Son of the Physician'.[42] By establishing a link between Livingstone and the Beatons, Carmichael successfully connected him to a Celtic 'golden age' and claimed him for the Gaelic world. Indeed, in writing about Livingstone, Carmichael placed emphasis on the importance of heredity. He was sure to point out that 'The great traveller resembled his kinsmen and clansmen in Lismore in a remarkable manner, physically, mentally, and morally.'[43] Carmichael thus invested his descent from the Barons of Bachuill with meaning, insinuating that his was a basically Highland character. This point becomes much clearer as he offers Livingstone up as demonstrative of the Gaelic proverb 'heredity will cleave the rock':

The 'Clann an Liegh,' 'Clann an Leighean,' children of the physicians, Livingstones of Bachuill, are said to be descended, like the famous Beaton physicians of Mull, Islay, Skye, and Reay, from Beatan, the Columban medical missionary of Iona ... 'Sgoiltidh an dualchas a chreag' – Heredity will cleave the rock. David Livingstone cleaved his way through rocks harder than any that his kindred had ever faced.[44]

For Carmichael, Livingstone inherited his greatness from a long line of illustrious ancestors. By connecting him with some pre-eminent Highland traditions, Carmichael left his reader in no doubt that his subject was resolutely Celtic, best understood in terms of his Gaelic lineage.

In recent years, the Celtic revival has come under substantial criticism. Zumkhawala-Cook for example argues that it 'relied on a history that safely consigned Highland culture to a distant and romantic past'. It avoided the reality of contemporary Highland problems, like the effects of the 'improvement initiatives', and instead reduced 'its inhabitants to objects of historical study, characters in a quaint narrative of yesterday'.[45] At the same time, the revivalists projected a very idealised vision of Celtic culture. Some critics, for instance, have compared Carmichael's *Carmina* to the eighteenth-century *Ossian*, as a work of invention and imagination. Others, like John Lorne Campbell, think this is too dismissive and suggest that the work should be read as 'a literary and not as a literal presentation of Gaelic folklore': Carmichael may have adapted poems to heighten their appeal, but he was not bent on deception.[46] While the extent of Carmichael's interference is in question, the *Carmina Gadelica*, and projects like it, certainly romanticised the Celtic world and encouraged it to be perceived 'as a remote region of mystical (and misty) spirituality'.[47]

Despite these criticisms it must be acknowledged that in investigating Highland culture, the revivalists sought to combat negative conceptions of the Gaels. As Ian Bradley reminds us, some in Britain, particularly those enthralled by the country's Anglo-Saxon heritage, were unenthusiastic about things Celtic: 'It was against such notions that Celtophiles sought to champion the claims of a marginalised and peripheral people.'[48] Zumkhawala-Cook too concedes that in the 'recovery of Highland folklore there is a subtle edge of critique aimed at the still strong anti-Celtic sentiment in Britain'.[49] Certainly, this was the case with Carmichael, who was himself a Gaelic speaker and a vigorous defender of the crofters. As Bradley points out, he was 'fired by an almost evangelical enthusiasm to show that the Gaels were not the barbaric savages that they were so often portrayed as being in the predominant Anglo-Saxon culture'.[50]

The Celtic revivalists who hunted down traditions of Livingstone's ancestry thus incorporated him into a project that aimed to enhance the prestige of the Gàidhealtachd. By linking him with Highland heritage they were able to represent one of Britain's foremost heroes as one of their own. This was certainly K.W. Grant's purpose as she cast the net wider into Gaelic legend, going beyond Duncan Livingstone and Carmichael in unearthing Livingstone lore. First she provided an additional heroic tradition from the 'Barons of Bachuill' by recounting a notorious feud between 'Maclean of Duart' and 'Stewart of Appin' which eventually resulted in the murder of the latter. His body, left hanging on the castle wall, was daringly rescued by the Baron of Bachuill and his daughters. While escaping 'they came up to the Livingstone skiff as it was running through the narrow channel that separates the islet of Mùsdal from Lismore ... The Livingstones rowed their hardest, reached a creek where they landed and hastily buried the body in the shingle.'[51] Livingstone's ancestors were clearly prepared to risk life and limb for a comrade and so demonstrated the capacity for 'devoted friendship which characterised Livingstone families'. For Grant, the famous explorer possessed the same trait: the depth of his bond with Susi and Chuma, manifested most famously in the transcontinental transportation of his withered remains, was 'a glorious sequel' to the example of his predecessors.[52]

Grant did not stop there, but went on to explore connections with a second branch of the Livingstones, those of 'Achnacree in Benderloch.'[53] The tradition of this family, which was also known as the 'Livingstones of Ballachulish', had a place 'of special and peculiar interest' in the annals of Scottish legend: 'It is believed to be the true answer to the question frequently asked, "who buried the bones of 'Seumas a Ghlinne,' James Stewart of Glen Duror?".'[54] Falsely accused of shooting Colin Campbell of Glenure in Lettermore Wood, this 'James of the Glen', whose estate had been forfeited after the '45, was condemned to death in a rigged trial 'by a packed jury of Campbells'. After the execution, his body was hung in chains and put on display as an 'example of official power' and would remain there for several years before mysteriously disappearing.[55] According to Grant, it was three brothers, Neil, Donald and John, of the Ballachulish Livingstones, who succeeded in retrieving the remains. One brother distracted the sentry while the others hurriedly captured the body; they then fled the mainland together to bury the bones and later took a croft in Ulva. Grant links this courageous episode most explicitly to David Livingstone, by contending that one of the brothers, Neil, would remain in Ulva and eventually become the explorer's grandfather.[56]

According to Andrew Ross, a version of this oral tradition first emerged when Livingstone returned home from his expedition on the Zambesi. He suggests that it originated during his stay with the Duke of Argyll at Inverary Castle, where he found himself embraced by the local people. Since the episode cannot be found in the official records, Ross speculates that the flowering of the Livingstone connection should be seen as *'the Gaels* claiming him as their own'.[57] Certainly, this was Grant's purpose in putting the myth down on paper. By the time she wrote her *Myth, Tradition and Story*, the tale of 'James Stewart of the Glen' had gained in colour, having being famously retold in Robert Louis Stevenson's *Kidnapped* and *Catriona*. But it is at the very end of her chapter on 'Some of David Livingstone's Gaelic Kindred' that Grant makes her purpose most explicit. After pages of information relating to Livingstone's lineage, she writes: 'There were traits in the character of David Livingstone that puzzled his biographers – Lowland Scot, Englishman, and American alike – and that they could not account for. They are no enigma to his Highland country-men.'[58] After positioning him at the end of a long line of Highlanders, she is now able to argue that Livingstone could be clearly comprehended only by those attuned to Gaelic character. Furthermore, embedding him within Celtic lore allowed Grant to directly oppose rival claims that paid insufficient attention to the Gaelic influence. She complained that he 'has been held up to admiration as an example of "the highest type of the Anglo-Saxon race" by those who persistently ignore the old race to which the British Empire to-day owes so much'.[59] She explicitly combated the Anglo-Saxon construction and instead used Livingstone as a vehicle to parade the importance of the Gaels within the fabric of Britain. By presenting him as a Celtic representative, Grant sought to resist the marginalisation of Gaelic culture and to argue for the significance of a people too often dismissed as peripheral.

The truth or falsity of the connection between Livingstone and these different Highland legends is of course not the primary question, although it is correct to regard them with a healthy dose of suspicion. As R.J. Campbell pointed out when he first surveyed the various Highland pedigrees in the 1920s, a considerable amount of conjecture and romance is amply detectable.[60] However, the important question concerns not veracity, but the purpose these stories served. As I have argued, the impulse to connect Livingstone with Highland heritage emerged out of the Celtic revival, a movement ambivalent in nature. While it idealised and reified Celtic culture, it also sought to combat anti-Gaelic prejudice. In the same way, the revivalists who keenly linked Livingstone to Highland traditions may have romanticised their subject, yet they simultaneously succeeded in making him a vehicle for Celtic aspirations.

A fusion of races: a unifying hero for Scotland

In contrast to these polarised representations, Anglo-Saxon and Celtic, certain Scottish authors found Livingstone attractive because he could be interpreted as representing a fusion of races. While Livingstone had sketched a brief picture of his paternal lineage in *Missionary Travels*, he had failed to give any account of his mother's ancestral history. As certain authors happily brought to light her Lowland and Covenanting pedigree, they were able to suggest that Livingstone be understood as an amalgam of Highland and Lowland, a compound of Gael and Saxon. As R.J. Campbell summarised the matter:

> Livingstone came of Scottish Highland stock on his father's side. On the mother's he derived from a no less virile but widely different race, that of the Lowlanders of Strathclyde, with their tenacious democratic traditions and stern Calvinistic faith. It was to the blend of these two that he owed the qualities that chiefly distinguished him throughout life.[61]

Livingstone could best be understood as a blend of races. 'Heredity does not explain everything in a great man ... But it explains much.'[62]

Campbell was not the originator of this idea, and he merely drew attention in explicit fashion to a dimension of Livingstone's Scottish legacy that had long been in existence. It was already being emphasised by the time the 'official' biography of David Livingstone was published in 1880. The author, Professor William Garden Blaikie of New College, Edinburgh, argued that 'the influence of his Highland blood was apparent in many ways in David Livingstone's character. It modified the democratic influences of his early years, when he lived among the cotton-spinners of Lanarkshire'.[63] Indeed, 'It showed itself in the dash and daring which were so remarkably combined in him with the Saxon forethought and perseverance. We are not sure but it gave a tinge to his affections, intensifying his likes, and some of his dislikes too.' On his maternal side, his grandfather 'was a doughty Covenanter', converted by the preaching of 'Secession Erskine'.[64] His mother 'had a great store of family traditions, and, like the mother of Sir Walter Scott, she retained the power of telling them with the utmost accuracy to extreme old age'. She was a repository of Lowland tradition, whose stories gave 'an illustration of the social condition of Scotland in the early part of the eighteenth century'.[65] For Blaikie, both sides of Livingstone's family tree participated in making him the man he was. The tribal influence of the Highlands supposedly 'enabled him to enter more readily into the relation of the African tribes to their chiefs', and 'the genial, gentle influences' that he learnt from his mother 'enabled him to move the savages of Africa'.[66]

The significance of this construction is that Livingstone was able to represent the whole of the Scottish nation. As Neil Davidson points out, Scotland has a long history of internal division. To some degree, the Highlands and Lowlands can be considered distinct societies even after the Union of Parliaments in 1707. Lowland Scotland tended to think of the Highlands as a place of disorder and lawlessness, an identification that was heightened by 'the distinctiveness of their language', Gaelic, and, while the Highlands were still predominantly Catholic and Episcopalian, by differences in religion.[67] Highlanders, too, perceived the Lowlands as alien and as a society that had more in common with the English than with themselves.[68] The deep-seated divisions in Scotland were most famously enacted in the '45, which succeeded in further heightening the animosity.[69] Indeed for Davidson, the very 'name of Scotland concealed the existence of two regions whose inhabitants had been antagonistic to each other for centuries'.[70]

Of course, by the time Livingstone shot to national fame there was no longer such an acute sense of distinction to speak of. A number of factors contributed to this. After the final defeat of Jacobitism, many supporters of the Stuarts shifted their allegiance to the Hanoverians. And as Tom Devine points out, with the spectre of republicanism in the French Revolution, the distinction between Stuart and Hanoverian no longer seemed quite so significant. In this context, Jacobitism could be reinterpreted to signify commitment to the idea of monarchy in an 'abstract sense'. Furthermore, the increasingly important role that Highland regiments played in imperial service helped to undermine Lowlander hostility. The Jacobite Highlanders thus underwent a rapid 'metamorphosis from faithless traitors to national heroes'.[71] This process continued into the nineteenth century, as Walter Scott began to romanticise the Highlands and to employ them as a symbol of the whole of Scotland. The construction of Scotland as a Highland country, as curious as it may seem given the historic antipathy, enabled the assertion of a Scottish identity that would distinguish it from England without jeopardising the Union.[72] As Paul Scott writes, Walter Scott 'created an image of the Scottish past which welded the Highlands and Lowlands together in a heightened national consciousness'.[73]

In the wake of a history of feud and reconciliation, however, it was appropriate that Scotland's foremost hero could represent both Highland and Lowland. The discovery of Livingstone's dual ancestry meant that he could embody a unified national identity that was still relatively new. In the decades following Blaikie, others would take up the theme. In his 1900 biography, for instance, T. Banks Maclachlan, a Glaswegian journalist and the editor of the *Weekly Scotsman* and the *Edinburgh Evening Dispatch*, pointed out the traits that Livingstone's parents possessed and attributed them to their descent. Livingstone's father Neil 'had something of the excitable temper, but also much of the Celt's sensitiveness, insight, gentleness and imagination', while his mother Agnes 'had the blood of the Covenanters in her veins'.[74] This dimension of the Livingstone myth would receive renewed and vigorous attention from the late 1920s, the period in which his Scottishness was most avidly asserted. James I. Macnair, the mind behind the Scottish National Memorial to Livingstone, which opened in 1929, would later write:

> To his Celtic forebears he owed much of his impulsive generosity, his imagination and fire ... From his Lowland ancestry he inherited traits not less valuable: determination and tenacity, hatred of oppression, a self-reliant practical temper, and a sense of humour, and from both sides, his marvellous powers of endurance.[75]

A full exploration of Macnair's particular re-casting of Livingstone, however, must wait until later in the chapter.

The Scottish Briton

While Livingstone symbolised the unity of Highlands and Lowlands, certain nineteenth-century Scottish authors also had a larger purpose at hand. Many of them sought to use Livingstone to demonstrate the significant role that Scotland had played in Britain's international and imperialist projects. Livingstone thus served as a vehicle to assert a Scottish national consciousness, but one that operated within the confines of the Union.

On Livingstone's return from his first trans-continental African journey, he was instantly launched to fame across the whole of Britain, being celebrated with as much fervour in London as in the Scottish cities. Indeed, when Livingstone delivered his famous speech in Cambridge in 1857, it was staged as an event of national (British) significance. For the Professor of Geology, Adam Sedgwick, his visit was on a par with some of the university's most momentous occasions. At the beginning of the century, wrote Sedgwick in his preface to the published lectures, 'England saw nation after nation falling before the sword of the first Napoleon ... Again and again, I have seen those good, stout-hearted men who, under God, had helped to work out the deliverance of Europe from military servitude, greeted in the Senate House with our loudest acclamations.'[76] The Senate House too had even been 'honoured by the presence of our sovereign', who was met with 'a loyalty that carried us almost beyond ourselves'. Yet despite the grandeur of these occasions, on none of them 'were the gratulations of the University more honest and true-hearted than those offered to Dr. Livingstone'.[77] Livingstone's position as a British champion could not have been more clearly stated. His reception in the nation's principal academy equalled those offered to Britain's foremost military heroes and even to royalty, visitations which were sure to excite the highest degree of patriotic fervour.

Within this avid British celebration, a number of Scottish authors sought to stake their claim to Livingstone. He was used to convey a pride in Scottish nationhood, a pride, however, which was firmly compatible with loyalty to the crown and the empire. The period following Livingstone's death was in many ways a time of significant civic confidence in Scotland. In the closing decades of the nineteenth century, Glasgow was on the path to becoming 'the second city of the Empire'.[78] With rapid developments in its heavy industries, Scotland gained international pre-eminence in several areas and developed an important role in the global economy.[79] Despite its flourishing international position, however, some scholars have interpreted this period as one of crisis in Scottish identity. Tom Nairn, for instance, bemoaned Scotland's failure to follow other small nations in Europe by pursuing nationalism. In his understanding, Scotland compromised on its distinctive identity, paying the price of Anglicisation and developing 'grave cultural and psychological problems' in order to benefit economically from the Union.[80] More recently, scholars have contested this understanding of nineteenth-century Scotland, arguing, as Devine puts it, that 'it does not follow that because the basis for a strong *political nationalism* did not exist in the Victorian era Scottish national identity was therefore in itself inevitably emasculated'.[81] While the middle classes did not seek independence, since they possessed considerable political autonomy and prosperity, the economic success they had achieved was a major source of national pride. Furthermore, the empire, rather than quashing Scottish national sentiment, actually provided a platform for it. It bolstered esteem because it enabled the Scots to demonstrate both their national distinctiveness and the parity of their partnership with their Southern neighbours:[82] 'within the imperial relationship the Scots could feel that they were the peers of the English'.[83]

The Scottish representation of Livingstone in this period reflects the contemporary impulse to assert the country's contribution to the empire and thus heighten its prestige within the British state. Perhaps the best example of this construction is John McGregor's seventy-two-page epic poem *The Hero of an Unknown Land* (1875). It begins very much in epic fashion, with a hymn to a Muse who has inspired him to lift the authorial pen. In McGregor's version of heroic poetry, this Muse is the Scottish nation:

> O Scotland, dear, my own loved land,
> With thoughts of thee, emotions grand
> . . .
>
> Such love, dear land, dost thou inspire –
> A bard's pure love, a patriot's fire.[84]

The author thus commences the poem by expressing his own identification with Scotland. In a declaration of pride, he declares that all Scotsmen 'Have on their souls engraven – "free"': 'And still thy sons proud boast shall be / That thou art Scotia and they free.'[85] After extolling the nation, and the powerful sentiments it could inspire within true patriots, McGregor goes on to recite the familiar scenes from Scottish history that so popularly serve as signposts of national identity. He would:

> envy those their happy lot
> With Bruce or Wallace wight that fought;
> Or those that sleep 'neath cairn and sod,
> Martyrs for Scotland and for God.[86]

While these heroes of Scotland's past had received their share of panegyrics, McGregor felt the pressing need for a 'bard of modern time', 'To sing another hero's worth'. With inflated rhetoric, he construes himself as the laureate of Scotland's present, proclaiming that 'for a hero's noble fame / I'd dare to light the holy flame / Of poesy'. And the new heroic figure for the modern age, comparable with the champions of the distant past, would be 'thy noblest son, / Old Scotland, David Livingstone!'[87]

The life of Livingstone that McGregor recites is thus from the outset enmeshed within a Scottish frame of reference and a heroic narrative of its history. As the poem goes on, Livingstone is also represented as embodying a specifically Scottish character. He was one of the many 'sons' of 'old Scotia' who succeeded through their commitment to 'proud ambition's fervid flame'. Most of all, it was in 'self-denial grand' that lay the secret to 'the independence of our land'. Livingstone was of course the pre-eminent embodiment of this quality:

> Nor least of these was Livingstone,
> To toil to reach the mighty throne
> Of learning and to spurn
> The mountains that before him lay
> Of trial or difficulty.[88]

Part of what made Livingstone great was thus his Scottishness, his status as the supreme representative of the national character.

The interest of this poem does not merely consist in its construction of Livingstone as exemplary Scot. In fact, once he is firmly fixed as Scottish in the consciousness of the reader, McGregor's language begins to change. Generally there is a shift from the restricted praise that had been reserved for Scotland, to a broader encomium on England and 'Albion'. McGregor now can write:

> hail, old England! hail to thee
> That first hath set the captive free,
> And struck his shackles down
> Hail, Albion! Noble thou as brave,
> To break the fetters of the slave.[89]

By equating England and 'Albion', McGregor seeks to extend his praise to Britain as a whole. He makes this clearer when he lauds 'England's' desire to 'disperse the haze of night' with the 'glorious sun' of 'Enlightened civilisation', a lofty aspiration foremost in 'British hearts and British life.'[90] The point is that as McGregor's poem progresses there is a gradual broadening of horizons, a shift from the Scottish to the British.

Mirroring this is an adjustment in the descriptors surrounding Livingstone. Where he had formerly been firmly a Scot, Livingstone now becomes a 'Briton';[91] earlier in the text he had been Scotland's 'son', but now he is portrayed as the 'brave son' of 'Brave Albion, land of liberty'.[92] Reporting Livingstone's return to the United Kingdom in 1856, McGregor writes of the enthusiasm with which 'Britain greets her noble son'.[93] Having first established Livingstone as a model Scot, the poem progressively asserts his status as a British hero. By so doing, McGregor's epic works to emphasise that it was the Scottish nation, with its attendant character, that had provided the Union with the most honoured of Britons.

In drawing on Livingstone to display Scotland's contribution to Britain's empire, McGregor's work does not stand alone. In the early 1880s, for instance, a series of readings and sixteen songs, written and composed by Charles Allan and John Guest, was published with the title *David Livingstone; or, Scotland's Soldier of Christ*. While the collection was firmly evangelical in intent, being designed for church use, Scottishness was clearly an additional critical horizon. 'No name appeals more to every good instinct in our breast', the authors assert at the outset, 'than that of Scotland's soldier of God, David Livingstone.'[94] In the same vein, the first song contains the lyrics 'Would you hear the Thrilling Story, of our Scottish hero bold', while another urges its listeners to attend to the lessons 'the grand old Scotchman teaches'.[95] But once again, the larger framework of Britishness remains present.

Even though this champion was from the 'Land O' Cakes', as the authors put it following Burns, 'The heart of Britain throbb'd with pride, When [he] went forth the lost to guide.'[96] The Scottish hero had a hold on British hearts.

The same line of construction is also apparent in an 1877 biography by Jabez Marrat, a Methodist minister who frequently wrote on Scots themes. Rather than shying away from Livingstone's loyalty to the crown, this author capitalised on Livingstone's decision to name the Victoria Falls after the reigning monarch. For Marrat, this amply illustrated the presence of 'the loyal feeling, which even in regions remote from British dominion swelled high in his heart'.[97] Yet, while British allegiance was not in question, Marrat, like McGregor, was very keen to draw attention to Livingstone's more specific national identity. His mind, argued Marrat, had a distinctly Scottish quality, being 'characterised by vigorous common sense' and by 'no small share of that grand Scottish obstinacy'.[98] Furthermore, a Scots upbringing had been crucial in the formation of Livingstone's talents and character. A diet of 'oatmeal and hardwork had given him a compactness of fibre enabling him to endure excessive heat and fatigue with impunity'.[99] Even more important was the trajectory of Livingstone's education. The well-known story of his purchase of a Latin grammar with his first week's wages demonstrated for Marrat 'a Scottish avidity for mental improvement'.[100] In aspiring to attend university and determining to pay his own way, Livingstone revealed his independent nature, but at the same time he 'knew he was only doing what many other brave Scottish youths had done'.[101]

In emphasising Livingstone's course of education, Marrat ensured that his biography resonated with what Robert Anderson has described as a key 'marker of Scottish identity'. As Anderson points out, the myth of a unique Scots form of education is 'associated with various supposed qualities of the Scottish character such as individualism, social ambition, respect for talent above birth, or "metaphysical" rationalism'.[102] Livingstone's cultivation of knowledge and strenuous efforts towards academic achievement thus became, in Marrat's text, national characteristics. As he put it in one of his other books, *Northern Lights*, Livingstone's 'difficulties in the acquisition of learning were great; but he was a thorough adept in the Scotch way of putting a stout heart to a steep hill'.[103] Since many others had walked the path before him, Marrat implies, Livingstone profited from a society that valued learning and made space for his talent to flourish. The notion of the Scottish enthusiasm for education, as David McCrone points out, has historically functioned to confirm the country's distinctive nature, particularly in relation to its southern neighbour. The myth thus helped 'to confirm a sense of identity by saying who Scots are and what they value'.[104]

By connecting Livingstone with a prominent myth of Scottish identity, Marrat reveals a longstanding strategy that authors employed in their efforts to claim Livingstone for Scotland. As many scholars have observed, the notion of Scottish distinctiveness has been constructed around the particularity of the country's legal, educational and ecclesiastical systems. Together, these three components constitute what has been called the 'holy trinity' of Scottish identity.[105] The idea was that, despite the Union of 1707, Scotland remained perennially separate in the triune spheres of law, college and Kirk. Authors wanting to yoke Livingstone firmly to his country of origin thus made sure to connect him with the latter two of these institutions.

Perhaps the best instance of this occurs in G. Watt Smith's 1913 biography *David Livingstone: The Great Heart of Africa*. Written on the centenary of Livingstone's birth, Smith's book was published as the 'Blantyre Edition', so named after the explorer's hometown. It is thus no surprise that considerable space should be given to the local features of Livingstone's life. Again, Smith paraded Livingstone's Scottish education, explaining that 'his school contributed its share to his general training'.[106] And like Marrat, Smith made it clear that Livingstone was not unique in his drive towards erudition: rather, he was just Scottish. While his decision to pursue a degree 'was a bold proposal', 'Fortunately it is not difficult to do something heroic when you know that others have done it before. Many Scotch lads had won their way to a coveted degree ... who had as few advantages as Livingstone had.'[107] Smith went further than Marrat, however, by using his biography to comment on the respective natures of English and Scottish higher education. 'Scotland is fortunate in the number and character of her universities', he wrote: 'They never had that cloistered exclusiveness which has been characteristic of Oxford and Cambridge. The shrines were not reserved for the gentle born, but open to any, with fine fingers or horny hands, whose brains were equal to the exercises of the professors.'[108] In this, Smith tapped into a major dimension of the myth of Scottish learning: that it has historically been much more democratic than England's. As McCrone points out, 'Few myths are more powerful and prevalent in and about Scotland than that it is a more egalitarian society than England.'[109] Smith thus claimed Livingstone as a product of the Scottish democratic intellect and used him to consolidate Scotland's identity against its 'other', England. He was a product of the Scottish 'genius for education which ... has become part of their very blood'.[110]

Smith also fixed Livingstone to that other keystone of Scots identity, the ecclesiastical tradition. He argued that one of the primary explanations for 'the peculiar eminence' of Scotsmen was 'what has been euphemistically called the faculty for religion'. 'Among the Scottish people', he suggested, 'this produces a sense of duty which helps them to do what lies to their hand to the best of their ability.'[111] Smith recognised that the terminology of Scottish Christianity could seem impenetrable to the outsider, but he contended that 'not one of these terms has ever stood for a passing emotion, an intellectual fad, or a theological quibble'. Instead, 'They are the signs which represent movements which stirred certain people to their depths and give them a firmer grip on some section of the volume of Divine truth.'[112] The Scottish penchant for sect and schism was a sign not of unhealthy division, but of a passion for theological accuracy. It was this environment that played perhaps the biggest role in shaping Livingstone: he 'received all the benefits he could from this distinctively Scottish characteristic'.[113] More specifically, Smith felt that much of Livingstone's greatness lay in the religious concepts that he imbibed early in life from his 'priest-like father'.[114] Indeed, 'All his later achievements ... were just the development of what the precept and example of his father had set before him.'[115] Throughout his biography, Smith routinely makes Livingstone's local context, educational and theological, the foundation of his greatness.

G. Watt Smith's work marks the culmination of the Scottish representation of David Livingstone before the outbreak of the First World War. While, as Tom Devine points out, the years preceding 1914 saw the 'resource endowment' that had given Scotland its competitive edge begin to weaken, the nation nevertheless remained confident about its international position.[116] As Angus Calder puts it, 'In 1914, Scots were by and large complacent about their status in the world.'[117] Smith's biography, in addition to connecting Livingstone with markers of Scottish identity, reflects the confidence of Edwardian industrial Scotland within Britain. He paints a picture of the 'majestic Clyde', which passed Livingstone's home and then progressed to become a 'fabled highway of the Argosies of Commerce ... moving messengers from other nations'.[118] The text parades Scotland's global standing, celebrating the imperial connections of Glasgow. The Broomielaw Quay, the city's historic harbour, takes on romantic significance: 'BROOMIELAW!' Smith exclaims, 'What associations are called up by that name', by that 'point of contact between the second city of the empire and all the rest of the world.'[119] Smith is keen to remind his readers that Livingstone's nation of birth was a major player on the world stage and vital to British commerce and imperialism.

Throughout the Victorian and Edwardian periods, Scottish authors staked their claim to Livingstone by vigorously asserting the country's importance in shaping him into the figure that so captured the British imagination. Envisaging him as a representative Scot, the product of a distinct educational and ecclesiastical system, many of these biographies show a depth of national pride. Yet this Scottish construction should not be considered part of a nationalistic project, since it operated firmly within the parameters of the Union relationship. It is useful to bear in mind here Neil Davidson's distinction between the political project of nationalism and a sense of national consciousness.[120] It is possible to have a strong and distinct awareness of national identity without the concomitant aspiration to achieve independence. Livingstone was drawn on to express and enhance Scottish identity, with the primary purpose of consolidating prestige within the British imperial project.

A Kailyard story

One of the effects of the focus on Livingstone's Scottish background is that many of the biographies manifest traits reminiscent of the 'Kailyard' genre. The term 'Kailyard' was originally associated with a group of Scottish authors in the 1890s, notably Barrie, Crockett and Maclaren, but as Andrew Nash points out it has subsequently come to define a 'tradition'.[121] In one of the first systematised studies of Kailyard, Ian Campbell identifies the themes conventionally associated with its writing: 'education, religion, strong social fabric and family ties, Burns worship, local boys getting on'.[122] It is a literature that focuses primarily on rural communities of the 'comfortable working class', whose values are that of 'Churchgoing, decent rational practical Christianity'.[123] The Kailyard genre was exceptionally popular and indeed was one of the major forms of literary output in Scotland during the late Victorian period. This mode of writing and the image of the nation that it presented, however, would persist well beyond the confines of the nineteenth century.

In some ways, it is obvious that Livingstone's childhood and development correspond with Kailyard themes. From an evangelical and working-class background, it is undeniable that he succeeded in changing his circumstances through hard work and application in education. Certain authors, however, capitalised on these resonances to give Livingstone's success a mythic quality. The emphasis on Scots education and the Kirk that I disclosed in Jabez Marrat and G. Watt Smith is assuredly evocative of the genre, but in other biographies it intrudes in even more palpable fashion.

Several texts position Livingstone in a Kailyard world by fictionalising scenes from his Scottish youth. For instance, James J. Ellis's *David*

Livingstone begins by fabricating a conversation between Livingstone's mother, Agnes, and her father, David Hunter.[124] Discussing her son's recent employment in Blantyre Mill, Agnes dolefully remarks: 'He's but a little lad to begin the toil that always falls to the poor. It went to my heart like a knife; and yet I was as proud as a queen when last Saturday night he brought me his first week's wages ...'[125] The scene locates Livingstone within the honest poor, hard-working and content with their lot. But while the child is compelled by poverty to heavy toil, he belongs to a family that values learning. David Hunter, reflecting on his grandchildren, mentions to his daughter that they 'come here and rummage my books over, and "let them," say I': 'I'm glad that your husband himself reads, and sets them reading too.'[126] The Scottish provincial social space is represented as one of hard labour but in which the democratic intellect thrives.

Ellis ensures, in Kailyard fashion, that the Scottish working-class home is presented as a realm of domestic harmony. Agnes is a faithful wife whose devotion to her husband is boundless. She tells her father: 'It's main hard I know to make the little bit o' money answer all our needs; but when he comes in from his rounds, however worried I am, I forget all about it and about his tea-selling, and his gentle, winning face looks like an angel's.'[127] Agnes thus appears as the conventional Kailyard angel in the house who, as Zumkhawala-Cook puts it, is at once 'delicate, energetic, generous, wholesome, idle, charitable and subservient while simultaneously demonstrating qualities of strength, hardiness, efficiency, skill'.[128] Agnes also indicates the role of Christian principles in her homestead and marriage, announcing: 'When we are one in the Lord, it is as nigh heaven as may be here below.'[129] The whole scene is saturated in religion, and the Church maintains pride of place at the centre of their social domain. Both David Hunter and his son-in-law Neil are portrayed as men of staunch Christian character, although of different theological persuasions: the former 'love[d] the presbytery', while the latter was a Sunday school teacher and deacon in an independent church.[130] The denominational discord, however, only functions to heighten the reader's perception that this is a community in which Church and faith are integral to the fabric of daily affairs.

Other biographies of Livingstone also invented scenes that were deeply redolent of Kailyard fiction. Robert Smiles's work, published in 1885 when the genre was on the ascent, opens outside the Blantyre factory on a day when the mill machinery had unexpectedly ground to a halt. In the pages that follow, Smiles imagines the experience that young 'Davie Livinstin' and two of his factory workmates might have had on being released from their daily labour. One boy wants to go to

Hamilton to 'see "the sojers" and what was going on in "the toon"', while another wants to go to Cathlin Brae on the Clyde, where they could enjoy the views and gather some rare plants.[131] The second more elevated suggestion, proffered by Davie, wins the day, and the boys set off on their journey. Along the way they decide to perform some music to raise money to buy lunch. And so one of them, playing the tin whistle, 'struck up "Maggie Lauder," following in succession with "The Laird O'Cockpen" and "Whistle, and I'll come to you, my lad"'.[132] On hearing the music, a woman from a nearby house emerged to ask them whether they were there to beg. Davie took it upon himself to respond: 'No, no, mem; we're no beggars. The mill that we work at's stoppit, an' we cam' frae Blantyre to see the new road. We're unco hungry, an' we have nae siller; but we dinna want siller. We thocht ye micht like a tune.' The woman replied with peasant charm: '*You* are a pawkie loon; but come awa; yese no want for a bit bannock.'[133]

This fictionalised beginning certainly squares with Kailyard features by rooting Livingstone's youth in a rural setting of homely values. Indeed, as Thomas Knowles points out, the 'classic' Kailyard 'is characterised by the sentimental and nostalgic treatment of parochial scenes'.[134] By constructing such a provincial setting, Smiles's text works to accentuate the transformation that was effected in Livingstone's life. He thus becomes the apotheosis of the 'lad o' pairts': the story of the poor Scottish boy who makes good. As Ian Campbell argues, in one Kailyard plot the local boy who progresses to 'the wider world' does so 'without losing his loyalty to the kailyard village'.[135] This feature appears in Smiles, as he assures his readers that Livingstone maintained his domestic values: 'He lived a transparent life, never seeking places or associations in which he would be ashamed for his mother, sisters, or anybody else to see him.' While he achieved greatness in Africa, he never departed from the ethics of his early experience: 'He lived as if in the sight of the family.'[136]

In representing Livingstone in terms of the Kailyard, these authors indicated that he could best be understood within a Scottish context: he was seen as the fitting subject for the country's best-known literary genre. Yet the Kailyard has come under substantial censure in recent years and, as Andrew Nash points out, the very term has become one 'to sum up what critics take to be wrong ways of writing about Scotland'.[137] Much of this hostility dates to the Scottish Renaissance, when Hugh MacDairmid and others sought to combat what they saw as the misrepresentation of the nation. Kailyard was so vigorously resisted because 'the diversity of Scottish life was not being given cultural voice'.[138] It had come to provide 'a definition of Scotland' that was profoundly limited, one that was by no means representative of the lived experience of the majority of Scots, and so it needed to be rebuffed in the interest of national authenticity.[139]

The Kailyard genre, it is now argued, can be understood as meeting a series of turn-of-the-century anxieties. As Ian Campbell puts it, in a period of transition and industrialisation, it 'looks back to a just vanished comfortable certainty'.[140] With the rapid rise of the city, the countryside and village offered an imagined location of security. In the midst of end-of-the-century unease about the rise of new social movements and challenges to established moral perspectives, Kailyard novels performed an 'essentially conservationist' role in Scottish culture.[141] As the subject of Kailyard representation, Livingstone was thus conscripted into a vision of Scotland that was deeply conservative. Nevertheless, despite their reactionary impulse, these authors were engaged in staking a claim to Livingstone, in representing him in no uncertain terms as a Scot. Indeed, it would be wrong to dismiss Kailyard out of hand. As Campbell observes, its authors at least 'invited pride in a Scottish Church, social fabric, educational system and historical sense'.[142] One might not like their vision of Scotland, but they at least tried to articulate a version of national identity. According to Zumkhawala-Cook, some critics have detected a nationalistic current at work in Kailyard, a construction of Scottish distinctiveness that was not dissimilar to Walter Scott's literary attempts to prevent the 'cultural erasure' of Scotland.[143] It seems best then to view Kailyard literature as a problematic and ambivalent form of cultural expression. This ambivalence is mirrored in the Kailyard construction of Livingstone: on the one hand, the authors ensured that attention was directed towards his Scottish identity, yet on the other hand they used him as a vehicle for a vision of the nation that was nostalgic and even semi-mythical.

One of the conspicuous features of Robert Smiles's depiction of Livingstone, and of Kailyard texts in general, is its extensive use of Scots language. In the scene outlined above, 'Davie's' Scottish pronunciation is conveyed almost phonetically, and a certain amount of Scots vocabulary is incorporated into his speech. But it is significant that Smiles often chooses to translate the words and phrases he uses into Standard English. For example, when Livingstone is offered some 'bannock' by the Scottish housewife whom the boys serenade, Smiles explains in parenthesis that this refers to 'unleavened cakes of flour'.[144] The same thing occurs in the description of Livingstone's birthplace: it was near the 'dookit', or 'dove-cote', in Blantyre and had a 'roondle', or 'a roofed spiral stone stair'.[145]

What then was Smiles's purpose in writing in Scots? Certainly, as Emma Letley points out, many authors have been able to use the language as 'a gesture of resistance, a political, nationalist reproach against the union, against London, and against the ascendancy of Standard English'.[146] Particularly in the late eighteenth and early nineteenth centuries, those who wrote in Scots had to resist a longstanding cultural convention that excluded the language from serious discourse: they had to combat a lengthy history of 'linguistic prejudice' against writing in any 'regional' language.[147] Such political statement, however, played at most a small role for a writer like Smiles. By the late nineteenth century there was no longer such animosity towards Scots and, while it remained possible to use the language to radical effect, the 'foreignness' of literature in 'dialect' now had broader appeal. In translating Scots words into English, Smiles attempted to meet this appetite for the exotic. Of course, the very need to provide a translation presumed a readership for whom the language was unfamiliar: Scots thus became a spectacle, offered up for the titillation of a non-local audience. The parenthetical definitions, a familiar Kailyard device, made the Scots more immediately accessible to its readers, but as Letley points out, they actually serve to make the speech seem much more foreign.[148] The quotation marks used to demarcate the Scots vocabulary further heighten the sense of the alien. Compounding this too is the implied distance between the language of the characters and the mediating voice of the narrator. While the former speak Scots, Smiles is in control of perfect English. The effect of all this is to emphasise 'the linguistic contrast between Scots and English', which, as Letley argues, 'tends to isolate the Scots words and to patronise the speakers of the dialect'.[149] In his use of Scottish language, Smiles did venture to ensure that Livingstone's background could not be overlooked. Yet, for all that, the text appears more preoccupied with satisfying an appetite for the foreign and, in so doing, reproduces a parochial image of Scotland and its language.

Instances of the Kailyard portrayal of Livingstone, with its Scots linguistic context, can be found well into the twentieth century. In 1931, Mary A. Maclennan's play *David Livingstone: A Simple Drama* was published posthumously by her husband.[150] The work was a dramatic rendering of various scenes from Livingstone's life, but a significant proportion was devoted to his Blantyre upbringing. Like the authors of the earlier texts we have examined, Maclennan invented episodes from Livingstone's youth, opening her play with a vision of his grandfather telling stories from Culloden. Following the pattern established by earlier Kailyard constructions, Scots religion remains pre-eminent and Livingstone is again the 'lad o' pairts', who departs from the village sphere but holds onto the values imparted at the hearth. More interesting, however, is the way in which the text is encoded linguistically.

In fact, an intriguing language plot can be traced across the pages of Maclennan's short dramatisation of Livingstone.[151] To explore this dimension, it would be useful to follow John Corbett and adopt a 'stylistics' analysis, a mode of criticism that is 'concerned with showing how the selection of options from the language system can result in a particular interpretation'.[152] A stylistics approach would pay attention to the various effects that can be achieved within a text by employing different varieties and registers of language. In Maclennan's play there are two such linguistic levels; Standard English and Rural Scots. While his family use Scottish diction and vocabulary, Livingstone speaks with perfect Received Pronunciation. This is even the case, to some degree, while he is a child. When his grandfather pauses in his tale 'o' Prince Chairlie' and 'the field o' battle fighting for the tartan', Livingstone politely urges him in polished Queen's English, 'Do go on, Grandpa.'[153] The discrepancy at this point is only slightly detectable, but as the play progresses the linguistic gulf becomes more apparent. In a later scene, Livingstone's father comes to visit him while he is studying in Glasgow. He asks his son if he is busy with work, to which Livingstone replies, 'Never too busy to see you, Father. Sit down. How's mother?' Livingstone's Standard English differs from the Scots of his father, who says, 'Aye at it, my boy, Aye at it!' on seeing his son engrossed in his books. By this stage, when Livingstone uses Scots, the words appear in quotation marks. To his father's enquiries about the difficulty of his studies, he replies: 'Oh, it's all right, Father! "A stout heart to a stey brae".'[154] Scots is thus a discourse that he can draw on and quote at will, but it is not his own mode of speech. In the later part of the text, Livingstone almost speaks like an English gentleman. When he returns to Blantyre after his first African expedition, and his mother delights that he has 'come back unspoiled', Livingstone says: 'What a *cad* he would be who didn't, and to such a mother' (emphasis added).[155] While the textual content tells us that Livingstone remained true to his home values, the code-mixing of the language plot lends another shade of meaning. Livingstone's anglicised speech, which sits in contrast to his family's Scots, suggests a narrative of maturation: it implies that he transcended the people and culture of small-town Scotland. Moreover, since Livingstone spoke differently even while a child there is a sense in which the text insinuates his natural superiority. He is marked off as an exception to the culture of his provenance, which by default appears restricted and unsophisticated.

It is worth mentioning that it was possible to devise a language plot that could be put to more constructive use. John McGregor, for example, already discussed at length, integrated a positive linguistic narrative into *The Hero of an Unknown Land*. While the vast majority of the work is in Standard English and consists of a single epic poem, McGregor offsets one short separate piece in Scots that addresses the death of Livingstone's wife. Beginning with Livingstone's oft-quoted words of lament, 'Poor Mary sleeps in Shupanga brae, And beeks fornent the sun', the poem goes on to imaginatively express his loss in Scots. After her passing, the beauty of nature and 'the balm o' ilka flower' 'bring nae joy to me', but only 'thoughts o' grief an' wae'. Other stanzas reflect on Mary's character: 'Her heart was ay sae leal an' kind, / Her love sae pure and true.'[156] While the poem cannot be considered any great work of literature, it is stylistically provoking. McGregor privileges Scots as the language of Livingstone's most deeply felt emotion, the most appropriate vehicle to convey pain and loss. Here, Scots is not translated and made foreign, nor represented as a limited language that Livingstone culturally supersedes. Instead, it is his natural medium of expression and has the qualities required to express the depths of lamentation.

What should now be clear from this survey is the longevity of the Kailyard form and its attendant vision of Scotland. From the late nineteenth century, and well into the twentieth, a number of authors chose to represent Livingstone in the familiar terms of this genre. He lent himself of course to this construction; it was not difficult to construe Livingstone as the 'lad o' pairts'. Furthermore, while his hometown Blantyre was actually fairly industrialised, it was enough of a threshold space between the country and the city, which lay only a few miles away, for authors to stress the rurality of his childhood domicile. But using the Kailyard genre to relate Livingstone's life was equivocal in its effects. In many ways it involved him in some of the most established of Scottish stereotypes. However, as Corbett points out, typecasts do not always have a purely negative function: 'it is salutary to remember that stereotypes can work for people as well as against them'.[157] Even tired and hackneyed depictions of Scotland have the function of distinguishing its culture from that of England and so asserting its independent identity. The Kailyard construction of Livingstone, while detrimental in many respects, at least served to claim him as a representative Scot.

The Scottish National Memorial to David Livingstone: a people's hero

Maclennan's 1931 dramatisation leads us into a particularly interesting period, for it is generally agreed that it was from the 1920s that Livingstone's Scottish identity was most vigorously asserted. As John MacKenzie argues, for example, it was in this period that Livingstone was re-appropriated for the contemporary Scottish cultural revival.[158] In a similar vein, Clare Pettitt suggests that the new emphasis can be related to developments in Scottish nationalism and the renewed sense of national identity made apparent in the cultural projects of the Scottish Renaissance.[159] While both scholars are correct in their observations, the purpose of this chapter has been to offer a longer history of the Scottish representation of Livingstone, and consequently to suggest that this period does not represent any entirely novel construction. The Scottish claim, so prominent in this period, was actually an intensification and modification of a long-established connection.

Those who have commented on Livingstone's Scottish reputation have attached importance to a cantata entitled *Livingstone the Pilgrim* by Hamish MacCunn – a composer best known for his overture *The Land of the Mountain and the Flood*. Written in 1913, the centenary of Livingstone's birth, the piece is sometimes seen as a key moment in his connection with Scottish national identity that would flourish in the next decade. Yet, in light of the numerous texts discussed in this chapter, it seems fair to say that it has been given undue significance. At most we can agree with Andrew Ross, who, touching on the matter, suggests that it represents 'a further step in an existing link between Livingstone and a renewed Scottish assertiveness' that can be traced into the previous century.[160] Even at that, it is not immediately clear that there is much to mark the text as distinctively Scottish. Its preoccupation is the sacred rather than the national, and it traces the course of Livingstone's spiritual trajectory in four movements. The following lines are indicative of its flavour: 'The selfless love of man, The fearless love of truth, These be, since time began, The beacon lights of youth.'[161] The cantata contains no references to particular details of Livingstone's life and notably none to his national identity. In light of the lack of Scots emphasis, it seems important to acknowledge that the text of the cantata was not actually written by MacCunn, but by Charles Silvester Horne, an English Congregationalist minister. Yet this piece was not the only evidence of MacCunn's interest in Livingstone. Arguably more important was a work entitled 'The Livingstone Episode', part of his larger *Pageant of Darkness and Light* written in collaboration with John Oxenham.[162] Commissioned by the LMS, however, 'The Livingstone Episode' was again primarily religious in theme. It focused on the Stanley encounter, ending by celebrating Livingstone's decision to refuse passage to Britain and retain his commitment to Africa. Clearly, then, the tone of this latter piece confirms that the Scottish significance of MacCunn has been somewhat overstated. Yet at the same time, there is one striking respect in which 'The Livingstone Episode' is noteworthy. This, I would argue, is less do with its lyrical content or

Scottish quality than with the notable occasions at which it was performed. First produced for 'The Orient in London: A Great Missionary Exhibition' in 1908, 'The Livingstone Episode' was later performed in the 'Pageant of Empire' at the 1924 British Empire Exhibition at Wembley.[163] These events suggest that, following the well-established pattern of Livingstone's Scottish biographers, MacCunn was engaged in parading the contribution of a Scot to British imperial glory: in fact, he did so at key events in the celebration of empire. In the story of Scotland's claim to Livingstone, MacCunn's work is certainly not as singular as has been sometimes been supposed: where it does have consequence, however, it resides primarily in the politics of performance.

By far the most notable contribution to Livingstone's evolving Scottish legacy in this period was his commemoration in a national memorial in Blantyre, opened on Saturday 5 October 1929. While Livingstone's religious credentials were given prominence, the new venture was, Andrew Ross argues, resolutely 'a *national* not a church or missionary memorial' (emphasis added).[164] This much is clear in the literature about its opening. In a pamphlet entitled *The Story of the Scottish National Memorial* by James I. Macnair, its founder, the national colour of the language is conspicuous. According to John White, author of the booklet's foreword, Macnair had stated when he first conceived of the project that 'Livingstone is a national figure and a movement like this should be national.'[165] The popularity of the memorial proved him right and amply demonstrated the appeal that Livingstone continued to exert 'upon the imagination and affection of the Scottish people'.[166] In the body of the text, Macnair continued to cast the story of the memorial in terms of Scottish nationhood. Describing the state of degeneration into which Livingstone's birthplace had fallen prior to the restorative initiative, Macnair wrote, 'The general surroundings were so disreputable that no Scotsman could take an overseas friend there, without an acute sense of shame.' Allowing Livingstone's home to descend into disrepair had brought dishonour on Scotland. But, according to Macnair, it was the Scottish national character that also sought to rectify the egregious situation: 'We felt sure that if this melancholy prospect were made known, the Scottish people would not permit such desecration.'[167] The success of the whole scheme was presented as a national triumph, for it drew the populace behind it. Indeed, 'There was no Scotsman however eminent but felt honoured to be associated with the name of the lad who began life as a "piecer".'[168] Even the architecture and landscape manifested a Scottish quality. Their possibilities were first envisaged by a man in possession of a 'fervid Celtic imagination' who recommended one of Scotland's eminent urban planners, Patrick Geddes, for the job. In the end it was his son-in-law Frank Charles Mears, another renowned planner and a man 'filled with the same idealism', who developed the scheme.[169] The 'shrine' to Livingstone was thus for Macnair a product of a Scots aesthetic imagination.

The memorial was itself structured to foreground Livingstone's Scottishness. The *Guide to the Scottish National Memorial*, published to accompany the exhibits, explained that the memorial was intended to be 'a pictorial biography'. On a tour of the building one would first encounter the 'Ancestry Room', which paraded Livingstone's historic 'connection with the two romantic incidents, in comparatively recent Scots history'; 'Prince Charlie and the gallant "Forty-Five"' and 'the heroism of the Covenanters'. Both periods, stated the brochure, 'appeal most vividly to the national temperament'.[170] From the outset, Livingstone was thus positioned within a Scottish historical framework and associated with two of the most celebrated moments in the nation's past. The emphasis on Livingstone's Scottish genesis did not stop there. Visitors would next enter 'The Blantyre Room', where 'pictures of the more outstanding men who influenced the explorer' were on display.[171] Livingstone's Lanarkshire youth was accorded a significant position in the exhibition. Indeed, as Macnair pointed out, local residents readily 'stripped their homes of cherished possessions' that related to Livingstone in order that his 'memory might be honoured'.[172] Livingstone was thus not only connected to Scottish history; he himself was Scottish history. As Macnair put it, the local Livingstone traditions were themselves 'stories that are part of Scotland's heritage'.[173]

The nature of this representation of Livingstone should be familiar from other constructions examined in the course of this chapter. The emphasis on his Scottishness intensified under the auspices of Macnair and the memorial, but the underlying intention was broadly similar. Once again the purpose was to uphold Scotland's national identity, but once again this national consciousness was expressed in order to assert the country's contribution to the Union and empire. This could be clearly seen in the staging of the memorial's opening ceremony, at which none other than the then Duchess of York officiated. 'Ours was a national movement', wrote Macnair, 'and it was fit that some royal person should be asked to preside.'[174] The words of Dr Alexander Hetherwick, the head of the Church of Scotland's Malawi mission, whose duty it was to thank the future Queen Mother for her presence, epitomised the ceremony's tone as he addressed her in glowingly patriotic terms: 'It is fitting that you should perform this ceremony', he said, 'since you hold in your hand the heart of every true Scotsman and Scotswoman.'[175] The commemoration of Livingstone as a Scottish national figure was seen to be in no way incompatible with Union loyalty; rather, one of the British state's foremost representatives was deemed the appropriate figure to solemnise the occasion.

The question, then, is why the Scottish representation of Livingstone intensified in the 1920s. Of course, the inter-war period was one of economic hardship for Scotland. While the country had been dominant in various industrial sectors leading up to and during the First World War, the demands of the global conflict had increased its dependence on a narrow range of interdependent industries. As Devine points out, this meant that Scotland was particularly badly affected with the downturn in international trade in the aftermath of the war.[176] While Scottish industry stagnated, emigration and levels of unemployment rose to new heights. Jonathan Hyslop suggests that some degree of nationalist sentiment developed in response to this period of austerity. Scotland had formerly supplied the industrial needs of the empire, as well as providing it with a significant proportion of its servants. As these connections faltered after the war and in the midst of heightening industrial competition, the empire no longer seemed to be such an advantage to Scotland. As Hyslop writes, 'brute economic realities contributed to a feeling that Scotland was not benefiting from imperial projects'.[177] Only a small proportion of the populace wanted to reject the empire, but there was a growing sense that Scotland's participation in imperialism needed to be more plainly acknowledged. The nationalist sentiment that flowered was not separatist in nature, but one that sought, sometimes with a 'sting in the tale', greater accreditation from the British state.[178]

The Scottish National Memorial to David Livingstone broadly reflected these developments in national consciousness. As Hyslop points out, the memorial celebrated Livingstone as an imperial figure while simultaneously asserting 'the distinct claims of Scotland'.[179] In this way, the memorial registered 'The complexity of the strengthening nationalist sentiment in Scotland, and its relation to empire'.[180] It should be remembered that the National Party of Scotland, a forerunner of the Scottish National Party, was founded in 1928, only one year before the opening of the memorial. At the same time, the literary revival of the Scottish Renaissance was beginning to inaugurate a spirit of cultural nationalism. While the memorial to Livingstone certainly lacked the tinge of radicalism of these political and cultural projects, it nonetheless manifested the broader simmering of Scottish national sentiment.

The period of the Scottish National Memorial to David Livingstone thus marked an extension of the purpose that Livingstone had long served for those who sought to parade Scotland's prestigious participation in the empire. Yet, with Macnair and the memorial, Livingstone's Scottish reputation also experienced a degree of modification. As Andrew Ross argues, it adapted to take on 'a new and class twist'.[181] Livingstone, it was emphasised, was a hero from the working classes and a hero of the working classes. Macnair certainly stressed that the majority of the required funds came from ordinary people: 'probably no national scheme in Scotland owes so little to the gifts of the rich', he wrote. For Macnair, 'this [was] as it should be. Livingstone was a man of the people, and proud of the fact, and he is still a great people's hero.'[182] In view of his status as a champion from the working classes, it was only appropriate that his commemoration should be supported first and foremost by the general populace: 'It is so obviously right that the privilege of honouring their great countryman should belong to the ordinary folk of Scotland.'[183] The fact that the majority of the funds were raised domestically, through numerous small contributions rather than a select number of large donations, was truly a notable achievement given the economic hardship in Scotland in the years following the General Strike.[184]

As John MacKenzie suggests, efforts were made to make the Livingstone legend 'more accessible to the Scottish working class'.[185] With the political shifts of the period, the moment was ripe to recast Livingstone in this way. The Labour Party was making advances at the beginning of the twentieth century; there was also some evidence of left-wing developments on the Clydeside and in the famous rent strikes of 1915, in which workers protested against the poor quality of Glasgow's over-crowded housing.[186] After the First World War, Labour had its major breakthrough, profiting from the sitting Liberal government's failure to provide the promised 'homes fit for heroes' in the aftermath of the war. In the 1922 election, Labour ended Liberal hegemony by becoming the largest party in Scotland: as Devine writes, 'the national political landscape had changed'.[187] With the increase of leftist support in Scotland, Macnair's emphasis on Livingstone's working-class credentials was clearly timely.

In his 1940 biography, published eleven years after the opening of the memorial, Macnair continued to construe Livingstone in a manner amenable to workers. Although in many ways his text perpetuates dimensions of the myth of the 'lad o' pairts', he insisted that his 'story is not the usual "kail-yard School" romance'.[188] His attempt to differentiate his text from Kailyard demonstrates that he aimed for his Livingstone to have appeal across Scotland's industrial belt. Macnair went about this in the way he represented Livingstone's juvenescence, suggesting that he grew up at 'a time of unrest and political agitation' in a town where 'there was much intelligent interest in the progress of the Reform Bill'.[189] The factory was something of a political hothouse, 'since the Scottish Weaver was always a man of radical leanings'.[190] Macnair could find little evidence of Livingstone's own political interest, aside from his once having carved 'no state Church' upon a tree. Nonetheless, he gave him something of a progressive flavour, speculating that there 'might perhaps be a hint of politics of the radical colour in the story ... of how David once bagged a salmon'.[191] While Macnair acknowledged that his family's interests were more religious than political, he made sure to give Livingstone at least some proximity to a radical working-class tradition.

Macnair also hinted at connections between Livingstone's factory youth and the projects of the social reformer Robert Owen, 'one of the inaugurators of the Co-operative Movement'.[192] Owen's enterprises, including his unsuccessful attempt to establish 'a communistic settlement' nearby at Orbiston, 'gave the politically minded much food for discussion'.[193] But Macnair went further and argued that Owen's New Lanark 'social experiments ... had their influence in Blantyre'. Although he 'had no connection with the Blantyre factory', the suggestion of indirect influence was plausible because Owen's father-in-law, David Dale, was its founder.[194] To some degree, then, Macnair sought to connect Livingstone to a radical and equitable system of labour, an environment that would appeal to the Scottish working classes. Yet in all this, he was not very seriously trying to represent Livingstone as a political radical. This much is indicated in the conservative language into which he lapsed when describing the habits of James Monteith, the factory owner from 1797, who continued the 'kindly traditions' and 'paternal' system of management established by his predecessors.[195] This implies that Macnair forged connections to radical traditions less out of political conviction than out of a desire to create a hero who would be amenable to working sensibilities. In fact, I would argue that he aimed to use Livingstone as a reconciling figure, to mediate Christianity to Scotland's populace. In his biography, he often took it upon himself to commend his subject's faith. 'To understand Livingstone aright', he wrote, 'the depth and power of his religious convictions must be recognised.'[196] Speaking at the opening ceremony of the national memorial, Macnair made it clear that his primary vision was the evangelisation of Scotland: his prayer was that the refurbished birthplace would help to promote 'the ideal that Livingstone followed with such tremendous concentration, the ideal of a Christian Scotland and a Christian world'.[197] In hoping that Livingstone could represent Christianity to the masses, Macnair was influenced not only by changes in Scotland's political structure, but, most likely, by the waning of Christian belief following the

First World War. While religious identities continued to play an integral role in British culture following the conflict, it did contribute significantly to Christian decline and disillusionment. In a period of political and religious flux, Macnair sought to construe Livingstone as a people's hero who could help revive religious enthusiasm.[198]

The commemoration of Livingstone executed by Macnair did not occur in a vacuum. As I have argued, it is important to place it in the context of a longer course of representation in which Livingstone was made to work on behalf of Scottish identity. To this extent, the memorial marks the apogee of an intensifying emphasis on Livingstone's Scots credentials that, I would suggest, mirrors the contemporary simmering of national sentiment. At the same time, it was up to Macnair to establish the major modification within the Livingstone legend in Scotland by ensuring that he became enshrined in the public consciousness as the country's foremost working class hero. His success in developing and adapting Livingstone's reputation, and capturing the national imagination in a period of political change, is amply illustrated in the visiting figures of the memorial's opening year. As Hyslop states, the 51,000 who passed through its doors in 1929–30 surpassed the numbers visiting Walter Scott's Abbotsford and even those visiting the cottage birthplace of Scotland's bard, Robert Burns.[199]

Livingstone today

Livingstone's reputation in Scotland has quietened since Macnair and the early years of the memorial. Indeed, it is interesting to note that while he has often served as the politically charged vehicle of Scottish sentiment, Livingstone has never come under a sustained nationalist construction. Perhaps closest to this is his place in the genre of 'famous Scots' books, in which he stands alongside any and every Scottish person of note. For instance, in 1943 the nationalist William Weir Gilmour published his *Famous Scotsmen*, which was simply a long list of achievements by Scots. Livingstone, like all the others, is given his single sentence: 'It was a Scotsman, David Livingstone, who explored the Zambesi.'[200] In an expanded edition of the book in 1979, the year of a failed referendum to form a devolved Scottish Assembly, the nationalist objective is evident. As the author of the preface, William Wolfe, Chairman of the Scottish National Party, put it, the hope was that the timely book would encourage 'Scots to shake off their dependent outlook, and to raise their eyes to a prospect of new and greater possibilities for Scotland.'[201] While not all 'famous Scots' books necessarily had quite the devolutionary intent found in Gilmore, the genre did become more prevalent in the years leading up to the formation of the Scottish

Parliament in 1997: the political message of the literary form, as is to be expected, is nationalist for the most part. While Livingstone is not much developed in texts of this ilk, he is at least granted a place in the majority of them. In *Famous Scots* by Ian Fellowes Gordon (1988) and *Famous Scots* (1992) by Raymond Lamont-Brown, in *Famous Scots: The Pride of a Small Nation* (1984) by Forbes Macgregor and *Baxters Book of Famous Scots* (1995) by Bill Fletcher, Livingstone is described in anything from a sentence to a paragraph.[202] The rather facile nationalism that such texts express, in their undiscriminating impulse to employ any Scottish worthy as a marker of national identity, is as close as Livingstone has come to serving the cause of separatist nationalism. Perhaps the longevity of his heroic status as a British and imperial icon would have made a vigorous nationalist construction just too uncomfortable a fit.

Attempts, however, can occasionally be found in recent criticism at least to make Livingstone more amenable to contemporary Scots. For instance, in his essay 'Livingstone, Self-Help and Scotland', the historian Angus Calder made an unusual connection between the Victorian explorer and one of Scotland's foremost literary luminaries, Hugh MacDiarmid. By first linking Livingstone to 'Walter Scott, whose techniques of description he imitates', Calder situated him within a Scottish aesthetic tradition.[203] As an example of Livingstone's prose, he quoted his description of the water breaking at Victoria Falls, which 'gave off several rays of foam, exactly as bits of steel, when burnt in oxygen gas, give off rays of sparks ...'. Calder then argued that such expression is reminiscent 'of Scott's twentieth-century successor as the dominant figure in Scottish arts and letters, C.M. Grieve (Hugh MacDiarmid), a Marxist and materialist who attempted in his later verse to put poetry and science together again after their rupture in the late Nineteenth century'. He went on: 'In his combination of inspiration and matter-of-factness Livingstone prefigures characteristics of twentieth-century Scottish intellectual life ... The image of steel burning in oxygen would have appealed to MacDiarmid.'[204] It is probably fair to say that the relation between Livingstone and MacDiarmid that Calder established is not a particularly obvious one. The unusual nature of the allusion suggests a desire to resist the image of Livingstone as Victorian religious hero and 'lad o' pairts'.[205] Calder's piece was first published in *Livingstone and the Victorian Encounter with Africa*, a volume of essays which was published by the National Portrait Gallery in accompaniment to its exhibition, and which clearly aimed to address a readership beyond the academic community.[206] Perhaps the nature of this publication presented Calder with an opportunity to recast Livingstone before a wider audience and particularly in a manner appealing to twentieth-century Scots. While his essay can probably not be described as a nationalist construction, it is significant that Calder, who was himself a nationalist and socialist, chose to connect Livingstone with the foremost proponent of Scottish cultural nationalism at a time when questions of Scottish identity and statehood were being hotly debated.[207]

Despite such efforts, Livingstone's popular reputation has undoubtedly diminished since Macnair's commemorative endeavours. Following the empire's decline, imperial heroes increasingly lost their appeal and became ever more problematic figures. Scholarly work has of course abounded, particularly under the aegis of significant dates such as the centenary of Livingstone's death in 1973.[208] In the public arena, however – in Scotland as in the rest of Britain – Livingstone was seldom celebrated with quite such vigour. Yet although such a retreat has taken place, and although he has receded in the popular imagination, where he is commemorated today it does tend to be in Scotland. In fact the 2013 bicentenary of Livingstone's birth was marked by a surprising number of events. And it was striking that the vast majority, aside from a memorial service in Westminster Abbey, took place in Scotland. The major exhibition was held in Edinburgh's National Museum and was accompanied by the major publication. The events listed by 'Livingstone 200', a partnership established between various institutions to coordinate the bicentenary, included public lectures at the museum, the University of Glasgow, the Royal Society of Edinburgh and the Royal College of Physicians and Surgeons of Glasgow.[209] Conferences and symposiums took place on themes as diverse as Livingstone's legacy, Christian mission and ecumenism, and tropical medicine. Memorial services were held in Blantyre and Hamilton, and outreach events, predominantly at the National Museum of Scotland and the David Livingstone Centre, included story-telling, craft sessions and even an African drumming workshop. The major funder, moreover, was the Scottish government, which provided over £250,000 in support. This state of affairs suggests that while Livingstone's public stature has experienced decline, his repute has remained somewhat stronger in Scotland than in the rest of the United Kingdom. As his reputation has diminished, it has – naturally enough – become increasingly restricted to his country of origin. But it may not only be that Livingstone's memory has been a little more persistent in the north. Rather, the extent of the Scottish bicentenary celebrations could be interpreted as an effort to rehabilitate his reputation. It might be too much to say that his brief, government supported, resurgence bears explicit relation to the 2014 'Homecoming' and approaching bid for independence. Nevertheless, the restoration of an important national icon cannot be entirely divorced from a contemporary political environment in which Scottish distinctiveness is often given voice.[210]

This chapter has taken as its subject a major strand of David Livingstone's posthumous reputation. His Scottish legacy, it should now be clear, was by no means homogenous in nature or in stasis. By beginning with certain representations in which Livingstone was held up as a paragon of 'English' character, I sought to show that not everyone has been interested in his Scottish identity. Even as late as 1939, Livingstone could be performed as English in the Hollywood film *Stanley and Livingstone*; Cedric Hardwicke, who performed the role, did so with perfect Received Pronunciation. The late Victorian and Edwardian texts that I examined at the outset of this chapter, which were deeply Anglocentric, reflected both the tendency of the period to describe things British as 'English' and the proclivity of the contemporary historiography to recite a narrative of English ascendancy. In a similar vein, I drew attention to those who were preoccupied with Livingstone's embodiment of supposedly Anglo-Saxon traits. While these biographies did not quite perform an act of historical amnesia, since they did not altogether ignore his Highland ancestry, it was the Anglo-Saxon dimension of his character that was of pre-eminent importance. Such constructions of Livingstone, however, were not left unchallenged. In the years of Britain's Celtic revival, there was considerable research into Livingstone's ancestry which ultimately connected him with a range of heroic Highland traditions. For these Celtic enthusiasts, who were sometimes responding directly to the Anglo-Saxon representation, Livingstone could be understood only within a Gaelic context. By assiduously tracking down lore that related to Livingstone, and by emphasising his Gaelic character, the Celtic revivalists sought to claim one of Britain's foremost heroes as their own.[211]

Livingstone can thus be seen as a site of conflict. But in contrast to the polar extremes of the Anglo-Saxon and Celtic constructions, it was more common to celebrate him as a fusion of races. His patrilineal descent was Highland and Jacobite, while his maternal ancestry was Lowland and Covenanting. Thus, as both Gael and Saxon, Livingstone could act as a reconciling figure and stand symbolically for the whole of Scotland. It is clear then that he was subject to a plurality of representations, which served a series of different political purposes. Yet, without doubt, in the late nineteenth century and the years leading up to the First World War one major construction of Livingstone was more significant than the rest. A considerable number of Scottish biographers, who took him as their subject, aimed to display Scotland's significant contribution to the British Empire. Livingstone was used as a vehicle of Scots pride and national consciousness, but one that co-resided with support for the Union and empire.

One way in which authors articulated Livingstone's Scottishness was by writing about him in the well-known terms of the Kailyard genre. Biographies influenced by this literary form set his youth in a world in which religion monopolised the social sphere. They fictionalised scenes of the provincial working-class and mythologised Livingstone as a 'lad o' pairts'. As with his portrayal by the Celtic revivalists, I suggested that the Kailyard representation should likewise be considered ambivalent in nature. While presenting a deeply conservative and arguably 'inauthentic' vision of Scotland, the genre at least aimed to give voice to Scottish identity and to cultivate pride in the nation.

A distinctive feature of the Kailyard construction of Livingstone was, simply put, its longevity. It broke the confines of the late Victorian era, the period of 'high' Kailyard, and persisted well into the twentieth century. Indeed, Livingstone's Scottish identity was actually asserted most vigorously from the 1920s. It was at this time that James I. Macnair began to campaign and raise funds to renovate Livingstone's birthplace into a national memorial. There has rightly been a considerable amount of scholarly emphasis on the relationship between Livingstone and a renewal of Scottish identity in this period. I sought, however, to argue that this was not something altogether new, but was rather an intensification of a longstanding connection that mirrored contemporary developments in national consciousness. At the same time Livingstone's Scots reputation was also modified as he was recast, in timely fashion, as the nation's foremost working-class hero.

The evolutionary nature of Livingstone's Scottish reputation, its adaptability across socio-political time and space, should now be abundantly clear. At certain moments, he was subject to conflicting constructions that were starkly opposed to one another. Yet it is also possible to discern a significant degree of consistency in Livingstone's Scottish mobilisation. Across a considerable period of time, he was put to work to express national sentiment and to heighten Scots prestige. And as the bicentenary celebrations suggest, this continues to occur. Consistency, however, should not be mistaken for uniformity. While perhaps subject to fewer developments, re-presentations and points of conflict than his imperialist legacy, the Livingstone legend in Scotland was historically malleable and adapted in response to a variety of political contexts.

Notes

1. The first expression is taken from Henry Y. Pickering's *Scotia's Noblest Son: The Romance of the Man who Died for Africa* (Glasgow: Pickering & Inglis, 1913). The second comes from James Hannan, a partner of Blantyre works, who described Livingstone in this way when he visited the mill in 1856. Quoted in Stephen Mullen, 'One of Scotia's "Sons of Toil": David Livingstone and the Blantyre Mill', in Sarah Worden (ed.), *David Livingstone: Man, Myth and Legacy* (Edinburgh: National Museums Scotland, 2012), p. 15.
2. George Shepperson, 'David Livingstone the Scot', *The Scottish Historical Review*, 39 (1960), 116.
3. Angus Calder, *Scotlands of the Mind* (Edinburgh: Luath, 2002), p. 120.
4. Andrew Ross, *David Livingstone: Mission and Empire* (London: Hambledon and London, 2002), p. 1.
5. Andrew Ross, *Livingstone: The Scot and Doctor* (Glasgow: University of Glasgow, 1990), p. 9.
6. Clare Pettitt, *Dr. Livingstone, I Presume? Missionaries, Journalists, Explorers, and Empire* (Cambridge, Mass.: Harvard University Press, 2007), p. 21.
7. John M. MacKenzie, 'David Livingstone: The Construction of the Myth', in Graham Walker and Tom Gallagher (eds), *Sermons and Battle Hymns* (Edinburgh: Edinburgh University Press, 1990), pp. 36–7.
8. Ibid., p. 36. For information on the 'Livingstone Centenary Loan Exhibition, 1913' at the Royal Scottish Museum, see Sarah Worden, 'Introduction: Exhibiting Livingstone', in Worden (ed.), *David Livingstone*, pp. 1–4.
9. Andrew Ross, 'David Livingstone', *Études écossaises*, 10 (2005), 100.
10. Brian H. Murray, 'H.M. Stanley, David Livingstone and the Staging of "Anglo-Saxon" Manliness', in Justin D. Livingstone (ed.), 'Livingstone Studies: Bicentenary Essays', *Scottish Geographical Journal*, 129: 3–4 (2013), 158.
11. William H.G. Kingston, *Travels of Dr. Livingstone* (London: Routledge, 1887), p. 121.
12. Anne Manning, *Heroes of the Desert: The Story of the Lives and Labours of Moffat and Livingstone* (London: Thomas Nelson, 1885), pp. 267–8.
13. Ibid., p. 254.
14. Robert Cochrane, *The English Explorers Comprising Details of the More Famous Travels, by Mandeville, Bruce, Park, and Livingstone* (London: William P. Nimmo, 1875), p. 607.
15. Stephanie L. Barczewski, *Myth and National Identity in Nineteenth-Century Britain: The Legends of King Arthur and Robin Hood* (Oxford: Oxford University Press, 2000), p. 6.
16. Ibid., p. 49.
17. Peter Mandler, *The English National Character: The History of an Idea from Edmund Burke to Tony Blair* (New Haven and London: Yale University Press, 2006), pp. 66–7.
18. Reginald Horsman, *Race and Manifest Destiny: The Origin of American Racial Anglo-Saxonism* (Cambridge, Mass.: Harvard University Press, 1981), p. 62.
19. Robert Knox, *The Races of Men* (Philadelphia: Lea & Blanchard, 1850), p. 7.
20. Edward Beasley, *The Victorian Reinvention of Race: New Racisms and the Problem of Grouping in the Human Sciences* (London: Routledge, 2010), pp. 6, 1.
21. Horsman, *Race and Manifest Destiny*, pp. 73–4.
22. Basil Mathews, *Livingstone the Pathfinder* (London: Oxford University Press, 1912), p. 127.
23. Ibid., p. 144.
24. Ibid., p. 196.
25. Barczewski, *Myth and National Identity*, p. 124.
26. Mathews, *Livingstone the Pathfinder*, p. 41.

27 For discussion of Stanley's 'Anglo-Saxon' construction of Livingstone, see Murray, 'Staging of "Anglo-Saxon" Manliness', pp. 152, 158.
28 Richard Zumkhawala-Cook, *Scotland as We Know It: Representations of National Identity in Literature, Film and Popular Culture* (Jefferson, NC: McFarland, 2008), p. 39.
29 The term 'Celtic' is to a large extent a constructed concept. As Joep Leerssen points out, the notion of the Celts is linguistically and ethnically 'a highly disparate one'. 'The similarities between Breton, Irish-Gaelic, and extinct Gaulish ... is by no means obvious'. See Joep Leerssen, 'Celticism', in Terence Brown (ed.), *Celticism* (Amsterdam: Rodopi, 1996), p. 1. With an awareness of these real differences, the term 'Celtic' should be understood in this chapter as signifying an invented cultural tradition.
30 Duncan Livingstone, 'The Stewarts of Appin at Culloden', *Celtic Monthly*, 4: 5–7 (1896), 120.
31 Ibid.
32 Ibid., p. 131.
33 Ibid., p. 132.
34 Ibid., p. 120.
35 Ibid., p. 132.
36 Katherine White Grant, *Myth, Tradition and Story from Western Argyll* (Oban: Oban Times, 1925), p. 63.
37 Ibid.
38 Ibid., p. 64.
39 Ian C. Bradley, *Celtic Christianity: Making Myths and Chasing Dreams* (Edinburgh: Edinburgh University Press, 1999), p. 137.
40 Alexander Carmichael, *Carmina Gadelica: Hymns and Incantations*, vol. 2 (Edinburgh: T. and A. Constable, 1900), p. 259.
41 Ibid., p. 79.
42 This was suggested in William Garden Blaikie, *The Personal Life of David Livingstone* (London: John Murray, 1880), pp. 1–2.
43 Carmichael, *Carmina Gadelica*, vol. 2, p. 260.
44 Ibid.
45 Zumkhawala-Cook, *Scotland as We Know It*, p. 41.
46 Quoted in Bradley, *Celtic Christianity*, p. 158.
47 Ibid., p. 160.
48 Ibid., p. 119.
49 Zumkhawala-Cook, *Scotland as We Know It*, p. 48.
50 Bradley, *Celtic Christianity*, p. 137.
51 Grant, *Myth, Tradition and Story*, p. 63.
52 Ibid., p. 68.
53 Ibid., p. 61.
54 Ibid., p. 64.
55 Ibid., p. 65.
56 Ibid., p. 66.
57 Ross, 'David Livingstone', p. 96.
58 Grant, *Myth, Tradition and Story*, p. 68.
59 Ibid.
60 Reginald John Campbell, *Livingstone* (London: E. Benn, 1929), pp. 27–39.
61 Ibid., p. 22.
62 Ibid., p. 26.
63 Blaikie, *The Personal Life*, p. 4.
64 Ibid., pp. 4–5.
65 Ibid., p. 7.
66 Ibid., pp. 4, 6–7.
67 Neil Davidson, *The Origins of Scottish Nationhood* (London: Pluto, 2000), p. 65, 68–9.
68 Ibid., p. 72.

69   Ibid., p. 78.
70   Ibid., p. 75.
71   Thomas Martin Devine, *The Scottish Nation, 1700–2000* (London: Penguin, 2000), p. 237.
72   Ibid., p. 244.
73   Paul H. Scott, 'The Malachi Episode', in Walter Scott, *The Letters of Malachi Malagrowther*, ed. Paul H. Scott (Edinburgh: W. Blackwood, 1981), p. xxix.
74   T. Banks Maclachlan, *David Livingstone: The Factory Lad who Became Africa's Greatest Missionary* (Kilmarnock: John Ritchie, 1900), p. 10.
75   James Irvine Macnair, *Livingstone the Liberator: A Study of a Dynamic Personality* (London: Collins, 1940), p. 25.
76   Adam Sedgwick, 'A Prefatory Letter', in William Monk (ed.), *Dr. Livingstone's Cambridge Lectures* (Cambridge: Deighton, Bell, 1860), p. 53.
77   Ibid., p. 54.
78   John M. MacKenzie, '"The Second City of the Empire": Glasgow – Imperial Municipality', in Felix Driver and David Gilbert (eds), *Imperial Cities* (Manchester: Manchester University Press, 1999), p. 215.
79   Devine, *The Scottish Nation*, p. 252.
80   Tom Nairn, *The Break-Up of Britain: Crisis and Neo-Nationalism*, 3rd ed. (Altona, Vic.: Common Ground, 2003), p. 118.
81   Devine, *The Scottish Nation*, p. 289.
82   John M. MacKenzie, 'Essay and Reflection: On Scotland and the Empire', *The International History Review*, 15: 4 (1993), 732.
83   Devine, *The Scottish Nation*, p. 289.
84   John McGregor, *The Hero of an Unknown Land: Being a Moral and Descriptive Versification of the 'Life & Labors of Dr. Livingstone' and Other Poems* (London: Otley, 1875), p. 13.
85   Ibid., p. 14.
86   Ibid., p. 16.
87   Ibid., p. 17.
88   Ibid., p. 25.
89   Ibid., p. 34.
90   Ibid., p. 35.
91   Ibid., p. 57.
92   Ibid., p. 46.
93   Ibid., p. 58.
94   Charles Allan and John Guest, *David Livingstone; or, Scotland's Soldier of Christ* (London: J. Guest, 1881), p. 2.
95   Ibid., pp. 2–3.
96   Ibid., pp. 3, 6.
97   Jabez Marrat, *David Livingstone, Missionary and Discoverer* (London: Wesleyan Conference Office, 1877), p. 65.
98   Ibid., pp. 8–9.
99   Ibid., p. 8.
100 Ibid., pp. 2.
101 Ibid., pp. 5–6.
102 Robert Anderson, *Scottish Education since the Reformation* (Stirling: Economic & Social History Society of Scotland, 1997), pp. 2–3.
103 Jabez Marrat, *Northern Lights: Pen and Pencil Sketches of Modern Scottish Worthies*, 3rd ed. (London: T. Woolmer, 1885), p. 168.
104 David McCrone, 'Culture, Nationalism and Scottish Education: Homogeneity and Diversity', in T.G.K. Bryce and W.M. Humes (eds), *Scottish Education: Beyond Devolution*, 3rd ed. (Edinburgh: Edinburgh University Press, 2008), p. 226.
105 Davidson, *The Origins of Scottish Nationhood*, p. 51.
106 G. Watt Smith, *David Livingstone: The Great Heart of Africa* (London: A.H. Stockwell, 1913), p. 22.
107 Ibid., p. 27.

108 Ibid., p. 28.
109 McCrone, 'Culture, Nationalism and Scottish Education', p. 226.
110 Smith, *David Livingstone*, p. 13.
111 Ibid.
112 Ibid., p. 15.
113 Ibid.
114 Ibid., p. 56.
115 Ibid., p. 21.
116 Devine, *The Scottish Nation*, p. 264.
117 Calder, *Scotlands of the Mind*, p. 112.
118 Smith, *David Livingstone*, p. 11.
119 Ibid., p. 34.
120 Davidson, *The Origins of Scottish Nationhood*, p. 13.
121 Andrew Nash, *Kailyard and Scottish Literature* (Amsterdam: Rodopi, 2007), p. 15.
122 Ian Campbell, *Kailyard* (Edinburgh: Ramsay Head, 1981), p. 9.
123 Ibid., p. 13.
124 There is some ambiguity over the date on which Ellis's text was first published. It was definitely released in the mid- to late 1920s, but it seems likely that this was a reprint or revised edition, since several catalogues list earlier publication dates ranging from 1891 to 1910.
125 James J. Ellis, *David Livingstone: The Factory Boy who Became a Great Missionary* (London and Glasgow: Pickering & Inglis, 1928), p. 3.
126 Ibid., p. 4.
127 Ibid., pp. 4–5.
128 Zumkhawala-Cook, *Scotland as We Know It*, p. 58.
129 Ellis, *David Livingstone*, p. 4.
130 Ibid., p. 5.
131 Robert Smiles, *David Livingstone* (London: Cassell, 1885), p. 6.
132 Ibid., p. 7.
133 Ibid., p. 8.
134 Thomas D. Knowles, *Ideology, Art and Commerce: Aspects of Literary Sociology in the Late Victorian Scottish Kailyard* (Göteborg: Acta Universitatis Gothoburgensis, 1983), p. 13.
135 Campbell, *Kailyard*, p. 96.
136 Smiles, *David Livingstone*, p. 63.
137 Nash, *Kailyard and Scottish Literature*, p. 14.
138 Ibid., p. 46.
139 Nairn, *The Break-Up of Britain*, p. 145.
140 Campbell, *Kailyard*, p. 15.
141 Ibid., p. 87.
142 Ibid., p. 16.
143 Zumkhawala-Cook, *Scotland as We Know It*, p. 33.
144 Smiles, *David Livingstone*, p. 8.
145 Ibid., p. 14.
146 Emma Letley, *From Galt to Douglas Brown: Nineteenth-Century Fiction and Scots Language* (Edinburgh: Scottish Academic, 1988), p. 6.
147 Ibid., p. 3.
148 Ibid., pp. 229, 245.
149 Ibid., p. 231.
150 While dramatic and fictional representations will be the subject of Chapter 6, this play is mentioned here for its especial interest in a Scottish context.
151 The notion of a 'language plot' is borrowed from Emma Letley. See Letley, *From Galt to Douglas Brown*, p. xii.
152 John Corbett, *Language and Scottish Literature* (Edinburgh: Edinburgh University Press, 1997), pp. 3–4.
153 Mary A. Maclennan, *David Livingstone: A Simple Drama* (London: Edinburgh House, 1931), p. 18.

154 Ibid., p. 22.
155 Ibid., p. 76.
156 McGregor, *The Hero of an Unknown Land*, p. 63.
157 Corbett, *Language and Scottish Literature*, p. 189.
158 MacKenzie, 'David Livingstone: The Construction of the Myth', p. 34.
159 Pettitt, *Dr. Livingstone, I Presume?*, p. 57.
160 Ross, 'David Livingstone', p. 100.
161 Hamish MacCunn, *Livingstone the Pilgrim*, 1912, p. 3, MS MacCunn 11, Special Collections, University of Glasgow Library.
162 Hamish MacCunn, *The Pageant of Darkness and Light* (London: Weekes & Co., 1908).
163 Angus Calder notes that MacCunn was represented at the British Empire Exhibition by 'Livingstone Episode' and 'Camp and Kaffir Melodies'. See Calder, *Scotlands of the Mind*, p. 174.
164 Ross, 'David Livingstone', p. 100.
165 James I. Macnair, *The Story of the Scottish National Memorial to David Livingstone* (Blantyre: Scottish National Memorial to David Livingstone Trust, 1951), p. x.
166 Ibid., p. xi.
167 Ibid., p. 2.
168 Ibid., p. 8.
169 Ibid., p. 16.
170 James Irvine Macnair, *Guide to the Scottish National Memorial to David Livingstone*, 2nd ed. (Hamilton: Hamilton Advertiser, 1932), p. 6.
171 Ibid., p. 9.
172 Ibid., p. 7.
173 Macnair, *The Story of the Scottish National Memorial*, p. 20.
174 Ibid., p. 39.
175 Ibid., p. 43.
176 Devine, *The Scottish Nation*, p. 266.
177 Jonathan Hyslop, 'Making Scotland in South Africa: Charles Murray, the Transvaal's Aberdeenshire Poet', in David Lambert and Alan Lester (eds), *Colonial Lives across the British Empire: Imperial Careering in the Long Nineteenth Century* (Cambridge: Cambridge University Press, 2006), p. 330.
178 Ibid., p. 329.
179 Ibid., p. 331.
180 Ibid., p. 330.
181 Ross, 'David Livingstone', p. 100.
182 Macnair, *The Story of the Scottish National Memorial*, p. 10.
183 Ibid., p. 11.
184 This is mentioned by MacKenzie in 'David Livingstone: The Construction of the Myth', p. 37, and by Ross in 'David Livingstone', p. 100.
185 MacKenzie, 'David Livingstone: The Construction of the Myth', p. 35.
186 Devine, *The Scottish Nation*, pp. 305, 311.
187 Ibid., p. 313.
188 Macnair, *Livingstone the Liberator*, p. 35.
189 Ibid., p. 39.
190 Ibid., pp. 39–40.
191 Ibid., p. 40.
192 Ibid., p. 33.
193 Ibid., p. 40.
194 Ibid., p. 34. For discussion of the working conditions in Blantyre Mill, drawing on official records, see Mullen, 'One of Scotia's "Sons of Toil"', p. 19.
195 Macnair, *Livingstone the Liberator*, p. 34.
196 Ibid., p. 59.
197 Macnair, *The Story of the Scottish National Memorial*, p. 42.
198 Macnair was the key figure in the period that marks the highpoint of Livingstone's Scottish reputation. Nonetheless, the quickening of national sentiment was

detectable in other biographies of the inter-war years. In 1918, R.B. Dawson presented Livingstone as though he were a member of a Highland clan. In his account of the infamous lion attack, Livingstone's coat became a 'Highland jacket' and the pattern became specifically 'Livingstone's tartan'. He used tribal language, describing how some of the 'Livingstones of the old clan' had pioneered in 'our distant colonies'. See R.B. Dawson, *Livingstone the Hero of Africa* (London: Seeley, Service, 1918), pp. 52, 32. Around the time of the opening of the Livingstone memorial, there was a greater concentration of biographies interested in Livingstone's Scottishness. In 1927, a book by Elizabeth Charles appeared, whose material, mostly plagiarised from Dawson, was rich in local colour. It began by painting a picture of Livingstone and his brother as two 'typical Scots boys in face and dress', attired in the garb 'of the Scottish schoolboy; the blue kilted bonnet, the cloth waistcoat'. See Elizabeth Charles, *David Livingstone* (Kilmarnock: John Ritchie, 1927), p. 9. Other authors pursued local flavour, tracking down traditions that circulated in Blantyre. In a 1929 biography of his namesake, W.P. Livingstone advertised a new story from the explorer's youth, telling how, at the Congregational chapel, 'The coins were slipped through an aperture ... David took to listening to the clink of the coins, and so expert did he become in guessing what they were that he could give a fairly accurate idea of the amount of the collection'. See William Pringle Livingstone, *Story of David Livingstone* (London: Livingstone, 1929), p. 12.
199 Hyslop, 'Making Scotland in South Africa', p. 331.
200 W. Weir Gilmour, *Famous Scotsmen* (Peebles: Manor Booklets, 1943), p. 9.
201 W. Weir Gilmour, *Famous Scots* (Glasgow: MacLellan, 1979), p. iii.
202 Ian Fellowes Gordon, *Famous Scots* (London: Shepheard-Walwyn, 1988); Raymond Lamont-Brown, *Famous Scots* (Edinburgh: Chambers, 1992); Forbes Macgregor, *Famous Scots: The Pride of a Small Nation* (Edinburgh: Gordon Wright, 1984); William Whigham Fletcher, *Baxters Book of Famous Scots who changed the World* (Glasgow: Lang Syne, 1995).
203 Calder, *Scotlands of the Mind*, p. 133.
204 Ibid.
205 Calder also tried to cast Livingstone's religious convictions in a quite different light, suggesting that 'he eventually became so thoroughly ecumenical and so little concerned with formal worship that he might be said to have moved away even from Protestantism itself'. See Calder, *Scotlands of the Mind*, p. 126.
206 Quotations here, however, are taken from the version printed in Calder's book *Scotlands of the Mind*.
207 The volume was published in 1996, one year before the formation of the Scottish Parliament.
208 The years around the centenary saw the publication of a considerable number of works on Livingstone. See, for instance: George Martelli, *Livingstone's River: A History of the Zambezi Expedition, 1858–1864* (London: Chatto & Windus, 1970); Tim Jeal, *Livingstone* (London: Heinemann, 1973); *David Livingstone and Africa: Proceedings of a Seminar Held on the Occasion of the Centenary of the Death of David Livingstone at the Centre of African Studies, University of Edinburgh, 4th and 5th May 1973* (Edinburgh: University of Edinburgh, Centre of African Studies, 1973); Bridglal Pachai (ed.), *Livingstone: Man of Africa: Memorial Essays, 1873–1973* (Harlow: Longman, 1973); Judith Listowel, *The Other Livingstone* (New York: Charles Scribner's Sons, 1974); Isaac Schapera (ed.), *David Livingstone South African Papers, 1849–1853* (Cape Town: Van Riebeeck Society, 1974); Oliver Ransford, *David Livingstone: The Dark Interior* (London: John Murray, 1978).
209 Livingstone 200 (The National Trust for Scotland, Scotland Malawi Partnership and The Scottish Government), www.davidlivingstone200.org (accessed 10 December 2012).
210 Interestingly, in the David Livingstone bicentenary lecture at the University of Glasgow (28 February 2013), entitled 'Livingstone's Legacy: Lessons for Today', Scotland's former First Minister Lord Jack McConnell speculated that in the run-up

to the independence referendum, both sides of the debate might seek to claim Livingstone for support. While McConnell was trying to foreclose such appropriations, his own predilections were clear when he suggested that Livingstone would have wanted the nation to remain outward-looking and international, and to resist insularity. McConnell also put Livingstone to work in political fashion on behalf of Scotland's foreign affairs and development projects, arguing that he would have been angered by the conditions of poverty in Malawi today and that he would have been a staunch supporter of the Scotland Malawi Partnership.

211 The less constructive dimensions of the Celtic construction of Livingstone, however, have had lasting effect. In numerous biographies it is assumed that his Gaelic blood tells us something about the kind of person he was. To this extent he has been the subject of 'Celticism', the stereotyped and exoticised representation of 'Celtic' peoples. See Leerssen, 'Celticism', p. 5. For instance, Edward Hume could write about Livingstone's 'Celtic emotionalism', while James Macnair could discuss his 'Celtic melancholy' and the 'imagination and fire' inherited from his 'Celtic forebears'. See Edward Hume, *David Livingstone: The Man, the Missionary, and the Explorer* (London: Sunday School Union, 1904), p. 184; Macnair, *Livingstone the Liberator*, pp. 249, 25. Reginald Coupland, writing in the 1940s, felt that Livingstone displayed 'the Gael's reputed gift of "second sight"'. See Reginald Coupland, *Livingstone's Last Journey* (London: Collins, 1945), p. 241. Even contemporary scholarship is not entirely free from Celticist representation. For instance, Andrew Ross suggests that his 'Gaelic roots may also explain the fact for him his good things were always very very good and the bad were always terrible, but isn't that always the way with a good Celtic storyteller'. See Ross, *Livingstone: The Scot and Doctor*, p. 9.

CHAPTER SIX

Fiction: laughing at Livingstone?

> It's easy to point at other men, conveniently dead, starting with the ones who first scooped up mud from riverbanks to catch the scent of a source. Why, Dr. Livingstone, I presume, wasn't he the rascal! He and all the profiteers who've since walked out on Africa as a husband quits a wife, leaving her with her naked body curled around the emptied-out mine of her womb.
>
> (Orleana Price, in Barbara Kingsolver, *The Poisonwood Bible*)

The biographical portrait, the predominant mode in which Livingstone has been posthumously portrayed, has proven itself to be a literary genre flexible enough to accommodate an array of perspectives and politics. This chapter, however, moves away from professedly 'factual' representations to consider the consciously fictional. Surprisingly, studies of Livingstone have almost universally ignored the creative literature that the missionary explorer generated. Certain scholars – Clare Pettitt and John M. MacKenzie among them – do draw attention to several of the novels and plays inspired by Livingstone, but for the most part they have been passed over without sustained engagement. This absence of analysis is conspicuous, for even while the fictional portrayals appear few in number beside the tens and hundreds of biographical studies, they certainly constitute a significant dimension of Livingstone's reputation. Indeed the range of his fictive imaginings, in various kinds of literature and for various ideological ends, is actually quite considerable. By providing a detailed discussion of Livingstone's creative constructions, this chapter aims to fill in a glaring lacuna and so provide a fuller understanding of his multivalent legacy. While I have argued throughout this book for the socio-political embeddedness of the biographical 'lives of Livingstone', it will become clear that the agendas in fictional and dramatic formations are often even more explicit, frequently operating less at the level of subtext than as primary subjects.

FICTION: LAUGHING AT LIVINGSTONE?

Livingstone and postcolonialism

It is notable that for a long time – until the later twentieth century – there were very few fictionalisations of Livingstone to speak of. MacKenzie points out that, unlike some other Victorian heroes, he 'seldom if ever made an appearance in the "faction" of the period'. He suggests that 'To a certain extent, Livingstone's failure to appear in topical fiction so typical of the age was a tribute to the power of the myth, the saint-like character of the subject.'[1] It is possible, then, that Livingstone was just too significant a figure, with too great a political utility in the service of empire, for authors to play fast and loose with him creatively. This likely compounded a more general aversion to the fictional representation of historical characters in the late nineteenth century. As Naomi Jacobs argues in her book *Character of Truth*, 'Under realism, which assumed that historical materials and characters must be treated with objectivity and accuracy, such figures have been regarded as presenting formidable aesthetic or creative difficulties.'[2] In other words, many authors were concerned about blurring the boundary between fact and fiction and losing the truth of a character within an invented tale. When the historical subject carried as much saintly baggage as a David Livingstone, of course, the risk was all the greater.

Very occasional fictional treatments of Livingstone, however, can be found in the first half of the twentieth century. One of these, *Livingstone the Empire Builder* by Jane Agnes Staunton Batty, a children's book published by the Society for Promoting Christian Knowledge in 1913, told the story of a class of young students in an obscure countryside school avidly learning about the life of David Livingstone.[3] He does not himself appear as an actual character, but rather as the subject of continued discussion and a series of lessons. Broadly speaking, Livingstone serves to inculcate moral values and to induct the children into an understanding of British imperial duty. The text's acculturating purpose is similar in intent to that of many juvenile books before the Second World War, which, as Daphne Kutzer argues, 'reflect imperialism and empire as a normal part of the world and often encourage child readers to accept the values of imperialism'.[4] Later in the century, in 1949, Livingstone again appeared in fiction, this time in *Black Crusade* by Mary Mitchell, a novel that was heavily intertextually reliant on Reginald Coupland's celebratory historiography.[5] Following two world wars and Indian independence, and in the midst of Islamic nationalist stirrings and the Labour government's 'new policy' in Africa, Mitchell followed Coupland in using Livingstone and Kirk to assert a triumphal narrative of the British colonial heritage. The contemporary anxieties of the empire are an ever-present current in her historical novel. While these two books intervened at different moments in the history of empire they are united in purpose, both seeking to employ Livingstone and the narratives related to him for the consolidation and transmission of imperial values. In marshalling his iconic status for the empire's work, whether projecting an easy colonial confidence or shrouding seeds of discontent with unchastened imperial rhetoric, these books broadly shared the goals of many Livingstone biographies.

Yet before the second half of the twentieth century fictional Livingstones are conspicuous by their absence. Batty's and Mitchell's novels are the exceptions that prove the rule. Indeed, it would take significant cultural and intellectual shifts for imaginative rewrites to finally begin to flourish. On the one hand, the contestation of objective representation in the later twentieth century played its part. The difficulties surrounding historical characters had been 'tied to certain assumptions of the modern age: that fiction is (or can be) distinguishable from fact, that documentable subjects should be treated only in objective or factual ways, and that, indeed, rational objectivity is possible'.[6] But with the rise of creative anti-realism in the academy, the notion thrived that 'identity and what we call "reality" are no less constructs of language than are the most fantastic fictions'.[7] Fact and fiction were not quite so easily distinguished as had been presumed. The project of history, some argued, was at bottom a fictional endeavour, reliant upon constructed narratives that were invariably selective. The integrity of the historical character was no longer so sacrosanct; a famous figure's public persona could itself be conceived of as a fiction, far from objective, and so it lay open to rewriting, revision and even violence.

If this environment permitted authors to take Livingstone as their subject, the primary motivating factor lay in another quarter. Indeed, the most noteworthy feature of the creative rewrites is the substantial number produced under the auspices of postcolonialism; its politico-intellectual stance enabled a very different incarnation of Livingstone to come into being.[8] For Robert J.C. Young, the postcolonial movement can be described as a reconsideration of the violent history of colonialism 'particularly from the perspectives of those who suffered its effects, together with the defining of its contemporary social and cultural impact'.[9] Postcolonialism is a committed critique, 'united by a common political and moral consensus towards the history and legacy of western colonialism'.[10] Its origins are bound up with the political anti-colonial and nationalist struggles in the era leading towards decolonisation, and as such postcolonialism is firmly rooted in an activist past.

But central to postcolonial critique is the marriage of the cultural and the political. As Elleke Boehmer has argued, it stresses that 'cultural representations were central first to the process of colonizing other lands, and then again to the process of obtaining independence from the colonizer'.[11] Frantz Fanon, in his seminal text *Black Skins, White Masks*, was among the first to concentrate on the internal effects of the colonial environment, 'the arsenal of complexes' that it left in its wake.[12] For him, resisting colonialism was not only about achieving political freedom, but about emancipating the consciousness; the oppressed had to 'insult' and 'vomit' up the values imposed upon them. Culture, seen in this light, became a critical arena of struggle and a potential site of psychic transformation.[13] It played a crucial role in decolonising the mind, a process that necessarily remains ongoing even after the achievement of formal independence. And so a characteristic feature of much postcolonial literature is its oppositional impulse towards the imperial centre, its contestation of the values of European civilisation, and its denigration of 'the West' as an ideology.[14] The reconstructions of Livingstone that will occupy the bulk of this chapter are deeply embedded in this context. While many biographies had valorised colonial values, these postcolonial revisions would seek to deconstruct them.[15]

Marlene NourbeSe Philip's *Looking for Livingstone* (1991), Lennart Hagerfors's *The Whales in Lake Tanganyika* (1989) and David Pownall's *Livingstone and Sechele* (1979) all rework the missionary-explorer in order to inflict damage upon his reputation or at least complicate his heroic status.[16] In revising a cherished icon, these authors implement a key postcolonial strategy, which Boehmer describes as the 'adaptation and mutation' of Europe's defining myths.[17] By reconceiving such tales, postcolonial writers express their rejection of European cultural pre-eminence and of established and authoritative versions of history.

In re-presenting Livingstone, NourbeSe Philip, a Caribbean author originally from Tobago but now resident in Canada, sought to revise the European 'myth of discovery'. Rewriting and inverting the conventional exploration narrative, she tells the tale of a nameless female 'Traveller' traversing the African continent in search of David Livingstone. Through the text's structure, the masculine explorer becomes the object rather than the subject of discovery and is thus removed immediately from his place of primacy. In contrast, as Adetayo Alabi points out, an African woman, formerly 'an object that was "discovered" by colonialism', instead 'locates herself in a resistant subject position'.[18] The travelling woman passes through many tribal communities whose names, all anagrams of the word 'silence', express their history of oppression. From these kinship groups she learns crucial lessons to aid her journey to Livingstone and to self-knowledge. Denise deCaires Narain argues that Philip's text sets up a dichotomy 'between the woman's version of "the quest", her openness to suggestion, to difference and to sharing' and 'the single-minded determination of Livingstone and Stanley's attitudes'.[19] Philip's Traveller departs from the icons of exploration in the ethos of her journeying.

Looking for Livingstone is thus, in its very form of composition, opposed to the European exploration narrative. Within this antitravelogue, David Livingstone's role is to stand as the archetypal emblem of discovery, a figure through whom to focalise her broader critique. For the most part the text is less concerned with the details of Livingstone's life than with what he signifies as a type. Jacobs detects this pattern in many contemporary texts that deploy historical figures; they often 'are interesting less for who they were than for what they represent', serving their authors as 'ready-made allegorical characters'.[20] And while of course I have been arguing for the multiplicity of meanings attached to Livingstone, he has been perpetually a symbol of discovery. Philip's book relies upon the resonance of this popular image, but slants it with a new significance. She radically reinterprets the discovery mission, ripping it away from all its grandiose associations and depicting it as a European mechanism of appropriation.

As part of her revision of discovery, Philip has room for gentle satire. She routinely belittles Livingstone's achievements and adopts a scathing tone when describing his accoutrements of travel:

> His supplies alone would have kept me going for centuries – a thermometer; quinine for malaria; a magic lantern to frighten and impress the 'savage heathen' with God; guns for killing … Thomson's Logarithm Tables; and, of course, the 'good book' … as well as sugar, coffee, and tea – 'elevenses' in the deep, mysterious African jungle! … And finally his arrogance – his insurmountable arrogance.[21]

In detracting from the feats of exploration by poking fun in its direction, Philip already defies some of our preconceptions and shocks us with the irreverence of her comments.

But Philip makes more serious points. Discovery was a spurious endeavour, she argues, because its achievements were so reliant on indigenous assistance. All the credit that men like Livingstone unduly received must be wrenched from them and redistributed: 'what support he had!' rants the Traveller, 'African porters to carry his baggage, to interpret and lead the way'.[22] And when the unnamed sojourner finally encounters Livingstone, she berates him: 'You're nothing but a cheat and a liar, Livingstone-I-presume. Without the African, you couldn't have done anything.'[23] Indeed, Philip imagines Livingstone admitting as much to Stanley: 'I *always* travel with native guides myself – don't know where we would be without them. Between you, me, and the jungle, Stanley, it is they who should get the credit.'[24] The success of Livingstone's claims to 'discovery' are thus revealed to be the dubious product of European power. His claim to have found the Victoria Falls was certified as true, says the Traveller, because 'a fact is whatever anyone, having the power to enforce it, says is a fact. Power – that is the distinguishing mark of a fact.' Livingstone's discovery is thus simultaneously 'a lie, *and* a fact, because you and you supporters, your nation of liars, had the power to change a lie into a fact'.[25] For Philip, European discovery was a case of appropriating indigenous knowledge; essentially it was an authorised fiction.

The Traveller gives Livingstone a new name to reflect the logic she sees underlying exploration. Satirising H.M. Stanley's infamous greeting, the new appellation 'Livingstone-I-Presume' sums up discovery as a presumptuous endeavour. The Traveller rechristens Livingstone just as he had 'renamed' his African discoveries and so forces him onto the receiving end of his own power mechanics of labelling and analysis. The Traveller revokes Livingstone's other titles too, rejecting 'foe of darkness' in favour of 'thin end of the wedge'.[26] This second novel name suggests that Livingstone was merely the first small stage of something that would soon become much larger and more significant. The implication is that his explorations were the initial steps towards the imperial rush that would soon grip the continent.

Both Livingstone's new titles, of course, insist that discovery was no innocent endeavour. In fact, for Philip, it amounted to conquest. Listing Livingstone, Henry the Navigator, Columbus 'And all those other explorers', she summarises their endeavours: 'Discover and possess – one and the same thing. And destroy.'[27] Later in the text, the Traveller rejects Livingstone's claim to have filled in the spaces on the blank canvas of the African map, and sets him straight on the true nature of his cartography: 'You captured and seized the Silence you found – possessed it like the true discoverer you were – dissected and analysed it; labelled it – you took their Silence – the Silence of the African – and replaced it with your own – the silence of the word.'[28] Philip frequently makes this oscillation between 'silence' and 'Silence'. With an upper-case letter the word implies, as Isabel Hoving puts it, 'the deepest personal point of authenticity' and 'the irrepressible possibility of otherness'.[29] The lower-case word, however, connotes a silence forced by others, the state of being silenced. What Philip suggests is that by representing Africa in Western terms, Livingstone domesticated the radical otherness he encountered: he, and the many explorers that he stands for, wrote 'the other' into silence.

Livingstone thus served Philip as a figure through whom she could deconstruct the European discovery narrative. But by representing

Livingstone as the 'word', she also used him to revisit the linguistic problematic of colonialism. This theme has preoccupied much of her work, and for good reason. As a descendant of African slaves who were ripped from their indigenous locales, exported to the Caribbean and forced into an English-speaking melting pot, Philip has tried to come to terms with the cultural and linguistic alienation brought about by 'the middle passage'. In the wake of this history, Philip describes herself as writing in 'exile': 'It's exile from a number of things on many layers – your original language, your mother tongue, your culture, your spirituality.'[30] English is for Philip an oppressive force, an alien tongue, the language that stole away her African heritage. Yet it is simultaneously her 'native' tongue, the language in which she is most at home and in which she writes. Her relationship to English is fundamentally ambivalent; it is at once a language that is and is not her own. Philip captures this duality in her poem 'Discourse on the Logic of Language', where she writes, 'English is my mother tongue / is my father tongue.'[31] The imposing 'father tongue' of the coloniser is also the language with which she is most intimate. In an interview with Barbara Carey in 1991 she described English as an 'abusive parent': 'The problem is that you cannot pretend that you didn't have an abusive parent. You have to find some way of resolving the experience or coming to terms with it.'[32]

By referring to Livingstone as the 'word', Philip construes him as a signifier of the 'father tongue'. The Traveller's search for Livingstone is part of Philip's attempt to come to terms with that abusive parent, the colonial language. In much of the text, she explores the possibility of an altogether different mode of communication, valorising the language of 'Silence' in place of speech. She rebuffs the assumption that silence equates to powerlessness and instead turns it into a resource of 'infinite potentiality and possibility'.[33] While this seems counterintuitive, Isabel Hoving reminds us that 'In non-Western traditions, one may discern different epistemologies wherein silence is highly esteemed.'[34]

But at the same time, dealing with the colonial language entails vengeance. Philip inflicts imaginative violence on Livingstone to the extent that it almost becomes a revenge fantasy. This is at its clearest in the traveller's recurring sexual dream. She imagines that she and Livingstone 'COPULATE LIKE TWO BEASTS – HE RIDES ME – HIS WORD SLIPPING IN AND OUT OF THE WET MOIST SPACES OF MY SILENCE'.[35] The graphic scene obviously draws upon the notion of the colonial relationship as an exploitative sexual encounter. But the rape is soon inverted as the Traveller becomes the dominant partner: 'I TAKE HIS WORD – STRONG AND THRUSTING ... I TAKE IT INTO THE SILENCE OF MY MOUTH – AND IN A CLEARING IN A FOREST HE SITS AND WEEPS.'[36] Livingstone's sexual aggression is turned back upon himself as he finds himself orally castrated and rendered impotent. Commenting on this scene, 'a rigorous rewriting of a history of victimism', Hoving suggests that Livingstone is not himself victimised in a retributive manner, but that he experiences a 'wholesome castration'.[37] This seems to me unconvincing. Even writing Livingstone into a sexual scene of this ilk is iconoclastic. Philip's purpose is to violate the figure who for her represents the invasive colonial language that has alienated her from her cultural roots. Philip almost seeks imaginative catharsis. As she put it to Barbara Carey, her project of rewriting history is 'like talking to Livingstone and telling him a few things'.[38]

Nonetheless, despite Philip's clear enjoyment at violating Livingstone, the text makes a more productive point. After the Traveller has berated Livingstone at length, the book closes with some approximation to reconciliation. At the end, the two lie uneasily together with hands clasped. While Silence reigns supreme, there is the suggestion of some alliance, however strained. This ambiguous ending could be read, as Hoving suggests, as a statement of the impossibility of speaking without the word of the father tongue.[39] Indeed Arwhal, the Traveller's lover-mentor, has taught her at an earlier point in the text that 'to use your silence, you have to use the word'.[40] However contaminated the colonial language is, 'you need the word – whore words – to weave your silence'.[41] Even while Livingstone and his language must be violated, it is only by appropriating his resources, the resources of the 'word', that the Caribbean experience can be expressed: English must be beaten and abused, but still used. In showing the deeply uncomfortable, but irrevocable, connection to the father tongue, *Looking for Livingstone* ultimately emphasises the hybridity of postcolonial identity. As Hoving writes, for Philip 'The dominant discourse is always present, even in one's deepest inner self.'[42] By reaching a point of uneasy coexistence with Livingstone, Philip attempts to come to terms with an integral dimension of her selfhood that is both deeply familiar and irrevocably alien.

NourbeSe Philip's re-figuration of Livingstone was not met without resistance. In fact, her publication sparked off a protracted debate in the pages of *Books in Canada*. It began with a letter to the editor in November 1991 by a member of the public, Eleanor Parkes, who forcefully rejected Philip's book: 'The anti-slavery activist and explorer Dr David Livingstone (1813–1873) did not silence her people; he opened their country to medical missionaries, teachers, and engineers, and exposed her people to stimulating change. To sneer at his accomplishments is absurd.'[43] Philip swiftly replied to the letter herself, accusing her critic of a xenophobic undercurrent: Parkes's reaction proved 'the existence of the bedrock racism that surfaces as soon as there is any attempt to present a fuller and more detailed picture of what has been a thoroughly Eurocentric *and* inaccurate view of Africa'. Philip went on to argue that *Books in Canada* had shown little editorial responsibility in publishing a letter that was on the level of 'the down and dirty'.[44] This point was picked up as other names entered the debate. One correspondent, Richard Sanger, rebuked Philip for interfering with free speech: 'That someone who has herself suffered racism and exclusion at the hands of Canadian publishers should now call on the editors of *Books in Canada* to suppress such letters for reasons of "bad taste" is a sad irony'.[45] Philip responded by arguing that she had not at all called for the letter's suppression, but that since editors customarily had 'discretionary powers' it could be expected that they might 'point out to a letter writer that a letter does not really raise any issues and suggest that the writer make a substantive point'.[46]

Philip was perhaps a little caught up with the rage-filled pen, because it seems obvious that substantial issues were indeed raised by Parkes's arguably reactionary letter. If nothing else it reveals the risky nature of reinterpreting history and, as Philip herself recognised, of debunking a 'sacred cow'.[47] But it also shows that Livingstone's identity remained a space for debate. And even though she was probably right to detect an unpleasant undertone in Parkes's letter, this debate is one that Philip seems too keen to shut down. In responding to Parkes, Philip defended her book as an essentially accurate depiction of Livingstone, by directing her opponent to Tim Jeal's well-known biography: 'She might be surprised to find there, in Livingstone's own words, his plans for Africa: destroy the indigenous way of life – including their customs, religions, and mores – the better to bring Commerce ... And he a Christian man at that!'[48] It seems to me, however, that Philip places herself on weak terrain here by defending her book on the wrong grounds. Jeal's biography, one of the first critical studies of Livingstone, might consolidate some of Philip's points, but it is in no way comparable to her own sustained character destruction. In fact, Philip's book is at its strongest where Livingstone functions as a type – as a figure of discovery and the colonial language. The violence done to Livingstone makes sense because of what she sets him up to signify. To defend her book on its historical accuracy is somewhat superfluous: her primary points do not hinge on what Livingstone really was or was not like.

Yet if Philip does intend her book to be an accurate representation of the historical figure, rather than a colonial symbol, her hypercritical approach is arguably as reductive as those texts that sing solely to the tune of greatness. It has to be said that the boundary between Livingstone as type and as historical personage is blurred in Philip's work. She does strike out at Livingstone on a personal level, consistently attributing his actions to unflattering motives and unconscious drives. Any biographical details that Philip chooses to import are the conspicuously negative ones. For instance, before Livingstone can fully spit out his claim to be 'the first European to –', the Traveller sharply intercepts him: 'You lie, Livingstone-I-Presume. The Portuguese were there before you.' When Livingstone insists they were 'half-castes', she yells 'Bull-shit! – you made that up so you could capture the glory yourself.'[49] Livingstone's attempts to consolidate his own reputation are thus brought under the microscope for inspection. Philip also weaves into the text an imagined letter from Mary Livingstone, in which she protests against her abandonment: 'I, who have travelled the Kalahari with a child at my breast and one in the womb to be with you, want more than silence ...'.[50] Philip chooses to foreground, once again, the familiar complaint that Livingstone was neglectful of his familial duties. Driven by an excoriating impulse, she interprets her subject in a way that leaves little room for complexity.

Perhaps, then, we see in Philip something of the potentially reductive nature of postcolonial reading practices. As Brian Musgrove has observed, postcolonialism often interprets exploration and travel 'as a version of Freud's "instinct of destruction"'.[51] Even though Philip uses Livingstone to make some powerful anti-colonial points she somewhat reductively presents discovery, the English language and Livingstone's individual actions as manifestations of an unambiguous Western will to power. Philip reveals something of her totalising mindset in *Books in Canada*. She accuses Parkes, for her 'unsolicited, unwanted, and useless advice', of falling 'squarely within that missionary tradition that David Livingstone so notoriously embodies'.[52] In characterising a 'missionary tradition', Philip lapses into cliché and a postcolonial 'grand narrative' that typecasts missionaries as agents of cultural imperialism.[53] Nonetheless, Philip did set out with very political and polemical intentions, and so in forcefully reconstructing Livingstone, and rejecting what she considers to be European mythologies, she successfully achieved her aim.

The Whales in Lake Tanganyika, penned by the Swedish author Lennart Hagerfors, similarly sets out to distance Livingstone from his heroic legacy. Hagerfors's European origin demonstrates that as a space of commitment, postcolonial critique is not the domain solely of the formerly colonised; it is transcultural, not confined by race or region.[54] His novel retells H.M. Stanley's expedition to 'find Livingstone' from the perspective of John William Shaw, a work-shy drunkard. As a figure about whom little is known historically, Hagerfors is presented with an opportunity to re-imagine the enterprise from the inside. Yet again, the journey to Livingstone and the man himself are used as a means to elaborate on key postcolonial themes and to envision a different version of history.

Like *Looking for Livingstone*, *Whales* challenges the European discovery narrative by parodying the conventional travelogue. While the book begins in typical diary format, dated 'Zanzibar *15 January 1871*', the systematised approach is short-lived.[55] Shaw narrates as if in a dream, but his almost hallucinatory perspective permits clarity of vision and an altogether different outlook on exploration. At points, Shaw writes much about a small number of days, but at others vast chunks of time are barely narrated. Describing his journey between Kingaru and Simbamwenni, Shaw concedes: 'In my memory, the days that followed blur into one another in a feverish fog. I have no idea of the chronology of events ... I have only a few fleeting but extremely clear images.'[56] Shaw thus departs from routinised recording practices that recount the monotonous detail of daily affairs. Instead, his narrative emphasises subjective rather than 'real' time, time as experienced rather than calibrated by the clock. Early in the text he muses:

> According to the calendar, it's been two weeks since Stanley hired me. They have been so eventful that I've lost my sense of time. Perhaps it was two *years* ago that we met in the shack? ... Time's own motion, however, has swept onward like a storm: the two weeks have swirled away in a temporal space equivalent to two days.[57]

Shaw refuses to domesticate his experience to the requirements of the travelogue. Indeed, his unusual recording ethic enables some critical commentary on standard documenting practices. He relates the horror of the expedition's trek through the Makata swamp, and the feverish expiration of Asmani, an African porter who had become something of a friend.[58] Shortly after all this, Shaw 'sneaked an illicit look at Stanley's notes. In them, he says simply that the dog and a few porters died.'[59] The juxtaposition of two versions of events sharply highlights the selective nature of exploration narratives. For Hagerfors, like Philip, travelogues can silence. Or as Shaw puts it, 'I record in order to erase. Writing is the most exact instrument for forgetting.'[60]

Hagerfors's quest for Livingstone is Conradian in sentiment, but with a few twists. He too revisits the myth of the 'heart of darkness' and positions Europeans as a corruptive presence. But Hagerfors takes the dichotomy of light and darkness and inscribes it with a new meaning: he reverses the binary so that light no longer stands for enlightenment, but instead becomes an invasive and destructive force. Stanley is consistently attached to this imagery of brutal light. When he first bursts into Shaw's chamber, 'a terrible blinding white light entered ...

I glimpsed a figure bathed in this torrent of light'.[61] Later, when Stanley is engaged in war with the Arab chief Mirambo, the same 'white light shone around his body'.[62] And when he calls himself 'the bright light', Shaw sums up his overblown self-description as 'so many dark words'.[63] In a powerful reversal, metaphors of light and enlightenment are ironically revealed to be truly 'dark'.

Stanley continually relies on the categories that Hagerfors reveals to be so hollow. He paints his hunt for Livingstone as a search for 'The light that shineth in the darkness'.[64] But while Livingstone may be light for Stanley, *Whales* alienates the reader's expectations by offering other ways of seeing him. When Stanley and Shaw dine with a caravan of wealthy Arab noblemen, their hosts tell the tale of 'a strange white man who was staying in Ujiji'. Brought up at the end of an evening, 'as if to entertain' their guests, Livingstone is reduced to an after-dinner anecdote.[65] Stanley becomes excited nonetheless, exclaiming to Shaw that 'Livingstone is alive!', 'He is one of the most important men in the world.' At this, the Arabs laugh in surprise: 'Oh, so you regard him as an important man. Interesting.' They assume that Stanley is either a kinsman or confused, for to the Arabs Livingstone is 'just a peculiar old man'.[66] Like NourbeSe Philip, Hagerfors explores a possible world in which Livingstone's African excursion might be counted unremarkable. When Stanley protests that his hero is 'one of the world's greatest explorers', the Arab replies, 'Perhaps we who have done business here for a few generations see matters a little differently.'[67] Livingstone is removed from pride of place; to those already in Africa, Livingstone was only a recent and inexperienced guest.

The Arabs' description of Livingstone prepares us for a debunking representation. Nevertheless, his first appearance still shocks in its conspicuous departure from received notions. When Stanley and Shaw arrive in Ujiji, 'a strange figure staggered forth and set out on a limping run to the water's edge'; 'He looked like an injured bird that couldn't fly.'[68] As William Ferguson puts it, there is an almost 'Darwinian reversal' as the beast-like imagery is developed.[69] Livingstone 'resembled a chimpanzee' with his 'skinny and bowed' legs, 'apelike arms' and 'clawlike hand'.[70] On one level, the point is simply to make Livingstone pathetically laughable. In recent years, humour has grown as a subject of interest to postcolonial studies, as scholars have interrogated the ways in which authors 'laugh back' to the imperial centre. Theorists have come to focus on the connection between humour and agency, the way in which seemingly frivolous laughter can do serious work.[71] As Ulrike Erichsen points out, much of this research is Bakhtinian in perspective, emphasising the antinomian potential of humour to subvert official ideologies.[72] In laughing at Livingstone, Hagerfors aims to invert the heroic image of Livingstone so as to detach him, and the European mission in Africa, from associations of grandeur. A Freudian perspective might shed further light. While he considered joking to be an outlet for the repressed and tabooed, Freud also argued that it was primarily hostile in intent; it relied on a coalition between teller and listener at the expense of a third party, and as such was a symbolic victory over an enemy.[73] Hagerfors's subversive ridiculing of Livingstone is aggressive in purpose, an attempt to forcefully 'abrogate' European authority by mocking one of its canonical figures.[74]

Hagerfors, however, does not just make Livingstone animal-like in order to pour forth scorn. The imagery also implies that instead of taming the continent, Livingstone has been made wild. Or, to put it another way, he has failed to colonise Africa; instead it has colonised him. The *New York Times* critic Michiko Kakutani is misleading on this point in her review. She says that Livingstone 'appears to have succumbed to the darkness at the heart of the continent'.[75] But, as I have shown, Hagerfors resists the notion that Africa is a place of darkness. In becoming beast-like, Livingstone has not at all been corrupted by Africa. Rather, his degeneration indicates that his categories and mythologies have been vanquished; notions of discovery and civilisation do not hold in the centre of Africa.

That Livingstone's decrepit appearance signifies the breakdown of once-dear European values is confirmed at the close of the novel, when he finally breaks silence and gives voice to his disillusion in a lengthy monologue. He has become estranged from his 'native tongue', which can no longer express his identity: 'I no longer speak it.' While Stanley has reintroduced him to the language, to Livingstone 'It sounds frightful.'[76] His homeland has become alien, a place of fear. 'The terror I feel when Stanley talks about Europe gives me stomach cramps', he confesses.[77] Indeed Livingstone has altogether lost faith in his own mission. He describes the chastening experience of communicating the Christian message: 'The Negroes have spoken the name of Jesus, and sung songs about him too', but only because they 'care for me'.[78] In truth, his efforts were utterly domesticated: 'since they live in the jungle, their god lives in the jungle too'. 'Into the Negroes' inexhaustible storehouse of gods and spirits, my god disappeared, accepted and tolerated to the point of anonymity.'[79] In other words, Livingstone was confronted with the ability of an encountered culture to appropriate the message in unpredictable and hybrid ways. While once he had preached to the continent with 'a mouth as large as a cathedral', now 'all that remains of me is an ear'.[80] Livingstone can no longer espouse a European vision; instead he has been chastened, compelled to listen and learn.

FICTION: LAUGHING AT LIVINGSTONE?

Having been subdued by Africa, the simian-like Livingstone is now able to critique his former code. As he prepares to survey Lake Tanganyika with Stanley, he reflects upon discovery: 'We are playing. I must play again. I used to play that the Lualaba ran north. If it runs west, someone else must play that.'[81] While Stanley has continually attached lofty associations to exploration, Livingstone reduces it to the level of a trivial game. This perspective is consolidated by Shaw, who thinks that Livingstone, 'decked out as an explorer', looks 'like a circus animal dressed up as a person'.[82] Throughout the text, moreover, Shaw depicts the exploratory mission as performative posturing. Stanley is perpetually theatrical, even greeting Shaw in their first meeting with a practised spiel: 'My name is Stanley. Henry Morton Stanley. I am a correspondent for an American paper, the *New York Herald.*'[83] Later in the book, too, when Stanley has waxed at length about his enlightening ideals, Shaw writes, 'It was as if we were acting in a play.'[84]

Livingstone becomes almost prophetic and advances from his critique of discovery to a critique of colonialism. He realises that the 'raging passion' with which he traversed Africa had 'brought with it a monster'. And this 'monster', which 'has only begun to show its face', is the stirrings of colonialism.[85] Livingstone is far-sighted and forecasts the way in which he would be put to work in the future colonial project. He realises that for Stanley he is 'the soft fingertips of his firm hand, the gentle smile on his determined face'.[86] In other words, Livingstone predicts that he will play the moral face of imperialism, masking its brutal reality. As Shaw muses, 'the warm' and 'soft' hand of Livingstone and the 'cold' and 'hard' hand of Stanley would together be 'invincible'.[87] This aspect of Hagerfors's representation is particularly intriguing, for it suggests that even while Livingstone paved the way for colonialism, he was to some degree appropriated. While Hagerfors has removed Livingstone from his heroic heritage, it seems that he detects a degree of ambivalence in his historical subject. Despite Livingstone's all-consuming passion for discovery, colonialism remains to him a 'monster'.

This element of ambivalence, which is a quiet note in Hagerfors's text, is clearer in David Pownall's play *Livingstone and Sechele.* Discussing his dramatic representation, Pownall suggests that 'the transfiguration of Britain's colonial power' in the 1960s resounds in the performance like an 'ironical chorus'. Having spent what he calls his 'apprenticeship to the stage' in the Zambian theatre scene, Pownall was well suited to his role as commentator.[88] In *Livingstone and Sechele*, he is partly concerned with psychologically interrogating a real historical character, but like the other authors in this section he primarily uses his subject as a locus for particular thematic preoccupations. This time,

Livingstone becomes the focal point for an examination of the complex relationship between Christianity and colonialism.

As the title suggests, Pownall's play is as much about Sechele as about Livingstone. As with the other postcolonial re-visions, Livingstone's pre-eminence is contested. By forcing the missionary to share the centre stage with the chief of the Kwena, Pownall is able to envision the dynamic of their interaction and, in so doing, to explore a collision of cultures. This clash is first represented on stage in spatial terms. In his stage directions, Pownall indicates that Sechele's rondavel should be depicted on the right by a 'large circle chalked on the floor', while Livingstone's cabin should be signified by 'a square of equal dimension' on the left.[89] By using shapes to characterise the different thought-worlds, Pownall suggests a degree of incommensurability. It is as difficult to make these worlds fit as it is to square a circle.

Within this cultural clash, Pownall examines the functioning of Christianity as a tool of colonial power. Livingstone strives to use his religion to control Sechele and to construct him egotistically in his own desired fashion. Finding Mokoron, Sechele's wife, impossible to teach, Livingstone appeals against polygamy in order to get rid of her. 'You're a polygamist man, a sinner in depth ... How can I teach her, or you, anything while we're still fighting this problem.'[90] Later on, when Livingstone discovers that Sechele has still been sleeping with Mokoron after their divorce, he exerts his power by banning his convert from communion: 'No, no,' Sechele protests, 'you are casting me out.'[91] Livingstone threatens to abandon Kolobeng in order to bend Sechele to his will, giving him an ultimatum for his genuine conversion. 'If you won't accept Christ in the next seven days,' he warns, 'you and your Crocodile People will have to come down with the dust and I'll move on.'[92] By presenting conversion as a catch-all solution to tribal problems, he entices Sechele to embrace Christianity: 'Accept Christ and civilisation will follow, protection from the Boers, trade, the tribe will get stronger ...'.[93]

Nonetheless, Pownall does not settle for a facile appraisal in which Christianity operates solely in terms of domination. The play posits considerably more complexity by showing how Livingstone's efforts to regulate, and to colonise the mind, continually result in failure. He is unable to determine the way in which Sechele receives the message, and indeed the chieftain adopts utterly heretical perspectives. In one hilarious episode, Sechele decides to barter with God. He confesses before his redeemer that he sent one treacherous relative a 'present' of gunpowder, which led to its intended calamitous conclusion. He prays, 'If I am forgiven for this, Lord, then I am prepared to forgive you for the last twenty years.'[94] Even as David protests at his blasphemy, Sechele persists, ending his intercession by assuring God that 'we have balanced things out'.[95] His expression of faith is a syncretic blend of Christian and indigenous systems. In one entreaty, he muses on 'the Duke of Wellington, a great soldier whose spirit I must consult as to my strategy of defence ...'.[96] This uncontrollability disturbs Livingstone, and he frets that Sechele's profession of faith is bogus. 'You don't take your own soul seriously ... I see the twinkle in your eye.'[97] Certainly, Sechele does receive Christianity for his own purposes, and not least because he treasures David. Livingstone is Sechele's true god, his 'father' and his 'angel', who surpasses Christ in greatness: 'Christ would not come down here from Jerusalem, but David has come all the way from Glasgow.'[98] He confesses to Mokoron, 'I love God because he is David's.'[99] At his most honest, Sechele indicates that Livingstone is valuable as a political asset: 'He is good for the tribe. Count how many guns we have since he came. If the Matabele or the Boers attacked tomorrow I would kill them with eighty quick shots.'[100] Both Sechele's beliefs and his reasons for adopting them lie markedly beyond the parameters of Livingstone's control.

Pownall further troubles a glib connection between Christianity and colonialism by parading the ways in which the religion could actually facilitate critique. Livingstone's actions are consistently admonished by the faith he espouses. While he rages about Sechele's and Mokoron's noisy sexual antics, his wife's humble spirituality sits in critical commentary. She gently urges him to 'finish our prayer' and completes it herself when he continues to vent: 'We ask to be forgiven. By the power of your Spirit turn us from evil to good, help us to forgive others.'[101] Mary's request for absolution and the bestowal of grace reveals Livingstone's unrelenting anger to be fundamentally unchristian. Later, Livingstone is censured by the very words he recites from the Eucharist: 'He who comes to me I will not cast out.'[102] Yet Livingstone has just threatened to expel Sechele from the communion and eventually does so. Some reproof of Livingstone's uncompromising standards is provided too by one of the most celebrated authors in Christian history, the Puritan John Bunyan. After Livingstone has railed at Sechele for his backsliding regression, the chieftain and Mokoron read a dialogue from *Pilgrim's Progress* on the struggle with the sinful nature. In this passage Hopeful tells Christian that, on conversion, 'Sin was yet very sweet to my flesh, and I was loth to leave it'; from time to time, we learn Hopeful relapses and becomes 'as bad, nay worse than I was before'.[103] It is exactly for this battle in Sechele, between the spirit and the flesh, that Livingstone offers no quarter. By New Testament criteria, he is in danger of becoming a

Pharisee. Mary, opening the Bible and stabbing her finger, stumbles on a passage from Luke: 'Beware of the scribes, which desire to walk in long robes, and love greetings in the markets, and the highest seats in the synagogues and the chief's room at feasts.'[104] Confusing the words 'chief' and 'chief's', Mary unconsciously applies these verses directly to her husband.

Through Sechele's fiery wife, Mokoron, Pownall explores the polyvalent power of scripture, its capacity to be wielded as a weapon. Livingstone and she go tête-à-tête, jousting with each other using biblical quotation. Citing Isaiah 'fifty-five, twelve!', Livingstone tries to assure Sechele that the tribe's conversion will result in prosperity. 'For ye shall go out with joy and be led forth with peace', he exclaims, 'the mountains and the hills shall break forth before you into singing.'[105] Mokoron, however, knows her Bible well enough to employ it in an act of defiance. She reminds him of other words from Isaiah: 'I will make waste mountains and hills, and dry up all their herbs; and I will make rivers islands ... their fish stinketh because there is not water, and dieth of thirst!'[106] In Mokoron's interpretation, God is not a deity of mercy but one of drought and pestilence; she unsettles David by showing how the coloniser's book can be exercised against him. At the close of the text, Mokoron does seem to accept Christianity, but she does so for its radical potential. She mumbles to herself, 'Isaiah, one, seven and eight: your land, strangers devour it in your presence and it is desolate, as overthrown by strangers ... I take Christ now.'[107] She almost adopts a form of liberation theology, finding in the Bible the resources to resist the alien presence in her homeland.[108]

Pownall's exploration of ambivalence is reflected in the way in which he chooses to cast Livingstone. Certainly, he is more critical than favourable; that much is clear from his castigation of Livingstone's abusive spiritual rhetoric. Yet Pownall does not paint his subject purely with the broad brush of villainy and instead creates a character of psychological complexity. By imagining several honest conversations with Mary, Pownall endows Livingstone with a deep-seated vulnerability. He asks his wife, 'Do you think I'm cut out for this work?' and 'can I preach?'[109] In a moment of self-reflexive angst, he tells her, 'I'm a very unattractive personality, I know that ... Listening to my own voice is as painful to me as it is to my audience.' He goes on, 'God gave me few natural talents for some reason.'[110] Pownall makes clear the real frustrations of the struggle to impact a reticent people. '[T]here are a thousand jobs to be done here,' Livingstone complains. 'Gardening. Digging. Engineering even. Mending guns, always mending guns ... I'm not a missionary, Mary, I'm a handyman.' In a despairing moment he questions the value of his labours: 'If I handed the whole lot back to the witch-doctor, how many more would perish?'[111] The point is that, despite having a will to power, the colonist lacks full control and is by no means self-assured.

But Pownall does not put Livingstone to work purely as a vehicle for ideas. Rather, it seems that he detects ambivalence in him as a real historical personage. While for Pownall, Livingstone did have some colonial aspirations, it was concern for the impoverished working classes that impelled him. In Africa, Livingstone muses, 'There's room': 'My millions at home don't have to live like mice in a meal-kist. Out here they can stretch themselves.'[112] And Pownall complicates the colonial picture further by granting Livingstone some anti-imperial sentiments. At the play's outset, he urges Sechele to maintain his independence: 'give up your reliance on Europe, keep yourself pure and uncontaminated by all kinds of heathenism, and be independent. Accept no interference from British, Dutch, Matabele, anyone!'[113] Rather than advocating the advent and intrusion of imperial power, Livingstone stands in opposition to it: he cautions against the corrupting effects of European influence, which he equates to other manifestations of 'heathenism'. Livingstone is also at pains to differentiate himself from both the Boers and the British colony at the Cape. 'When I met the Boers you know what they asked me to do? Preach to you a text that you were below them! Then, they said, I can stay. They'd hang all us missionaries on the same gibbet, as would the governor of Cape Colony if he could. We're a nuisance because we don't teach subjection.'[114] While there is a trace of irony here, for Sechele dubs himself the missionary's 'slave', Pownall highlights the complexity of Livingstone's imperial motivations and something of the fraught dynamic between missionaries and colonial authorities.

It would be misleading, however, to overestimate the ambivalence that Pownall detects in Livingstone. Writing at a time when gender studies was on the ascent, Pownall construes his subject as excessively patriarchal in his exercise of authority. Livingstone tells his student at the beginning of the play, 'the ladies might get about their household chores while we do this detailed work on the Scriptures, Sechele. It is not for the superficial mind.'[115] Ultimately Livingstone makes his resolution to quit Kolobeng, abandoning his wife and children, while Mary is in the throes of childbirth. Ignoring her anguish and protests, he shrouds his decision in sanctimonious rhetoric: 'Let your affection be towards God, much more than towards me.'[116] The real heroes of the play, and by far and away the more impressive characters, are the two women: Mary, the voice of true faith and earthy wisdom, and Mokoron, the impassioned voice of defiance.

The play too, treats Livingstone in an almost diagnostic fashion. He is overly irascible, flaring up at the least provocation before sinking to the depths of self-doubt and despair. Indeed, he is unstable to a degree that suggests bipolarity. Pownall may well have been influenced by Oliver Ransford's *David Livingstone: The Dark Interior*, which posthumously diagnosed Livingstone with manic depressive disorder and was published just the previous year.[117] Pownall at least shared its psychological preoccupation, tracing Livingstone's growing obsession with achievement and envelopment within his own ego. Sechele detects his consuming desire to be a 'great man' and prays, 'Give him fame, God! Give him fame!'[118] Eventually Livingstone's scientific aspirations become so integral to his being that they infringe on his prayer life. In a sudden outburst, he abandons his usually sacramental language and addresses God in scientific speech:

> Dear Jesus, in the midst of this dreary drought it is wonderful to see the ants running about with their accustomed vivacity! ... this broiling heat only augmented the activity of the long-legged black ants ... Can it be that they have the power of combining the oxygen and hydrogen of their vegetable food by a vital force so as to form water, H_2O?[119]

Livingstone slumps forward, exhausted after this powerful release of repression: his science has become spiritual, his desire for discovery has supplanted the sacred. By the end of the play, the suppressed yearning for prominence has altogether trumped his Christian incentive: he removes the picture of the crucifixion from his magic lantern, replacing it excitedly, and in a symbolic gesture, with a map of his proposed route from Kolobeng to Lake Ngami.[120] For Pownall, then, Livingstone's declared missionary intentions masked more fundamental urges.

The politico-intellectual climate of postcolonialism spawned some of the most creative reinterpretations of Livingstone. In defiance of European mythology and historical narrative, the story of Livingstone was appropriated and rewritten for political purposes. With a moral imperative to critique all things imperial, he came under fire as one of empire's most celebrated symbols. In all this, Livingstone's identity as an historical figure was less important than what he could signify as a type. In his symbolic capacity, he was used in order to evaluate the discovery narrative, to 'laugh back' at the imperial centre and to revisit both the linguistic legacy of imperialism and the complex interaction between colonialism and Christianity. Of course, this is not to say that the historical character of Livingstone was irrelevant to all this; he was of course considered by each author to be an appropriate vehicle for her or his critique. In fact one danger in all these texts, even those which posit a degree of ambivalence, is their tendency towards almost libellous debunking. In reacting against a cult of celebration, their acts of textual violence risk becoming as reductive as the narratives they seek to rebut.

Livingstone and liberalism: a view from apartheid

In contrast to these sustained postcolonial revisions, several creative representations of Livingstone emerging from South Africa stand out as distinctive. Written by a pair of the nation's most celebrated authors, Alan Paton and Nadine Gordimer, these texts mobilise Livingstone for liberal and radical purposes in the context of apartheid. In an environment of racial discrimination and violence, Livingstone came to symbolise, in varying degrees for the two authors, the possibility of racial harmony and the breakdown of segregation in practice.

Alan Paton, the author of *Cry, the Beloved Country* (1948), was a central figure within South African oppositional politics and a founding member of the short-lived Liberal Party. The brand of liberalism that he espoused, as he argued in *Hope for South Africa* (1958), was primarily characterised by a 'particular concern for racial justice'.[121] And indeed, it was the governing National Party's increasingly restrictive racial legislation that spurred a group of liberals to create a new party in 1953. As Peter F. Alexander points out, from 1950 the government had enacted a series of repressive statutes, the Mixed Marriages Act and the Suppression of Communism Act among them. The first of these, forbidding sexual relations between races, was regarded by Paton to be an inhuman and 'iron law'. The second granted the minister of justice extraordinary powers, authorising him to ban anyone deemed to be furthering the 'aims of communism' from public life.[122] Such legislation, as Alexander observes, seemed to Paton to escalate repression radically: it was becoming increasingly clear that the Nationalists were seeking to remove non-whites permanently from political life.[123] Paton was never overly optimistic about the Liberal Party's potential for success and he was right; the party would never succeed in getting one of its candidates elected before it was disbanded in 1968. Nonetheless, he felt it was essential to take this stand in order to oppose Verwoerd's hyper-nationalism and apartheid schemes.

It was in this context of quickening segregation and the developing liberal response that Paton decided to write on Livingstone. His efforts resulted in two plays: *David Livingstone* – begun during a spell in Long Island in 1956 – and *The Last Journey*, which he completed in late 1958.[124] In the intervening period, between the conception and conclusion of his work on Livingstone, the repressive edicts continued to intensify and the Liberal Party itself came under increasing state pressure. The first of Paton's plays exists in almost complete typescript form, although it was never performed and Paton ultimately abandoned it as unsatisfactory. The second, like its predecessor, remained unpublished but was performed on at least one occasion in Lusaka in Northern Rhodesia. Unfortunately no full script has survived and no critical edition has been formed; as it stands, it consists of several incomplete handwritten manscripts which often contain variant versions of the same scenes. As Mary Rosner points out, in the only existing critical analysis of these plays, this suggests that Paton engaged in extensive reworking and rewriting.[125]

In *David Livingstone*, Paton's clear agenda was to use his subject to endorse liberalism and racial accord. The play retells the story of the indigenous porters who carried Livingstone's body to the coast, after his death at the village of Chitambo, for transportation to his home nation. It foregrounds the valour of these men, and particularly of Susi, whom Paton envisaged in the 'heroic mould'.[126] In the first scene, the men cross through hostile territory paved with uncertainty. Susi tells his companions to 'sleep, all of you. I shall watch'; while the others put down their loads and lie down to rest, Susi remains standing and alert.[127] In an apartheid climate, even choosing to make a black African the central protagonist, and heroic at that, had radical implications. And Paton ensures that the Africans appear superior to the Englishmen they encounter. When the men meet Lieutenant Cameron, in command of an expedition searching for Livingstone, he immediately tries to force them to bury the body in Unyanyembe. As Susi attempts to explain the hazards they have faced in their efforts to send the body home, Cameron is monosyllabic, merely repeating an abrupt and uninterested 'yes' with 'impatience not altogether concealed'. In his stage directions, Paton instructs Susi to stand bowed 'in a dignified manner' that is 'neither servile nor arrogant'.[128] He seems comfortably superior to the presumptuous and unthinking white man.

There is a similar scene later in the play, when the men arrive at the coast. They greet a British captain at the port, saluting him with 'upraised hands and the title "Bwana"', only to be barely noticed while he congratulates Cameron. The captain coolly barks out an instruction, 'Men, take over', and leaves the carriers behind. 'Susi and his company', writes Paton, are left 'looking after them in anger, hurt, and astonishment.' Chuma reminds Susi, who can barely 'control his anger', that 'there are stupid men in every nation'.[129] The play thus castigates the blithe and habitual nature of white racism and, by Susi's fury, suggests that it may have violent consequences. This was of course a pertinent message in the 1950s, as the decade witnessed increasing militancy in

FICTION: LAUGHING AT LIVINGSTONE?

the African National Congress and other black protest groups. In the final scene of the play, which depicts Livingstone's funeral service in Westminster Abbey, the white and elite pall-bearers are symbolically substituted for the more deserving Susi and his men. The episode highlights their forgotten role and attempts to make some sort of posthumous reparation. Paton clearly wrote this play, like *Cry, the Beloved Country*, to 'stab South Africa in the conscience'.[130]

In much of his writing Paton argued that the only alternative to dictatorship, black or white, was for South African people as a whole to live alongside one another and work together.[131] The same concern motivates *David Livingstone*; he retells the story in order to highlight its potential as a paradigm for racial cooperation. At the play's outset, Chuma and Jacob, two of the carriers, remind themselves of a conversation between the young Livingstone and the missionary Robert Moffat, in which the 'old man' asks the new recruit, 'who will be your helpers in making God's plan?' Jacob and Chuma recite Livingstone's response like an anthem: 'Men are working there / To be my helpers / Black men and white men.'[132] Throughout the play, flashbacks to Livingstone's life provide images of this racial amity. One scene depicts Livingstone and Sechele in conversation. In contrast to Pownall's image of a chaotic power struggle, Paton portrays a friendship of mutuality. The two men greet each other with familiarity, while Livingstone affectionately grasps Sechele's hand. The leader of the Kwena takes Livingstone under his wing, bantering with him and even offering him a little marriage advice. He urges him to get on with proposing to Mary: 'Why do you not do it?' When Livingstone replies that he is 'getting together [his] courage', Sechele adopts a fatherly tone telling him that 'The young woman is returning, and she is returning for one reason only ... To find out if you have gathered your courage.'[133] In their friendship, Paton presents a sodality in which racial differences are insignificant and in which the limits of apartheid do not hold. Another moment of analepsis takes the viewer to London, where Livingstone regales his children with the tale of his famous lion attack. In Paton's version of events, Livingstone describes himself as 'luckily' rescued by another man who 'rushed up with a spear and struck at the tremendous beast'.[134] But this departs from Livingstone's actual account of the incident in *Missionary Travels*, where the lion's death is ultimately attributed to his own bullets finally taking effect. The tale is translated from a narrative of personal triumph to one of indigenous assistance. By amending this small detail Paton ensures that the story projects an image of mutual dependence.

Much of *David Livingstone* consists of lengthy speeches by a narrator figure, whose monologues consolidate the play's message of racial unity. The narrator casts an image of Livingstone, stepping into the 'blinding and bright' sun of South Africa, where:

> walk men of many nations, Englishmen
> And Scots, and Dutch and Boers from the Kamoo;
> Brown folk whose veins hold blood of Hottentot
> And European and slaves from far Malaya;
> And here there walks a native African
> Come down with some white hunter from the north.[135]

The beauty of the country, for the narrator and for Paton, lies in this diversity. It is through the narrator, too, that the play's narrative is most directly applied to contemporary South African affairs. In one lengthy disquisition, he decides to 'step down / A moment and converse with you', presenting himself to his audience as an 'Everyman' who might 'speak for all of us, for all our griefs / And joys ...'. The speech begins in ambiguity:

> The one half of myself is anxious
> The other half is anxious too, trying to hide
> The half's that anxious, so the world won't see
> That there's a prisoner here ...[136]

While it is somewhat unclear, the 'Everyman' narrator seems to be speaking for South Africa, for a racially dichotomised nation that he thinks has turned against itself. It becomes more obvious that he is preaching to his country's divisions when he says: 'something here's awry / That touches Everyman, something not good.' And it becomes most palpable when he tells his audience that:

> Man was not born to live in such a slavery.
> Captor and captive locked in this embrace
> One watching always to make good escape
> One watching always to prevent it ... [137]

For Paton, the South African racial battle was harmful to captor and captive, and their mutually destructive 'embrace' constituted enslavement. The narrator urges instead the pursuit of the 'good rich life', one of 'eating, drinking, loving, worshipping'. He urges a love for 'women, children, strangers, outcasts' and joy in 'strange countries and / Strange peoples'.[138] In place of conflict, Paton's narrator hopes for a world of Christian unity and peace.

Indeed, the deeply religious nature of the play is integral to its meaning. Many commentators have of course observed the centrality of the Christian perspective to Paton's art and politics. As David Levey argues, Paton envisaged himself as a pilgrim and prophet, seeking to apply the 'immanence of God in the world ... to current political and social issues'.[139] Colin Gardner also points out his prophetic intentions: 'Like the biblical prophets, he wrote warnings and denunciations precisely because he thought they might be heeded, and because he believed in the possibility of fulfilments that might be earthly as well as heavenly.'[140] His philosophy is better described, then, as liberal Christian than as liberal humanist, for his distinctive worldview emanates from the 'interconnectedness of liberal politics and Christianity'.[141] It is out of this combination that his perpetual call for justice emerges.

The connection between Paton's Christianity and political commitment is particularly clear in *David Livingstone*. Written for performance in a church, the whole play has the feel of worship and almost takes place as a prayer for Africa. Very early in the drama the narrator actually does offer up intercession. He praises God 'For all the wonders of Africa' and its 'diversity of races', to which the congregation-audience responds, 'We thank thee, good Lord.' The prayer exalts God for 'delivery from slavery, and the life of David Livingstone' and asks, in the midst of apartheid, that the people 'may guard our inheritance'. The narrator prays that they would 'cherish love, mercy and justice' and be delivered from 'hatred and fear' and 'blindness of heart'.[142] The message of racial unity that Paton communicates through 'this simple tale of Livingstone' is thus deeply rooted in Christian ethics. And by actually compelling his audience to join in liturgical response, in a profession of unity and faith, Paton suggests that the only hope for the future of the collective peoples of South Africa lies in embracing the wedded Christian and liberal worldview.

The end of the play deepens the prevailing mood of religiosity. The scene becomes Livingstone's funeral service, with a priest appearing to read the 'Psalm De Profundis' and to commend 'the soul of our brother departed' to God.[143] Once again the congregation joins in, reciting the Lord's Prayer before the play closes with the Benediction. The audience thus participates in mourning David Livingstone. They do not mourn just a man, but they mourn what he has stood for in the play; the sense of loss is for the Livingstonian spirit, for the symbol of racial unity. As Rose Moss argues, one of the most distinctive features of Paton's most famous work, *Cry, the Beloved Country*, is its instruction to lament. In a situation of political hopelessness he instructs readers 'how to respond: cry'.[144] Moss suggests that in his writings Paton chooses to grieve rather than to 'intervene to change or repair'. The 'cadences of mourning' seemed appropriate for Paton and for the writers who later followed him in detecting a political impasse.[145] But it seems to me that in *David Livingstone* mourning, and reflecting with sadness on the state of the nation, do not preclude action. Livingstone not only is lamented but is upheld as an example of another way of being.

Ultimately, Paton decided to set this play to one side. Given its near-completion and the intrinsic interest of the liturgical drama, his decision is surprising. Yet in an essay sharing the title of his second play, 'The Last Journey', Paton explained that while he found the material provided by Livingstone's life 'fascinating', it eventually proved 'quite intractable'. Livingstone was too complex an individual to be put to use for 'didactic or churchly purpose'.[146] While Paton applauded him for having a more progressive attitude to Africans than many of his Victorian contemporaries, he also detected a moral problematic in the great traveller's commitment to exploration at the expense of familial duty. This is not to say that Paton's second play is without didactic intent, but his concerns were enough to make him rethink and recast his drama. There was, however, a more important reason underlying his decision to start afresh. As Paton described it in his essay, he abandoned the concept of a 'play for performance in churches' because of a lack of evidence 'that either Susi or Chuma was a Christian'.[147] He chose to resist, in other words, coopting Livingstone's African retinue into his explicitly Christian framework. While he does not elaborate on this logic in much detail, Paton perhaps felt that such a move would have been an unacceptable act of appropriation.

The Last Journey retains the broad purposes of the earlier play, while also manifesting shifts in tone and content. The liturgical dimension is eradicated, as is the narrator figure who provided much of the important moral commentary. As Rosner points out, the flashbacks to Livingstone's life are removed and the drama concentrates more exclusively on the exploits of the carriers.[148] In place of the sacramental accents, Paton gave *The Last Journey* a more distinctively epic quality. Even more than *David Livingstone*, it is a story foregrounding the outstanding efforts of the Africans and the heroic quality of their journey. Susi continues to command considerable respect, and he appears as an epitome of control and rationality. In the play's first scene, when the company learn of Livingstone's death, Susi instructs Chuma to tell the others that 'they are not to speak to any stranger of our father's death. If they do not hide their grief, then all of us are lost.'[149] While deeply moved by Livingstone's passing, Susi exhibits exemplary leadership qualities.[150] Paton ensures that he is at a far remove from the stereotype of the emotional, rash and unreasonable African. This is true of the whole retinue, who engage in reasoned discussion and debate about how to proceed with Livingstone's remains. In the second scene, various members of the company advance arguments for and against the transportation of the body to Zanzibar. One senior figure, Dazuka, reminds them all that Livingstone had often said to them 'Put me down, let me rest forever', and he articulates forcefully the series of obstacles they will be sure to encounter. He also makes an impressive and dramatic appeal to the company: 'People, my time will come to die ... But when I die, then bury my body as it is.'[151] Chuma, on the other hand, advocates the daring scheme to make for the coast, winning others to his plan one by one in spite of their initial reluctance. The scene thus works to show just how unlikely the events that unfolded actually were, and so compounds the epic quality that Paton aspired to convey. At the same time the considerable disagreement and the thoughtful and moving dialogue militate against African typecasting and the Victorian mythology of simple, 'faithful' servants. As Rosner points out, Paton refused to homogenise the collective; instead we are met with the 'cultural subtleties and ethical richness' and 'the diversity of personalities and values that make up even one group of Africans'.[152] To achieve this, Paton expanded the cast of black characters, including a host of voices that are absent in the earlier drama. And what is more, as he indicates in his essay, while writing *The Last Journey* he made sure to consult the various available accounts of the events provided by Africans themselves.[153]

The apartheid context remains important in understanding this play, and Paton continues to use the narrative to comment on race relations. Again, he is disapproving of the white attitude to those who risked so much to deliver Livingstone's body. W.E. Dillon, for instance, the naval surgeon who accompanied Lieutenant Cameron's expedition, is reluctant to accept advice from the carriers despite their considerable travelling experience. And he is portrayed as unable to bridge the divide between black and white. He says to Susi in Act 3 Scene 1, 'When I come out in the morning, there you are all waiting with your loads so – separate – separate. As though one couldn't get near you.'[154] Again, as in the previous play, Lieutenant Cameron is unable to truly engage with Susi and the others (see Fig. 10). As Paton put it, he 'failed to understand the meaning of SUSI's expedition';[155] his actions in opening the boxes of Livingstone's possessions, and Captain Prideaux's way of taking command at Zanzibar, fit 'into a pattern recognizable of any person who understands Africa'. While they were undoubtedly 'upright & decent gentlemen', they simply assumed that they 'had every proprietary right to take over the body'.[156] Such actions may have been unexceptional in their own time, but Paton was acutely aware of the damage 'that a superior white attitude can inflict upon Africans'. Cameron and Prideaux manifested 'a total inability to integrate the epic African journey with the great British ceremonial that lay ahead'. Indeed, the lieutenant was fundamentally unable 'to see that the body & the boxes belonged to Susi & his company in a way that they could never belong to him or to any other official'.[157] For Paton the actions were indicative,

10. 'Susi's Party Meets Cameron's at Unyanyembe'. Photograph from Alan Paton, *The Last Journey*.

to some extent at least, of the racial prejudice he set out to combat in his writings and political action. 'I think it would be harsh', he wrote, 'to describe it as the master–servant attitude that has so bedevilled Africa, but I am content to drop that as a hint, an approximation, that may make the situation clearer for those who do not fully live in Africa.'[158] Commenting on Horace Waller's partial defence of Cameron – that 'It cannot be conceded for a moment that these poor fellows would have been right in forbidding this examination' given the 'relative position' of 'natives' and 'English officers' – Paton again made broader political reference. Such an 'ultra-conservative attitude', he wrote, might be considered 'baasskap' – the assumption that the white man was the 'boss' and should naturally dominate the black.[159] In the essay manuscript, Paton also equated the attitude to 'apartheid' but then scored it out in making subsequent corrections. Nonetheless, it is clear that the play shares the intent of the earlier work in seeking to combat and critique racial prejudice.

In spite of this, Cameron is portrayed much more favourably in *The Last Journey* than he is in *David Livingstone*. He is no longer quite so presumptuous or uncommunicative. Speaking to his companion Lieutenant Murphy, he says: 'I like that fellow Chuma. And that Susi must be a good fellow ... Damned wonderful fellows.'[160] In fact, in the second play Paton was careful to moderate his criticisms of the white party, aware that he was dealing with contentious and potentially

FICTION: LAUGHING AT LIVINGSTONE?

incendiary material. In the stage directions, he emphasised that 'CAMERON was a resourceful & courageous man' and that he 'should not be portrayed as a pompous caricature of an English gentleman'. To do so 'would have the effect in Africa, of embarrassing & perhaps antagonising the white members of the audience'.[161] Likewise, while Dillon could be portrayed as 'tense and troubled', he should not appear 'as a neurotic personality' lest he became 'embarrassing to the white audience'. In fact, to avert such a possibility he actually directed that both Cameron and Dillon be played by actors equal in physical stature to those playing Chuma and Susi.[162] Underlying this was concern that dwelling too much on deplorable white behaviour might undermine the purpose of the play, 'turning it from an epic story of African courage & persistence into a complaint against the insensitivity & overbearingness of European officials'.[163] Since Paton felt that hope for South Africa lay in genuine racial cooperation, he was wary of alienating his white audience. While he felt bound to criticise racial prejudice, antagonising viewers would not serve the purposes of partnership and unity.

Racial cooperation would, however, be facilitated by showing the possibility of genuine interaction. While Livingstone's role is diminished in *The Last Journey*, with the flashbacks to his life excised, he still stands as a symbol of collaboration. For his companions, he is an object of real affection and they genuinely mourn his passing (see Fig. 11). Susi

11. 'Livingstone Dies at Ilala'. Photograph from Alan Paton, *The Last Journey*.

[249]

tells Chuma that 'You & I will not see such a man again', and recalls how, when he had to be carried in his weakness, Livingstone said, 'I am grieved to burden you.'[164] They read passages from his journals, reminding themselves of his suffering, and they act out his final hours in a moving ritual of remembrance.[165] Later, too, a survivor of the Nyangwe massacre, Salomi, describes in poignant detail how Livingstone came to her aid after her whole family was exterminated.[166] Despite the ambivalence that Paton detected in Livingstone, he recognised his devotion to Africa and that he 'loved her people'; his human kindness allowed him to see Africans 'primarily as fellow humans, even though their languages & customs & beliefs were different'.[167] Most European characters in the play fall short of such an example. But it is precisely this kind of attitude that eventually flourishes in Lieutenant Murphy. Murphy manages to surmount the divide, supporting the plan to transport the remains to Zanzibar when Cameron opposes it; in his effort to know 'the other', he even learns KiSwahili. By the end of the play, he sees the injustice in appropriating Livingstone's body and in failing to provide passage to Britain for its carriers. He tells Susi in despair, 'I do not know what to say to you', but promises them all that he will tell the people of Britain 'I had never met such men before. My children – if I have any – will know about every one of you and the journey that you made.'[168] And in an important symbolic gesture, he returns one of Livingstone's instruments – a sextant – in recognition that the European party never had the right to assume command.[169] Murphy's story, then, is a narrative of maturation into the spirit of racial unity, a spirit embodied in Livingstone's relationship with his men. While this play lacks the liturgical form of the earlier drama, positive interaction is again underpinned by the liberal Christian vision. At the end of *The Last Journey*, a religious figure named Father Mercier suggests to Murphy that he has 'learned the lesson – or perhaps you knew it already – that no gift wins love, except the gift of ourselves .... Christ ... put a duty on us, that we shall love others'.[170] The reconciliation between black and white, and the reparation for European wrongs, offered by Murphy essentially stems from Paton's political theology.[171]

David Livingstone and *The Last Journey* are quite different plays, but are governed by the same imperative – to advocate racial cooperation in an apartheid context. In the latter drama, Paton emphasised the epic dimensions of the heroic journey more than he had in his first play. In the former, however, he was arguably more forthright in his critique of white abuses. Yet, it is important to remember one crucial distinction: *The Last Journey* actually made it to the stage. Indeed, I would suggest that its very performance was an important act of political resistance. In 1957 J.G. Strijdom's government had

FICTION: LAUGHING AT LIVINGSTONE?

passed the Native Laws Amendment Act, which forbade any multi-racial meeting in white areas, including church services. While *The Last Journey* was produced in Northern Rhodesia and so did not technically break the law, it can be read as an expression of opposition to the bill. It is an example of what Michael Black has called, in another context, 'The Patonesque principle of protesting against unjust laws whilst respecting the law itself'.[172] We can gather from the play's programme that it was performed using a multi-racial cast. Most likely, the audience was also un-segregated, for as Alexander points out, Paton felt it was 'better to have no theatre than colour-bar theatre'.[173] By producing Livingstone's last journey, in which races mixed both on stage and off, Paton expressed his defiance in an act of performative rebellion.

Nonetheless, certain limitations in Paton's vision can be detected in his plays. Even while he deploys Livingstone in order to critique the apartheid regime, he remains somewhat paternalistic. In one episode in *David Livingstone*, Paton consciously aimed to dramatically re-create a scene from the statuary at the Scottish National Memorial to David Livingstone. The piece it imitated, *Mercy*, by C. d'O. Pilkington Jackson, portrays a slave cartel run by an Arab with 'a crook and a whip' (see Figs. 12 and 13). After this iconic moment is emulated in the performance, Paton's stage directions

12. C. d'O. Pilkington Jackson, *Mercy: Freeing a Slave Gang*.

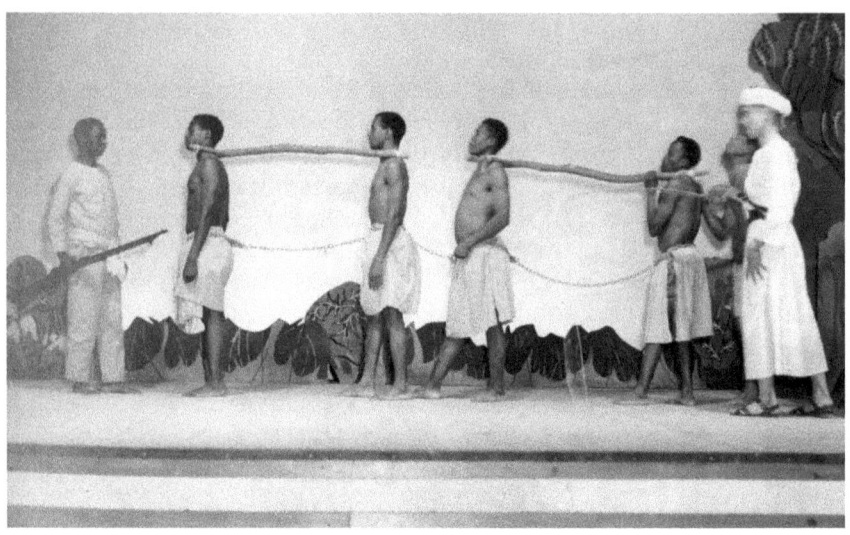

13. 'Slaver and Slaves'. Photograph from Alan Paton, *The Last Journey*.

instruct Livingstone to stand and stare after the procession 'with a look of great resolve'.[174] The play thus persists, to some degree, in hagiographic and romantic staging. Furthermore, Paton's portrayal of Africans is also quite limited. Depicting Livingstone and his men arriving at the sea after months of travel, Paton instructs the carriers to act like children, 'laughing' and 'generally behaving in a lunatic fashion'. As they engage in this 'pantomime', Livingstone loses his 'grave manner' too, but remains much 'more subdued in action'.[175] Despite the play's message of equality, the notion of the juvenile native and paternal white man is not entirely eradicated. As an attempt to write an African epic, *The Last Journey* falls into such traps less frequently. Nevertheless, a character named Farijala does act as a comic butt, engaging in trivial antics and general 'fooling' throughout the performance.[176] As David Ward points out, black intellectuals such as Ngugi wa Thiong'o have criticised Paton's 'imaginative failure' in representing Africans as 'good Christian souls' who lack any significant connections to an historical thought-world of their own.[177] Ward further argues that in *Cry, the Beloved Country*, Paton perpetually conveys the subtle and complex Zulu language using rudimentary English sentence constructions.[178] There is a similar tendency in both Livingstone plays, where African characters speak in short and staccato sentences that inevitably indicate naiveté.

A project like Paton's thus remains in danger of engaging the sympathy of a white readership, while failing to challenge its deepest prejudices.[179]

Ward's analysis is indicative of the ideological critique that has been directed against Paton and his liberalism in recent years. In spite of this, John O. Jordan thinks there are things worth defending in the liberal vision. He concedes that 'In its emphasis on non-violence and on gradual change through parliamentary reform, the liberal program proved ineffective for dealing with the intransigence of a government that did not hesitate to abridge civil rights or use violence.'[180] Furthermore, the party could never quite escape the fact that it sought to speak for an oppressed majority while remaining a primarily white-run party. But even while it was significantly less important in bringing political change than African-led resistance, the Liberals provided a white voice that was prepared to demand one man, one vote. There was a brief moment in the 1950s when they represented the real possibility of a multi-racial democracy. Jordan urges us to remember that this was a period in which the distinction between the moderate liberals of the United Party and the 'true' or 'radical' liberals was of critical importance.[181] While there are clear limitations to Paton's vision, it is perhaps too easy from an historical vantage point to undermine the significance of his opposition and indeed the radical nature of the Livingstone he constructed.

Another South African author to turn her attention to David Livingstone was the Nobel laureate and anti-apartheid activist Nadine Gordimer. Her writing has continually been characterised by its commitment to the oppressed races of South Africa. As Steven Clingman writes, even while she is distanced from the marginalised black classes by colour, position and privilege, she has persisted in writing '*in favour* of that world'.[182] He frames her ambiguous position in Gramscian terms, as a 'non-organic' intellectual, describing her as one 'linked mentally to the oppressed classes but not physically or materially'.[183] Gordimer's literary career has been distinctive too for her continued presence in South Africa. She persisted in writing controversial literature from her homeland in a period when, as Michael Wade points out, many other authors chose exile:[184] 'In an age when political exile is often a mark of respectability for the creative artist, she chooses to stick to her post in the face of a situation of moral, cultural and political repression'.[185] For a time, Gordimer was involved in the sort of liberal response to racism that was characterised by Paton. But she can be identified with such politics only to a limited extent, for she has been more radical in inclination and has fostered closer links with the black community.

Her commitment to the world of the oppressed is clear in her short story 'Livingstone's Companions' (1972). It tells the tale of Carl A. Church, a newspaper reporter based in a newly independent central African state, who is instructed to retrace Livingstone's last journey for a three-thousand-word 'special feature'.[186] Getting lost on the way to Old Moambe, where Livingstone 'had talked with chiefs whose descendants were active in the present-day politics of their country', Church eventually finds himself at the Gough's Bay Hotel, an establishment owned by an affluent and seedy widow, Mrs Palmer.[187] The text focuses on several lazy days that Church whiles away, working through Livingstone's journals and eventually visiting the graves of his 'companions'.

Race relations are the text's predominant theme. In contrast to much of Gordimer's other work, the text does not dissect the regime of formal apartheid, but instead, as Graham Huggan writes, explores 'the ironies of an emergent nation which claims to have thrown off the shackles of its former oppressors ... but which continues to be driven by social, political, and economic differences'.[188] When we first meet Church, he is listening lethargically to the minister of foreign affairs reporting on a recent presidential trip. While able to differentiate itself from 'the white-supremacy states south of our borders', this one-party state is soon revealed to be a neo-colonial nation.[189] Despite the minister's protestations to the contrary, Gordimer's symbolic representation of the parliament suggests that little has changed. The clerk, with his 'white pompadour, velvet bow and lacy jabot', continues to wear the very attire that was 'part of the investiture of sovereignty handed down from the British'.[190] The imitation of the colonial predecessor indicates that the same power structures remain intact. The minister, refusing an interview after the meeting, speaks with 'the volume of voice he had used in the House, as if someone had forgotten to turn off the public address system'.[191] In a world as yet unleashed from its colonial inheritance, politics are little more than performance. When he begins to retrace Livingstone's steps, Church flies into a bordering country whose capital city, and presumably its political makeup, 'were hardly distinguishable from the one he had left'.[192]

In the steamy space of the Gough's Bay Hotel, the reader meets a world in which white racism remains unaltered despite political change. Mrs Palmer's gormless son, Dickie, sets the tone by complaining to Church about the African servants: 'Where those boys are when you want one of them – that's the problem.'[193] His mother orders her 'boys' around too, repeating the familiar grumble: 'The trouble is, *they'll* never be any different, they just don't know how to look after anything.'[194] In reflecting this racially riven world, Gordimer offers the voice of middle-class racism up for inspection. As Dominic Head writes, she has often been preoccupied with representing 'the consciousness of the reactionary white landowner'.[195]

It is for purposes of critique that Gordimer deploys Livingstone. As Church reads from Livingstone's journals, extracts from the text reflect critically on the circumstances around him. In contrast to a milieu where Africans are perpetually servile, Livingstone's journals represent some possibility of a different mode of relation. As Huggan puts it, Church focuses on those sections where 'the celebrated explorer pays rich, if patronizing, tribute to those who died on his behalf'.[196] One extract, close to the beginning, is most important for understanding the text: *'Our sympathies are drawn out towards our humble hardy companions by a community of interests, and, it may be, of perils, which make us all friends.'*[197] Despite the paternalist tone, the respect and cooperation enshrined in these words are deeply alien to the likes of Dickie and his mother. The short passage sits in ironic reflection on the divided world of the lakeside hotel, in which the white community values the black community only for its labour. As Huggan writes, describing 'Livingstone's Companions' and another story, 'Jump', 'a voice from elsewhere impinges upon the protagonist's consciousness, defamiliarizing the world of his everyday experience'.[198] The deep-seated nature of white racism is rendered clearer to Church as it is estranged through his encounter with Livingstone's text.

But the journals are not just used to interrogate the voice of the racists. Rather, the textual fragments also reveal the limitations of Church, the primary narrative voice, who sees himself as a racial liberal. As Dominic Head argues, Gordimer often uses short stories to explore 'an unreliable or incomplete narrative perspective'.[199] While Church claims to identify with the oppressed, and clearly despises the crudeness of Mrs Palmer and her brood, it becomes clear that his radicalism stretches only so far. Gordimer highlights this by what Robert Haugh calls the 'juxtaposed "life-style"'.[200] Livingstone's energetic commitment sits in contrast to the insufficiency and apathy of Church. It becomes his habit to read of Livingstone's intense activities 'before falling stunned-asleep'. Livingstone can declare, *'Now that I am on the point of starting another trip into Africa I feel quite exhilarated: when one travels with the specific object in view of ameliorating the condition of the natives every act becomes ennobled.'* Church, by contrast, lounges around while 'The afternoon heat made him think of women.'[201] Where Livingstone proclaims that *'The effect of travel on a man whose heart is in the right place is that the mind is made more self-reliant ... there is greater presence of mind'*, Church sleeps through the heat of the day and wakes to a 'feeling of helplessness'.[202] Livingstone represents one '"plane" of dignity' and purpose while the world of the hotel represents another '"plane" of shallow trivia'.[203] Church is actually quite self-reflexive about his own limitations, and he admits that his sexual weaknesses have led him to compromise his liberal ideals. In the past he has offered an African woman money for sex, and thereby participated in commodifying both the female and the black body: 'when it came to women, whom he loved so well, his other passion – the desire to defend the rights of the individual of any colour or race – did not bear scrutiny'.[204] On the whole, Livingstone's racial collaboration is almost as alien to Church, the liberal, as it is to Mrs Palmer. To him, the African servants remain essentially nameless; he never crosses the racial barrier and remains profoundly detached from the black world.

All this is not to say that Gordimer simply establishes Livingstone as a standard of unambiguous goodness. There is undoubtedly a hint of satire in the comparison between Livingstone's grandiose declarations and Church's less elevated, and more lewd, experience in central Africa. The text is certainly no act of simplistic celebration. Gordimer's words of introduction to her collection of stories are revealing on this point: 'we who live in or travel in Africa' are Livingstone's companions, 'because Livingstone, more than any other individual, was responsible for bringing Africa and Europe into confrontation and that confrontation, in reality and in irony, is still being worked out today'.[205] Livingstone, Gordimer recognises, represents a crucial moment of cultural encounter. And what she does in her story, rather than settling for the extremes of celebration or condemnation, is to revisit and reread this moment. As Huggan puts it, the extracts from Livingstone serve to 'alert the reader to a submerged consciousness within the primary narrative: a consciousness which speaks the silences of the colonial past'.[206] That certain dimensions of the Livingstone story have been repressed is symbolised by the quite forgotten graves of his companions. Even after reading the journals, Church can barely stir himself from his lethargy in order to look for them. He eventually stumbles on them when he is leaving Gough's Bay, where they lie neglected at the end of an obscure and meandering track.

But Gordimer's story warns of what Steven Clingman calls 'the return of the repressed'. He points to 'the persistent reappearance in her work of that politically repressed world separated from her at a deep level in the domain of her fictional "unconscious"'.[207] While we may or may not agree with Clingman that this is part of the narrative unconscious, the text certainly suggests, on a number of levels, that the latent black world might reassert itself. Church himself recognises this, musing that the political plans being laid in the capital would soon ensure that Mrs Palmer's African servant would 'lose the standard that had been set by people who maintained it by using him to pick up their dirt'.[208] This resurgence is hinted at too in the text's imagery. At the end of the story, the graves are pictured looking out towards the lake, which stretched 'as far as one could see, flat and shining; a long way up Africa'.[209] While hidden from sight, the forgotten men of Livingstone's travels look down almost ominously from their hilltop vantage, and seem to call with silent strength up through the African continent. It is not just the graves, moreover, that speak of an oppressed world in abeyance. Gordimer most powerfully communicates it by using nature to metaphorically represent the marginalised. As Clingman points out, 'where a white political culture has its historical roots in a colonial or *settler* culture, the land "naturally" becomes a sign of the people'.[210] In 'Livingstone's Companions', the bush surrounding Gough's Bay seems portentously close, as if seeking to reclaim the land Mrs Palmer has intruded upon. When Church wanders down a beaten path to find himself 'among ruined arcades' of a recently abandoned hotel construction, the looming bush has already reclaimed them: 'The bush was all around; as far as the Congo, as far as the latitude where the forests began.'[211] This encroaching resurgence of nature forecasts the inevitable return of a subjugated people.

In Paton and Gordimer, we find a truly distinctive implementation of David Livingstone. It is, of course, important to note the shared appeal of a white British hero to two white, liberal South Africans. Whether Livingstone would have proven so amenable to authors from South Africa's other racial communities is somewhat doubtful. Nevertheless, these two authors – notwithstanding the significant ideological differences between them – were politically united in their status as vocal opponents of apartheid. It was this political commitment, in a nation torn by racial hatred, that enabled them both to read, in varying degrees, the radical possibilities in Livingstone's life. Even though Gordimer can be considered a postcolonial writer, she differs from the authors in my previous section by focusing on the enabling qualities of Livingstone and his travels. Both Paton and Gordimer also used their subject to engage with South African liberalism. For Paton, Livingstone served as a means to espouse a liberal response to apartheid, which he grounded in a Christian view of human fraternity. For Gordimer, Livingstone similarly provided a voice with which to critique racism, but at the same time he granted her a means by which to reveal the failure of radical vision in the liberal politics of her protagonist.

Possible or implausible worlds? Livingstone in science fiction

The final fictional Livingstone belongs in a category of its own, for it does not mobilise him for any of the political reasons examined so far. Its concern is neither to engage in postcolonial critique nor to respond to an apartheid context. Instead, writing in the science fiction mode, this author draws on Livingstone to ask one of the genre's governing questions: what if the world were different? Robin Wayne Bailey's short story entitled 'The Terminal Solution' tells an alternative history in which David Livingstone has recently brought AIDS back to the United Kingdom from the 'darkest heart of Africa', initiating an epidemic that sweeps with catastrophic effect across the Victorian world.[212] The fact that Livingstone can be imported into such a bizarre scenario is indicative of the anti-realist epistemological shifts that I recounted at the beginning of this chapter. In such a climate, where history itself is demoted to a form of fiction, the accurate representation of historical figures declined in importance. It was this situation that enabled Bailey to set the question of his subject's 'true' identity to one side in order to write a piece of 'recombinant fiction', in which Livingstone is freely positioned alongside the likes of Conan Doyle and Jack the Ripper.[213]

'The Terminal Solution' thus ignores Livingstone's actual life and instead uses him as a plot device in order to broach some interesting questions. As Matt Hills among others has pointed out, the science-fiction subgenre of alternative history provides a good means of studying counterfactual possibilities, the divergent ways in which the world might have unfolded had a moment in history occurred differently. In exploring the implications of counterfactuals, science fiction 'can destabilize ontological perspectives and compel readers to see the "real" historical world in different, perhaps more critical ways'.[214] In other words, in showing the possibility of a very different outworking of history, such narratives can highlight the contingent nature of our own reality and encourage a more critical attitude to the historical processes by which the present has been constituted. Barney Warf describes alternative history as anti-teleological, for it rejects the assumption that 'the present is as it is precisely because it could be no other way'.[215] In its denial of the inevitable and its exploration of the possible, science fiction has the potential to serve as 'a tool of critical social analysis'.[216]

Bailey's story does have some limited analytical interest. The title of the collection in which it appears, *ReVISIONS*, indicates that the volume's prerogative is to revise history and to do so with vision. Unifying the stories is one thematic question: '*what if* scientific or technological discoveries had happened differently, in different cultures or times'.[217]

FICTION: LAUGHING AT LIVINGSTONE?

By making Livingstone the vehicle of AIDS, Bailey explores what might have happened if such an epidemic had arrived in Britain 125 years early. The text focuses on several vulnerabilities of the Victorian world that would have permitted calamity to ensue.

Bailey highlights contemporary medical limitations. In a brief explanation of his story, he wrote, 'In modern times, after twenty years of effort, our science and medicine have barely made inroads against Acquired Immune Deficiency Syndrome. What chance would the Victorian world have had?' In a culture that did not yet know either of viruses or of basic sterilization techniques, the answer resounds: 'none at all'.[218] The text shows how ignorance of transmission by bodily fluid would have allowed infections to multiply thick and fast. Dr Joseph Bell and Dr Arthur Doyle, the two men undertaking a Sherlock Holmes-style exploration of the Livingstone-carried disease, are unaware of a vital piece of information; it is transmitted by blood. The reader is horrified by the viral cesspit of Doyle's surgery, where he practises cupping and blood-letting, collecting the communal 'crimson liqueur' of his patients in a single small pan.[219] When Bell picks up a 'blood-smeared' scalpel, lightly 'nicking the skin' and sucking the 'tiniest drop of blood', the reader knows that he too has caught the disease.[220] The text ends on an ominous note, when Doyle shares an opium needle with his mentor and presses 'the point deep into his arm', unconsciously initiating his own path to decline and death.[221]

The social makeup of Victorian London would also have furthered the 'massive and rapid spread of the infection'.[222] The abysmal conditions of the 'sewage filled' East End were a 'breeding ground for disease and all manner of contagion'.[223] With widespread prostitution, and without knowledge of sexual protection, the effects would be far-reaching: the 'contagion' would spread from illicit union to the marriage bed, right 'from the lowest Whitechapel doxy up to the throne itself'.[224]

In this alternate history, the greatest manifestations of British power would instead become an Achilles heel. The technological advances of the industrial revolution and global imperial networks would facilitate the diffusion of disease. As Doyle complains, 'The new railways that link our cities carry it from one end of the island to the other. Our soldiers and sailors, our merchants and businessmen, have transported it to all corners of the empire.'[225] Bell fears that 'the world as they knew it was coming down around their ears'.[226] The epidemic was 'exhausting the empire';[227] this was an enemy against whom imperial strength counted only as weakness.

But what critical reflection does Bailey's alternative history provide? We might describe its primary effect as 'estrangement' of the present. As Darko Suvin famously argued, in exploring the logical consequences of 'novum', those differences between the fictional world and the world of reality, science fiction texts could disrupt the familiar and that which we unreflectively take for granted.[228] In exploring a possible world in which Britain's empire would have crumbled over half a century early, 'The Terminal Solution' leaves the reader speculating on the repercussions that this might have had on world affairs; it reveals the contingent nature of the present and of the British role on the international stage. The text's alienating effect is to disrupt the uncritically held notion that Britain's pre-eminence was an historical inevitability.

Incorporating Livingstone into this alternate history enhances, to some degree, the reflective dimension of the text. As Naomi Jacobs points out, historical figures prove conducive to the science fiction genre's pursuit of alienation. By meeting a familiar figure in a deeply unfamiliar context, readers are forced to make a comparison between their own world and the alternative universe before them: it establishes 'a "feedback oscillation" ... between accepted reality and fictional reality'.[229] By violating our expectations, and departing from preconceived notions of Livingstone, Bailey aims to shock his readers into evaluating their own world in terms of the other before them. By ironically transforming an iconic figure of empire into the unwitting agent of its destruction, Bailey forces his readers to follow through the repercussions of his imagined counterfactual history.

It must be pointed out, however, that despite provoking some degree of estrangement, certain aspects of the text are deeply troublesome. For one thing, its treatment of AIDS falls into familiar stereotypes. Steven F. Kruger argues that there are two structuring cultural narratives by which AIDS is understood in the public domain. The first charts the course of the illness in the individual, relying on a vocabulary of inevitable decline and death. While grounded in truth, since AIDS obviously does kill, it emphasises 'inexorable suffering' and passivity to the extent that it suggests degeneracy.[230] The second, which Kruger calls an 'epidemiological' narrative, tracks its endemic spread until it reaches apocalyptic proportions as an 'unstoppable plague'.[231] While again there is some truth in the narrative, for AIDS is spreading fast, it focuses 'fear and fascination' by promoting a 'worst case scenario'.[232] Although 'The Terminal Solution' is concerned with alternate history, and is undoubtedly correct in speculating that AIDS would have devastated the Victorian world, the text panders to contemporary fears that surround the syndrome. From the first mention of the 'purplish lesions' on 'Livingstone's torso', clearly Kaposi's sarcoma, it becomes apparent that Bailey will emphasise physical decline.[233] And the whole tale is structured around uncontrollable contagion. Like many AIDS narratives, 'The Terminal Solution' also posits an origin for the disease.

FICTION: LAUGHING AT LIVINGSTONE?

This is probably the most troublesome aspect of the text, for in the story AIDS stands for 'African Invasive Disease', a name which projects blame and risks perpetuating a damaging racial stereotype.[234] As Kruger points out, such 'origin' stories often concentrate on foreignness and in so doing create scapegoats of those deemed 'culpable'.[235]

In light of this, the selection of Livingstone as a 'patient zero', the infectious carrier of disease, can be seen as double-sided.[236] While it may alienate and shock, Bailey's decision to make the source of disease an African explorer perpetuates a virulent image of the continent. Of course, the text does some violence to Livingstone's reputation: linking him with HIV insinuates sexual scandal. However, the story does less harm to Livingstone than it does to Africa. The explorer has been infected by a continent that really remains, to all intents and purposes, a heart of darkness. As Clare Pettitt comments, the text pulls 'together the nineteenth-century fantasy of Africa (Livingstone) and the twenty-first (AIDS)': 'The old fear of possible contamination by the "savage" – or the revenge of the colonised – is reinflected through the fear of a modern epidemic that respects no boundaries.'[237] Responding to Bailey's comment that the story 'sprang from a dream', Pettitt notes that 'such stereotypes often function at the level of the unconscious'.[238] Perhaps because it stemmed from a nightmare, the whole fantasy has a sense of being just too implausible. But it is of course plausibility, as Barney Warf argues, that characterises the best counterfactual analysis: the most powerful social criticism is achieved when the alternative world is one that actually might have come into being. Without this, alternative history can easily 'degenerate into idle speculation'.[239] While Bailey's story does pose some interesting questions, his use of Livingstone just seems too arbitrary to be convincing. On the whole, the story is less thought-provoking than it is revealing of the persistent nature of contemporary typecasting.

The diverse creative representations of Livingstone sharply highlight the located nature of interpretation and the malleability of an historical life. As with the biographical constructions, the horizons of these authors inevitably impinged on the meaning they found in him. While there were several novelists in the early twentieth century for whom Livingstone provided a means to transmit and perpetuate imperial ideology, significant fictive and dramatic renditions really began to burgeon only with the rise of postcolonialism. In this literature, Livingstone took on an entirely new set of meanings; the political and intellectual reorientation against imperialism meant that, for many, he became the object of critical revision. I focused here on texts in which Livingstone occupied centre stage as a principal character, but it is significant that he also made occasional cameos in the ideological critique of other works. For instance, in *The Trial of Mallam Ilya*, a play by Mohammed Ben Abdallah that examines Ghana under Nkrumah's rule, Livingstone appears as part of a marionette in the middle of the performance.[240] An actor dressed as David Livingstone controls the strings of a puppet clothed as an African Christian preacher, who is then seen to hit a carved figure of a traditional priest on the head with his Bible.[241] In this brief scene, Livingstone is imported to epitomise religion as a tool of control, coercion and psychological colonisation. Another Ghanaian author, Ama Ata Aidoo, incorporates a verse on Livingstone into her novel *Our Sister Killjoy*, where, in a manner reminiscent of NourbeSe Philip, he emerges as an exploitative agent:

> Livingstone the Saint
> Opening
> Africa up for
> Rape.[242]

Since Livingstone's explorations never led him to Ghana, it was clearly his symbolic value that attracted these authors. Indeed, for all those who rewrote Livingstone it was his status as a popular signifier of empire, the moral face of imperialism, that made him a suitable figure through whom to focalise anti-colonial analysis. Yet, as we have seen, the postcolonial implementation of Livingstone was by no means homogenous: he was mobilised in order to interrogate the discovery narrative, the 'heart of darkness' mythology and the workings of both language and Christianity in the colonial project. His symbolic function thus proved polyvalent. In all cases, Livingstone served as a vehicle for critique that stretched well beyond his historical person. These authors were all less interested in his actual life than in what he represented in the public consciousness and what he could be made to signify. Nonetheless, as Naomi Jacobs points out, the fascination with historical characters in contemporary fiction is actually 'a mixed response to extraordinary individuals and to the broader types they seem to represent'.[243] All of these texts encountered the problem of dealing with a real figure that they also wanted to employ typologically. The haziness of the boundary line between symbol and historical individual means that the postcolonial portraits are in danger of appearing excessively disparaging and reductive in tendency.

The freedom with which Livingstone was represented in these texts was not just granted by the rise of postcolonialism. While it was certainly an anti-imperialist agenda that primarily influenced these authors, philosophical challenges to objectivity and historical narrative permitted their creative projects. And this epistemological climate facilitated other uses of Livingstone too that were not bound to postcolonial politics. Robin Wayne Bailey's 'The Terminal Solution' was able to draw Livingstone into a bizarre counterfactual alternative history in which Victorian England was brought to its knees by an unstoppable epidemic. While there seems to be no specific political agenda underlying his representation, the text is indicative of an intellectual environment that permits the most free and even arbitrary implementation of historical figures.

In a South African context, however, the representations of Livingstone were resolutely political. In contrast to postcolonial condemnation, the Livingstone that emerged from the racially divided society of apartheid was found to provide an alternative to conflict. For Paton, Livingstone – despite his character flaws – embodied a Christian liberal response to the racist political formation that he spent so much time and energy resisting. Gordimer, while less celebratory, saw in Livingstone's explorations a quiet narrative that had been repressed, but which sat in critical reflection upon both racism and a certain kind of liberal response.

The polyvalence of Livingstone's fictional legacy reminds us that interpretation is never innocent and never takes place in a vacuum: the socio-political and cultural milieu and the specific commitments of the individual author are inextricably connected to the ways in which Livingstone has been endowed with significance. While this book has perpetually drawn attention to the plurality of Livingstone's afterlives, it is perhaps in these imaginative works, which serve so self-consciously as vehicles for ideas, that diversity and ideological embeddedness are at their most explicit.

Notes

1. John M. MacKenzie, 'David Livingstone: The Construction of the Myth', in Graham Walker and Tom Gallagher (eds), *Sermons and Battle Hymns* (Edinburgh: Edinburgh University Press, 1990), p. 31.
2. Naomi Jacobs, *The Character of Truth: Historical Figures in Contemporary Fiction* (Carbondale: Southern Illinois University Press, 1990), p. xiv.
3. Jane Agnes Staunton Batty, *Livingstone the Empire Builder; or, 'Set Under the Cross'* (London: SPCK, 1913).
4. M. Daphne Kutzer, *Empire's Children: Empire and Imperialism in Classic British Children's Books* (New York: Garland, 2000), p. xiii.
5. Mary Mitchell, *Black Crusade* (London: Methuen, 1949).
6. Jacobs, *The Character of Truth*, p. xix.
7. Ibid., p. xvi.
8. These two influences should not perhaps be thought of as entirely separate, for various scholars have argued that postcolonial and poststructuralist thought are deeply related. For instance, Robert Young suggests that much poststructuralist thinking itself emerged out of an anti-colonial critique of Western intellectual structures. See Robert J.C. Young, *White Mythologies: Writing History and the West* (London: Routledge, 1990), p. 1. Furthermore, theorists such as Bhabha

and Spivak have found it productive to draw insights from poststruturalism into their analysis of the postcolonial situation. Yet it is important to note that certain critics have seen the dynamic between these intellectual currents in less favourable terms. Anne McClintock, for one, suggests that the term 'postcolonial' borrows from 'the dazzling market success of the term "postmodernism"'. See Anne McClintock, 'The Angel of Progress: Pitfalls of the Term "Post-Colonialism"', in Patrick Williams and Laura Chrisman (eds), *Colonial Discourse and Post-Colonial Theory: A Reader* (Hemel Hempstead: Harvester Wheatsheaf, 1993), p. 299. Others such as Meenakshi Mukherjee have framed the relationship between postcolonialism and Western theoretical advances in terms of complicity. Those who were once politically colonised are now re-colonised with a terminology forged in Western universities. See Meenakshi Mukherjee, 'Interrogating Post-Colonialism', in Harish Trivedi and Meenakshi Mukherjee (eds), *Interrogating Post-Colonialism: Theory, Text and Context* (Shimla: Indian Institute of Advanced Study, 1996), pp. 3–11. As John McLeod observes, some worry that postcolonialism has conceded too much to anti-foundationalism and its critique of 'grand narratives'. They argue that this line of thought undermines oppositional discourses at a time when they would prove most useful. See John McLeod, *Beginning Postcolonialism* (Manchester: Manchester University Press, 2000), pp. 251-2. In a different vein, some scholars have suggested that while postcolonial writers might appear to be doing similar things to the 'postmodern', the source of their motivation is quite different. Kwame Anthony Appiah argues that the 'post' of postcolonialism, 'like postmodernism's, is also a post that challenges earlier legitimating narratives'. But it does so 'in the name of the ethical universal; in the name of humanism'. In this case postcolonialism 'is not an ally for Western postmodernism but an agonist'. See Kwame Anthony Appiah, 'The Postcolonial and the Postmodern', in Bill Ashcroft, Gareth Griffiths and Helen Tiffin (eds), *The Post-Colonial Studies Reader* (London: Routledge, 2003), p. 123. The relationship, then, between the two influences – the postmodern and the postcolonial – that permitted Livingstone to be radically rewritten is strained and complex.
9 Robert J.C. Young, *Postcolonialism: An Historical Introduction* (Oxford: Blackwell, 2001), p. 4.
10 Ibid., p. 5.
11 Elleke Boehmer, *Colonial and Postcolonial Literature: Migrant Metaphors* (Oxford: Oxford University Press, 1995), p. 5.
12 Frantz Fanon, *Black Skin, White Masks* (London: Pluto, 1986), p. 30.
13 Boehmer, *Colonial and Postcolonial Literature*, pp. 183–4.
14 Young, *Postcolonialism*, p. 6.
15 'Postcolonialism' is a contested term. Anne McClintock has challenged it for relying on a notion of linear development and for orienting 'the globe once more around a single, binary opposition: colonial/post-colonial'. The singularity of the term focuses global history through the 'rubric of European time' and makes colonialism the 'determining marker of history'. Neither does it sufficiently differentiate between different experiences of colonialism and global domination. The 'post' of postcolonialism is too celebratory, for it belies the continuity of inequality in international power relations. See McClintock, 'The Angel of Progress', pp. 292, 293 294. Ella Shohat suggests that giving diverse peoples the label 'postcolonial' effaces critical differences between and within nations. See Ella Shohat, 'Notes on the "Post-Colonial"', *Social Text*, 31-2 (1992), 102. Yet while the term is problematic, there are also good reasons for holding onto it. John McLeod, for example, argues that postcolonialism encourages comparative thinking. All terms have to generalise, and 'postcolonialism' can be defended on the grounds that it 'serves as a constant reminder of the historical contexts of both oppression and resistance which inform literature in the colonial period and its aftermath'. It also provides 'a challenging, innovative set of concepts which we can bring to bear in our reading practices'. See McLeod, *Beginning Postcolonialism*, pp. 246, 258. Thus, while I am

aware that 'postcolonialism' is a fraught term, I use it here to point to a shared impulse that is manifest across a diverse body of texts.
16 *Livingstone and Sechele* was first performed in 1979, but was published later in a volume of collected plays. David Pownall, *Livingstone and Sechele*, in *Plays One* (London: Oberon Books, 2000).
17 Boehmer, *Colonial and Postcolonial Literature*, p. 204.
18 Adetayo Alabi, 'Recover, Not Discover: Africa in Walcott's *Dream on Monkey Mountain* and Philip's *Looking for Livingstone*', in Isidore Okpewho, Carole Boyce Davies and Ali A. Mazrui (eds), *The African Diaspora: African Origins and New World Identities* (Bloomington: Indiana University Press, 1999), p. 334.
19 Denise deCaires Narain, *Contemporary Caribbean Women's Poetry: Making Style* (London: Routledge, 2002), p. 209.
20 Jacobs, *The Character of Truth*, pp. 69, 106.
21 Marlene NourbeSe Philip, *Looking for Livingstone: An Odyssey of Silence* (Toronto: Mercury, 1991), p. 16.
22 Ibid.
23 Ibid., p. 62.
24 Ibid., p. 32.
25 Ibid., p. 68.
26 Ibid., p. 66.
27 Ibid., p. 15.
28 Ibid., pp. 69–70.
29 Isabel Hoving, *In Praise of New Travelers: Reading Caribbean Migrant Women Writers* (Stanford: Stanford University Press, 2001), p. 275.
30 Kristen Mahlis, 'A Poet of Place: An Interview with M. NourbeSe Philip', *Callaloo*, 27: 3 (2004), 690.
31 Marlene NourbeSe Philip, 'Discourse on the Logic of Language', in *She Tries her Tongue, her Silence Softly Breaks* (London: Women's Press, 1993), p. 32.
32 Barbara Carey, 'Secrecy and Silence: Marlene Nourbese Philip's Struggle to Connect with her Lost Cultural Heritage Fuels her Writing', *Books in Canada*, 20: 6 (1991), 19.
33 Ibid.
34 Hoving, *In Praise of New Travelers*, p. 275.
35 Philip, *Looking for Livingstone*, p. 25.
36 Ibid.
37 Hoving, *In Praise of New Travelers*, p. 291.
38 Carey, 'Secrecy and Silence', p. 19.
39 Hoving, *In Praise of New Travelers*, p. 312.
40 Philip, *Looking for Livingstone*, p. 52.
41 Ibid., p. 53.
42 Hoving, *In Praise of New Travelers*, p. 303.
43 Eleanor G. Parkes, 'Livingstone Presumed', letter, *Books in Canada*, 20: 8 (1991), 8.
44 Marlene NourbeSe Philip, 'Q.E.D.', letter, *Books in Canada*, 21: 1 (1992), 5.
45 Richard Sanger, 'Other Voices', letter, *Books in Canada*, 21: 3 (1992), 6.
46 Marlene NourbeSe Philip, 'Discretionary Powers', letter, *Books in Canada*, 21: 5 (1992), 12.
47 Philip, 'Q.E.D.', p. 5.
48 Ibid.
49 Philip, *Looking for Livingstone*, p. 66.
50 Ibid., p. 29.
51 Brian Musgrove, 'Travel and Unsettlement: Freud on Vacation', in S.H. Clark (ed.), *Travel Writing and Empire: Postcolonial Theory in Transit* (London and New York: Zed Books, 1999), p. 31.
52 Philip, 'Q.E.D.', p. 5.
53 An extensive literature now resists the simplistic cliché of 'the Bible and gun'. See Lamin Sanneh, *Translating the Message: The Missionary Impact Upon Culture* (New York: Orbis, 1989); R.S. Sugirtharajah, *The Bible and Empire: Postcolonial*

Explorations (Cambridge: Cambridge University Press, 2005); Brian Stanley, *The Bible and the Flag: Protestant Missions and British Imperialism in the Nineteenth and Twentieth Centuries* (Leicester: Apollos, 1990); Andrew N. Porter, *Religion versus Empire? British Protestant Missionaries and Overseas Expansion, 1700–1914* (Manchester: Manchester University Press, 2004).
54 Simon During argues that when we use the term 'postcolonial', we need to bear in mind the distinction between the 'post-colonized' and the 'post-colonizers'. See Simon During, 'Postmodernism or Post-Colonialism Today', in Thomas Docherty (ed.), *Postmodernism: A Reader* (New York and London: Harvester Wheatsheaf, 1993), p. 460.
55 Lennart Hagerfors, *The Whales in Lake Tanganyika* (London: Penguin, 1991), p. 3.
56 Ibid., p. 66.
57 Ibid., p. 10.
58 Ibid., pp. 81–90.
59 Ibid., p. 91.
60 Ibid., p. 111.
61 Ibid., p. 4.
62 Ibid., p. 141.
63 Ibid., p. 28.
64 Ibid., pp. 56–7.
65 Ibid., p. 70.
66 Ibid., p. 71.
67 Ibid.
68 Ibid., pp. 162–3.
69 William Ferguson, 'In Short: Fiction', review of Lennart Hagerfors, *The Whales in Lake Tanganyika*, *New York Times* (30 July 1989), www.nytimes.com/1989/07/30/books/in-short-fiction-109089.html?ref=bookreviews. (accessed 6 September 2010).
70 Hagerfors, *The Whales*, p. 163.
71 Susanne Reichl and Mark Stein, 'Introduction', in Susanne Reichl and Mark Stein (eds), *Cheeky Fictions: Laughter and the Postcolonial* (Amsterdam: Rodopi, 2005), p. 2.
72 Ulrike Erichsen, 'Smiling in the Face of Adversity: How to Use Humour to Defuse Cultural Conflict', in Reichl and Stein (eds), *Cheeky Fictions*, p. 30.
73 Virginia Richter, 'Laughter and Aggression: Desire and Derision in a Postcolonial Context', in Reichl and Stein (eds), *Cheeky Fictions*, p. 63. For Freud, the exclusionary power of joking could assist oppression. He also felt that humour permitted the alleviation of tension. Since it was an accepted outlet for repressed impulses, it was unlikely to be conducive to social change. See Richter, 'Laughter and Aggression', pp. 62–3.
74 Postcolonial theorists of humour now tend to point towards its polyvalent potential. They have given up, argue Susanne Reichl and Mark Stein, on a '*grand récit*' of laughter and universalising generalisations. Instead they point to the importance of a 'multi-dimensional conceptualisation' that will do justice to its diverse possibilities. See Reichl and Stein, 'Introduction', pp. 4, 6, 8.
75 Michiko Kakutani, 'Books of the Times: The Heart of Darkness Beats Again', review of Lennart Hagerfors, *The Whales in Lake Tanganyika*, *New York Times* (11 April 1989), www.nytimes.com/1989/04/11/books/books-of-the-times-the-heart-of-darkness-beats-again.html?pagewanted=1 (accessed 6 September 2010).
76 Hagerfors, *The Whales*, p. 168.
77 Ibid., p. 170.
78 Ibid., p. 168.
79 Ibid., p. 169.
80 Ibid., p. 168.
81 Ibid., p. 167.
82 Ibid., p. 170.
83 Ibid., p. 6.
84 Ibid., p. 28.

FICTION: LAUGHING AT LIVINGSTONE?

85 Ibid., p. 168.
86 Ibid.
87 Ibid., p. 171.
88 David Pownall, 'Introduction', in *Plays One* (London: Oberon Books, 2000), p. 6.
89 Pownall, *Livingstone*, p. 76.
90 Ibid., p. 86.
91 Ibid., p. 117.
92 Ibid., p. 87.
93 Ibid.
94 Ibid., p. 100.
95 Ibid., p. 101.
96 Ibid., p. 106.
97 Ibid., p. 88.
98 Ibid., pp. 88, 89.
99 Ibid., p. 121.
100 It is too much to say that Sechele adopts Christianity for purely manipulative ends since his sentiment at times seems strikingly genuine. When he learns that Mokoron is pregnant, he kneels, 'seizes his fly-switch and starts to flagellate himself' in self-loathing and repentance. Even after Livingstone has rebuked him at length, he finds comfort in dejectedly singing, 'Give me joy in my heart, keep me praising ... sing Hosanna!' See Pownall, *Livingstone*, pp. 14, 119.
101 Ibid., p. 91.
102 Ibid., p. 103.
103 Ibid., p. 122.
104 Ibid., p. 98.
105 Ibid., p. 86.
106 Ibid.
107 Ibid., p. 128.
108 This is reminiscent, to some degree, of the body of research that emphasises the way in which scripture can be indigenised by colonised people and, in certain cases, provides the impulse for nationalist stirrings. See Adrian Hastings, *The Construction of Nationhood: Ethnicity, Religion and Nationalism* (Cambridge: Cambridge University Press, 1997), pp. 195–6.
109 Pownall, *Livingstone*, p. 91.
110 Ibid., p. 109.
111 Ibid.
112 Ibid., p. 83.
113 Ibid., p. 82.
114 Ibid.
115 Ibid., p. 78.
116 Ibid., p. 127.
117 Oliver Ransford, *David Livingstone: The Dark Interior* (London: John Murray, 1978), p. 3.
118 Pownall, *Livingstone*, p. 97.
119 Ibid., p. 107.
120 Ibid., p. 125.
121 Quoted in John O. Jordan, 'Alan Paton and the Novel of South African Liberalism: *Too Late the Phalarope*', *Modern Fiction Studies*, 42: 4 (1996), 698.
122 Peter F. Alexander, *Alan Paton: A Biography* (Oxford: Oxford University Press, 1994), p. 271.
123 Ibid., p. 278.
124 Ibid., p. 314. The first play's full title is *David Livingstone: Being a Dramatic Representation of the Life of the Great Missionary and Explorer, Designed for Performance in Churches*.
125 Mary Rosner's article has helped to impose order on the various manuscripts of the play, which are held in The Alan Paton Centre & Struggle Archives at the University of KwaZulu-Natal. See Mary Rosner, 'Revising a Victorian Convention:

Alan Paton and the Final Journey of David Livingstone', *English Studies in Africa*, 54: 1 (2011), 44–60.

126 Alan Paton, 'Author's Note' to *The Last Journey*, 1959, Alan Paton Centre & Struggle Archives, University of Kwazulu-Natal (Pietermaritzburg). Here Paton is speaking about *The Last Journey*, but his remark applies equally to the earlier play, *David Livingstone*.

127 Alan Paton, *David Livingstone: Being a Dramatic Representation of the Life of the Great Missionary and Explorer, Designed for Performance in Churches*, c.1956–58, PC1/3/6/5, p. 2, Alan Paton Centre & Struggle Archives.

128 Ibid., p. 38.

129 Ibid., p. 42.

130 E. Callan, *Alan Paton* (Boston: Twayne, 1982), p. 29.

131 Alexander, *Alan Paton*, p. 313.

132 Paton, *David Livingstone*, p. 7.

133 Ibid., p. 10.

134 Ibid., p. 20.

135 Ibid., p. 8.

136 Ibid., p. 27.

137 Ibid., p. 28.

138 Ibid.

139 David Levey, *Alan Paton: Pilgrim and Prophet?* (Shrewsbury: Feather Books, 2001), p. 9.

140 Colin Gardner, 'Alan Paton and the Bible', *Bulletin for Contextual Theology*, 4: 3 (1997), 29.

141 Levey, *Alan Paton*, p. 15.

142 Paton, *David Livingstone*, p. 4.

143 Ibid., p. 45.

144 Rose Moss, 'Alan Paton: Bringing a Sense of the Sacred', *World Literature Today*, 57: 2 (1983), 234.

145 Ibid.

146 Alan Paton, 'The Last Journey', essay, c.1959, PC1/3/6/3, p. 4, Alan Paton Centre & Struggle Archives.

147 Ibid., p. 7. James Chuma, however, had been baptised in 1865 and had spent time at a Christian school in Bombay, established by the Free Church, while Livingstone was in Britain after the Zambesi expedition. See Clare Pettitt, *Dr. Livingstone, I Presume?: Missionaries, Journalists, Explorers, and Empire* (Cambridge, Mass.: Harvard University Press, 2007), pp. 156–7.

148 Rosner, 'Revising a Victorian Convention', p. 55.

149 Alan Paton, *The Last Journey*, incomplete manuscript, c.1958–9, PC1/3/6/1, p. 5, Alan Paton Centre & Struggle Archives.

150 In his essay, Paton acknowledges that he may have 'idealized' Susi. See Paton, 'The Last Journey', essay, PC1/3/6/3, p. 17.

151 Alan Paton, *The Last Journey*, incomplete manuscript, c.1958–59, PC1/3/6/4, p. 17, Alan Paton Centre & Struggle Archives.

152 Rosner, 'Revising a Victorian Convention', p. 55.

153 The essay mentions F. Holmwood's transcription of 'Majwara's Account of the Last Journey and Death of Dr. Livingstone', *Proceedings of the Royal Geographical Society*, 18: 3 (1873–74), 244–6; William Joseph Wright Rampley, *Matthew Wellington: Sole Surviving Link with Dr. Livingstone* (London: SPCK, 1930); and 'The History of Carus Farrar of Finding Dr. Livingstone in Central Africa', which was discovered in the archives of the Church Missionary Society in London. The latter was published in H.B. Thomas, 'The Death of Dr. Livingstone: Carus Farrar's Narrative', *The Uganda Journal: The Journal of the Uganda Society*, 14: 2 (1950), 115–28.

154 Paton, *The Last Journey*, incomplete manuscript, c.1958–59, PC1/3/6/2, p. 2, Alan Paton Centre & Struggle Archives. In this manuscript there is more than one p. 2. The quotation above is taken from Act 3, Scene 1.

FICTION: LAUGHING AT LIVINGSTONE?

155 Paton, *The Last Journey* incomplete manuscript, PC1/3/6/1, p. 32.
156 Paton, 'The Last Journey', essay, PC1/3/6/3, p. 14.
157 Ibid., p. 15.
158 Ibid.
159 Ibid., p. 11.
160 Paton, *The Last Journey*, incomplete manuscript, PC1/3/6/1, p. 33.
161 Ibid., p. 32.
162 Ibid.
163 Paton, 'The Last Journey', essay PC1/3/6/3, p. 12.
164 Paton, *The Last Journey*, incomplete manuscript, PC1/3/6/1, p. 4.
165 Ibid., pp. 15–16; Paton, *The Last Journey*, PC1/3/6/4, n. pag. While the relevant pages in this document have no page numbers, they appear as the tenth and eleventh pages of the manuscript.
166 Alan Paton, *The Last Journey*, incomplete typed draft, c.1958–59, PC1/3/6/4, Alan Paton Centre & Struggle Archives, n. pag. This typescript is unpaginated, but the scene described appears on the thirteenth and fourteenth pages.
167 Paton, 'The Last Journey', essay, PC1/3/6/3, p. 5.
168 Paton, *The Last Journey*, incomplete manuscript, PC1/3/6/2, pp. 9, 12.
169 Ibid., p. 12.
170 Paton, *The Last Journey*, incomplete manuscript, PC1/3/6/1, p. 43.
171 As Rosner points out, Paton also wrote another ending to the play with a rather different and 'darker' inflection. In the version discussed above black culture is open to reconciliation, and Susi tells Murphy that they will 'receive any man' with only one condition: 'He must want to be received.' See Paton, *The Last Journey*, incomplete manuscript, PC1/3/6/1, p. 44. The other version is less optimistic. Here, Murphy's 'heart aches' for the company 'because having performed their epic task, they are now bearers to whom wages will be paid'. He says to Chuma, 'we shall meet tomorrow' and is met with a mere 'yes, Bwana', spoken 'impassively'. On the final page the play closes with Susi and Chuma staring out, again 'impassively', to the sea and the ship that will bear Livingstone's body. See Paton, *The Last Journey*, incomplete typed draft, PC1/3/6/4, n. pag. As Rosner puts it, 'The separation between the Africans at the shore and the only Englishman who could understand them seems final.' See Rosner, 'Revising a Victorian Convention', pp. 54, 55. With the alienation and disenchantment of Chuma and Susi, the conclusion seems pessimistic about the possibilities of the ultimate reconciliation between black and white.
172 Michael Black, 'Alan Paton and the Rule of Law', *African Affairs*, 91: 362 (1992), 70.
173 Quoted in Alexander, *Alan Paton*, p. 316.
174 Paton, *David Livingstone*, p. 15.
175 Ibid., p. 17.
176 Paton, *The Last Journey*, incomplete manuscript, PC1/3/6/1, pp. 13–14.
177 David Ward, *Chronicles of Darkness* (London: Routledge, 1989), p. 70.
178 Ibid., p. 74.
179 Ibid., p. 73.
180 Jordan, 'Alan Paton', pp. 699–700.
181 Ibid., p. 700. According to Jordon, this was a distinction made by Nadine Gordimer.
182 Stephen Clingman, *The Novels of Nadine Gordimer: History from the Inside* (London: Allen & Unwin, 1986), p. 214.
183 Ibid., pp. 217–18.
184 Michael Wade, *Nadine Gordimer* (London: Evans Bros., 1978), p. 3.
185 Ibid., p. 228.
186 Nadine Gordimer, 'Livingstone's Companions', in *Livingstone's Companions* (London: Jonathan Cape, 1972), p. 5.
187 Ibid., p. 11.
188 Graham Huggan, 'Echoes from Elsewhere: Gordimer's Short Fiction as Social Critique', *Research in African Literatures*, 25: 1 (1994), 70.

189 Gordimer, 'Livingstone's Companions', p. 4.
190 Ibid., p. 4.
191 Ibid., p. 5.
192 Ibid., p. 10.
193 Ibid., p. 13.
194 Ibid., p. 28.
195 Dominic Head, *Nadine Gordimer* (Cambridge: Cambridge University Press, 1994), p. 171.
196 Huggan, 'Echoes from Elsewhere', p. 69.
197 Gordimer, 'Livingstone's Companions', p. 9.
198 Huggan, 'Echoes from Elsewhere', p. 70.
199 Head, *Nadine Gordimer*, p. 169.
200 Robert F. Haugh, *Nadine Gordimer* (New York: Twayne, 1974), p. 32.
201 Gordimer, 'Livingstone's Companions', p. 26.
202 Ibid., p. 22.
203 Haugh, *Nadine Gordimer*, p. 32.
204 Gordimer, 'Livingstone's Companions', p. 7.
205 These words appear on the dust jacket of Gordimer's volume of stories *Livingstone's Companions*.
206 Huggan, 'Echoes from Elsewhere', p. 70.
207 Clingman, *The Novels of Nadine Gordimer*, p. 212.
208 Gordimer, 'Livingstone's Companions', p. 28.
209 Ibid., p. 37.
210 Clingman, *The Novels of Nadine Gordimer*, p. 220.
211 Gordimer, 'Livingstone's Companions', p. 24.
212 Robin Wayne Bailey, 'The Terminal Solution', in Julie E. Czerneda and Isaac Szpindel (eds), *ReVISIONS* (New York: Daw Books, 2004), p. 122.
213 'Recombinant fiction' is Naomi Jacobs' term for fiction that freely incorporates characters from history alongside those from popular culture, literature, and myth. See Jacobs, *The Character of Truth*, p. 105.
214 Matt Hills, 'Time, Possible Worlds, and Counterfactuals', in Mark Bould, Andrew M. Butler, Adam Roberts and Sherryl Vint (eds), *The Routledge Companion to Science Fiction* (London: Routledge, 2009), p. 437.
215 Barney Warf, 'The Way it Wasn't: Alternate Histories, Contingent Geographies', in Rob Kitchen and James Kneale (eds), *Lost in Space: Geographies of Science Fiction* (London: Continuum, 2002), p. 19.
216 Ibid., p. 36.
217 Julie E. Czerneda and Isaac Szpindel, 'Introduction', in Czerneda and Szpindel (eds), *ReVISIONS*, p. 2.
218 Bailey, 'The Terminal Solution', p. 143.
219 Ibid., p. 130.
220 Ibid., p. 131.
221 Ibid., p. 142.
222 Ibid., p. 143.
223 Ibid., p. 134.
224 Ibid., p. 140.
225 Ibid., p. 127.
226 Ibid., p. 140.
227 Ibid., p. 129.
228 Darko Suvin, 'On the Poetics of the Science Fiction Genre', *College English*, 34: 3 (1972), 373–5.
229 Jacobs, *The Character of Truth*, p. 113. Jacobs is borrowing the terminology of Darko Suvin.
230 Steven F. Kruger, *AIDS Narratives: Gender and Sexuality, Fiction and Science* (New York: Garland, 1996), p. 73.
231 Ibid., pp. 75, 77.
232 Ibid., p. 76.

FICTION: LAUGHING AT LIVINGSTONE?

233 Bailey, 'The Terminal Solution', p. 123.
234 Ibid., p. 123.
235 Kruger, *AIDS Narratives*, p. 80.
236 The term 'patient zero' belongs to Steven Kruger. See Ibid.
237 Pettitt, *Dr. Livingstone, I Presume?*, pp. 68–9.
238 Ibid., p. 69.
239 Warf, 'The Way it Wasn't', p. 26.
240 The play examines Nkrumah indirectly, but it does so quite clearly. As John K. Djisenu points out, it is set in a land named 'Angah' under the leadership of 'Mwake Kumrahn'. The first is an anagram of Ghana, and the second of Kwame Nkrumah. See John K. Djisenu, 'Some Political Lessons from Abdallah's *The Trial of Mallam Ilya*', *Journal of Performing Arts*, 3: 1 (1998–99), 19.
241 Mohammad Ben Abdallah, *The Trial of Mallam Ilya, and Other Plays* (Accra: Woeli, 1987), p. 117.
242 Ama Ata Aidoo, *Our Sister Killjoy* (New York: Longman, 1977), p. 92.
243 Jacobs, *The Character of Truth*, p. 113.

CHAPTER SEVEN

Revisionism: sins, psyche, sex

Who was the real David Livingstone? This is a question I have aimed to render problematic. The complexity and multifaceted nature of his posthumous identity reveals the extent to which the matter defies easy resolution. While the issue of Livingstone's true essence may continue to be worth pursuing, it is something that I have resolutely set to one side in the course of this project. Since Stanley met Livingstone with the words, 'Dr. Livingstone, I presume?', his biographers have routinely 'presumed' knowledge and command over his identity. He has been an occupied space, and I have sought to resist the urge to colonise him further. Instead, this book has approached Livingstone's reputation with the methodology of metabiography, a framework which Thomas Söderqvist has aptly described as a 'supergenre'.[1] Metabiography, it is crucial to remember, does not set itself the task of dispelling myths about the biographical subject in order to offer the truth about a life. Rather than pursuing 'authenticity', the point is instead to expose 'the relational nature of a biographical account – the relation it has to the biographer's location'.[2]

It might be argued that the critical examination of biographical heritage has long played a role in academic enquiry. For the most part, however, scholars have examined previous biographical portraits as a preface to their own work, which inevitably claims to supersede its predecessors and avoid their catalogue of errors. Metabiography departs from this tradition in altogether abandoning what Rupke calls its 'propaedeutic function'.[3] In other words, metabiography is no preparatory endeavour that aims to assess the inadequacy of prior research so as to pave the way for one's own 'definitive' work. It is in this respect that my own study differs most sharply from other appraisals of Livingstone's reputation. His 'myth' has previously been discussed, often receiving the attention of a solitary chapter, but the almost universal aim has been to reveal the 'real' Livingstone.[4] My project, in contrast, does not accumulate an inventory of myths and mistakes, but instead offers reflections on 'the essential instability of historical lives'.[5] It excavates the process of reinterpretation and reinscription by which Livingstone has been re-formed in order to meet diverse and historically discrete political agendas. The focus has been on the located and contingent nature of representation: I have argued that the socio-political prejudices of Livingstone's interpreters, from biographers to novelists, have been decisive in governing his many formulations. Or to put it more precisely, he has been constructed out of a synthesis of both subjective and collective horizons. According to Gadamer, any act of understanding emerges out of 'a fusion of one's own horizon with the historical horizon'.[6] In other words, while there is clear historical progression in Livingstone's legacy, his biographers actually constructed him in dialogue with their contemporary moment. This interaction, between the subjective and the historical, accounts for the competing versions of Livingstone that can be identified at any one chronological moment. While there is discernible development in his legacy, at no time is he ever represented in uniform fashion.

By way of conclusion, I would like extend my argument by bringing the story of Livingstone's afterlife into the present. At this point, it might be tempting to suppose that metabiography's insights are only confined to hagiographical writings or at least to work whose political intent is barely concealed. Yet given its insistence on the located nature of all biographical representation, even contemporary work cannot evade metabiographical analysis. While the research on Livingstone in the past forty or so years has productively expanded our understanding of his life and character, I would suggest that it is possible to discern underlying patterns of thought even in recent work.

Much of this literature has abandoned the heroic approach of the past, often offering a critical view of its subject. Of course, debunking biography is no new phenomenon. It has existed since at least Lytton Strachey's scathing book of 1918, *Eminent Victorians*, in which he re-evaluated and subjected to mockery a series of nineteenth-century heroes. He flouted a culture of Victorian adulation by, as Nigel Hamilton puts it, 'one by one knocking his targets off their pedestals'.[7] Yet, while critical biography subsequently became prevalent across the twentieth century, it was quite some time before such an approach was taken to Livingstone. Just as fictional portrayals were slow to proliferate while the empire was at its height, it is possible – as I suggested earlier – that Livingstone remained sacrosanct for so long because of the utility he offered in imperialist contexts: perhaps he was too valuable an icon to deflate. By the 1970s, however, a new image of Livingstone was established in which he appeared less than saintly. An important book in this shifting tide was *Livingstone's River*, by George Martelli. Reacting to the 'hero-worshippers or clergymen' who had for the most part constituted Livingstone's biographers, Martelli aimed to write a book 'free of the excessive adulation which has characterised its predecessors'.[8] Without denying Livingstone's 'imaginative enterprise, grit' and 'outstanding genius', Martelli presented an individual 'ruthless in pursuit of his goal; unimaginative to the point of callousness ... authoritarian and secretive; spiteful and vindictive'.[9]

Much of this reappraisal depended on excellent scholarly work, which made Livingstone's primary documents more easily accessible. For instance, Isaac Schapera's critical editions, *David Livingstone: Family Letters, Livingstone's Missionary Correspondence, 1841–1856* and *Livingstone's Private Journals, 1851–1853*, helped to provide the material that would grant biographers a broader perspective. Yet the development of the critical approach was not only governed by the availability of sources. Instead, it reflects a growing trend in biographical studies, which Joyce Carol Oates has aptly described as 'pathography'.[10] By this term Oates refers to the almost diagnostic approach that many biographers now take to their subject, in which the focus is primarily on aberration. As Peter Gibbon writes, pathographers 'excoriate any hint of impurity, prejudice, sexism, or hypocrisy'; they are only interested in stripping away 'mythology'.[11] At its worst, the desire to puncture reputations can lead to little more than scandal-mongering. In an amusing and completely unverified statement, for example, a recent article in the *Daily Mail* was able to pronounce coolly that Livingstone's 'Christian morals did not prevent him from sleeping with African women on a regular and prolific basis'.[12] My concern here, however, is not with such scurrilous assertions, but rather with a broader cultural phenomenon that revels in demythologising. While this, of course, is part of the afterlife of almost any public figure to a certain extent, such efforts, like some of the more forceful postcolonial revisions, run the risk of becoming as reductive as the hagiographical portraits they seek to replace.

One prime example of scholarly pathography is Judith Listowel's *The Other Livingstone*. By its very name, the work declares its opposition to the established iconography and its intention to explore an unknown side of Livingstone's identity. Listowel claims to offer a more even-handed approach, contending that 'By recognising his defects as well as his admirable qualities, we can see David Livingstone as a more credible person than the sentimentally pious Victorian presented by his biographers.' Nevertheless, the vision that she projects is overwhelmingly negative. Listowel concentrates particularly on his reluctance to acknowledge 'that he had been helped in his explorations by others who had lived or travelled in Africa'.[13] She argues that Livingstone failed to give due credit to William Cotton Oswell for collaborating in the expedition to Lake Ngami and that he strove to deny that Candido Cardoso had visited Lake Nyasa, even after pressing him for useful information. Given that Livingstone was prone to describe the Portuguese traders he encountered in the interior as 'half-castes', and since he refused to see the Hungarian traveller Lásló Magyar when he visited Linyanti, Listowel argues that Livingstone was greedy for the limelight and driven by a 'pathological determination to be the "the first"'.[14] All this does cast interesting light on Livingstone, but Listowel's selection of episodes reveals much about her approach. Primarily, she chooses to discuss Livingstone's less estimable moments, and her focus is heavily weighted towards blunders and bad relations. Listowel is also intent on vandalising his character. Discussing Livingstone's commitment to the Congregationalist Church, she suggests that its 'creed suited David's wilful and individualistic character'.[15] While he 'appeared respectful to his parents', in reality he was 'thoroughly self-centred and self-absorbed';[16] his nature was 'obsessive' and his disposition 'suspicious'.[17] In routine fashion, Listowel reiterates and castigates Livingstone's ignoble qualities.

The most famous biography of Livingstone, authored by Tim Jeal, is characterised by the same mentality. While the book offers the best-researched account of Livingstone's life and concedes that he was undeniably 'very great', it subjects his character to sustained and sometimes hostile revision. In his days at Glasgow University, Livingstone was a 'stodgy Scottish student' and an 'awkward, sullen young man'.[18] By twenty-eight 'Livingstone was intolerant, narrow and self-opinionated', and while he may have been 'courageous and resilient' this 'did not make him likeable'.[19] Jeal revisits various episodes of Livingstone's life, offering new evaluations that cast him in unfavourable light. For instance, he notes that 'At twenty-one he had been ready to walk through a snowstorm rather than miss a single lecture.' Instead of commending Livingstone's determination, as earlier biographers had done, Jeal writes: 'sometimes it is hard not to be chilled by his resilience and almost inhuman perseverance'.[20] In the same way, Livingstone's brief sojourn at Rio de Janeiro, where he distributed temperance tracts at a local bar, is mentioned not purely because it 'proved his courage', but because it 'underlined his priggishness'.[21]

Despite the rigour of Jeal's research, then, his sometimes scathing comments evince the authorial stance of pathographer. This is actually clearest in the remarks he makes about Livingstone's wife, Mary, who apparently 'lacked in refinement'.[22] While their marriage, perhaps justly, is described as one of 'convenience', Jeal also comments that

'Livingstone knew that a man in his position could not afford to be fussy.'[23] He remarks too that since Mary was 'fat and plain', she 'probably felt fortunate to be getting married at all'. Indeed Mary's appearance arguably receives undue consideration. Jeal notes that she 'grew extremely fat' in later life and that 'it is interesting that this should already have been such a feature in her early twenties'.[24] Both her body image and countenance are offered up for readerly inspection. By 1857, he writes, 'she was a stout, heavy-jowled woman, slightly coarse-featured and with a large nose'.[25] Livingstone, argues Jeal, told himself he would never expect too much of his wife, and 'in the romantic sense he kept his word'. 'But, considering her appearance', he goes on, 'he cannot be given too much credit for his achievement.'[26] Jeal's sustained descriptions of Mary verge on the callous. He even rather unfairly conjectures that she might have left Livingstone dissatisfied. Discussing one enigmatic letter in which Livingstone mentioned a mysterious 'guilt' to a friend, Jeal speculates that 'The "guilt" could have been over some wish that he could enjoy prettier women.'[27]

Jeal's pathographic tendency is also indicated in his hermeneutic of suspicion, which leads him to question Livingstone's stated motives and insinuate deeper incentives at work. He points out that, from the beginning of his time in Africa, Livingstone displayed 'an ambition to excel personally: a very questionable motive for a young man ostensibly about to begin a grinding and largely frustrating life of humble service'.[28] His eventual decision to leave his work with the Kwena in order to pioneer new missions, seems, for Jeal, to have been a choice of 'a far more attractive role, that of a man who opened the way for others': 'The important thing was that he should lead and others follow.'[29] Under this conception, Livingstone was less motivated by duty than by ego and self-oriented zeal. Finally, as Jeal puts it, 'Livingstone was not the first nor the last religiously motivated man to see his own wishes and personal preferences in terms of the dictates of Providence.'[30] Operating with a cynical *modus operandi*, Jeal casts aside Livingstone's sense of divine calling as little more than a shroud for naked ambition.

These revisionist biographies, while productively challenging, and perhaps enlarging, our conception of Livingstone, should thus not be seen as definitive. They reflect a contemporary pathographic mentality dominated by an impulse towards unmasking, a trend in life-writing in which greatness is deemed to be a veneer. In the same way, other recent biographies of Livingstone can be located as instances within biographical paradigms rather than authoritative interpretations. A good example of this is Oliver Ransford's *David Livingstone: The Dark Interior* (1978). Taking a medicalised approach to his subject's mental state, Ransford diagnoses Livingstone with 'Manic Depressive

Disorder' also known as 'Cyclothymia, and *Folie Circulaire*'.[31] Sufferers of the condition, he notes, 'show alternating phases of depression and hypomania (excitable exuberance)'. The symptoms of the depressed phase consist of 'guilt, pessimism ... inability to reach decisions, querulous anxiety, and periods of inertia'. The '"striving" periods of hypomania' in contrast are manifested in 'increased flight of ideas, enterprise, elation of mood ... ruthlessness ... violent likes and dislikes, lack of insight into people's minds ...'.[32]

In diagnosing Livingstone's condition, Ransford presents him as a psychological case study. To this extent, his work can be considered a late example of a genre that primarily thrived between the 1920s and 1960s: psychobiography.[33] Like debunking biography, psychobiography dates back to the early twentieth century, when Freud approached his life of Leonardo da Vinci, 'not as an idealized Victorian exemplar', as Nigel Hamilton puts it, 'but as a psychological *riddle*'.[34] While there was considerable resistance to Freud's 'colonization' of life-writing,[35] psychobiography began to burgeon as authors sought to try to 'uncover the inner self behind the public figure'.[36] Ransford is not Freudian in approach, but his text is psychobiographical to the degree that it prioritises the internal mental state and focuses on interiority.[37] On the one hand, Ransford's diagnosis provides a compelling explanation for the inconsistencies in Livingstone's character that scholars had long found troubling. Yet, on the other hand, while remaining quite laudatory, his work reflects a mode of biographical practice in which the biographee is less a subject for celebration than one for interrogation.

Several problematic issues in Ransford's approach indicate that psychobiography cannot offer the final word on Livingstone. Firstly, Ransford comes to his diagnosis by examining Livingstone's diary and correspondence, which provide 'a unique record of a man's day-to-day mood'.[38] He assumes that when Livingstone 'neglected his journal' it signals 'a depressive phase'.[39] In the same way, 'terse and uninteresting' entries are said to reflect 'Livingstone's depression'.[40] The analysis of private writings of course offers one of the few ways to diagnose a posthumous subject, but the potential unreliability of such an endeavour is clear, at least as it appears in Ransford. Indeed, he assumes, too confidently, that he can accurately trace the course of Livingstone's mental illness through his journal entries; the link between mental state and written word is thus deemed to be obvious and uncomplicated. In fact, this reveals what David Ellis considers to be a fundamental problem with the methodology of the psychobiographer. He complains that 'biographers who act as analysts ... lack access to its most characteristic method': free association. Since they are unable 'to ask their subjects questions', they are 'deprived therefore of all the new material which the *process* of analysis throws up', an altogether 'crippling drawback' to their endeavour.[41] Without denying that one can diagnose and analyse an historical individual successfully, the detailed inferences of the psychobiographer should perhaps be considered partial and provisional.

Furthermore, Ransford presents cyclothymia as the key to understanding Livingstone and so attributes much of his action to the effects of the cyclic phases. Livingstone's disputes with Baines and Bedingfeld, during the Zambesi expedition, are credited to his condition: 'As always, Livingstone's suspicions about a colleague's intentions were most sharply expressed during one of the hypomanic phases.'[42] Similarly, his tirade against Kirk in the aftermath of Stanley's visit is assigned to his 'manic mood'.[43] Indeed, when Livingstone decided to emancipate a slave coffle, it was once again a 'hypomanic phase' that led him to intervene.[44] In contrast, it was 'one of his "downs"' that prevented him from relishing his pioneering voyage on Lake Nyasa:[45] generally, 'during a depressed phase, Livingstone showed apathy'.[46] The problem here is that almost everything is attributed to his depressive disorder and the cyclic phases; Livingstone's free agency is radically circumscribed by his presumed condition. This is another problem of the whole approach, for as Hermione Lee puts it, psychobiography 'placed its subjects on the couch and fitted their behaviour into a pattern'.[47]

David Ellis makes a similar observation about the way in which biographers treat illness, noting 'that a medical explanation has a tendency to invade all the available interpretive space'. Once an ailment enters the equation, 'every feature of their behaviour which strikes an observer as abnormal tends to be attributed to their disease'.[48] Yet as Ellis observes, substantiating that an individual suffered a condition is not the same as establishing the extent to which it affected them.[49] Even if Ransford is correct in his diagnosis of Livingstone, it is less clear that we need give it the same degree of explanatory value.[50] For Ransford, Livingstone's condition serves not only to resolve his irregularities but to explain his successes. Since hypomania led to 'dynamism', Livingstone's 'cyclothymic temperament' actually 'fathered his achievements'.[51] Indeed, Ransford describes cyclothymia as 'a creative illness which often leads to great achievement' and whose sufferers 'may be most valuable members of society'.[52] In making this suggestion, Ransford buys into one of the more persistent paradigms for the discussion of illness. As Ellis argues, biographers often insinuate 'that there is some natural connection between the pathological and the creative: that no person who is completely "healthy" is likely to do important work'.[53] The fluctuating mental state is given almost deterministic explanatory power: it serves to decode an enigma, to complete what Ransford calls the 'jigsaw puzzle' of Livingstone's life.[54] The point here of critiquing Ransford's methodological approach is to demonstrate that more recent biographical interpretations are every bit as much located and ephemeral as those of the past. Now that the penchant for psychological exploration has waned somewhat, and we are left with 'vestigial traces of its language', we can see that biography continues to be transient, framed by the concerns of the present.[55]

While the preoccupations of pathography and psychobiography have inflected the way in which Livingstone's life-narrative has been written, another major source of revisionism has been provided by the rise of feminist and gender criticism. By those concerned with the ethics of biographical practice, it has often been argued that the tendency to focus on one 'great life' as particularly worthy of record is 'hierarchical, anti-egalitarian' and therefore socially conservative. It has been castigated, moreover, as a 'patriarchal form', one predominantly consisting of male authors writing about other men.[56] To some extent, such accusations run the risk of masking the considerable number of biographies written by women and about women. In some non-Western contexts – notably in Arabic literature – there are actually significant traditions of women's biography. And in Europe, Elizabeth Gaskell's idealised *Life of Charlotte Brontë* opened the floodgates to other female biographers and biographees in the Victorian period. Nevertheless, the charge that the history of biography is largely made up of records of prominent men is – in the broadest sense – legitimate. The rise of feminism in culture and the academy has thus led both to critiques of the genre and to changes within biographical practice itself. Such criticisms of course are not altogether new: the advent of literary modernism saw Virginia Woolf pointing to the significant exclusion of women from the roll-call of biographical worthies. But this critique, and new ways of writing biography, would gather momentum with the feminist movement of the 1970s and 1980s and the development of women's history.

A new awareness of gender politics clearly fed into the rise of the critical approach taken to Livingstone discussed above. While Livingstone was acutely aware that decisions he made on his family's behalf left him open to condemnation, his subsequent celebratory biographers tended to paper potential criticism over by opting either for silence or for apologetic.[57] The 'canonical' debunking biographies of the 1970s, however, foreground the domestic, arguing that Livingstone's public success came at the expense of private failure. Jeal, for instance, traces his 'failure as a husband and a father', while Listowel charges him with 'putting his wife and children after the achievement of his own obsessive plans'.[58] Feminism, as Susan Tridgell argues, has the capacity to radically alter established interpretations of 'acclaimed men', and while neither of these texts amounts to a sustained feminist critique, they do bear the diffused traces of its prevailing concerns.[59]

There is another set of texts, however, that is much more embedded in feminist ethos. These books do not take Livingstone himself as their primary subject, but instead turn the focus in the direction of his wife. Judith Zinsser writes that as 'woman's history' became established, it drew attention to the reality that 'all but a few women had been quietly eliminated from the formal and informal stories of our past'.[60] Its first task was thus 'recovery history', retrieving those lives lost to the historical record. Where feminism meets biography, then, it radically expands the potential number of subjects worthy of exploration. The biographers of Mary Livingstone are invested in this process, telling the life of one woman whose story has lurked in the background and been dominated by her husband's.

Edna Healey's collective biography *Wives of Fame* charts the lives of Mary Livingstone, Jenny Marx and Emma Darwin – the spouses of three renowned Victorians. The book is very much a retrieval project, bringing these 'invisible and forgotten' wives 'out of the shadows, to share their husbands' place in history'.[61] While Healey's treatment of Mary perhaps comes close to the cliché that behind every great man stands a great woman, her work is laudable for addressing an absence in historical memory. Exploring the consequences of Mary's 'years of privation', the 'cultural shock' of her period in Britain and the accumulated effects of Livingstone's constant itinerancy, Healey traces her progressive mental decline.[62] But rather than presenting her as a purely passive subject, acted upon by her husband, Healey follows the pattern of other feminist biographers by drawing attention to her achievements and individual agency. 'She had travelled thousands of miles by ox wagon across deserts hitherto believed to be impassable for white men. She had journeyed ... to regions where no white woman had been before.'[63] Alongside her husband, Mary also had claim to be the 'first' European visitor. Likewise, Healey contends that Mary was instrumental to the success of Livingstone's meeting with the Kololo chief, Sebituane. Her status as the daughter of Robert Moffat, a confidante of Mzilikatze, chief of the Matabele, immediately aroused his interest. Mary endowed Livingstone with political significance and, Healey suggests, 'made possible the first step towards her father's dream – that his family should unite the two warring tribes, the Makololo and the Matabele'.[64] Healey's character study of Mary, which presents courage and fortitude as her primary qualities, also enlarges her importance within Livingstone's story. Indeed, her death on the Zambesi in 1862 becomes his chief crisis point and the start of a downward spiral. From this fundamental moment, 'Nothing would be the same again, neither his simple faith in Heaven nor his confidence in his own mission.'[65] As though initiating the beginning of the end, Healey writes that after brief respite in Britain, 'he returned to die in Africa'.[66]

Margaret Forster's book of 2001, *Good Wives?*, similarly investigates Mary alongside other spouses – this time, Fanny Stevenson and Jennie Lee. The fact that both Healey and Forster chose to approach their subject not in isolation, but in tandem with others, is significant in itself. As Marilyn Booth and Antoinette Burton point out, the collective impulse in much feminist biography stands in contrast to the tendency 'at least traditionally and in Euro/American literary traditions – to highlight the single (and male) hero'.[67] Collective biography, they argue, has been 'indispensable to the writing of women's history' and particularly to its 'popularization'. A characteristic of many feminist biographies – although by no means all – has been an interest in historical figures not only for their exceptional status, but for the ways in which their individual life-narratives illuminate the more general social situation of women. Approaching a biographee within a collective text, argues Barbara Caine, 'serves to remove the "exceptional" framework from the study of women's lives'. A case-study approach enables the author to use 'the situation, experiences and life-course of one woman ... to concretise the broader situation of women generally'.[68] Forster's interest in Mary Livingstone treads the line between the exceptional and the representative. While she did not lead an 'ordinary' life, Mary's marital situation reflected 'the standards of her own time'; 'Few women had to endure what she did in her marriage but on the other hand her spirit of submission to her husband was shared by millions.'[69] Forster's aim is to subject the category of 'wife' to interrogation and examine its shifting meanings between 1845 and 2001. The analysis of Mary is primarily designed as criticism of a marital model, based on subservience, to which she is fundamentally opposed. While her historical insights are limited, and border on caricature, Forster engages in committed critique with an imperative to advance egalitarian gender politics. More than Healey, she castigates Livingstone for his patriarchal conduct. Livingstone 'exploited Mary's natural tendency to obey and to put him first at all costs'; he 'sacrificed his family's happiness and security in the cause of his own self-fulfilment'.[70] Like Healey, Forster extends the project of recovering Mary's forgotten history, yet her relationship with her subject is clearly ambivalent. On the one hand, she sees Mary as a victim whose chief tragedy lay in her lack of self-determination. However, in her submissive obedience Mary privileged her husband and neglected her children; 'she seemed forced to put being a wife before being a mother'.[71] For Forster, Mary's crippling 'dependency' on

Livingstone did not make her admirable. Mary 'couldn't challenge him. She didn't have the courage.'[72]

Although caught between the poles of recovery and critique, Forster had as one of her major aims to defend Mary from the 'wonderful male arrogance' with which she had hitherto between written about.[73] She set out with the determination to write against the 'prejudice' of men such as John Kirk, who never warmed to Mary, and, most explicitly, the biographer Tim Jeal. It was, apparently, both the 'insulting terms' that Livingstone used to describe Mary in his letters and Jeal's unflattering account of their marriage that raised Forster's hackles.[74] Primarily her objection is to the claim that their union was 'a marriage of convenience', and she accuses Livingstone's biographers of the tacit assumption that 'men cannot love fat, plain women'. 'It is insulting to them both', she argues, 'to doubt that their marriage lacked genuine mutual attraction.'[75] In crafting Mary's narrative, and in polemically challenging established perspectives, Forster – like many feminist authors – is clearly attuned to 'the political valences of writing a life'.[76] Yet while her feminist revisionism was undoubtedly timely, her analysis does tend to attribute too much to issues of gender and the 'good wife' ideology. Forster, for instance, suggests that Mary was sent to boarding school by her parents explicitly to prepare for wifely duty. Apparently, argued Forster, this decision showed that her mother felt 'A wife should be educated to a sufficient standard to be of use to her husband.'[77] Likewise, Mary's scant enthusiasm for the paeanistic gatherings in honour of her husband supposedly revealed her internalisation of the dictum that 'A wife's job was to keep in the background.'[78] Such comments are, of course, unsatisfactory – both speculative and simplifying. Forster's political investment, however commendable, leads her to commit what Booth and Burton call the error of 'reducing everything to gender as a causal explanation'.[79]

The turn away from Livingstone and towards his wife was taken one step further in Julie Davidson's recent publication *Looking for Mrs Livingstone*. The book, as the author points out, is 'not an orthodox biography'. Rather, it is a compelling formal experiment, a blend of lifewriting and travelogue, which unfolds Mary's story within the chronicle of Davidson's own African travels. It is, Davidson writes, 'a journey through her life by way of her own journeys and those I've made in her footsteps'.[80] If Livingstone has inspired his share of African travels and even pilgrimages to his place of death, south of Lake Bangweulu, Davidson's quest in search of Mary's grave can be read as a counter-pilgrimage. Her travels in Mary's trail and the text itself are acts of respect honouring a neglected woman. It is a tribute to Mary, not to David: 'this is not his story', she writes.[81] Throughout the book, however, the sense emerges that Mrs Livingstone is not an easy subject to grasp. While all biographies are underdetermined by the available facts, this is particularly true of any attempt to write Mary. Unlike Livingstone, whose voluminous writings present his biographers' biggest challenge, Mary is represented by a written record which exists only in traces. Her other biographers make fairly confident statements about their subject, but Davidson draws attention instead to Mary's elusive nature. Routinely, she tells us that Mary is 'as usual, silent', that we have only 'fragments of text', that she is 'a phantom in her own story'.[82] As Tridgell points out, the dearth of documentation is a problem often confronted in writing women's lives. It is, however, one that can 'present an opportunity for experimenting with the form of biography'.[83] To some extent, Davidson's bio-travelogue does just that, as she raises questions and foregrounds the gaps, silences and uncertainties in Mary's life history. Understandably, Davidson is frustrated by the paucity of the record. Advancing a conspiracy theory, she suggests that Mary's letters – which surely would have given voice to her unhappiness – might well have been destroyed by Livingstone himself or 'by self-appointed guardians of the Livingstone reputation'.[84] For Davidson, then, this historical absence is a case not just of Mary's silence, but of her silencing. Yet she does not allow indeterminacy to limit her construction of Mary, but rather uses it as an opportunity for re-imagination. Taking well-known scenes from her life, Davidson offers subversive interpretations. Revisiting Mary's death-bed and the comfort that her husband took as she 'looked up towards Heaven thoughtfully', Davidson suggests another way of reading Mary's expression. 'Could it be that, badgered beyond endurance, Mary simply rolled her eyes to the skies in the time-honoured manner of long-suffering wives everywhere?'[85] Likewise, her 'impassive appearance' at public functions might have been less 'submissive modesty' than 'a reservoir of resentment, a private contempt for the unctuous claims for her character and virtue made by people who didn't know her'.[86] Instead of simply accepting the given image of submissive wife, Davidson looks for signs of resistance. And where Mary's thoughts and emotions are undocumented – concerning, for instance, the death of her daughter Elizabeth, or her experience of religious crisis – Davidson fills these spaces with possibilities.[87] Refusing claims to certainty, by acknowledging that her own 'deductions' 'can't be verified by [Mary's] own testimony', she presents the reader with re-imaginings that are at least plausible.[88]

While such lengthy focus on Mary might seem odd in a metabiography of her husband, these books are an important part of Livingstone revisionism. Together they wrest attention away from the 'great man' in favour of one who has remained subordinate in his many biographies:

these texts rewrite Livingstone by positioning him as the background figure in his wife's story. As Zinsser points out, the majority of feminist biographers have a mandate to 'break the cultural traditions that have erased women from historical memory'.[89] While the lives of celebrated figures will probably never lose their appeal, these texts are part of an effort to divert attention away from the 'powerful and prominent' in favour of marginalised and '"minority" subjects'.[90] Nonetheless, Livingstone will continue to attract biographers. The popular industry will no doubt live on, but the way is open too for more radical projects. As formal experiments in biography continue to emerge in the wake of challenges to 'essential character', the 'coherent subject' and 'the linearity of the life story', it is possible that Livingstone will be rewritten in altogether novel ways.[91]

Certainly, it is clear that from psychobiography to pathography and to gender critique, the way in which Livingstone's life has been told over the past forty years has been influenced by the changing aesthetics and politics of biography itself. Revisionist biographies – such as Jeal's and Ransford's – have been hailed in their time as 'definitive' by the reviewers, yet this excellent work actually reflects contemporary predilections, whether it be an appetite for demythologising or for interrogating psychological states. In an expanded edition of his book, published for the bicentenary of Livingstone's birth (2013), Jeal describes his critical account of the explorer as a 'revised orthodoxy'.[92] While there is some justice to this claim, the fact that as serious an academic biography as Andrew Ross's *David Livingstone: Mission and Empire* (2002) explicitly set out to contest his perspective – arguably re-romanticising Livingstone's life in the process – suggests that a truly 'definitive' biography can never be written. Established portraits always provoke response – not least, in this case, from the less well-known pens of Mary's feminist biographers. Indeed, contemporary works, it is vital to realise, do not transcend metabiographical commentary; instead, they mark important moments in the subject's ongoing posthumous production and reproduction.[93]

The terrain covered in this book has been extensive. While it has given the fullest account of Livingstone's reputation to date, however, it has necessarily still been selective and discriminatory. As Steven Aschheim observes, in order to achieve a 'synoptic perspective' it is essential 'to sacrifice some of the complexity and creative intensity' of the numerous 'individual encounters' with the historical subject.[24] Consequently, I have imposed order on the heterogeneity of Livingstone's afterlife by adopting a thematic approach, distinguishing several of his dominant legacies and then tracing the evolution of each. The most significant of these, perhaps, situated in the centre of the book and at the crux of my argument, is Livingstone's imperialist identity. No dimension of his reputation has been more sustained or better exposes his political utility. As the face of the British Empire changed, over a period of eighty years, Livingstone was habitually reconstructed in order to meet its shifting requirements. Yet, at concurrent historical moments, his reputation was actually conflicted; he was deployed on behalf of competing imperialisms, for empire has never been a unified endeavour. Even while Livingstone became a firmly established colonial icon, however, it is important to note that there were also occasional counter-hegemonic constructions that used him to provide at least some element of imperial critique. The next chapter took Livingstone's Scottish legacy as its subject and investigated his significance for Scots national identity in a variety of literary and historical contexts. While some biographers have been completely uninterested in Livingstone's northern heritage, others have used him to gain prestige for the Gaelic peoples of Scotland, to symbolise the union of Highland and Lowland, and to negotiate the nation's role within the United Kingdom and its imperialist affairs. From the Celtic revival to Kailyard, and until its apotheosis in the national memorial at Blantyre, Livingstone provided a means to express Scottish sentiment.

While these two chapters traced dominant strands in Livingstone's legacy, the two others framing them dealt with lesser-known aspects of his reputation. The second chapter was unique in bringing to light a body of unexplored literature, in the form of elegiac poetry and eulogistic obituaries. By analysing the year of his interment, it became clear that Livingstone was the site of debate even in a restricted time frame, a subject who was claimed by a variety of interest groups who at times competed with one another. The brief historical juncture on which this chapter focused was counterpoised by the breadth of reflection that such commemorative writing offered, not only on the Victorian celebration of Livingstone, but also on the period's culture of death and mourning. Chapter 6 likewise explored new avenues of Livingstone's legacy, by offering the first discussion of his fictional representation. It concentrated particularly on how he was reconfigured in the postcolonial era, as the values of empire came under sustained critique. In contrast to this rewritten version of the hero, however, was the Livingstone who emerged out of an apartheid context, to represent resistance to racial segregation. Both these chapters aimed to extend the notion of biography beyond the conventional documentary approach: they suggest that to gain the fullest picture of a posthumous reputation we need to examine a broader spectrum of representative practices and to take account of other forms of life-writing.

LIVINGSTONE'S 'LIVES'

Before interrogating these many afterlives, this study examined Livingstone's self-representation particularly as it is manifested in *Missionary Travels*. A discussion of this travelogue seemed vital, for it was Livingstone's major platform before the British populace and consequently played a critical role in shaping his public perception. What emerged was a heterogeneous text, influenced by a number of generic models, which presented a multifaceted persona to its audience. The text was also revealed as complex and ambivalent, capable of sustaining a variety of different interpretations: as has been seen, this is particularly relevant to the question of Livingstone's imperialist legacy. Indeed, while my argument has primarily been about the interpretive and constructive practices of Livingstone's many biographers, it does seem likely that his diverse posthumous reputations were facilitated by his mutable text. As other metabiographers have observed, afterlife images are not entirely arbitrary and do not emerge purely out of thin air. Steven Aschheim, in his study of the Nietzsche legacy, and David B. Dennis, in his investigation of Beethoven's reputation, both suggest that the generations who appropriated these figures proceeded with a hermeneutic of 'selective scavenging'.[95] Wearing 'selective blinders' and adopting a 'filtering system' they were able to construe their subjects to suit their own ends.[96] The purpose, then, of examining Livingstone's travelogue at the outset was to offer a detailed interrogation of one of the central sources which later biographers would scan in order to construct their subject. Such scavenging was not always a sophisticated process. The manner by which an historical figure is re-created can be forceful, or can even rely on mere assertion. Rupke, for instance, observes that Humboldt's 'life and oeuvre were aggressively recreated to suit contemporaneous needs',[97] while Dennis notes the 'blatant, sometimes humorous, even embarrassing' efforts to link Beethoven to various political developments.[98] The protean nature of Livingstone's text, which surely made him conducive to competing constructions, is thus only part of the story. The agendas and horizons of his biographers, analysed in the other chapters, were decisive factors.

By offering an extended treatment of Livingstone's legacies, this book has sought to engage with the field of biographical studies. In filling out the methodology of the metabiographical framework, it hopes to direct further study to the changing nature of historical lives. It meets existing demands in the field of biography for comparative analysis, by following the development of a single biographical tradition. The insights of this project have thus been not only theoretical, but empirical. Furthermore, my particular subject of enquiry, David Livingstone, also helps to bridge a gulf in biographical studies, since, as Ben Pimlott notes, the majority of criticism on the subject has been devoted to 'literary biography', life-writing about novelists, poets and dramatists.[99] This of course reflects the predilections of the academics, often literary critics by trade, who have led the way in theorising the genre. The result, Pimlott complains, is that 'there is a growing academic literature on "biography" that takes no account of the biographies of scientists or statesmen'.[100] By studying Livingstone's 'lives', I hope to go some way towards fostering a deeper understanding of the legacies of public figures. In fact, it is arguable that such subjects are particularly conducive to comparative analysis, especially when the overarching concern is the political utility of the biographical record. Representations of those who lived their lives in the public and political arena are likely to have a particular investment in the institutional and ideological apparatus of their time.

While my preoccupation has been the embeddedness of biographical portraits – which I have now traced even into contemporary writing – this research cannot close the debate on Livingstone. As Rupke remarks of his own representation study, it 'joins the long list of publications in which particular Humboldts have been enacted'. His book 'itself now becomes part of the raw material for a further metastudy, namely of the politics and socio-political purposes of the metabiographical approach'.[101] In a similar manner, Lucasta Miller comments that the interpretive practices she brought to bear on the evolution of the Brontë myth would likely be traced to her 'background as a literary critic'.[102] In its preoccupation with reception and representation, construction and contingency, this study inevitably reflects current academic proclivities. My project is open to the same analysis to which I have subjected others, and can be dissected for its own politics and assumptions. Such reflexivity is a crucial part of metabiographical practice: *Livingstone's 'Lives'* does not stand outside the textual production of Livingstone, but rather itself has become a part of it.

Notes

1 Thomas Söderqvist, review of Nicolaas A. Rupke, *Alexander von Humboldt: A Metabiography*, Isis, 98: 1 (2007), 203.
2 Nicolaas A. Rupke, *Alexander von Humboldt: A Metabiography* (Chicago: University of Chicago Press, 2008), p. 214.
3 Ibid.
4 See, for example, Meriel Buxton's reflections on 'Livingstone's legend'. She engages in a brief critical biography in order to argue that Livingstone should be understood as 'exceptional, a complex man of extraordinary contradictions'. See Meriel Buxton, *David Livingstone* (Basingstoke: Palgrave, 2001), p. 198. Andrew Ross, one of the authors most attuned to the subtleties of Livingstone's legacy, is similar in approach when he argues that 'David Livingstone was a more complex person than can be captured by any of these myths'. See Andrew Ross,

David Livingstone: Mission and Empire (London: Hambledon and London, 2002), p. 239. More particularly, his aim is to contend that Livingstone's construction as an 'icon of imperialism' was a distortion of his real identity. See also Andrew Ross, 'David Livingstone', *Études écossaises*, 10 (2005), 92. Other biographies, by their very titles, tacitly claim to transcend the mythos. This is the case with Timothy Holmes's *Journey to Livingstone: Exploration of an Imperial Myth* (Edinburgh: Canongate, 1993) and Rob Mackenzie's more conventional *David Livingstone: The Truth behind the Legend* (Fearn, Ross-shire: Christian Focus, 2000).

5 Rupke, *Alexander von Humboldt*, p. 214.
6 Robert C. Holub, *Reception Theory: A Critical Introduction* (London: Methuen, 1984), p. 42.
7 Nigel Hamilton, *Biography: A Brief History* (Cambridge, Mass.: Harvard University Press, 2007), p. 147.
8 George Martelli, *Livingstone's River: A History of the Zambezi Expedition, 1858–1864* (London: Chatto & Windus, 1970), p. ix.
9 Ibid., pp. 242, x.
10 Joyce Carol Oates, 'Adventures in Abandonment', *New York Times* (28 August 1988), www.nytimes.com/1988/08/28/books/adventures-in-abandonment.html (accessed 2 August 2011).
11 Peter Hazen Gibbon, *A Call to Heroism: Renewing the American Vision of Greatness* (New York: Atlantic Monthly, 2002), p. 112.
12 Annabel Venning, 'The Dark Side of Dr Livingstone: A Fascinating New Letter Casts the Great Explorer in a Very Different Light', *Mail Online* (29 July 2010), www.dailymail.co.uk/news/article-1298546/Dark-Dr-David-Livingstone-New-letter-casts-explorer-different-light.html#ixzz1Lqwe8uX1 (accessed 9 May 2011).
13 Judith Listowel, *The Other Livingstone* (New York: Charles Scribner's Sons, 1974). Listowel makes these comments in the book's unpaginated preface.
14 Ibid., p. 190.
15 Ibid., p. 4.
16 Ibid., p. 5.
17 Ibid., pp. 56, 148.
18 Tim Jeal, *Livingstone* (New Haven: Yale University Press, 2001), pp. 19, 20.
19 Ibid., p. 24.
20 Ibid.
21 Ibid., p. 25.
22 Ibid., p. 59.
23 Ibid., pp. 60, 58.
24 Ibid., p. 60.
25 Ibid., p. 61.
26 Ibid.
27 Ibid., pp. 61–2.
28 Ibid., p. 42.
29 Ibid., p. 108.
30 Ibid.
31 Oliver Ransford, *David Livingstone: The Dark Interior* (London: John Murray, 1978), p. 2.
32 Ibid., p. 3.
33 Both Jeal and Listowel are influenced, like many contemporary biographers, by what David Ellis calls a 'popularly diffused Freudianism'. This is not to say, by any means, that they explicitly adopt psychoanalysis, but rather that its pervasive influence inclines them to treat their 'subjects' own explanations of their behaviour' with a dose of suspicion. Even 'unFreudian' biographers today tend to assume that their subjects are likely to yield to 'the temptation to disguise the truth'. See David Ellis, *Literary Lives: Biography and the Search for Understanding* (Edinburgh: Edinburgh University Press, 2000), p. 9. Listowel and Jeal both signal in the direction of psychological conjecture. Discussing Livingstone's 'almost childish enjoyment of aristocratic circles', Listowel attributes it to a 'sense of

inferiority' from which he never escaped. See Listowel, *The Other Livingstone*, p. 208. Jeal comments that Livingstone was 'prone to moods of manic-depression', and that after Mary's death his native determination became an 'almost masochistic desire to push himself to the limits of human endurance'. He also comments on Livingstone's emotional maturation, suggesting that he had been stunted in a vital part of his development. Whereas most young men discover the importance of 'compromise and concession' in human relationships, and that their previous ambitions have been set too high, these were lessons that Livingstone never acquired. Having studied so intensely until he was twenty-seven, Jeal suspects, Livingstone 'never had time to make these normal adjustments, and as a result he would never really understand people'. See Jeal, *Livingstone*, pp. 224, 261, 372. Nevertheless, while both Jeal and Listowel are inclined to comment on mental states, and are infused with psychological suspicion, neither text constitutes a psychobiography.

34 Hamilton, *Biography*, p. 136. As I argued in Chapter 4, discussing D.C. Somervell's biography, Livingstone evaded psychological examination for a surprisingly long period. George Seaver would similarly resist such an approach as late as 1957. 'The psychologist, seeking ulterior motives and rational explanations for human behaviour ... would doubtless say that Livingstone was the victim of self-delusion', he argued. But, Seaver went on, 'For a true comprehension of the significance of Livingstone's life we must look deeper than psychological analysis and envisage it against the background of eternal values.' See George Seaver, *David Livingstone: His Life and Letters* (London: Lutterworth, 1957).

35 Hamilton, *Biography*, p. 144.
36 Hermione Lee, *Biography: A Very Short Introduction* (Oxford: Oxford University Press, 2009), p. 72.
37 Some of Ransford's reviewers wished that he had been even more psychological in his approach. James Casada desired further systematic discussion of manic depression: 'one only wishes he had carried his examination one step further to include a table or graph tracing Livingstone's behavior throughout his life and relating his successes and failures to the varying effects of cyclothymia'. See James Casada, review of Oliver Ransford, *David Livingstone: The Dark Interior*, *The International Journal of African Historical Studies*, 13: 1 (1980), 142. R.S. Roberts suggested that the 'psychological explanations' of the book would have been enhanced had it delved into 'the whole question of the sexual behaviour of these missionaries'. See R.S. Roberts, 'Another Livingstone?', review of Oliver Ransford, *David Livingstone: The Dark Interior*, *Zambezia*, 8: 1 (1980), 83.
38 Ransford, *David Livingstone*, p. 2.
39 Ibid., p. 165.
40 Ibid., p. 191.
41 Ellis, *Literary Lives*, p. 62.
42 Ransford, *David Livingstone*, pp. 146–7.
43 Ibid., p. 291.
44 Ibid., p. 185.
45 Ibid., p. 190.
46 Ibid., p. 4.
47 Lee, *Biography*, p. 87.
48 Ellis, *Literary Lives*, p. 93.
49 Ibid., p. 88.
50 Some of Ransford's evidence seems quite weak. Describing the hereditary nature of cyclothymia, he notes that 'Livingstone himself described one of his sisters as "dottie" and Janet, the other, as "daft"'. He also attaches weight to Kirk's description of Livingstone as 'out of his mind'. In these cases, Ransford is in danger of over-interpretation. The same could be said of his suggestion that Livingstone's occasional use of the third person 'reflects the exalted concept of self seen often in the hypomanic phase'. See Ransford, *David Livingstone*, pp. 3, 4, 286.
51 Ibid., p. 5.

52 Ibid., p. 4.
53 Ellis, *Literary Lives*, p. 83.
54 Ransford, *David Livingstone*, p. 4.
55 Lee, *Biography*, p. 87.
56 Susan Tridgell, 'Biography', in Victoria Boynton and Jo Malin (eds), *Encyclopedia of Women's Autobiography: K–Z* (Westport, Conn.: Greenwood Press, 2005), p. 101.
57 See, for instance, the strategies adopted by D.C. Somervell and James I. Macnair discussed in Chapter 4.
58 Jeal, *Livingstone*, p. 2; Listowel, *The Other Livingstone*, p. 56.
59 Tridgell, 'Biography', p. 103.
60 Judith P. Zinsser, 'Feminist Biography: A Contradiction in Terms?', *The Eighteenth Century*, 50: 1 (2009), 43.
61 Edna Healey, *Wives of Fame* (London: Sidgwick & Jackson, 1986), pp. x, xiii.
62 Ibid., pp. 31–2, 29.
63 Ibid., p. 27.
64 Ibid., p. 26.
65 Ibid., p. 53.
66 Ibid., p. 16.
67 Marilyn Booth and Antoinette Burton, 'Critical Feminist Biography II', *Journal of Women's History*, 21: 4 (2009), 9.
68 Barbara Caine, 'Feminist Biography and Feminist History', *Women's History Review*, 3: 2 (1994), 252.
69 Margaret Forster, *Good Wives?* (London: Vintage, 2002), p. 8.
70 Ibid., pp. 89, 94.
71 Ibid., pp. 103–4.
72 Ibid., p. 106.
73 Ibid., p. 25.
74 Ibid., p. 8.
75 Ibid., pp. 26, 27.
76 Booth and Burton, 'Critical Feminist Biography II', p. 11.
77 Forster, *Good Wives?*, p. 18.
78 Ibid., p. 58.
79 Marilyn Booth and Antoinette Burton, 'Critical Feminist Biography', *Journal of Women's History*, 21: 3 (2009), 9.
80 Julie Davidson, *Looking for Mrs Livingstone* (Edinburgh: Saint Andrew Press, 2012), p. xxii. Davidson acknowledges that her work is reliant on Janet Wagner Parsons's scholarship. Certainly Parsons did unearth much of what is known about Mary, and like the other authors, she does criticise Livingstone for pursuing 'personal fulfilment'. I have not focused on her book here, however, since its theme is not only Mary, but rather the Livingstone family as a whole. Parsons sees their story as a 'tragedy' and the 'wreckage of a family sacrificed to an ideal'. See Janet Wagner Parsons, *The Livingstones at Kolobeng 1847–1852* (Gaborone: Pula Press, 1997), p. 175.
81 Davidson, *Looking*, p. 230.
82 Ibid., pp. 151, 152, 116.
83 Tridgell, 'Biography', p. 103.
84 Davidson, *Looking*, p. 117.
85 Ibid., p. 54.
86 Ibid., pp. 231–2.
87 Ibid., pp. 184, 223, 242.
88 Ibid., p. 243.
89 Zinsser, 'Feminist Biography', p. 47.
90 For discussions of this trend, see Miles Ogborn, *Global Lives: Britain and the World 1550–1800* (Cambridge: Cambridge University Press, 2008), p. 9; David Lambert and Alan Lester, *Colonial Lives across the British Empire: Imperial Careering in the Long Nineteenth Century* (Cambridge: Cambridge University Press, 2006), p. 19.

91 Lambert and Lester, *Colonial Lives*, p. 19; Booth and Burton, 'Critical Feminist Biography', pp. 8, 7.
92 Tim Jeal, *Livingstone*, rev. ed. (New Haven: Yale University Press, 2013), p. xii.
93 While the current climate has demanded a new vision of David Livingstone, the celebratory has never quite disappeared. Rob Mackenzie's *David Livingstone: The Truth behind the Legend* aimed to 'redress the balance' in the wake of Tim Jeal and other critical biographers, but it is actually deeply redolent of Victorian adulation. See Mackenzie, *David Livingstone*, p. 17. His efforts to re-instantiate Livingstone's heroism and spiritual status show that the hagiographical inclination exists in any generation.
94 Steven E. Aschheim, *The Nietzsche Legacy in Germany, 1890–1990* (Berkeley: University of California Press, 1994), p. 3.
95 Ibid., p. 155; David B. Dennis, *Beethoven in German Politics, 1870–1989* (New Haven: Yale University Press, 1996), p. 22.
96 Aschheim, *The Nietzsche Legacy*, pp. 9, 15.
97 Rupke, *Alexander von Humboldt*, p. 208.
98 Dennis, *Beethoven*, p. 18.
99 Ben Pimlott, 'Brushstrokes', in Mark Bostridge (ed.), *Lives for Sale: Biographers' Tales* (London and New York: Continuum, 2004), p. 166.
100 Ibid.
101 Rupke, *Alexander von Humboldt*, p. 218.
102 Lucasta Miller, *The Brontë Myth* (London: Jonathan Cape, 2001), pp. x–xi.

INDEX

Note: 'n.' after a page reference indicates the number of a note on that page.
Note: page numbers in *italic* refer to illustrations.

Abdallah, Mohammed Ben 262
Aberdeen Journal 82
Aden 70
African National Congress 243
African Nationalism 163, 166–7, 243
Aidoo, Ama Ata 262
AIDS 258, 259, 260–1
Ajawa 95
'Alabama claims' 92
Alabi, Adetayo 225
Alexander, Peter F. 241, 251
Allan, Charles 193–4
Alpers, Svetlana 107n.59
American Civil War 92
Anderson, Robert 194
Anglo-Saxonism 13, 56, 93, 163, 179–82, 185, 187, 188, 213
Angola 128
Angra Pequena 130
Anthropological Society of London 111n.163
anti-realism 224, 258, 262
apartheid 241–57, 263
Appiah, Kwame Anthony 264n.8
Appin Murder 186
Arab–Swahili wars 131, 151
Argyll, Duke of 187
Arnold, Thomas 137
Aschheim, Steven 4–5, 284, 286
Asmani 232
Athenaeum 21, 31
Atkinson, Juliette 116, 117
Attlee, Clement 158
autobiography 27

Baden-Powell, Robert 142–4
Bagamoyo 12, 70
Bagehot, Walter 181
Bailey, Robin Wayne 258–61, 263

Bain, William 148, 158–9
Baines, Thomas 95, 120, 278
Bakalahari 49
Baker, Samuel 97
Bakhtin 50, 233
Bakwain *see* Kwena
Balfour Declaration of 1926 154
Balonda 44
Bangweolo, Lake (Lake Bangweulu) 129, 282
Barczewski, Stephanie L. 124, 180, 182
Barnett, Rev. J. L. 89–90, 110n.126
Barrie, J. M. 197
Barringer, Tim 24
Bashinje 49
Batoka 24, 46
Batty, Jane Agnes Staunton 223, 224
Beasley, Edward 133, 181
Beatons 184–5
Bechuana *see* Tswana
Bechuanaland 152, 176n.221
Bedingfeld, Norman 95, 120, 278
Benderloch 186
Bennett, James Gordon 93–4
Benson, Arthur 160
Benton, Michael 1, 9, 10, 18n.67
Berlin Conference (1884–85) 148
Beveridge, Craig 34
Bhabha, Homi K. 48, 50, 66n.188, 91, 263–4n.8
Binfield, Clyde 144
Binney, Thomas 26, 28
biography
  collective 281
  death in 74
  debunking biography and pathography 119, 125, 170n.50, 273–6, 279, 284

[292]

ethics of 170n.58, 279, 284
feminist 279–84
hagiography and exemplary lives 12, 116–26, 167–8, 273, 291n.93
illness in 278–9
modernism and 119, 279
psychobiography 119, 276–9, 284, 288–9n.33, 289n.34
recent theory 1, 8–11, 15, 63n.94
Victorian 116–18
see also metabiography
Birmingham, David 129
Bivona, Daniel 24, 60n.30
Black, Michael 251
Blaikie, William Garden 25, 118, 126, 169n.17, 171n.63, 188, 189
Blanton, Casey 21
Blantyre Mission (Malawi) 128, 132, 135–6
Blantyre (Scotland) 35, 91, 119, 178, 179, 195, 198, 199, 200, 201, 202, 203, 205, 206, 209, 212, 220n.198, 285
Boehmer, Elleke 143, 224–5
Boers 46, 153–4, 175n.189, 236, 237, 239, 244
see also Boer War
Boer War 141, 145, 153–5
see also Boers
Books in Canada 229–31
Booth, Marilyn 281, 282
Borm, Jan 22
Botha, Andries 40
Boyle, Robert 29
Boy Scout Movement 142–4
Boy Scouts of America 173n.138
Boys' Life: The Boy Scouts' Magazine 173n.138
Boy's Own Paper 144
Bradley, Ian 184, 185
Brantlinger, Patrick 84, 109n.88, 121
Breton, Rob 82, 108n.78
Brice, Arthur Montefiore 130, 131
Bridges, Roy C. 170n.58
Bright, John 97

Bristow, Joseph 108n.82
British Central Africa 128, 129, 135, 140, 145
British East Africa Company 130
British Empire Exhibition (1924) 205
British identity 91–2, 180, 190–1
see also Scottish identity
British Quarterly Review 87–8
British South Africa Company 135, 176n.221, 176n.223
Brotherhood Movement 144
Brown, Stewart J. 131–2, 136–7
Bruce, James 61n.53, 180
Bruce, Robert 192
Brussels Conference (1890) 148
Bryden, Inga 169n.40
Buckle, H. T. 34
Bulgarian atrocities 132
Bunyan, John 170n.46, 237
Burke, Edmund 148
Burke and Hare 181
Burns, Robert 35, 194, 197, 210
Burton, Antoinette 281, 282
Burton, Richard 22, 56, 69, 94, 97
Buxton, Meriel 287n.4
Buxton, T. F. (1st Baronet) 25, 50
Buxton, T. F. (3rd Baronet) 97

Cabora Bassa rapids 96
Caine, Barbara 281
Calder, Angus 178, 196, 211–12, 219n.163, 220n.205
Caledonian Mercury 19, 30
Cambridge, University of 158, 160, 164, 190
Cameron, Rev. C. Lovett 100–1
Cameron, Verney Lovett 70, 100–1
in drama 242, 247–50
Cameron – Livingstone Expedition 100–2
Cameroons 132
Campbell, Colin (of Glenure) 186
Campbell, Ian 197, 199, 200
Campbell, John Lorne 185
Campbell, Reginald J. 125–6, 149–55, 187, 188

Cape, South Africa 95, 130, 133, 151–2, 239
  see also Cape Frontier Wars
Cape Frontier Wars 11, 38–41, 64n.132
  see also Cape, South Africa
Cardoso, Candido 275
Carey, Barbara 228, 229
Caribbean 225, 228, 229
  Tobago 225
  Trinidad 155
Carlisle, Janice 64n.124
Carlyle, Thomas 82, 137
Carmichael, Alexander 184–6
Carr, E. H 7
Casada, James 289n.37
Celticism 221n.211
Celtic Monthly 182
Celtic revival 13, 182–7, 213, 214
Central African Federation 115, 158–67
Central African Journal of Medicine 161
Chard, Chloe 49
Charles, Elizabeth 220n.198
Chiboque 47
Chikumbi, Donald 166
children's literature 108n.82, 117, 180, 223
Child's Companion 108n.82
Chitambo (Chipundu) 12, 70, 242
Christian manliness *see* Muscular Christianity
Chuma, James 72, 100–1, 186, 268n.147
  in drama 242–3, 246–50, 269n.171
Church Herald 90
Clarendon, (Lord) (George Villiers) 41
Clark, Steven 51
Clifford, James 170n.58
Clingman, Steven 253, 256–7
Clyde, river 35, 196, 199, 208
Cochrane, Robert 180
Colenso, (Bishop) John William 79
Colley, Linda 91
colonial nostalgia 126, 170n.57
Comaroff, John and Jean 2–3, 53

Commonwealth 153, 154, 155, 175n.189
Congo Free State 131, 174n.155
Congregational Union of England and Wales 144
Cooper, Frederick 172n.98
Co-operative Movement 209
Corbett, John 34, 35, 36, 56–7, 202, 203
Cornhill 96
Coupland, Reginald 155–8, 165, 221n.211, 223
Crawford, Robert 35
Crimean War 71
Crockett, S. R. 197
Cubitt, Geoffrey 116–17, 118
Culloden, Battle of 35, 182–4, 201
  see also Jacobitism
Curl, James S. 72

Daily Mail 274
Daily News 77, 78–9, 109n.96
Dale, David 209
Danahay, Martin 82
Daniels, Stephen 11, 18n.74
Darwin, Charles 22, 79, 181
Darwin, Emma 280
Darwin, John 154, 159, 173n.124
David Livingstone Centre 212
  see also Scottish National Memorial
Davidson, Julie 282–3, 290n.80
Davidson, Neil 189, 197
da Vinci, Leonardo 119, 277
Dawson, Graham 113n.190, 117, 142
Dawson, R. B. 146, 147, 220n.198
Debenham, Frank 160–1, 165, 170n.46, 176n.221
de Kock, Leon 43, 44, 120–1
de Lacerda, José Maria 95
Democratic Republic of Congo 69
Dennis, David B. 286
Devine, Tom 189, 191, 196, 207, 208
Dick, Thomas 33
Dillon, W. E. 100
  in drama 247, 249
Djisenu, John K. 271n.240

INDEX

Dowding, W. H. 73, 75, 83, 85, 106n.15
Drayton, Richard 155
Dritsas, Lawrence 68n.226, 171n.58
Driver, Felix 27, 31–2, 94–5, 97, 110n.107, 111n.159, 126, 142
Dublin Review 61
Dugard, Martin 126
Duncan, James 51
During, Simon 266n.54

Edinburgh 92, 179, 188, 212
Edinburgh Evening Dispatch 189
Edwardian empire 115, 140–6, 167, 173n.124, 196
Egypt 131–2, 155
elegy 12, 71–86, 103, 106–7n.33, 109n.33, 285
Elizabeth the Queen Mother, Queen (Duchess of York) 206
Ellesmere, (Lord) (Francis Egerton) 89
Elliott, William A. 141, 144
Ellis, David 1, 9, 277–8, 288n.33
Ellis, James J. 197–8, 218n.124
Elwin, Whitwell 28
empire
  Scotland and 34, 63n.106, 91, 191, 196–7, 205, 206–7, 214
  see also Cape Frontier Wars; Central African Federation; Edwardian empire; imperial decline; partnership; scramble for Africa; trusteeship
epic poems 76, 84, 109n.96, 191–3, 202–3
Equiano, Olaudah 68n.229
Era 28
Erichsen, Ulrike 233
Essays and Reviews 79
Ethnological Society of London 111n.163
Evans, Richard J. 7
Evans-Pritchard, Edward 53
Examiner 82, 92

Fanon, Frantz 34, 225
Fara, Patricia 4

Ferguson, William (literary critic) 233
Fergusson, William (surgeon) 70, 86–7, 99, 102, 103
Finger, Charles 114
Finkelstein, David 41
First World War 13–14, 141, 145, 146–8, 196, 207, 208, 209, 213
Fish, Stanley 6
Fletcher, Bill 211
Forster, Margaret 281–4
Foucault, Michel 42–3, 65n.152
France, Peter 1–2
Fraser, H. C. 157
French Revolution 189, 109n.96
Frere, Bartle 85, 88–9, 96
Freud, Sigmund 119, 231, 234, 266n.73, 277, 288n.33
Frow, John 21
Frye, Northop 121
Fun 73, 74

Gadamer, Hans-Georg 5, 86, 88, 273
Gardner, Colin 245
Gaskell, Elizabeth 279
Geddes, Patrick 205
Gelfand, Michael 114, 161–2, 176n.223
gender studies 239, 279–84
General Strike (1926) 208
Genette, Gérard 31
German East African Protectorate 130–1
Germany 3, 4, 130–1, 132, 139, 140, 141
Ghana 262, 271n.240
Gibbon, Peter 274
Gilmour, William Weir 210
Glasgow 35, 85, 91, 92, 96, 113n.188, 140, 179, 180, 191, 196, 202, 208, 212, 220n.210, 237, 275
  see also Glasgow Herald
Glasgow, University of 140, 212, 220n.210, 275
Glasgow Herald 19, 30, 79, 80, 91, 92, 99, 101
Glenelg, (Lord) (Charles Grant) 39

Gluckman, Max 165, 167
Goffman, Erving 32–3
Goode, William J. 88
Gordimer, Nadine 241, 253–7, 263
Gordon, Charles George 129, 132
Gordon, Ian Fellowes 211
Graham's Town (Grahamstown) 39
Grant, James Augustus 94
Grant, K. W. 183–4, 186–7
Graphic 80, *81*, 93, 98
Gray, Erik 73, 106n.33
Green, Martin 47, 77
Gregory, Derek 43, 51, 126, 170n.57
Gregory, J. W. 140
Griffiths, James 162–4, 176n.231
Grimble, Arthur 150
Griqua 46
Guest, Charles 193–4

Hagerfors, Lennart 225, 231–5
Hamilton, Nigel 116, 118, 169n.20, 273, 277
Hamilton, Rev. H. W. 80, 108n.69
Hamilton (town) 108n.69, 199, 212
Hammond, Dorothy 107n.46
Hannan, James 215n.1
Hanoverian (House of Hanover) 189
Hardwicke, Cedric 213
Harrison, Debbie 103
Haugh, Robert 255
Havelock, Henry 113n.190, 117
Head, Dominic 255
Healey, Edna 280–1
Hector, Michael 63n.106
Heffernan, Michael 69, 102
Helly, Dorothy O. 16–17.n24, 21, 72, 127, 129
Helmers, Marguerite H. 48
Helmore, Holloway 111n.152
Hely-Hutchinson, C. 176n.223
Henderson, Louise 22, 26
Hetherwick, Alexander 206
Higgitt, Rebekah 17n.34
Hills, Matt 258
Holmes, Richard 1, 8, 9, 10, 15n.1
Holmes, Timothy 22, 27, 32, 33, 36, 38, 160, 288n.4

Holub, Robert 5
Hooper, Glenn 22, 44
Horne, Charles Silvester 114, 144–6, 204
Horsman, Reginald 181
Hoskyns-Abrahall, J. 75, 77
Houghton, (Lord) (Richard Monckton Milnes) 77, 103
Houghton, Walter 116
Hoving, Isabel 227, 228, 229
Howe, Stephen 158
Huggan, Graham 254, 255, 256
Hughes, Thomas 128, 130–2, 137–40
Hughes, William 82
Hulme, Peter 42–3
Humboldt, Alexander von 3–4, 286, 287
Hume, Edward 140, 141, 174n.161, 221n.211
Hunter, David 198
Hurnard, James 73
Hyam, Ronald 148, 152, 157, 158
hybridity 48, 50
Hymes, Dell 22
Hyslop, Jonathan 207, 210

imaginative geographies 76, 107n.59
imperial decline 115, 155–8, 166
imperial history
    imperial apologia 155–6
    'new' imperial history 136, 172n.98
Independent Labour Party 162
India 113n.190, 132, 155, 158, 223
indirect rule 148
    see also Lugard, Frederick D.
Iona 185
Ireland 155
Islam 131–2, 139, 171n.84, 223
Islam, Syed Manzurul 45, 51, 77
Islay 185

Jablow, Alta 107n.46
Jackson, C. d'O. Pilkington 251
Jacobitism 13, 56, 183, 189, 213
    Jacobite rising (1745) 186, 189, 206
    see also Culloden, Battle of

INDEX

Jacobs, Naomi 223, 226, 260, 262, 270n.213
Jalland, Pat 74
Jameson, Frederic 26, 33
Jameson Raid 153
Jauss, Hans Robert 5–6
Jeal, Tim 71, 168n.2, 230, 275–6, 279, 282, 284, 288–9n.33, 291n.93
Jenkins, Richard 15
Johanna men 98, 99, 112n.167
John, Christie 62n.78
John Bull 31, 73
Johnston, Harry H. 128, 129–30, 132–7, 139–40, 151, 167
  views on mission 134–5
Jones, Max 106n.11, 141, 142, 144–5
Jordon, John O. 253

Kailyard literature 14, 197–203, 208, 214
Kakutani, Michiko 234
Kalahari 120, 231
Kane, Elisha Kent 28, 61n.62
Kat River Rebellion 40
Kaunda, Kenneth 166
Khama III, Chief 176n.221
Khoikhoi *see* Kat River Rebellion
Kilimanjaro 132
Kingaru 232
Kingsolver, Barbara 222
Kingston, William H. G. 180
Kirk, John 68n.226, 95, 99, 111n.159, 156–7, 223, 278, 282, 289n.50
Knowles, Thomas 199
Knox, Robert 181
Kolobeng 46, 52, 236, 239
Kololo (Makololo) 47–8, 50, 52, 54, 68n.241, 111n.152, 151, 165, 280
Kruger, Steven F. 260–1
Kutzer, Daphne 223
Kwena (Bakwain) 49, 52–4, 66n.180, 154, 236, 243, 276

Labour Party 158, 208, 223
'lad o' pairts' 199, 201, 203, 208, 211, 214

Lambert, David 136, 170n.58
Lamont-Brown, Raymond 211
Lanarkshire 178, 188, 206
Lancet 86–7, 92
Last Journals 17n.24, 21, 72, 99, 106–7n.36, 127, 254, 255
Lawrence, T. E. 50
League of Nations 146–9, 152, 154
Lee, Alan J. 85–6, 109n.106
Lee, Hermione 8, 63n.94, 74, 116, 117, 126, 169n.20, 169n.24, 278
Lee, Jennie 281
Leeds Mercury 19, 27, 79–80, 110n.126
Leerssen, Joep 216n.29
Leslie, David 99, 101,
Lester, Alan 136, 170n.58
Letley, Emma 200–1, 218n.151
Levey, David 244–5
Lewis, Joanna 73–4, 105n.2
Leya 166
Liberal League 173
Liberal Party (South Africa) 241–2, 253
Liberal Party (UK) 153, 208
life-writing *see* biography
Lincoln, Arthur 142
Linge, David 94
Lismore 182, 184, 186
Listener 165
Listowel, Judith 34, 95–6, 274–5, 279, 288n.13, 288–9n.33
Livingstone, Agnes (daughter) 68n.226
Livingstone, Agnes (mother) 190, 198
  in drama 202
Livingstone, Charles 30, 54, 62n.76, 68n.226
Livingstone, David
  African reputation 166–7, 177n.256
  bicentenary of birth 212–13, 214, 220–1n.210, 284
  Cambridge lecture (1857) 164, 190
  Cape Frontier Wars 11, 38–41, 64n.132, 64n.134

Livingstone, David (*cont.*)
  centenary of birth 144, 145, 179, 195, 204
  centenary of death 166, 212, 220n.208
  Christianity, commerce and civilisation 25, 41–2, 70, 127, 141, 151, 152
  correspondence with John Murray 11, 19, 20, 26–9, 32, 40–1, 58, 62n.71
  death of 12, 69–105
    bodily remains 97–103, 105
    debates about 98–103
    funeral of 69–70, 80, 97
    idealisation of 72–5, 103, 106–7n.36, 112–13n.188
  and the evangelical tradition 55–7
  and feminist biography 279–84
  in fiction and drama 14, 285
    apartheid 14, 241–57, 263, 285
    colonial literature 223–4, 261
    postcolonial literature 224–40, 261–2, 285
    science fiction 258–61, 263
  imperialist reputation 12–13, 168n.2, 285, 288n.4
    Central African Federation 115, 158–67
    Edwardian empire 115, 140–6, 167
    imperial critique 115, 162–7
    imperial decline 115, 155–8, 166
    partnership 115, 158–67
    scramble for Africa 115, 127–40, 152, 155, 160, 166
    trusteeship 115, 146–55, 154–5, 158–9, 167, 174n.161
  Last Journey 69–70
  obituaries, elegies, epics 12, 15, 70–105, 285
  pathographies of 273–6, 279, 284
  psychobiographies of 276–9, 284, 288–9n.33, 289n.34
  recent scholarship on 2–3
  relationship with family 119–20, 231, 246, 279, 281, 290n.80

  Scottish influences on 34–6, 56–7, 64n.120
  Scottish reputation 13–14, 90–2, 285
    Anglo-Saxonism 13, 93, 179–82, 185, 187, 188, 213
    Celtic revival 13, 182–7, 213, 214, 285
    Kailyard literature 14, 197–203, 208, 214, 285
    recent reception 210–13
    as a Scottish Briton 190–7, 205–7, 214, 285
    Scottish National Memorial 14, 18n.275, 119, 179, 190, 203–10, 214, 251, 285
    unifying hero for Scotland 188–90, 213, 285
  statues of 3, 92, 166, 179
  Victorian commemoration 11–12, 69–105, 116–18, 127–40, 285
    abolitionist hero 72, 82–4, 104
    adventurous explorer 75–9, 104
    American reception 90, 92–4
    British national ideal 84–6
    Christian hero 79–82, 87, 89–90, 103–4
    competing images 86–96, 104–5
    contemporary criticisms of 94–7
    ecumenical appeal 33, 80, 89
    heroism and celebrity 71, 127
    medical hero 86–7
    scientist 87–9
    Scottish reception 90–2
    Victorian biography 116–18, 127–40
  views on race 54–7, 97
  Zambesi Expedition 62n.76, 95–6, 111n.156, 120, 140, 160, 171n.58, 268n.147, 278
  see also Missionary Travels; Narrative of an Expedition; Last Journals
Livingstone, Duncan 182–3, 184, 186
Livingstone, Elizabeth 120, 283
Livingstone, Mary 170n.58, 203, 275–6, 289n.33, 290n.80

biographies of 280–4
in fiction and drama 231, 237–9, 243
Livingstone, Neil 190, 198
in drama 202
Livingstone, Thomas 100–2
Livingstone, W. P. 149, 220n.198
Livingstones of Bachuil 183, 184, 186
Livingstones of Ballachulish 186
Livingstonia Mission 128
Lloyd's Weekly Newspaper 82, 85, 102
London 34, 70, 94, 105n.2, 108n.69, 149, 180, 190, 201, 205, 243, 259
London Missionary Society (LMS) 22, 33, 62n.76, 111n.152, 120, 141, 181, 204
    Helmore-Price Mission 95, 111n.152
Lowry, Donal 153
Lualaba 235
Lugard, Frederick D. 131, 148, 151, 163

Mabotsa 175n.189
McClintock, Anne 264n.8, 264n.15
McConnell, (Lord) Jack 220–1n.210
McCrone, David 194–5
MacCunn, Hamish 204–5, 219n.163
MacDiarmid, Hugh 199, 211
Macgregor, Forbes 211
McGregor, John 191–3, 194, 202–3
MacIntyre, Alasdair 15, 63n.94
Mackenzie, (Bishop) Charles 111n.152
MacKenzie, John M. 65–6n.168, 112n.186, 117, 149
    Livingstone's reputation 2, 12, 80, 115, 127, 128, 132, 140, 179, 203–4, 208, 222, 223
Mackenzie, Rob 170n.53, 288n.4, 291n.93
Maclachlan, T. Banks 130, 189–90
Maclaren, Ian 197
Maclean of Duart 186

Maclear, Thomas 32
Maclennan, Mary A. 201–2, 203
McLeod, John 264n.8, 264n.15
Macmillan, William M. 154
Macnair, James I. 119–20, 125, 190, 205–10, 212, 214, 219n.198, 221n.211
Magabesberg 80
Magomero 111n.152
Magyar, László 275
Makata swamp 232
Malawi 69, 166, 206, 221n.210
    see also Nyasaland
Malory, Thomas 121, 169n.40
Malpas, Simon 17n.50
mandate system 146, 149
Mandler, Peter 180
Manning, Anne 180
Marcus, Laura 21, 28, 63n.94
Markham, Clements 100
Marrat, Jabez 194–5, 197
Martelli, George 274
Marx, Jenny 280
Matabele 237, 239, 280
Mathema, Cain 166
Mathews, Basil 121–5, 142–4, 146, 169n.38, 181–2
Maxwell, William Stirling 85
Mazzeo, Tilar J. 48
Mears, Frank Charles 206
Mebalwe 66n.168
metabiography 3–11, 71, 86, 272–3, 283, 284, 286–7
    biographical studies and 8–11
    postmodernism and 6–8
    reception theory and 5–6
    see also biography
Miller, Lucasta 4, 8, 10, 287
Mills, Sara 42
Milton, John (literary advisor) 28, 61n.65
Mirambo 233
Missionary Travels 11, 19–59, 71, 75, 77, 84, 105n.7, 121, 164, 165, 167, 184, 188, 243
    Cape Frontier Wars 11, 38–41, 64n.134

Missionary Travels (cont.)
  dialogue with the 'rain doctor' 52–4
  ecclesiastical outlook 33–4
  humour in 49–50
  imagination of Africa 41–2, 71
  imperialist text 41–8, 58
  impression management in 32–41, 58, 121, 286
  landscape 35
  literary genre 21–7, 58, 75, 286
  literary style 27–32, 58
  manuscript of 11, 20, 36–42, 53–4, 57, 58
  resisting imperial discourse 50–8
  role in shaping reputation 57–8, 286
  Scottish national identity 34–6,
  social class 36–8
  textual hybridity 48–50
Mitchell, Mary 223–4
Moffat, Robert 22, 112n.171, 121, 280
  in drama 243
Monahin 46
Moretti, Frano 76
Morgan, Kenneth O. 163
Moss, Rose 245
Motheith, James 209
Mott, Albert J. 99
Mountains of the Moon 69
Mozambique 69, 128, 133
Mpende 181
Mufuzi, Friday 177n.256
Mugabeism 166
Mukherjee, Meenakshi 264n.8
Mukuni, Chief Silha 166
Mull 185
Murchison, Roderick 28, 31, 41, 171n.63
Murphy, Cecil 100–1
  in drama 248, 250, 269n.171
Murray, John 11, 19, 20, 26–9, 32, 40–1, 58, 61n.65
Musa 112n.167
Muscular Christianity 24–5, 79, 104, 108n.64, 137–9, 142

Mùsdal (Eilean Musdile) 186
Musgrove, Brian 50, 231
Mzilikatze 280

Nairn, Tom 191
Narain, Denise deCaires 225–6
Narrative of an Expedition to the Zambesi 30, 54, 55 60n.41, 62n.76, 64n.120, 68n.226
Nash, Andrew 197, 199
Nash, Catherine 11, 18n.74
National Heritage Conservation Commission (Zambia) 166
National Museum of Scotland 212
  see also Royal Scottish Museum
National Party (South Africa) 241
Neely, Alan 120
New College, Edinburgh 25, 188
new journalism 109–10n.106
New Lanark 178, 209
New Theology controversy 149
New York Herald 89, 92, 93, 235
New York Times 234
Ngami, Lake 240, 275
Ngoni 112n.167
Nicolson, Harold 117
Nigeria 151
Nineteenth Century 134
Njambi 47, 66n.180
Nkrumah, Kwame 262, 271n.240
Noel, Roden 76–7, 78, 82–3, 84, 103, 109n.96
Northcott, Cecil 159–60
North-Eastern Rhodesia 141
  see also Zambia
Northern Echo 78, 89–90
Northern Rhodesia 159, 160, 161, 242, 251
  Lusaka 242
  see also Zambia
North-Western Rhodesia 141
  see also Zambia
Nowes, John 67n.207
Nyangwe 156, 175n.197, 250
Nyasa, Lake (Lake Malawi) 128, 131, 275, 278

INDEX

Nyasaland 128–9, 130, 131, 135, 140, 151, 159, 160–1, 179
  see also Malawi

Oates, Joyce Carol 170n.50, 274
obituary 12, 15, 57, 70–1, 75–105, 285
Ogborn, Miles 170n.58
Oil Rivers District 132
Oliver, Roland 132, 134
Ongar 33
Orbiston 209
Orient in London exhibition (1908) 205
Ossian 185
Oswell, William Cotton 275
Outram, Dorinda 59n.20, 99
Owen, Richard 28
Owen, Robert 178, 209
Oxenham, John 204

Pachai, Bridglal 166
Park, Mungo 49, 87, 180
Parkes, Eleanor 229–30, 231
Parliament, Scottish 210–11
Parsons, Janet Wagner 290n.80
partnership 115, 158–67
Paton, Alan 241–53, 257, 263, 268n.126, 268n.150, 269n.171
Petrusic, Christopher 39
Pettitt, Clare 35, 57, 130, 179, 204, 222, 261
  celebrity 111n.151, 127
  Livingstone's death and funeral 97, 102–3
  transatlantic relations 92, 94
Philip, John 22, 55
Philip, Marlene NourbeSe 225–31, 232, 233, 262
Phillips, Richard 78, 107n.59
Pickering, Henry Y. 178
Pimlott, Ben 10, 287
Pinto, Serpa 129
Polo, Marco 50
Porter, Andrew N. 131
Porter, Bernard 141, 145
Porter, Dennis 50

Portugal 87, 128–30, 132, 135, 139, 140, 179, 231, 275
  Portuguese criticisms of Livingstone 95
postcolonialism
  colonial discourse 42–3
  criticisms of 231, 264n.8, 264n.15, 266n.54
  European discovery 43–4, 225–7
  humour and 50, 233–4, 266n.74
  language and 228–9
  cultural critique 224–5
  postcolonial literature 224–40, 261–2
  postmodernism and 263–4n.8
  see also imaginative geographies
Pownall, David 225, 235–40
Prater, Ernest *122*, *123*, *143*
Pratt, Mary Louise 43, 44, 65n.157, 78
Price, Roger 111n.152
Prideaux, W. F.
  in drama 247
Pryde, John Marshall 140
Punch 73, 78, 82, 85

Quarterly Review 28

Ransford, Oliver 25, 95, 240, 276–9, 284, 289n.37, 289n.50
Reay 185
Reichl, Susanne 266n.74
Renema, Sybren 113n.188
rent strikes, Glasgow (1915) 208
Rhodes, Cecil 114, 133, 151–2, 163, 166, 176n.221
Richards, Jeffrey 137, 139
Rio de Janeiro 275
Roberts, R. S. 289n.37
Robbins, Keith 153
Rohrer, James 125
romance form 120–5, 168
Rosen, Harold 32
Rosenberg, John D. 109n.103
Rosner, Mary 242, 246, 247, 267n.125, 269n.171

[301]

Ross, Andrew 52, 54, 55–6, 71, 112n.167, 168n.2, 170–1n.58, 178–9, 186–7, 204, 205, 208, 221n.211, 284, 287–8n.4
Rovuma, river (Ruvuma) 130
Rowley, Henry 95, 96
Rowse, A. L. 155
Royal College of Physicians and Surgeons of Glasgow 212
Royal Geographical Society (RGS) 26, 31, 32, 70, 78, 88–9, 94, 100, 105n.2, 108 n.69, 130, 171n.63
  Proceedings of 88–9
Royal Scottish Museum 179
  see also National Museum of Scotland
Royal Society of Edinburgh 212
Rupke, Nicolaas, 3–4, 5, 6, 8, 272, 286, 287

Said, Edward 42–3, 50, 65n.152, 76
St Clair, William 2
Salisbury, (Lord) (Robert Gascoyne-Cecil) 129, 130
Sandile 39–40
Sanger, Richard 230
Sansawe 49
Schapera, Isaac 2, 25, 60n.40, 274
Schreuder, D. M. 130
Schwer, Mary Angela 139
science fiction
  alternative history 258–61, 263
Scotland–Malawi partnership 221n.210
Scots language 200–3
Scotsman 61n.53, 97
Scott, David Clement 135–7, 140
Scott, Paul 189
Scott, Robert Falcon 106n.11, 142, 160
Scott, Walter 188, 189, 200, 210, 211
Scottish identity 34–6, 189, 190–1, 194–7, 203–4, 206–7, 210, 214
  see also British identity
Scottish National Memorial 14, 18n.275, 119, 179, 190, 203–10, 214, 251, 285

Scottish National Party (and National Party of Scotland) 207, 210
Scottish Renaissance 199, 204, 207
scramble for Africa 115, 127–40, 152, 155, 160, 166
  British rivalry with Germany 130–1, 140
  British rivalry with Portugal 128–30, 135, 140
Seaver, George 289n.34
Sebituane 52, 280
Sechele 23, 52
  in fiction and drama 235–40, 243, 267n.100
Second World War 115, 155, 177–8, 223
Sedgwick, Adam 190
Seeley, John Robert 155
Sekeletu 47, 111n.152
Shapin, Steven 27, 29, 61n.56
Sharp, John Alfred 171–2n.84
Shaw, John William 231–5
Sheakondo 54
Shepperson, George 34, 178
Shinte 24
Shire highlands 64n.120, 111n.152, 128, 160
Shohat, Ella 264n.15
Shuttleworth, Sally 62n.78
Simbamwenni 232
Simmons, Jack 164–5
Skye 185
slavery 36, 92, 95, 97, 109n.88, 115, 124–5, 131, 144, 151, 152, 181, 193, 228, 229, 239, 251, 278
  abolition 84, 156–7
  factory workers and 38, 64n.124
  Livingstone's views and descriptions of 25, 42, 60n.41, 70
Smethurst, Paul 67n.205
Smiles, Robert 198–201
Smiles, Samuel 108n.82, 128
Smith, G. Watt 195–6, 197
Smith, J. Beverley 163

[302]

INDEX

Smuts, Jan C. 175n.189
Society for Promoting Christian Knowledge (SPCK) 223
Society for the Propagation of the Gospel (SPG) 89–90
Söderqvist, Thomas 272
Somervell, David C. 119, 125, 149, 150–2, 154–5, 167, 289n.34
South Africa *see* apartheid; Boers; Boer War; Cape, South Africa; Cape Frontier Wars; Union of South Africa
Southampton 69, 70, 77, 98, 103, 105n.2
Southern Rhodesia 159, 161, 163
  see also Zimbabwe
spaces of knowledge 110n.107
Speke, John 41, 94
Spivak, Gayatri Chakravorty 264n.8
Stanley, Brian 129, 135
Stanley, (Dean) Arthur P. 70, 80, 105n.2
Stanley, H. M. 24, 60n.30, 111n.159, 138, 139, 157, 204, 272
  and Anglo-Saxonism 93, 182
  construction of Livingstone 80, 82, 92–4, 179–80, 182
  in fiction 226–7, 231–5
  meeting with Livingstone 70, 92, 94, 95, 127, 278
Stanley, Oliver 159
Stanley and Livingstone (film, 1939) 213
Stein, Mark 266n.74
Stevenson, Fanny 281
Stevenson, Robert Louis 187
Stewart, James (missionary) 32, 95
Stewart, James (of the Glen) 186–7
Stewarts of Appin 182–3, 186
Stoler, Ann Laura 172n.98
Strachey, Lytton 119, 273
Strijdom, J. G. 250–1
Stuart (House of Stuart) 189
Sturrock, John 21
Sudan 132
Suez Canal 131

Sumpter, W. 74, 75
Susi, Abdullah 72, 100–1, 107n.36, 186
  in drama 242–3, 246–50, 268n.150, 269n.171
Suvin, Darko 259–60

Tanganyika, Lake 131, 235
Tanzania 69
Taylor, Charles 15, 17n.30
Tete 48
Thiong'o, Ngugi wa 252
Thornton, Richard 95
Timbuctu (Timbuktu) 39
Times, The 57, 80, 82, 83, 91, 93, 95, 100–1, 150
Tlapane 45
Todorov, Tzvetan 21
Toynbee, Henry 26
Transvaal 175n.189
Transvaal republic 176n.221
travel writing
  credibility and 28–32, 61n.56
  genre and 22, 121
  process of publication 40–1, 62n.71
  recent theory 50–1, 67n.205
Tridgell, Susan 279–80, 283
trusteeship 15, 146–51, 154–5, 158–9, 167, 174n.161, 174n.167
Tswana (Bechuana) 3, 23, 25, 50
Tucker, Herbert F. 84, 109n.96
Turnbull, Ronald 34

Uganda 131, 151
Ugogo 101
Ujiji 70, 100, 157, 233
Ulva 178, 186
Union of Parliaments (1707) 189, 195
Union of South Africa 154, 176n.221
United Party (South Africa) 253
Universities' Mission to Central Africa (UMCA) 62n.76, 64n.120, 95, 111n.152, 138
Unyanyembe 70, 100–1, 157, 242
Updike, John 1, 15n.1
Usumbara 130

Vance, Norman 108n.64, 137, 138
van Zoelen, Timmy 113n.188
Verwoerd, H. F. 241
Victoria Falls (Mosioatunya) 35, 43–4, 163, 166, 194, 211, 227
Victoria, Lake 130
Victoria, Queen 70, 73, 129, 194
von Bismarck, Otto 130–1
Vovelle, Michel 74

Wade, Michael 253
Wainwright, Jacob 77, 83, 170n.58
  in drama 243
Wallace, William 192
Waller, Horace 16–17n.24, 68n.226, 72, 99, 106–7n.36, 111n.159, 127, 129, 156, 248
Ward, David 252–3
Ward, Paul 91
Warf, Barney 258, 261
Webb family 68n.226
Weekly Scotsman 189
Western Mail 79
Westminster Abbey 12, 69, 70, 73, 83, 91, 92, 97, 98, 102, 181, 212, 243
White, Hayden 6–7
White, John 205
Wilberforce, William 55
Wilberforce–Huxley debate 79
Wingfield, Chris 103, 112–13n.188
Wisnicki, Adrian 19, 25, 41, 44, 56, 71, 175n.197

Withers, Charles 27, 31
Wolfe, William 210
Wolffe, John 80, 105n.2
Woolf, Virginia 119, 279
World Missionary Conference (1910) 145
Wylie, Diana 161–2

Xhosa *see* Cape Frontier Wars

Young, Robert J. C. 66n.188, 224, 263n.8
Youngs, Tim 22, 44

Zambesi, river (and region) 25, 43–4, 95, 128–9, 130, 210, 280
Zambia 69, 70, 166, 177n.256, 235
  see also North-Eastern Rhodesia; Northern Rhodesia; North-Western Rhodesia
ZANU-PF 166
Zanzibar 69, 70, 100, 101, 111n.152, 112n.167, 125, 130, 131, 156–7, 232, 246, 247, 250
Ziff, Larzer 28, 61n.62
Zimbabwe 166
  Bulawayo 166
  see also Southern Rhodesia
Zinsser, Judith 280, 284
Zouga, river (Boteti) 35
Zumkhawala-Cook, Richard 182, 185, 198, 200

EU authorised representative for GPSR:
Easy Access System Europe, Mustamäe tee 50,
10621 Tallinn, Estonia
gpsr.requests@easproject.com

www.ingramcontent.com/pod-product-compliance
Ingram Content Group UK Ltd.
Pitfield, Milton Keynes, MK11 3LW, UK
UKHW042017140420
5217IPUK00015B/1227